PROJECT AND POLICY APPRAISAL:
INTEGRATING ECONOMICS
AND ENVIRONMENT

PUBLISHER'S NOTE

The following texts have been left in their original form to permit faster distribution at lower cost.

ORGANISATION FOR ECONOMIC CO-OPERATION AND DEVELOPMENT

ORGANISATION FOR ECONOMIC CO-OPERATION AND DEVELOPMENT

Pursuant to Article 1 of the Convention signed in Paris on 14th December 1960, and which came into force on 30th September 1961, the Organisation for Economic Co-operation and Development (OECD) shall promote policies designed:

— to achieve the highest sustainable economic growth and employment and a rising standard of living in Member countries, while maintaining financial stability, and thus to contribute to the development of the world economy;

— to contribute to sound economic expansion in Member as well as non-member countries in the process of economic development; and

— to contribute to the expansion of world trade on a multilateral, non-discriminatory basis in accordance with international obligations.

The original Member countries of the OECD are Austria, Belgium, Canada, Denmark, France, Germany, Greece, Iceland, Ireland, Italy, Luxembourg, the Netherlands, Norway, Portugal, Spain, Sweden, Switzerland, Turkey, the United Kingdom and the United States. The following countries became Members subsequently through accession at the dates indicated hereafter: Japan (28th April 1964), Finland (28th January 1969), Australia (7th June 1971) and New Zealand (29th May 1973). The Commission of the European Communities takes part in the work of the OECD (Article 13 of the OECD Convention).

Publié en français sous le titre :
ÉVALUATION DES PROJETS ET POLITIQUES :
INTÉGRER L'ÉCONOMIE ET L'ENVIRONNEMENT

Foreword

The path to sustainable development implies the consistent use of economic tools for the evaluation of projects, programmes and policies which are either designed to protect the environment or are likely to have an environmental impact. Over the last 10 years or so, the field of environmental economics has evolved considerably, in particular in the area of economic techniques for the valuation of environmental impacts, the pricing of natural resources and the choice of appropriate economic instruments for environmental policy. The OECD Environment Directorate has been closely involved in the development of these methods in OECD Member countries. Despite the evident need for more economic rationality in environmental policy, studies have clearly indicated that these economic techniques are still not widely used in practice. Furthermore, it is now clear that an economic evaluation of project, programmes and policies is crucial in developing countries to achieve sustainable development.

This is why it was decided to elaborate manuals for the application of economic techniques in both industrialised and developing countries. To this end, two manuals are being prepared: the present technical manual entitled "Project and Policy Appraisal: Integrating Economics and Environment" and a "Field Manual" which will provide a practical, step by step modus operandi on how to apply the valuation and other economic techniques. This Field Manual will be elaborated later.

The purposes of these manuals are threefold: first, to present a comprehensive state of the art assessment of existing techniques and of their applicability in industrialised and developing countries; second, to disseminate knowledge of these techniques and awareness to decision makers; and third, to promote the use of these methods in developing countries. This work was initiated by both the Group on Economic and Environmental Policy Integration and the Development Assistance Committee. Special funding was provided by Australia, France and the United Kingdom.

The present manual *Project and Policy Appraisal: Integrating Economics and Environment*, was written by **David Pearce** (Professor of Environmental Economics and Director of the Centre for Social and Economic Research on the Global Environment, University College London); **Dale Whittington** (Professor of Environmental Sciences and Engineering, and Professor of City and Regional Planning, University of North Carolina); **Steven Georgiou** (Research Fellow at CSERGE); and with contributions from **David James** (Director, Ecoservices Pty, Australia).

This manual is published under the responsibility of the Secretary-General.

Table Of Contents

Annexes

PART I

INTRODUCTION

Chapter 1

Introduction

Aims of this volume

There is now a widespread recognition that environmental quality and the integrity of the natural resource stock are of importance for human well-being now, and in the future. This recognition was enunciated in incipient form in the 1972 United Nations Conference on the Human Environment in Stockholm, but received its clearest expression 20 years later in the 1992 United Nations Conference on Environment and Development in Rio de Janeiro, the so-called "Earth Summit". Stripped to its barest, the basic message is that economic and social development is not "sustainable" unless the environment - natural and built - is afforded a much higher profile in national economic planning and management. That is, **the environment matters, not just for any "intrinsic value" it might have, but because failure to conserve and protect environmental resources imposes costs on the economy.**

Moreover, the Rio Conference was clear that this message applies to developed and developing countries alike. This is important since some developing countries have seen in catch-phrases like "sustainable development" a threat to traditional forms of development aimed at raising real per capita incomes. By stressing environmental quality - pollution control, the undesirability of tropical deforestation, the need to conserve biological diversity - the North could be construed as diverting · the South from its main objective of poverty alleviation. Defences to the effect that "sustainable development" means economic growth <u>and</u> environmental improvement, without the sacrifice of either, have not served to convince the Southern countries that the environment should be a priority. If it was that simple it seems likely that at least one country in the world could be identified as having pursued such a complementary set of goals. The reality is that environmental quality often <u>is</u> needlessly sacrificed in the name of economic growth, but that it can sometimes only be secured at the expense of growth, as traditionally defined. The "trade-off" may be between additional economic growth and maintained environmental quality; it may be between environmental quality and the social distribution of income; or between short-term gains in economic growth and sustainable economic growth. The basic fact is that, while much environmental improvement can be secured fairly costlessly, the rest will have to be paid for in forgone GNP as traditionally measured. That is why the environment and development debate is interesting. If these twin goals were completely complementary there would be little to argue about. It is the balance between the complementarity and the trade-off that defines the context of this volume. Basically, **the question is: given this context, how should we decide on economic and environmental policies and investments?**

The focus of the volume is on (a) investments, or **projects** and sets of projects (or **programmes**), and (b) **policies** which are either explicitly environmental in purpose, or which have a significant potential impact on the environment.

Why is a volume of this kind necessary? There are dozens of economics manuals purporting to offer guidance on how to evaluate policies and investment projects. Indeed, the OECD has been instrumental in producing one of the most famous of these manuals (Little and Mirrlees [1969], [1974]). Interestingly, however, and despite the twenty years or so of fervent environmental debate, these economic manuals still tend to ignore or downplay procedures for evaluating the ways in which environmental concerns affect economic decision-making. This is not to deny the existence of many manuals which are directly concerned with environmental appraisal, but few attempts have been made to integrate environmental issues into economic appraisal techniques. The underlying rationale of this volume is to try and correct this rather fundamental omission.

The approach adopted here is, as with the earlier manuals, economic. One rationale for this is that policy and investment decisions have to be seen as decisions about the **allocation of scarce resources**, and, since economics is the science of resource allocation, an economics approach appears most pertinent. A second rationale is that the economic approach has stood the test of time. It has an internal consistency and logic. It has been tested theoretically and empirically. Perhaps more to the point, no alternative approach has gained such widespread acceptance.

However, in adopting the economic approach, we are conscious that individuals, communities and nations have **multiple objectives**. These objectives are not all reducible to the traditional concern of economists with **economic efficiency** which basically amounts to trying to make people "better off" on the whole - see Chapter 3. One obvious objective which figures just as prominently, and some would say is prior to economic efficiency, is **fairness or justice**. Efficiency and fairness are often incompatible in the sense that the pursuit of the maximum amount of one of them will impair the achievement of the other. In this volume we therefore embrace the notion of fairness as it applies to people now, and as it applies across generations in time, and we show how the conventional economic decision rules could be modified to account for fairness objectives. However, we do not pursue these "non-efficiency" objectives very far. The reason for that is not discomfort at the need to embrace these objectives, but mainly a judgement that objectives like fairness are better pursued outside the remit of investment and environmental policy analysis. That is, fairness is better pursued at a macroeconomic level, as an item of national policy. Using investment at the microeconomic level, and policy appraisal to achieve goals of equity is unlikely to be the most efficient way of proceeding. But concerns about fairness are clearly relevant at all layers of decision-making so that it is neither possible nor desirable to reject totally these legitimate social concerns in the context of project and policy appraisal.

Two intellectual traditions

The development of project and policy appraisal has followed two broad intellectual traditions. In the first, prevailing markets are fairly competitive and the focus is therefore on **non-market** effects with a public dimension. This describes, albeit approximately, the evolution of the literature in the USA where non-market issues have dominated the literature: air and water pollution, amenity and conservation. In the second tradition the focus is on marketed goods and services in contexts where markets are very imperfect. Here the focus is on the rules for appraisal in distorted markets: simply put, shadow prices diverge markedly from market prices. It is perhaps no accident, then, that the literature on appraisal in distorted markets should have emerged first in the developing country context - see the UNIDO Manual (Dasgupta, Marglin and Sen [1972]), the OECD Manuals (Little and Mirrlees [1969, 1974]), and the World Bank Manual (Squire and van der Tak [1975]). Europe has gradually followed the US lead in focusing on non-market issues, and that defines the current preoccupation with valuation even if it has been even slower to get into official circles in Europe (Pearce and Turner [1992a]).

The matrix below shows a possible classification of issues according to whether the focus is on goods and services that are traded in markets, and whether the goods in question have significant public benefits or not. Then, cell I defines the scope of the traditional appraisal manuals. Cell 2 - goods that are often not marketed but which have private benefits (as well as public benefits, especially in the form of public health) - is the focus of much current work in developing countries. Cell 3 defines marketed goods with major public benefits, such as rural electricity; and cell 4 is the province of the "standard" economic valuation literature. Note that the common framework for the whole matrix is the need to secure measures of the 'true' demand for the goods in question, or the need to measure the true costs to the nation of using resources in a particular way. In turn, **valuation** is the process of measuring the true costs and the true benefits. This explains the emphasis given to valuation in this volume.

	Goods with Private Benefits	Goods with Public Benefits
Traded in Markets	"Conventional" goods e.g., cement, electricity. Issue is one of estimating shadow prices to correct for market price distortion	Marketed goods with significant public aspects, e.g., rural electricity, water, education
Not-marketed	Non-marketed private goods, e.g., some water resources	Non-marketed goods with public value, e.g., clean air, clean water, amenity. Focus of much of the valuation literature

The causes of environmental degradation

The factors at work which give rise to environmental degradation are many and complex. But without some understanding of them, policy measures aimed at improving the environment will risk failure, and the rate of return on investments may be less than expected if environmental impacts feed back negatively to the project. One route toward identifying the causes of degradation lies in an analysis of **property rights**. A property right is an **entitlement** on the part of an owner to a resource or good and where the entitlement is **socially enforced**. Such rights tend to be **attenuated** by various legal and customary restrictions which define limitations on the use or consumption of the good or resource. Such attenuation is embodied in the laws of a nation or in custom and prevailing morality. Some forms of attenuation will improve the efficiency of the property rights regime, but other forms may reduce efficiency.

If property rights are efficiently allocated in an economy it can be shown that the resulting allocation of resources will maximise the sum of individuals' well-being, or "social welfare" (we do not pursue this proof here - see Just, Hueth and Schmitz [1982]). It is generally recognised that four conditions must prevail for an efficient property rights structure to exist. These conditions (Tietenberg [1992]) are:

> **Universality**: all resources are privately owned and all the entitlements are completely specified.

> **Exclusivity**: all the benefits and costs arising from ownership of the resource must accrue to the owner.

Transferability: owners must be able to transfer property rights to another owner in voluntary exchange.

Enforceability: there must be a structure of penalties which prevent others from encroaching on or taking over property rights without the agreement of the owner.

Many environmental problems arise because these conditions do not all prevail. For example, in many cases property rights to land or a natural resource are not allocated or defined at all. This is so for **open access or non-property** resources such as the atmosphere or much of the world's oceans. Even where, in principle, property rights exist they may not be **enforceable** so that, de facto, an open access situation exists. Open access means that no individual has an incentive to conserve the resource since he or she has no assurance that others will do likewise (the **assurance problem**).

Often, resources are owned or managed by a reasonably well-defined group of people - a local community, for example. Rights are then exclusive in that individuals outside the community are not permitted to use the resource. This is a **common property** resource. The incentive for any one individual to conserve the resources arises because there is an assurance, enforced by the laws or customs of the community, that others will do likewise. Users of the resource have a **right** to the use and a **duty** to obey the rules of management. If, however, this assurance breaks down, this incentive will be lost and the common property regime may effectively become an open access regime. One way in which this assurance breaks down is through population growth which effectively adds new owners in the context of a finite resource (grazing land for example). The rights of existing users are then threatened and the assurance system may collapse. Note that common property differs from open access: the former has rules of use aimed at exclusivity and is backed by enforcement of those rules; the latter has no such rules (see Box 1.1).

Private property is the most familiar form of a property right in the developed world. In theory, private property secures a **right** to undertake a given use of the resource and a **duty** to refrain from socially unacceptable uses of the resource. In practice, private use rights often involve costs on third parties. The exclusivity condition breaks down in such contexts, the main class of which is known as **externalities**. Externalities are uncompensated costs (or unappropriated benefits) arising from the failure of private property rights to consider third party effects. Note that exclusivity will be difficult or impossible for certain classes of goods where the externality element is pronounced. These are **public goods** which are goods which, when supplied to one individual are automatically supplied to others ('joint supply') and where it is impossible or difficult to prevent others from benefitting from the good (non-exclusivity). Clean air has public good characteristics since the clean air breathed by individual A is also breathed by B, and A cannot exclude B from the benefit.

State property refers to the context where the resource rights are held by the state. The prima facie attraction of state property is that all externalities are "internalised": the one owner bears all costs and benefits and hence could be expected to seek the situation where the **net** benefits are maximised. In practice, state property has not proved to be to the advantage of environmental conservation - witness the environmental degradation in Eastern Europe and the old USSR. Clearly, state property offends the requirements of universality and transferability, even if it promises to embrace enforceability and exclusivity.

Fundamentally, then, environmental problems arise because of a failure of one or more of the various property rights regimes to fulfil the conditions for an efficient allocation of property rights. That is, one or more of the conditions of universality, exclusivity, transferability and enforceability are not met. There is a need, then, to check the type of the property rights regime in existence when assessing the chances of success in making policy recommendations or investing in a particular project. Thus, if the land tenure system that prevails does not give adequate enforceability of those rights, a project may fail because resource users do not have adequate incentives to take advantage of the project's benefits. This kind of failure is commonplace in environmental projects which seek to conserve a given habitat, for example. All potential users of the land must have incentives to honour the conservation status of the protected area. This can often be achieved by providing them with a legal or customary right to some of the benefits of the protected area -e.g., rights to offtake of wildlife products. Involving the local community in this way is often a precondition for a successful conservation policy, although it in no way guarantees it if other incentives to continue exploitation are still present. A further example of the importance of property rights regimes lies in identifying who has the property rights and who requires the incentive for a project to be successful. Assigning the benefits to male householders, for example, will not guarantee success if a project requires women to participate. Men's and women's property rights often differ in developing countries.

Box 1.2 summarises the discussion of property rights. Clearly, all environmental problems cannot be resolved by defining property rights. In the first place, no one system of property rights is exclusively good for the environment, although there must be a presumption against open access regimes and very probably against state property. The former lacks all incentives for conservation while the latter tends to assume benign behaviour on the part of governments when in fact nationally beneficial objectives are overtaken by the personal motives of the bureaucrats managing the state system. Secondly, other more general factors are at work. Environmental degradation may arise simply from population pressure, from over-reliance on single commodities (such that when the terms of trade are not favourable, greater pressure is exerted to exploit the resource to sustain revenues), from indebtedness, and so on. Nonetheless, property rights analysis is a powerful weapon in assessing the likely success or failure of investments and/or environmental policy. Certainly, many analysts have found **government failure** to be a pervasive force in causing environmental degradation. Such forms of failure are illustrated in Box 1.3.

The impact of environmental considerations on project and policy appraisal

Past policy appraisal has been severely criticised from an environmental standpoint on two major grounds:

> (a) the failure of appraisal to **account for environmental values** in the same terms as the conventional development costs and benefits;

> (b) the discrimination against the interests of future generations due, allegedly, to the practice of **discounting future costs and benefits**.

Failure (a) is often thought to result in a downgrading of environmental costs and benefits relative to conventional costs and benefits which are ultimately measured in terms of gains to real consumption now and in the future. The problem is one of "misplaced concreteness" because development benefits and costs appear to be more real than environmental gains and losses. What is quantified appears to be more important than what is not quantified. Since **development** costs and benefits are traditionally measured in monetary terms, the problem is that **environmental** costs and benefits are not similarly valued in monetary terms. The logic of this argument is either not to value benefits and costs in money terms at all, or to ensure that as many gains and losses are valued in money terms so that there is comparability. In this volume we take the second view, and this accounts for the emphasis that we put on techniques for measuring benefits and costs in money terms. The former option would, by and large, amount to choosing between policies and investments on generally irrational grounds since no other common units of measurement are available.

Failure (b) is more problematic. It is still a failure of **valuation** because it implies that conventional project appraisal fails to take account of **future values** in an adequate way. It is therefore tempting to think that the failure should be corrected by adjusting the implicit price of future consumption in terms of present consumption - the **discount rate**. In Chapter 12 we show that the role of the discount rate in lowering the "voice" of future generations is in fact quite complex.

In citing the two environmental concerns as being ones of valuation we are ignoring the more fundamental concern expressed by some environmentalists that economic valuation is **per se** a bad thing. Space forbids a detailed refutation of the view that monetising environmental values is inherently wrong. One of us has gone into those arguments in some detail elsewhere (Pearce [1993]).

Environment and sustainable development

The phrase "sustainable development" has done much to encapsulate concerns about the way in which economists have traditionally evaluated projects and policies. The term "development" is a deliberate diversion of attention from "economic growth" to a more embracing social goal. Unfortunately, development can mean whatever we want it to mean and the end result has been an obfuscation of what is useful in the overall phrase of sustainable development. The reality is that governments everywhere have multiple goals and some mixture of those goals is usually what is meant by development. Without question, development does embrace raising real per capita incomes, whether the context is developing or developed countries. But it also embraces advances in human capital - health and education notably - increases in human freedoms - and, increasingly, environmental quality improvements. This perhaps explains the attraction of new measures of development such as the UNDP "Human Development Index" (UNDP [1992]). For our purposes we accept that development is a multi-attribute concept, but we argue that securing economic efficiency is more than one attribute. It is an **enabling** attribute of development, i.e., it is a means of securing the various components of a human development index. If the goal of development is slightly nebulous, the idea of **sustainable** development has become quite controversial. It grew out of the long standing notions of "sustainable yield" in forestry or fisheries management whereby the stock of the resource itself is not allowed to decline, but the maximum economic rent from that stock is sought. As it happens, sustainable yields are consistent with many levels of stock in renewable resource management, so what is sought is the **optimal stock** of the resource, i.e., that stock corresponding to the maximum yield of rent. Translated to the overall sphere of national development sustainability appears to lose its meaning. Resources are heterogeneous and include non-renewable resources such as coal and oil. A "sustainable" resource base thus appears to be impossible. But this misses the importance of the valuation issue, since what sustainability means in this context, as we show below, is that the overall **value of the stock of capital** should not be declining if there is to be sustainable development. Determining the optimal national yield of economic rent also appears very problematic, and hence so does the idea of identifying the optimal stock of resources. All we can know is whether a movement from the existing position is good or bad since that can be determined by the measurement of gains and losses in monetary terms. We may know in which direction to move, but not where the optimum stock is.

This kind of consideration has led some writers to be critical of some of the prevailing notions of sustainable development. Others have been openly dismissive. Thus:

> "Sustainability has come to be used in recent years in connection with projects. This is more of a buzzword - probably derived from the environment lobby - than a genuine concept. It has no merit. Whether a project is sustainable (forever? -or just for a long time?) has nothing to do with whether it is desirable. If unsustainability were really regarded as a reason for rejecting a project, there would be no mining, and no industry" (Little and Mirrlees [1990, p365]).

If indeed anyone has suggested a terminology of "sustainable projects" then these strictures would be partly justified - only partly because investors are rightly concerned that projects should survive and prosper beyond the point where investment flows are associated with technical aid and capacity building, especially in developing economies. But the discussion has been about sustainable development, not projects. That said, sustainable development does have implications for project and policy appraisal.

The traditional focus in early manuals was on **government projects** since most economies were characterised by large public sectors. The modern focus is on those same public projects - especially infrastructure, energy supply, water and sanitation, etc - but has become much broader with the increasing role of private enterprise in the development process, and in the role that both domestic and international policy can play. Sustainable development simply means development that lasts. That this is a significant concern is evidenced by the number of economies in which all forms of investment capital are "mined" so that, ultimately, sustainable income levels above some minimum acceptable level are not secured. Lack of sustainable development in this sense can come about for all kinds of reasons, including war and famine, but also because of mismanagement at the macroeconomic level, poor project formulation and execution, and so on. That there is unsustainable development should not be doubted. The issue is whether project and policy appraisal needs to be changed in any way in order to avoid this unsustainability.

Sustainable development is a **macroeconomic objective** and it is very likely that securing it will mainly involve macroeconomic policy, not revisions to project appraisal. But there are implications for project and policy appraisal from the idea of sustainable development. Self-evidently, development is not sustained if, through time, the chosen index of development goes down. Ensuring that it rises, or is at least constant through time, and in per capita terms, means ensuring that future generations have no less capacity to generate "development" than current generations. That capacity lies in the capital stock and in technology, and in ensuring that rapid population growth does not quickly dissipate the benefits of growing capital stocks. One of the insights afforded by environmental economics is that environmental assets are as much capital as machines or roads or factories. A tropical forest has a great many ecological functions and all of those functions have economic value. Thus, the forest protects the watershed system and if removed that system may suffer damage, depending on the land use system that replaces it. At the global level, the ozone layer protects humans from amounts of ultra-violet radiation that would otherwise impair human health and ecosystem productivity.

If capital stocks are integral to future capacity to sustain development, then the overall maintenance of those stocks is an integral part of sustainable development policy. In essence, all that is being said is that future incomes are not sustainable if the capital stock is run down. Indeed, this is Hicksian "sustainable income" and we illustrate below how this might be computed. A main ingredient for the recipe for sustainable development is therefore not to let capital stocks runs down. How far the stock of **natural assets** should be run down depends on how far we think other assets substitute for them. It would be acceptable to destroy the tropical forests on this analysis if some other assets were built up in their place. Much of the modern debate about sustainability is in fact about exactly this issue - the extent to which capital assets are substitutable for each other. At the risk of oversimplification, the ecologists are saying that there are severe limits to substitution. Economists, by and large, probably believe in substitutability, but, it has to be said, they do so on the basis of assumption more than empirical evidence. If we are not sure of the degree of substitutability, and that seems a fair if limited statement of the truth, then risk aversion should dictate caution about depleting that natural capital stock. The fact that the existing stock may not be the optimal stock then seems largely academic in the pejorative sense, for if we cannot identify the optimum with reasonable certainty it barely seems worth the risk of reducing the stock in order to probe for an optimum less than the stock we have. In any event, no-one seriously suggests running down national capital stocks in the aggregate sense.

So, far from not being "a genuine concept", sustainable development does have interesting implications for the way national economies are managed. Moreover, conservation of environmental capital becomes more important still in the context of sustainable development, and this explains in part the emphasis it received at Rio in 1992 and earlier in publications such as *Our Common Future* (World Commission on Environment and Development [1987]). The implications are several and the fact that they are familiar from other contexts does not diminish their importance. We cite these implications as:

(a) revising the measure of National Real Income which traditionally underlies development policy. This is the **national income accounting** implication;

(b) the importance of measuring the **economic value of environmental assets and their flows of services** in project and policy appraisal;

(c) the importance of **correctly pricing goods, services and inputs so that environmental costs and benefits are fully reflected**.

(d) seeking the **maintenance of the economic value of the overall stock of capital** in value terms, and within that objective, paying special attention to the overall stock of natural capital.

How do these implications relate to project and policy appraisal? The national accounting issue helps redefine what it is that projects and policies aim to achieve. It helps set the context for project appraisal. Points (b) and (c) are similar in that they call for the proper economic valuation of both environmental assets and economic goods and inputs. One link here is that economic outputs have environmental assets as inputs. An obvious example is energy. If energy prices fail to reflect the pollution damage associated with energy production and use, then goods embodying that energy will be similarly **underpriced**. In terms of project appraisal, the prices of economic goods and inputs affect project returns. Hence, the proper pricing of those goods and inputs is integral to proper project appraisal.

The other link is that the **opportunity costs** of the development project will be wrongly defined and measured if **non-marketed environmental services** are ignored. As an example, a rural development project that involves the sacrifice of a tropical forest will generate a rate of economic return which will be exaggerated if the forgone benefits of the tropical forest in a "conserved" state are not calculated. Rather than underpricing of economic goods and services, the failure here lies in not accounting for **zero priced** but **positive economic value** assets.

Finally, the general objective of maintaining capital stocks sets the broad economic framework for policy in general. It affects policy and project appraisal in that all policies and projects must, when aggregated, comply with the overall objective of securing the conditions for sustainable development.

Box 1.4 summarises the implications of sustainable development as an objective of policy. Chapter 11 discusses how the underlying theory of national accounting might be changed to reflect changes in environmental assets.

Environmental problems and the policy options

Environmental problems range in terms of their impact from being **local to global**. While the distinction is not always a firm one, it is also useful to distinguish problems as they relate to **renewable resources** and **non-renewable resources**. The former have the capacity to regenerate, as with fish or forests; the latter do not, as with oil or copper. (The term "exhaustible" resource is eschewed here as all resources are exhaustible, depending on how they are managed.) Chapters 15 and 16 look at some of the ways in which the renewable/non-renewable distinction affects policy, notably with respect to the proper pricing of resources.

The matrix below suggests an elementary classification of issues in terms of the spatial range of the problem and the degree of renewability of the resource. Renewability here refers to the physical characteristic of the resource: all renewable resources are "exhaustible" in the sense that they can be over-used and hence can be extinguished. Notice that what is local, regional or global is not determined by the location of the resource as by the spatial <u>significance</u> of the resource. A tropical forest is purely a local resource in the former sense but can become a global resource if its value is global.

	Local	Regional	Global
Renewable Resource	e.g.: fishery; local forest; groundwater system; fuelwood	e.g.: shared water basin system;	e.g.: ozone layer; major tropical forest; genetic information
Non-Renewable Resource	e.g.: mineral deposits; oil, coal	e.g.: shared natural gas reservoir	

From the previous discussion it is possible to derive a similarly broad classification of policy measures that are relevant to managing resources in these categories. These are shown in the second matrix below for environmental problems <u>within a nation's boundaries</u>. The measures are: the redefinition of property rights and investment policies. The proper pricing of inputs and outputs can be viewed as a form of designation of property rights, whilst command-and-control measures (regulations, environmental quality standards etc.) are also means of defining property rights or of attenuating existing property rights. Examples are given of each type of policy measure. Note that, within a country, it is possible to redefine property rights: state or private property ownership would ˙ be shown by moving between the cells of the matrix.

Once property rights are established, the proper pricing of resources dictates that they be priced <u>at</u> <u>least</u> at marginal private cost, and ideally at marginal social cost. Given that developing countries are often characterised by output prices that are well below the private costs of production, the pricing at marginal cost option (P=MC) is emphasised in the matrix. But this should not be taken to mean that full social cost pricing (P=MSC) is not a longer term aim. Hence the pricing rule for the public sector is shown in two stages, P=MC and then P=MSC. If private sector conditions prevail then it is assumed that private costs are already covered and the policy measure is then to seek marginal social cost pricing through, say, environmental taxes. Quantity-based measures are shown as a separate policy option even though their effect is similar to price-based measures. Thus, a tradeable permit in emission rights has close similarities to an environmental tax: the price of the permit effectively acts as a surrogate for the environmental tax. Finally, under investment policy, the kind of approach developed in this volume, cost-benefit analysis, is applicable to all public sector operations. While a cost-benefit can, and often is, performed for a private sector operation, especially where the concern is with leasing of mining rights say, the most widely employed method of monitoring and assessing private sector performance in terms of environmental impact is through an environmental impact statement (EIA).

	LDCs Public Sector	DCs Public Sector	LDCs Private Sector	DCs Private Sector
Property Rights: (a) pricing	(a) $P = MC$ $P = MSC$	(a) $P = MSC$	(a) $P = MSC$	(a) $P = MSC$
(b) quantity trading			(b) possible emissions and resource quota trading	(b) emissions and resource quota trading
(c) command and control	(c) envtal quality objectives	(c) envtal quality objectives	(c) envtal quality objectives	(c) envtal quality objectives
Investment Policy	CBA	CBA	EIA	EIA

Box 1.1 **Common property and open access**

While common property contexts are often thought to result in environmental degradation - "the tragedy of the commons" - it is really *open access* that accounts for situations in which individuals have no incentive to manage resources widely. *Common property* differs from open access in that well defined communities of individuals manage the resource, and do so by setting up rules and regulations, backed by communal enforcement, for resource management. Many common property arrangements break down and the situation reverts to effective open access. Others survive and prosper. Explaining why some succeed and others do not is the subject of extensive study.

In South India, for example, some villages are organised to manage canal irrigation water and grazing land, but others are not. One explanation for effective management is that communal management emerges as a response to ecological risks: the greater the risk the more incentive there is to manage resources collectively and to create "assurance" rules whereby each individual knows that his or her rights will be respected. In South Indian villages, for example, landowners often have rights to their crops but not the stubble left after harvesting. The cost of excluding others from grazing the stubble is too high. The village therefore establishes rules for the grazing of the stubble land, including, for example, charging for grazing for agreed limited herds, and paying for the manure that these herds generate. Outside herders come to an agreement with village authorities. Some grazing rights are even auctioned to the highest bidders. And if some crops are still standing, and are therefore at risk from the grazing, additional rules of behaviour are sought and guards are posted.

Much the same happens for irrigation water, but, significantly, only with respect to water at the 'tail end' of the irrigation system. This means the water is scarce and this is the catalyst for communal management. One author concludes:

> "..where there are substantial individual benefits from joint action, that action is likely to be forthcoming. This is not to say that the free-rider problem, the temptation for self-interested individuals to go for immediate gain, is minor....the [village] council has developed formidable mechanisms for enforcing the rules, for precisely the purpose of convincing individuals that other people will probably abide by the rules, so that if they too abide by the rules they will not be the loser".

Source: Wade, R. [1986], "Common Property Resource Management in South Indian Villages", in National Research Council, *Proceedings of the Conference on Common Property Resource Management*, Washington DC: National Academy Press, 231-258.

Box 1.2 **A typology of property rights regimes and conditions for efficiency**

	Open Access	Common Property	Private Property	State Property
Universality	No	Defined for the group	Yes	No
Exclusivity	No	Defined for the group	Fails in the presence of externalities and public goods	No, but non-nationals excluded
Transferability	No	Applies for the group	Yes	No
Enforceability	No	Yes: legal and social sanctions	Yes: legal and social sanctions	Yes: legal sanctions
OVERALL EFFICIENCY	VERY LOW: NO INCENTIVE TO CONSERVE	MANY REGIMES ARE EFFICIENT, BUT INHERENT RISK OF BREAKDOWN	EFFICIENT BUT MARKET FAILURE OCCURS IN PRESENCE OF EXTERNAL-ITIES AND PUBLIC GOODS	OFTEN INEFFICIENT DUE TO GOVERN-MENT FAILURE

Box 1.3 Some examples of government failure

In the developing world free markets are very often not allowed to function. Governments intervene and control prices, but unlike the EC case they tend to keep prices down <u>below</u> their market equilibrium. They do this usually from well-meaning motives. For example, they wish to keep food prices low so as to subsidise food costs to the poor. Or they wish to stimulate industrial development and this leads them to keep energy prices down. Unfortunately, such interventions often cause more problems than they solve. The negative effects are:

- governments use up substantial tax revenues and other income in subsidies for price control, even though government revenues are at a premium because of the need to use them to develop the economy;

- the subsidies encourage over-use of the resources that are subsidised. While we tend to think that poor countries will use scarce resources wisely, the effect of keeping prices down is to encourage wasteful use;

- the subsidies make the economic activity in question appear artificially attractive. This tends to attract more people into that industry or sector because profits, or "rents", are high (this is known as <u>rent-seeking</u>). This diverts resources away from more important activities in the economy.

The impact on the environment can be illustrated in the context of the pricing of irrigation water and energy.

Irrigation Water

In many countries the prices charged for water that is used for irrigating crops are generally below costs of supply, and often lack incentives to conserve water, e.g., charges are often set on the basis of irrigated acreage regardless of water quantity consumed. One of the effects of such low charges is over-watering with the result that the irrigated land becomes waterlogged. Applications of irrigation water often exceed design levels by factors of three. In India 10 million hectares of land have been lost to cultivation through waterlogging and 25 million hectares are threatened by salinization. In Pakistan some 12 million hectares of the Indus Basin canal system is waterlogged and 40 per cent is saline. Worldwide, maybe some 40% of the world's irrigation capacity is affected by salinization. Irrigation from river impoundments has resulted in other environmental effects. Large dams produce downstream pollution, and upstream siltation as the land around the reservoir is deforested. Indigenous peoples are moved from their traditional homelands when the dammed area is flooded. Clearly, not all damage done by irrigation is due to low pricing, nor, by any means, can the environmental costs of large dams be debited to inefficient pricing. But there is an association between wrong pricing and environmental damage. By adopting prices that are too low more irrigation water than is needed is demanded, exaggerating the requirement for major irrigation schemes such as dams and for other schemes as well. Even if the scheme is justified, the amounts of water that are used are likely to be excessive because of the failure to price the resource closer to its true cost of supply.

Table 1.3.A. shows the ratio of actual revenues obtained from selected irrigation schemes to operating and maintenance costs (O + M) and to moderate estimates of capital plus O+M costs. While some countries succeed in recovering most or all of the O+M costs, the highest recovery rate of total costs is around 20% only.

The under-pricing encourages a wasteful attitude so that systems are kept in a poor state of repair. Inefficient irrigation negatively affects agricultural output. Because charges are low there is excess demand, giving a premium to those who can secure water rights, e.g., by being the first in line to receive water. This can be achieved by ensuring that the system irrigates particular parcels of land first, leaving the poorer farmer to secure whatever is left over after wasteful prior uses. Moreover, water tends to be allocated according to acreage, not by crop requirements. This results in the phenomenon of <u>rent-seeking</u>: the interest is in securing control of the allocation system. The high rents get capitalised in higher land values, making the incentive to compete for the allocation more intense. But the competition does not take place in the market place. It manifests itself as bribery to officials, corruption, expenditures on lobbying, political contributions, and so on. The allocators of rights similarly expand their own bureaucracies and secure benefits for themselves. Rent-seeking obviously favours the already rich and powerful and discriminates against the poor and unorganized. And because it encourages wasteful use of resources, rent-seeking harms the environment, adding to the social costs of policy failures in the price-setting sphere.

Energy

Commercial energy - coal, oil, gas, electricity - is widely subsidized in developing countries. As with irrigation water, the effects of the subsidy are to encourage wasteful uses of energy, and, hence in environmental terms to add to air pollution and problems of waste disposal. The economic impacts of the subsidies tend to be more dramatic, since they are a drain on government revenues and thereby divert valuable resources away from productive sectors, tend to reduce exports of any indigenous energy, thereby adding to external debt, and encourage energy intensive industry at the expense of more efficient industry.

There are two measures of subsidy. The <u>financial</u> measure indicates the difference between prices charged and costs of production. An <u>economic</u> subsidy measures the difference between the value of the energy source in its most productive use (the "opportunity cost value") and its actual price. A convenient measure of the opportunity cost value, or "shadow price", is either (a) the price the fuel would fetch if it were exported, or the price that has to be paid if it was imported (the "world" price), or (b) if the fuel is not tradeable (as with most electricity, for example) the <u>long-run marginal cost of supply</u>. The long-run marginal cost of supply is the cost of providing an additional supply in the long term. Financial subsidies measure the direct financial cost to the nation of subsidising energy, but the economic measure is more appropriate as an indicator of the "true cost" of subsidies since it measures what the country could secure if it adopted a full shadow pricing approach.

Table 1.3.B. shows the size of the economic subsidy for selected oil-exporting countries. Here the subsidies have an additional distortion in that they divert potentially exportable energy to the home market, thus adding to balance-of-payments difficulties and hence to international indebtedness. The scale of the distortion can be gauged by looking at the subsidies as a percentage of energy exports and as a percentage of all exports. In Egypt, for example, the subsidies are equal to 88% of all exports and are twice the value of oil exports.

Table 1.3.A. Cost recovery in irrigation schemes

(per cent)

Country	Actual Revenues O+M Costs	Actual Revenues Capital + O+M Costs
Indonesia	78	14
Korea	91	18
Nepal	57	7
Philippines	120	22
Thailand	28	5
Bangladesh	18	neg

Notes: neg = negligible. Capital costs are "moderate" estimates only.

Source: Repetto, R. [1986], *Skimming the Water: Rent-Seeking and the Performance of Public Irrigation Systems*, Washington DC: World Resources Institute, p5.

Table 1.3.B. Economic subsidies to energy in selected countries

	Size of Subsidy $m	Subsidy as % all exports	Subsidy as % energy exports
Bolivia	224	29	68
China	5400	20	82
Egypt	4000	88	200
Ecuador	370	12	19
Indonesia	600	5	7
Mexico	5000	23	33
Nigeria	5000	21	23
Peru	301	15	73
Tunisia	70	4	10
Venezuela	1900	14	15

Source: Kosmo, M. [1989], "Commercial Energy Subsidies in Developing Countries", *Energy Policy*, June, 244-253.

Box 1.4 The implications of sustainable development for policy and project appraisal

Sustainable development is simply the goal of ensuring that future generations are no worse off than this one. "Development" has various meanings but clearly involves raising individuals' well-being through increases in real income, educational achievement, health status, personal freedoms and environmental quality. Securing sustainable development involves making sure the next generation has the capacity to generate as much well-being as today. This means leaving them a stock of capital assets and technology no less than that possessed today. In practical terms, this "constant capital" means a constant or rising <u>economic value</u> of capital assets of all kinds. The implications of this view of sustainable development are set out below.

Implication	Context	Relevance to Project and Policy Appraisal
Redefine and Measure Modified GNP	New Measure Should Relate to Sustainable National Income as That Income Which Can be Secured Without Running Down Capital Assets	Primarily a Macroeconomic Concern, but Policy and Project Costs and Benefits Should be Measured in These Terms
Attach Economic Values to Environmental Services	Failure to Do So Will Lead to Excess Environmental Degradation	Emphasise Role of Environmental Assets in Projects and Policies, Especially Where They are Sacrificed by Development Projects
Correctly Price Economic Inputs and Outputs	The Polluter Pays Principle. Failure to Price Correctly Will Feed Back to Excess Environmental Degradation	Correct Shadow Pricing of Project and Policy Costs and Benefits
Establish Overall Goal of "Constant Capital Stock"	A Macroeconomic Goal of Constant or Rising Value of Assets	Generic Goal Underlying Modified GNP Approach
Avoid Investments and Policies Likely to Impose Major Irreversible Costs on Future Generations	Sustainable Development Means Not Making Future Worse Off Compared to Present	Importance of Correct Valuation. Possible Implication for the Discount Rate

Chapter 2

Environmental Information

Introduction: The nature of environmental information

All policy measures and investments require information. Environmental information is often the most difficult to assemble because it requires that a system of **environmental monitoring** be in place. In many developing countries such monitoring is often rudimentary, and what monitoring there is often has unknown bounds of uncertainty. Monitoring systems involve two dimensions:

(a)   the measurement of **emissions and waste arisings,** for example emissions of sulphur oxides (SOx) and the quantities of solid waste generated; and **land use change**;

(b)   the measurement of **environmental impact** from a given level of emissions or waste arisings, for example the reduction in water quality as measured by levels of dissolved oxygen (DO) in the water.

In turn, environmental impact can be measured in "biophysical" terms (as with the measure of DO) and in economic terms, i.e., with a money value attached to the impact. Part III of this volume looks in detail at the rationale for economic valuation and the techniques for achieving it. Typically, economic approaches require a biophysical measure to exist before any monetary valuation can be carried out. Monetary valuation can therefore be seen to be dependent upon detailed physical and biological information. In turn, the cost-benefit approach outlined in this volume requires that environmental impacts be valued in monetary terms whenever this is feasible and credible. Monetisation offers one way of assessing the **importance** of environmental impacts. Other means of doing this might include some indicator of ecological stress, or a measure of health impact.

A model of environmental information

The sequence of emissions - impacts - importance of impact is not the whole story of environmental information. Box 2.1 shows how this sequence fits into a wider model of information. Emissions and waste arisings are simply indicators of the **proximate pressure** on the environment. They reflect **underlying pressures** arising from sectoral change in the economy which in turn reflects population change, public policy (including any changes in property rights regimes and public opinion - the latter being especially important in developed economies) and macroeconomic changes to prices, international trade and overall GNP. The various sectoral impacts can then be measured in terms of **state of the environment (SOE) indicators,** e.g., changes in length of river with a particular classification of water quality, or change in DO levels in a given river over time, and so on. In order to make the transition to measures of importance, SOE indicators need to be translated into **effects indicators,** i.e., usually measures of **damage** (or improvement) in assets, natural and man-made, that have economic value to individuals. Thus, an SOE indicator might be the ambient level of SOx, but an effects indicator might be the rate of corrosion of exposed metal surfaces. In turn, the effects indicator can be measured in biophysical terms and monetary terms. At all stages, the monetary measure should relate back to the conceptual foundations for the measurement of changes in human well-being -i.e., the compensating or equivalent variation measures introduced in Chapter 3. Finally, the response dimension shows how various sectors of the economy respond to environmental change. Individuals and households, for example, may respond by increased political lobbying, and/or by spending money to avoid environmental damage (e.g., by relocating, installing water filtration equipment etc.). Governments may respond with policy measures, and so on.

Environmental indicators exist at various levels. At their simplest, indicators measure changes in the state of the environment, e.g., a change in ambient air quality. This is level 1. Level 2 links the state indicators to some measure of underlying pressure. The most common of these links measures of environmental quality or damage to a measure of economic activity such as GNP. While there are many reasons to engage in this linking operation, the most obvious is that it can facilitate **environmental impact forecasting**. An example would be the linking of SOx emissions to the level of energy consumption in the economy, the level of economic activity, the price of energy and the fuel mix in the economy. The resulting equation of the form:

$$SOx = f(E, Y, Pe, F)$$

might permit a general forecasting of sulphur emissions in the future. In turn, such a forecast could be linked to a model of impact (requiring some idea of how emissions translate into spatial ambient concentrations) and hence to importance. Note that equations of this form are especially useful for policy analysis if they cover time series in which different policy measures have been tried. In this case a policy variable, V, can be added to the determinants of SOx in the equation. The coefficient of the policy variable would then indicate the extent to which SOx emissions have been explained by policy measures, structural change in the economy, changes in fuel mix, etc.

Box 2.2 shows linked indicators of this kind but at the global level. The aim is to see how environmental degradation relates to income. While the analysis shown in Box 2.2 is global and is designed to illustrate a much broader relationship between environment and development, the same idea can be applied at national and regional levels.

A third level of indicators seeks to put them into an **accounting framework**. This would include monetised measures of damage since these are generally required in order to fit into some other schema such as cost-benefit analysis. But in some circumstances monetary measures may themselves be linked back to indicators of economic activity as in Level 2. The two most developed accounting frameworks, however, are : **satellite accounts** and **modified national income accounting**. While satellite accounts do **not** involve monetisation of impacts, modified national income accounting **does** involve monetisation. As such, we deal only with satellite accounting in this chapter and postpone discussion of national income accounting to Chapter 11.

Level 1 environmental indicators

Environmental indicators at level 1 simply show the "state of the environment" in terms of ambient qualities of the receiving environment, emissions and waste arisings, and land use. Such indicators may be presented for a single country, which is the most usual presentation for policy analysis, or in comparative terms, comparing indicators in several different countries. The usefulness of the latter is limited for policy analysis purposes. The most systematic collection of indicators for developed countries is that produced by the OECD: *Environmental Indicators: a Preliminary Set*, [1991], and OECD, *Environmental Data* [annually]. Similar comparative data are produced on a limited basis for the world as a whole in the World Bank's *World Development Report* [annually]; UNEP's *Environmental Data Report* [approximately every year]; UNDP's *Human Development Report* [annually]; and the World Resources Institute's *World Resources* [approximately annually and in conjunction with UNDP and UNEP]; and The UN Economic Commission for Europe's *The Environment in Europe and North America* [1992 is the first regular issue]. Many individual countries produce their own reports (e.g., the US Council for Environmental Quality's *Environmental Quality* report [annually] and Norway's *Natural Resources and the Environment* [annually]).

A selected illustration of these data is provided in Box 2.3. The example shown, waste paper recovery and consumption, could be used in evaluating feasible waste recovery targets in materials recycling investments. Thus, several countries are seen to make substantial use of recovered waste paper relative to their apparent consumption (output - exports + imports) of paper: Japan, Chile and Czechoslovakia at around 50%, for example, compared to less than 10% in Tunisia, Myanmar and Pakistan. It would be too simplistic to suggest that rates in the latter countries could be improved to the levels in the former since many factors affect feasible recycling rates -e.g., population density, the price of virgin pulp, the nature of industry etc. But analysts might compare recycling rates in countries where conditions are thought to be broadly similar, using these to establish a preliminary guess at feasible recycling targets in the country in question. As an example, it is unclear why Chile should achieve such a high recycling rate compared to Bolivia, although the data suggest that the lower is the absolute quantity of paper consumed, the lower is the recycling rate.

Level 2 environmental indicators

At level 2, level 1 indicators are related to some other variable, usually an economic one. An example is provided in Box 2.4 and shows how energy consumption per unit of GDP varies. Illustrations are given of comparative data and a time series for a few countries. There are many uses for such indicators. In order to evaluate energy investments, for example, it is essential to have some idea of future energy demand. Where quick and approximate calculations are required, energy per unit GDP is quite a useful indicator which can then be related to forecasts of GDP, expected structural change in the economy, and other factors. Time series help by showing how energy use per unit GDP might be expected to change with time given the state of development of the economy. In turn, pollution emissions tend to have fairly stable coefficients per unit of energy source. In this way, then, it is possible to get a rough estimate of the expected emissions of pollutants given the forecast of GDP.

Satellite accounts

The essence of satellite accounting is that environmental indicators (Level 1 and 2 types) are integrated into a wider accounting framework but without monetisation of environmental and resource changes. This is not a hard and fast rule, but generally holds. Essentially, then, a system of monetised accounts, based on the United Nations System of National Accounts (SNA), is supplemented by sets of physical accounts which usually show opening and closing stocks of natural resources and changes in environmental quality. Two countries in particular have developed these accounting procedures: France with its "natural patrimony accounts" and Norway, with its "resource accounts".

Box 2.5 illustrates the French system. The lower levels of information correspond approximately to what we have called Level 1 indicators: data on changes in ambient environmental quality, economic data and so on. Above these levels (level 3 and above in Box 2.5) attempts are made to integrate the various indicators into wider accounting frameworks. What the French call "satellite accounts" are in fact accounts relating to environmental expenditures: sources, flows and beneficiaries. These feed into the "patrimony" accounts along with the lower level environmental indicators. The patrimony accounts essentially record the opening and closing stocks of natural resources and changes in environmental quality. Above the level of patrimony and satellite accounts are larger models which simulate the two way interaction of environment and the economy - the effect of environmental change on macroeconomic magnitudes, and the effect of changes in the economy on the environment. This level (level 5 in Box 2.5) is essentially designed for environmental forecasting purposes. Level 6 in Box 2.5 goes to the final stage, integrated GNP and environmental accounts. As yet, France has not undertaken this stage.

The patrimony accounts are thus physical accounts. Ideally, they show not just the changes in the stock of any natural resource, but the immediate factors giving rise to those changes. Thus, a forest's growing stock would be estimated in year 1. Changes in that stock through natural growth will be recorded as a positive item, and reductions due to felling, natural tree death and accidents will then be deducted to give the growing stock in period 1. The link between this physical accounting of changes and the modified monetised national accounts will be indicated in the next section. Suffice it to say that patrimony accounts of this kind are needed before the full monetised accounts can be developed. Through the links to other accounts in the system it is possible, in principle anyway, to indicate how a given economic change will impact on an environmental or resource stock. That is, the primary purpose of the patrimony accounts together with the other accounts is to **describe the state of the environment** and to **predict the state of the environment**. This observation is important since it defines the difference between satellite accounting (a term we use to describe the general process of setting up physical and other subsidiary accounts) and full modified national income accounting. The latter has a different aim which is to **measure more accurately the state of human well-being and to offer initial indicators of sustainability of the national economy**. An additional feature of satellite accounts is that they serve to underline the physical interdependence of environment and economic activity since, again in principle, it should be possible to indicate the physical changes in the environment arising from changes in economic activity, and to indicate the impacts on the economy of changes in the environment. In practice these objectives are met only partially in the available satellite accounting systems.

Geographical Information Systems

In recent years it has become apparent that geographical information systems (GIS) have a significant role to play in the analysis of environment and economy interactions. A GIS is essentially a compilation of data on a spatial basis and such data might be presented as a map or in quantitative form on an outline map. A critical feature of a GIS, however, is that the data are computerised, thus facilitating manipulation using software programmes. The attraction of GIS's is that large sets of different data can be superimposed on the initial spatial layout. For example, the initial map might show forest cover for a given country or region. The source of such data is most likely to be thematic imagery from satellites or photographs from aerial surveys. One advantage of satellite imagery is that both past and current images can be called up, depending on the coverage of satellites, cloud cover and so on. From the images over two different periods it is then possible to show the same information but in terms of changes in forest cover. A further set of data might be the road system in the country. A map of this can be superimposed on the forest cover map, and an initial correlation might be sought between the presence of roads and the change of forest cover. The intuition behind the correlation is that road building "opens up" forest areas, first to logging concessions and then to agricultural colonists who follow the loggers and establish crop production farms, and perhaps livestock ranches after crop systems have become unproductive. One policy implication might then be that one of the social costs of road building projects is the deforestation they help facilitate.

In much the same way, a fairly complex picture of spatial information can be built up. Increasingly, socio-economic data are being added to what are primarily physical data GIS's. Population density and movements can be superimposed, as can information on agricultural systems, even prices. Two purposes are immediately served by such procedures: (a) a clearer understanding of environment and social and economic activity; and (b) insights into the causal factors at work giving rise to environmental change, and vice versa. It will be recalled that this is one of the main purposes of satellite accounting systems and it is no surprise therefore that information from GIS's is used in the construction of satellite environmental accounts. Similarly, any satellite account can be spatially differentiated to provide another dimension for policy makers to consider. Box 2.6 provides one example of the ways in which GIS's can assist policy decisions.

System models

Level 2 indicators link environmental change to some measure of economic activity. Such indicators can be developed for **national** activity measures, such as GNP, **regional and city** measures, and even **firm or industry** measures. Analysing the quantitative relationship between activities within any of these spatial units and the environmental impacts is an example of **activity analysis** (Hufschmidt et al., [1983]) and such analyses lend themselves naturally to **programming approaches**. For example, waste residual flows can be linked to economic activity across various kinds of industries and households in a region. By linking physical models, showing the relationships between inputs, outputs and residuals discharges and waste, with economic information on the costs of controlling waste flows, it is possible to analyse how to secure some desired objective, such as minimising the cost of control. Information of this kind may be embodied in specially commissioned engineering-economic studies, but in recent years much of this kind of information in richer countries is available from **environmental audits** carried out by companies. Usually, such information is confidential to the firm in question, but some audits are published.

Frequently, however, it will be necessary to evaluate the wider links between economic activity and environmental impact. These cases require **system wide models** where the system in question could be defined in economic terms (a specified economic region for example) but is better defined in environmental terms. The reason for this is that spatial environmental units will tend to capture the various inter-linkages between activities and impacts. For example, a river basin will tend to be the "natural unit of account" for an analysis of water pollution or land-use change that affects runoff to water. The focus of analysis may be on the individual receiving medium: an aquifer, a river basin, an airshed etc. But it is widely recognised now that environmental media are themselves linked: atmospheric emissions affect water acidification; waste that is burned on land affects air quality; sewage sludge not disposed of to the sea has to be burned or spread on land, and so on. The modern focus is therefore on **integrated** models in which the cross-media flows are also modelled. Hufschmidt et al [1983] distinguish **statistical black box models** from **conservation of mass-and-energy models**. The former relate dependent variables to some set of independent variables without detailing the **processes** by which the relationship occurs. The actual processes are, as it were, hidden in a "black box" which is not investigated. The conservation of mass/energy approach traces through the links between activities and flows of wastes and residuals to the environment using the principle that materials and energy cannot be destroyed. Thus, whatever is used up in a production or consumption process must reappear somewhere else in the system, albeit in altered form. A tonne of coal, for example, when burned, will reappear as ash and atmospheric gases.

System models may focus on a single activity or on many activities. Typical multi-activity models include **input-output analysis** and **programming models**.

In input-output models, the outputs of individual economic sectors are related to the inputs needed from other sectors. Thus, the steel industry buys coke from the energy sector, and so on. Extending this set of interlinkages, coefficients can be introduced which relate outputs of individual sectors to emissions to the atmosphere, water and land. Using computerised models it is then possible to simulate the effects on emissions of, say, a given percentage change in output in the economy as a whole or in a given sector. The effects of environmental controls can be simulated by reducing the coefficients linking emissions to activities, and so on.

Programming models permit multiple objectives and constraints to be integrated. For example, there may well be a target rate of economic growth and a desire not to allow environmental quality to deteriorate. In turn there may be several ways of achieving the target growth rate, e.g by expanding different industries. Programming models allow the "optimal" mix of industry expansion to be determined whilst observing the overall environmental constraint.

An excellent treatment of modelling approaches is to be found in Hufschmidt et al [1983].

Box 2.1 A model of environmental indicators

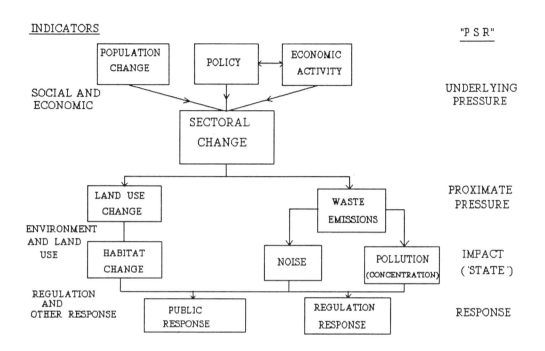

INDICATORS

"P S R"

POPULATION CHANGE

POLICY

ECONOMIC ACTIVITY

SOCIAL AND ECONOMIC

UNDERLYING PRESSURE

SECTORAL CHANGE

LAND USE CHANGE

WASTE EMISSIONS

PROXIMATE PRESSURE

ENVIRONMENT AND LAND USE

HABITAT CHANGE

NOISE

POLLUTION (CONCENTRATION)

IMPACT ('STATE')

REGULATION AND OTHER RESPONSE

PUBLIC RESPONSE

REGULATION RESPONSE

RESPONSE

P = Pressure   S = State of the environment   R = Response

31

Box 2.2 **Links between environment and economic development**

Population without safe water

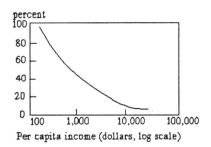

Urban population without
adequate sanitation

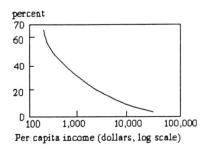

Urban concentrations
of particulate matter

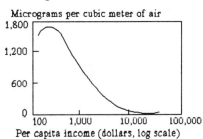

Urban concentrations
of sulphur dioxide

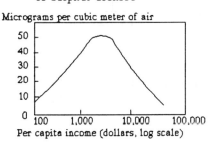

Municipal wastes per capita

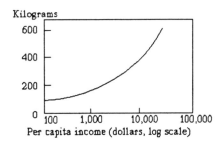

Carbon dioxide
emissions per capita[a]

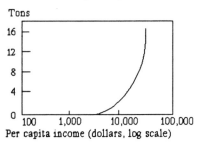

Note : Estimates are based on cross-country regression analysis
of data from the 1980's

a. Emissions are from fossil fuels

Sources: Shafik and Bandyopadhyay, background paper; World Bank data

Box 2.3 **Comparative environmental indicators: An illustration**

Most countries recycle waste products, but the extent to which this is done varies substantially between countries. One indicator of "recycling effort" is the ratio of waste paper used to the total amount of paper "consumed" in the economy. The latter is measured by production of paper less exports plus imports.

Country	Paper Recovered as % Apparent Consumption	Apparent Consumption 000 tonnes
Switzerland	61	1005
Netherlands	54	2800
Chile	54	370
Czechoslovakia	49	na
Austria	49	1083
Sweden	48	2050
Japan	48	24940
UK	30	9286
......		
New Zealand	18	561
Bolivia	17	26
Myanmar	14	20
Jordan	11	59
Tunisia	8	122
Pakistan	4	na

Source: UNEP, [1992], *Environmental Data Report 1991-1992*, 3rd edition, Oxford: Basil Blackwell, Table 8.12,

Box 2.4 Level 2 environmental indicators: An illustration

Energy use per unit of GDP tends to vary with the stage of economic development. As such we would expect economies in the early stages of development to use more energy per unit GDP as they industrialise. As service sectors grow so the "energy ratio" is likely to fall. Time series analysis indicate that, once an economy has gone beyond the peak of heavy industrialisation, the ratio falls systematically over time, indicating a higher and higher "efficiency" of energy use through time. These gains in efficiency reflect "autonomous" improvements in energy efficiency as technology improves, and structural change in the economy. The selected data suggests that this picture is broadly true, but for the 1980s a number of developing countries actually experienced a reduction in their energy ratio.

Country	Energy per Unit GNP: MJ/$ GNP	% Change in Energy Ratio 1979-1989
USA	17	-18
UK	12	-16
Germany(W)	9	-21
Japan	6	-22
Singapore	16	-51
Indonesia	34	-29
Dominica	25	-24
Bangladesh	27	- 2
China	84	-32
Malaysia	23	+25
Pakistan	36	+ 5
Greece	20	+34
Argentina	31	+47
Bolivia	24	+25
Congo	22	+40
Central African R	36	+40
Madagascar	34	+33

Source: World Resources Institute, [1992], *World Resources 1991-1992*, Oxford: Oxford University Press, Table 21.2.

Box 2.5 **The French Satellite and Patrimony account system**

The diagram overleaf shows the way in which the French accounting system proposes an ideal system of monetary and physical accounts. The two main building blocks are the patrimony accounts - essentially changes in the state of environmental variables, including land use - and the monetised national accounts. The aim is to show how each interacts with the other in a quantitative fashion, but without the environmental changes being monetised. The "satellite" account in the French system happens to relate only to environmental expenditures and the way they affect environmental changes. While the system is primarily designed to observe and measures changes in the environment, such physical accounts are essential precursors of a fully modified monetised national accounts system.

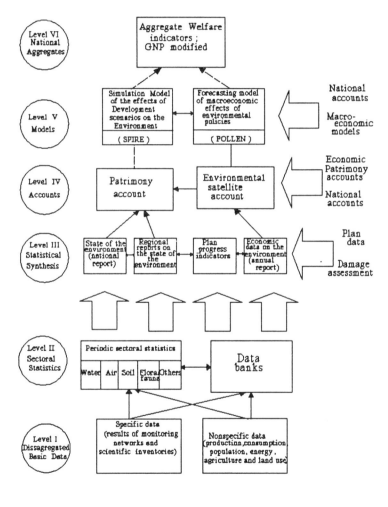

——————— Prospective relation; not yet implemented.

Source: Theys, J. [1989], "Environmental Accounting in Development Policy: the French Experience", in Ahmad, Y., S. El Serafy, E. Lutz, *Environmental Accounting for Sustainable Development*, World Bank, Washington DC.

Box 2.6 Using Geographical Information Systems

In case studies from Nigeria and Indonesia, Jagernathan [1989] uses GIS's to explore the relationship between poverty, public policies and environmental degradation. Poverty is perhaps the most widely cited "cause" of environmental degradation in poor countries. The poor, it is argued, have no option but to "mine" available natural resources, including soil and biomass, because of the absence of financial resources to invest in soil conservation and land productivity. Other commentators have shown that many poor groups still undertake conservation activities and longer-term investments (such as tree growing) even when there is famine pressure.

Using LANDSAT images from the mid 1970s and mid 1980s, Jagernathan quantified the changes in land use, particularly forest clearing and changes in human settlements. Socio-economic data on population migration, inequality of land holdings, non-farm income opportunities and public policies were then "superimposed" on the physical land use change observations.

For the Indonesia case study Jagernathan concluded that the change in land use was mainly accounted for by the growth of mixed-garden estates, built up areas and, in the more sparsely populated area, by the demand for wood. These land use changes are, by and large, sustainable. Moreover, the factors giving rise to the changes in land use appear to have more to do with government financial incentives to rice and tree crops. Poverty was generally not implicated in the changes that took place. Transport improvements "enabled" the land use changes to take place.

For Nigeria, Jagernathan concluded that the story was very similar. Infrastructural investment and changes in food prices appeared to account for land use change. Of course, the areas studied were microcosms of large areas and it would be dangerous to generalise. The issue here is not so much the causal links that emerged as the use of GIS to cast light on those links. Moreover, Jagernathan's studies were very modest in terms of cost and did not require a major resource input.

Source: Jagernathan, N.V. [1989], *Poverty, Public Policies and the Environment*, Environment Working Paper No.24, World Bank, Washington DC, December.

PART II

FOUNDATIONS

Chapter 3

The Economic Criterion for Policy Choice

Introduction

In a world with such a diversity of cultures, religions, languages, disciplines, professions, and moral philosophies, it is a complex undertaking to get people to agree on a course of collective action. This task is even more complicated if one wants to get them to agree on a **rationale** for a given course of action. This is in part because individuals have different beliefs about what will happen if particular investments are made, or specific policies adopted, but it is also because people have **different value systems** and world views. These value systems often clash, particularly in the environmental policy arena, and sometimes agreement on policy choice is simply not possible.

Democratic societies use two basic types of decision rules to resolve such conflicts and to decide on courses of collective action. The first and most common is some kind of **majority voting** rule in which the preferences of each person or group are counted equally. One problem with this rule is that weakly held preferences of one voter count as much in the decision as strongly - held preferences of another. To take account of the strength of individuals' preferences in the decision process, representative governments may impose a second kind of decision rule on government agencies: that actions only be undertaken for which the "benefits exceed the costs". The ethical justification for such a rule is that it gives greater weight in the decision to the magnitude of the effect of a policy or project on particular individuals or groups than do majority voting rules. This second decision rule thus allows some policies to be adopted that would not be approved by a majority vote because a few individuals may receive great benefits while a large number of individuals bear small costs. The decision rule may also approve policies with small benefits to a large number of individuals and high costs to a few, but such policies would be allowed by a majority vote as well.

In this chapter we examine this economic criterion of "benefits exceeding costs" **at the level of a single individual**. This criterion will be used throughout this volume to evaluate the wisdom or appropriateness of different environmental strategies. We propose that environmental investments, policies, and regulations be evaluated in terms of how they change the **well-being** or the **welfare** of the individuals affected. We do not advocate, however, that this be the sole criterion used to evaluate environmental strategies: just that it is an important one that should be given careful consideration. This criterion will be familiar to economists, who often think of or describe **human well-being** in terms of an individual's "utility" or "preference satisfaction". We prefer to use the term **human well-being** here in order to focus attention on the people themselves rather than a particular notion or conceptualization of how human welfare may be achieved. The proposal to use human well-being as a criterion raises three immediate questions:

(1) From a practical perspective, can human well-being be defined and measured?

(2) Even if we were able to develop accurate estimates of the changes in human well-being associated with different policies, would this be sufficient information on which to base a decision on the

appropriate policy to choose?

(3) How should information on changes in individuals' well-being be aggregated, synthesized, or summarized to aid in policy choice?

In this chapter we examine the first and second questions. We will examine decision rules for aggregating and summarizing this information in Chapter 4.

The criterion of increased human well-being

The notion of human well-being can be thought of in many ways, but is perhaps best conceived as an imprecise, multidimensional concept that cannot be measured directly. We can reasonably say that an individual's well-being increases when he or she moves from a state of hunger to being well - nourished, is better housed, lives a longer, healthier life, or indicates that he or she is happier and more satisfied with his life, community, and natural environment. There are in general two conceptually distinct ways one could go about the task of measuring well-being. First, one might attempt to define objective, measurable conditions, such as longevity, calorific intake, money income, and education level that would **be associated with** well-being. The UNDP social indicators are good examples of such objective measures that many people would agree are likely to **correlate** with our intuitive notion or general sense of human well-being (Box 3.1). Such indicators might enable an analyst to distinguish between individuals with high well-being and low well-being, or be a good "proxy" for well-being, but they would not provide a measure of the thing itself.

Second, a transformation of well-being into some other more general yardstick or numeraire can be attempted in order to measure well-being on a single scale or dimension. For example, Campbell et. al. [1976] attempted to measure people's subjective well-being with the use of surveys in which respondents are asked to use an ordinal number or category to describe or rank their level of happiness or well-being. Such indicators of subjective well-being have actually proved surprisingly robust, but as economists and others have pointed out, the meaning of interpersonal comparisons of well-being (or utility) using such approaches is unclear.

Applied welfare economists have proposed another such transformation in order to measure this multidimensional notion of an individual's well-being. For a **gain** in an individual's well-being, they propose that the **change** be measured by the maximum amount of goods or services - or money income (or wealth) - that he or she would be willing to give up or forego in order to obtain the change. Alternatively, if the change reduces well-being, it would be measured by the amount of money that the individual would require in compensation in order to accept the change.

Let us illustrate this approach for the monetary valuation of a change in environmental quality with the following "thought experiment". Consider an individual in an initial state of well-being W_0 that he achieves with a money income Y_0 and an environmental quality level of E_0:

$$W_0 (Y_0, E_0) \qquad\qquad [3.1]$$

Suppose that there is a proposal to **improve** environmental quality from E_0 to E_1. This improvement would increase the individual's well-being to W_1:

$$W_1 (Y_0, E_1) \qquad\qquad [3.2]$$

In order to assess the appropriateness of this policy, we would like to know **how much** the well-being of this individual is increased by this improvement in environmental quality, i.e., how large is W_1 minus W_0?

Since we cannot measure well-being in the two states directly (i.e., before and after the change in environmental quality), economists have proposed two different approaches. First, a policy analyst can try to determine the **maximum amount of income the individual would be willing to pay (WTP)** for the change. In effect, the individual is asked (or is hypothesized) to consider two combinations of income and environmental quality that both yield the same level of well-being (W_0): one in which his income is reduced and environmental quality is increased, and a second in which his income is not reduced and environmental quality is not increased:

$$W_0 (Y_0 - WTP, E_1) = W_0 (Y_0, E_0) \qquad [3.3]$$

The "rational" individual is assumed to adjust WTP to the point at which these two combinations of income and environmental quality yield equal well-being. At that point WTP is defined as the monetary **value** of the change in well-being, $W_1 - W_0$, resulting from the increase in environmental quality from E_0 to E_1, and is termed the individual's **compensating variation**. It is measured relative to the initial level of well-being, W_0.

The second approach yields an alternative monetary measure of this change in individual well-being. This second approach is to ask how much an individual would be willing to accept (WTA) in terms of additional income to forego the improvement in environmental quality and still have the same level of well-being as if environmental quality had been increased. In this case the individual is asked to consider the following two combinations of income and environmental quality that yield an equal level of well-being (W_1):

$$W_1 (Y_0 + WTA, E_0) = W_1 (Y_0, E_1) \qquad [3.4]$$

where WTA is an alternative monetary measure of the value to the individual of the change in well-being ($W_1 - W_0$) resulting from the improvement in environmental quality. This is termed the **equivalent variation** and is measured relative to the level of well-being after the change, W_1. Here the monetary measure of the value of the change in well-being could be infinite if no amount of money could compensate the individual for not experiencing the environmental improvement[1].

For a policy change that results in a **loss** in well-being, the correspondence between WTP and WTA, and the measures of compensating and equivalent variation is not the same. In this case the compensating variation is measured by WTA, and the equivalent variation is measured by WTP. Suppose, for example, that instead of an environmental improvement that the change in environmental quality from E_0 to E_1 results in a **reduction** in the individual's well-being.

The compensating variation is the amount of money the individual would be willing to accept as compensation to let the change occur and still leave him or her as well off as before the change:
$$W_0 (Y_0 + WTA, E_1) = W_0 (Y_0, E_0) \qquad [3.5]$$

Note that the required compensation could again be infinite if there was no way that money could fully substitute for the loss in environmental quality.

The equivalent variation is the amount of money the individual would be willing to pay to avert the change:
$$W_1 (Y_0 - WTP, E_0) = W_1 (Y_0, E_1) \qquad [3.6]$$

In this case the equivalent variation measure of the value to the individual of the change in well-being resulting from a deterioration in environmental quality from E_0 to E_1 is finite and limited by the individual's income. Box 3.2 summarizes the symmetry between WTP and WTA, and compensating and equivalent variation measures for welfare gains and losses.

Economists call both of these monetary measures of a change in an individual's well-being the **total economic value** of the change in environmental quality (to the individual). This usage of the word "value" has been a source of considerable confusion. For most laymen, philosophers, and members of other disciplines, the word "value" is used as a noun and means something or a quality that is **desirable**. This usage is equivalent to what we refer to here as a **criterion**. For economists the **value** of a good or service to an individual is established by an exchange transaction (either actual or hypothetical) and is the amount of something else (usually money) that the individual is willing to give up to obtain the thing in question (or accept as compensation to forgo or avoid the change). This definition of "value" does not allow for the possibility that to some individuals goods, qualities of things, or criteria may be "incommensurable" (Zeleny, [1982]). Economists may also use the word "value" as a verb to describe the activity or process of determining a monetary measure of the outcome of a policy intervention, and the noun "valuation" to refer to the process of assigning value to such effects in monetary terms.

Confusion often arises because a layman may refer to improved environmental quality as an important societal **value**, and economists may seek to determine or assign a monetary **value** to improved environmental quality. The uses of the word in these two cases are quite different. The layman's usage may imply nothing about our ability to assign a money measure to improved environmental quality, or even about our interest or inclination to think about what should be given up to maintain environmental quality.

It is useful to consider at this point the different reasons **why** an individual would be willing to pay for an improvement in environmental quality or services in order to disaggregate total economic value (as defined by economists) into two distinct components. Let us suppose the environmental change at issue is the creation of a national park, wilderness area, and wildlife reserve. One reason an individual might be willing to pay for the creation of such a national park is because he or she intends to go there and "use" it, i.e., hike, camp, and see the wildlife. The amount he would be willing to pay for such activities is termed the **actual use value**.

Alternatively, an individual may not be certain he would ever visit the national park, but might be willing to pay for its creation in order to have the possibility of using it in the future. The amount he would be willing to pay for this possibility of using the park in the future is called the **option value** of the resource. The **total use value** is the sum of the **actual use value** and the **option value** (Pearce, Markandya, and Barbier, [1989]).

Finally, an individual might be certain that he would never visit the national park, but he still might be willing to pay something for its creation. This might be because the individual is altruistic and wishes to provide others with the enjoyment of using the park, or it may be because he simply feels it is the "right" or "moral" thing to do. Whatever the reason, the amount such an individual is willing to pay is termed the **existence value**. One component of existence value might be the amount the individual is willing to pay to ensure that his or her heirs could use the park; this is termed **bequest value**. The **total economic value** of the resource to the individual is the sum of the actual use, option, and existence values:

Total Economic =	Actual	+	Option	+	Existence	[3.7]
Value	Use Value		Value		Value	

Many policy analysts, ourselves included, feel that these two monetary measures of the components of economic value have proved useful for thinking about the magnitude of changes in human well-being that result from policies or projects. However, it is clear that these measures of human well-being are not universally - or even widely - accepted by policy makers or citizens as building blocks for a decision rule for policy choice.

In the remainder of this chapter we examine the main limitations of using a monetary measure of changes in human well-being for policy analysis.

Obstacles to the use of monetary measures of human well-being

i) Which monetary measure of human well-being should be used: compensating or equivalent variation? WTP or WTA?

Since there are two different economic measures (compensating and equivalent variation) for the same change in an individual's well-being, the question naturally arises as to which one should be used. Most texts on cost-benefit analysis, applied welfare economics, and microeconomic theory devote considerable space to developing the concepts of compensating and equivalent variation, but then treat the decision on which measure to actually use in a cursory fashion. This is in large part because, until recently, most economists assumed that in most practical situations the difference between compensating and equivalent variation measures of change in well-being would be very small and of no practical policy relevance. This belief was based on the findings of two seminal articles. In 1960, in a discussion about appropriate policies for dealing with externalities, Nobel Laureate R.H. Coase showed that if:

(1) negotiations between the affected parties are costless;
(2) the property rights are well-specified; and
(3) the changes in the distribution of income resulting from payment and receipt of compensation for damages do not affect the parties marginal values,

then:

(1) the final level (amount) of the externality was not dependent on which party was legally liable for the damage from the externality, and
(2) the final level of the externality will be efficient, so the externality does not cause a problem that needs to be remedied.

The implication of Coase's third assumption above is that WTP and WTA, and compensating and equivalent variation, measures of value are the same. In effect, Coase assumed away the possibility of an income effect that could occur if a reallocation of resources resulted in a significant change in the well-being of the individuals affected by the policy change. This income effect arises because an individual's marginal valuation of a policy may change as his or her well-being (or income) changes; its presence results in a divergence between the compensating and equivalent variation measures of economic value. Willig [1976] developed a precise analytical expression of the size of this potential difference, and showed that in a wide variety of market situations, this divergence between compensating and equivalent variation measures would be very small.

However, a substantial body of empirical evidence has recently been developed that provides convincing evidence that WTP and WTA measures are often quite different (Hammack and Brown, [1974]; Gordon and Knetsch, [1979]; Meyer, [1979]; Rowe, d'Arge, and Brookshire, [1980];

Schulze, d'Arge, and Brookshire, [1981]; Knetsch and Sinden, [1984]). Typically **WTP measures turn out to be substantially less than WTA measures for the same policy change**. The initial reaction of many economists (and others) to this evidence was to argue that the WTA results were unreliable and should not be treated seriously (Dwyer and Bowes, [1979]; Kahneman, [1986]). The implication was that monetary estimates of well-being based on WTA measures should be not be used in policy analysis.

However, the difference between WTP and WTA measures has proven to be extremely robust in a wide variety of experiments, and appears to reflect a real difference in individuals' valuation of a policy change depending on how the policy is "framed" or the individual's "reference point" (Kahneman and Tversky, [1979]; Tversky and Kahneman, [1981]). Individuals weight (or value) losses from this reference point much more heavily than they do gains. In other words, the loss of $100 from current income will generally be perceived or felt to be much worse than a gain of $100 is perceived to be a benefit. This is not simply because of the declining marginal utility of income. Instead, the utility function appears to be "kinked" at the reference point.

This finding has three important implications. First, the gains from trade are likely to be **overstated** because people value highly what they must give up in the trade (Knetsch, [1990]). More generally, most WTP estimates of the value of losses will be too low, i.e., the losses will be of greater consequence to the individual than the economist would estimate.

Second, the decision on whether to use compensating or equivalent variation measures - or WTP versus WTA - would in many cases take on great practical importance because the losses associated with changes in the status quo - or the reference point - would weigh much more heavily than corresponding gains. Individuals tend to view compensation for a loss as two separate events: (1) a loss (which they greatly dislike), and (2) a money payment which is perceived as a gain from their new reference point (Knetsch, [1990]). Policy measures that mitigate or reduce losses may thus be more desirable than those that allow the damage to occur and then compensate the individuals affected.

Third, there is no justification **within economic theory** for choosing between the WTP and WTA measures - i.e., for judging whether the way in which an individual or group of individuals framed a particular problem was ethically justified or not. The economic measure of value thus depends upon a **political** judgment about the legitimacy of different reference points or endowments of property rights (Bromley, [1989a and b]).

Recently Hanemann [1992] has offered another explanation for the divergence between compensating and equivalent variation measures of economic value. He has shown that such differences are consistent with economic demand theory when there are few or poor substitutes for the goods or services in question (i.e., the goods or services an affected party might lose in a transaction or from the implementation of a policy) and when these goods or services are highly valued by individuals. These conditions are likely to be true for many environmental goods (e.g., global warming, ozone layer depletion, and species extinction).

The proper treatment of this disparity between WTP and WTA is particularly important in environmental policy analysis because private rights or entitlements to common property resources may not be well-defined or may be changing. Policy analysis may involve the resolution of disputes over entitlements and claims to public goods, and the evidence indicates that the allocation of entitlements can have a dramatic effect on economists' estimates of value. In such cases, the economists' estimates of benefits and costs may not yield unambiguous answers regarding which allocation of rights and entitlements will yield the greatest net benefits because the values themselves change with changes in allocations. Resolution of such disputes must thus often include appeals to criteria other than economic value, such as the ethical and moral justification for particular property rights regimes.

To illustrate the nature of the problem this disparity between WTP and WTA measures poses for environmental policy analysts, suppose an environmental protection agency is called upon to conduct an economic analysis of a proposed air quality standard. During the course of the policy analysis, the environmental economist finds that if an average individual believes he has a **right** to clean air, and is asked how much compensation he is willing to accept to have the air quality remain the same (i.e., degraded), his annual WTA is US$300. On the other hand, if he is asked how much he is willing to pay to have the air quality standard promulgated, he may answer only $100 per year. In the latter case the implicit reference point is not clean air, but the existing degraded air quality. Imagine the amusement of the agency administrator when the economist arrives in his office to pronounce the results of the economic analysis: it all depends on whether we assume that individuals have a **right** to clean air or industry has a **right** to pollute!

In summary, good economic analysis requires sound **noneconomic** judgement on the question of whether to use WTP or WTA measures of economic value in a particular situation.

ii) The appropriate treatment of an individual's preferences

The economic measures of changes in an individual's well-being are based on the assumption that the individual knows his own preferences and that satisfying them will advance his interests, however defined, or enhance his well-being. This is a reasonable assumption in many policy areas, but not in all, and for some, but not all, individuals. In fact, changing individuals' preferences may be an explicit goal of some environmental policies.

Consider, for example, the environmental problem of solid waste disposal. Households in industrialized countries generate large volumes of garbage that must be disposed of in some manner - either deposited in landfills, dumped in water bodies, or incinerated. All these options have adverse environmental consequences. Another option is recycling of household waste, which reduces the volume of materials that needs to be disposed of by other means. The success of recycling programs depends to a great extent on creating an awareness among citizens of the waste disposal problem and the need for collective action such as sorting garbage at the household level. Policy interventions thus often include media campaigns and educational programmes in schools. **Ex-ante**, before the initiation of a recycling programme, people may believe that sorting garbage is simply too much trouble for too little environmental gain. However, **ex-post**, after having experience sorting garbage, they may find that it is not as difficult as they expected. In such a case, an economic analysis based on households' **ex-ante** assessments of the inconvenience of sorting household garbage would overstate the social costs of the recycling programme.

As a second example, suppose that in a village in a developing country some valuation procedure is used to assess households' preferences for an improved drinking water system (MacRae and Whittington, [1988]). Assume that before the installation of the new water system that people were unaware of the health improvements that would result from the use of clean water from the new system, and thus **ex-ante** the value they assigned to the improvement in their water service was low. However, suppose that policy analysts were confident (based for example on experience in other similar villages) that after using the new water system, households would value it more highly. In this case, it might be reasonable for the policy analyst to use estimates of households' **ex-post** valuation of the water system in deciding whether it was a worthwhile investment or not. Such an approach is consistent with Tversky and Kahneman's [1981] suggestion that better decisions can be made by asking the affected individual "to focus on future experience and ask 'How will I feel then?' rather than 'What do I want now?'".

A goal of environmental policy analysis may not only be preference change, but also the setting of the terms of a policy debate by defining how people look at a problem (or what they regard as a reference point). For example, because people value reductions of losses more highly than corresponding gains, a water pollution control programme will be more highly valued if it is perceived by the public as reducing a harm that has already been incurred rather than improving water quality relative to a degraded status quo. In this context political leadership can shape or influence the outcome of an economic analysis by determining the reference point from which the public views the proposed policy change.

Not only can individuals' preferences change (with important policy consequences), but also some individuals' preferences may be judged "illegitimate" or "undeserving" from a social or policy maker's perspective. Decision makers may decide to exclude such preferences from an accounting of benefits and costs. In such cases monetary measures of individuals' willingness to pay or willingness to accept cannot be accepted at face value.

For example, suppose that a rural water supply project in a developing country would substantially reduce the amount of time that women spend fetching water from traditional sources. This time savings is a major benefit of the investment; women would have the opportunity to engage in a wide variety of new activities, possibly outside the home. The policy analyst might find that women were enthusiastic about the project, and thus assign a monetary value to the time savings based on what women would earn or produce outside the home.

Such a project could thus result in major changes in the traditional roles of women in society. Now suppose that a project economist determined that husbands saw little value in the project, or were even opposed to the project because it would change the power relationships in the family and disrupt the customary way of life. Should the preferences of the men to prevent the modernization process be considered legitimate? Or should the policy analyst count only the changes in well-being of the women in the appraisal of the project? Economic theory cannot provide ready answers to the appropriate treatment of such "interpersonal" preferences.

iii) The influence of income on WTP and WTA measures of economic value

In general the amount an individual is willing to pay for a particular policy change (or willing to accept to forego it) will be influenced by his income. This relationship between WTP and income is desirable in the sense that our ability to transform a change in human well-being into a monetary measure depends on the individual sacrificing something of value to him (in this case monetary income) in order to obtain the increase in well-being from the policy change. In other words, our measure of economic value has little meaning unless it is related to the individual's budget constraint.

However, the economist's monetary measures of compensating and equivalent variation may have serious limitations if they are used to compare the well-being of one individual with the well-being of another if the two individuals have different incomes. The problem of **interpersonal comparisons** will be examined in detail in Chapter 4, but it is important to note here that what the policy analyst would like is a measure of human well-being that could be used to compare the effects of a project on the well-being of different individuals. In some cases the economist's proposal to use compensating or equivalent variation as a measure of well-being is not well suited to this task because it is "coloured" or "filtered" by society's income distribution.

For example, suppose a policy analyst wanted to know how much two individuals' well-being would increase if radon levels were reduced in the air in their home and in their drinking water. Let us assume that the lives of both individuals would be increased by two years as a result of reductions in exposure to radon through breathing and ingesting pathways. One individual has an annual income of US$10,000 and would be willing to pay US$300 per year for reduced exposure to radon, and the second individual has an annual income of US$100,000, and would be willing to pay US$6000 for the policy change. Few people would argue that the second individual's increase in well-being from reduced exposure is 20 times greater than the increase in well-being of the first individual just because his willingness to pay for reduced exposure is 20 times larger. But that is what the WTP measures of well-being would suggest.

iv) Human versus nonhuman well-being

Environmentalists often object to the anthropomorphic character of economists' definition of value and of a criterion of increased human well-being. Many people feel that the effects of policies on the well-being of other living creatures should be considered in the decision process. In fact, in cultures throughout the world, notions of murder and sacredness of life extend beyond the human species (Whittington and MacRae, [1986]). Economists typically reply that the welfare of other living beings is, in fact, incorporated in the concept of economic value because people who value living creatures should be willing to pay to protect them. On the other hand, economists argue that people who do not value other living creatures should not be required to pay for their preservation.

Such a retort misses the fundamental nature of the environmentalists' criticism. Environmentalists do not accept the terms of the debate or the single - criterion decision framework structured by economists. Environmentalists (and others) are arguing that the well-being of other living creatures should be given **standing** in the policy analysis, not simply included to the extent that it affects the well-being of human beings. How the well-being of other living creatures affects the welfare of human beings can be included in measures of economic value, but another criterion is required to fully address the environmentalists' concerns about the **standing** of nonhuman entities. Economists should not expect a policy analysis carried out in terms of the single criterion of monetary measures of human well-being to provide convincing evidence to environmentalists who believe that the "preferences" of whales, monkeys (e.g., those used for scientific experiments), elephants, snail darters, salmon, and trees in tropical rain forests should be accorded **standing** in policy analyses. The criterion of human well-being is thus incomplete in the sense that it is not an all encompassing **value** to all individuals or groups, the measurement of which should not be expected to lead to consensus on collective action.

The appropriate treatment of nonhuman beings is not the kind of question that can be resolved by an appeal to economic theory or technical expertise, but must be openly discussed and debated on ethical, philosophical, and moral grounds (Whittington and MacRae, [1990]). Such value conflicts are best resolved by majority voting rules rather than benefit-cost rules.

Concluding remarks: The advantages of the economist's criterion of maximizing economic value

Despite the various attempts by economists and other social scientists to measure human well-being on a single scale, we must face the fact that to date this has proved impossible **in a fashion meaningful to a broad range of people**. Even if it were possible to measure human well-being quantitatively, many people are still concerned about other criteria. What then is the advantage of using the economists' measures of value for policy analysis?

We believe that there are two main arguments that favour the continued, judicious use of this criterion of maximizing economic value. First, the economists' criterion sometimes approximates the utilitarian ethic of the "greatest good for the greatest number". While there have been many philosophical and religious objections to this utilitarian ethic, it has proved to be a useful starting place for discussions of policy. Cost-benefit analysis has sometimes provided a convenient language for people from diverse philosophical and religious perspectives to find common ground. Few would reject this criterion out of hand as having **no** relevance to policy choice. The importance of this role of providing a language in which to talk about policy effects should not be underestimated. By focusing the attention of policy analysts, decision makers, and the public on the **ends** of policy rather than the **means**, and by being explicit about the criterion used to measure progress, the use of an economic criterion may foster communication between groups with differing viewpoints and often reduce areas of policy disagreement.

Second, the use of this criterion probably results in "pretty good" decisions most of the time. By "pretty good" we mean decisions that most of the people in society support and approve. The argument here is a practical one: whatever the limitations of the economists' criterion, it must be judged against the alternative approaches to policy analysis, and in this regard we do not believe that it has not been found wanting. There is considerable evidence to support this view. A broad political consensus exists among citizens in most democratic societies that the use of this economic criterion (and economic efficiency considerations in general) have an important role to play in public decision making. Representative governments continually **ask for** policy analyses based on this economic criterion (Mishan, [1982]).

One of the most important reasons why the use of an economic criterion has proved "practical" is that the procedures economists use to value policy effects deal relatively well with uncertainty. These valuation procedures will be discussed in Chapters 6 - 10. All of these valuation procedures are commonly used in situations in which the effects of policies or projects on the well-being of different individuals can only be estimated imprecisely. In the face of this uncertainty, a utilitarian ethic of "the greatest good for the greatest number" provides a relatively robust criterion for policy choice. If more was known about the exact consequences of policies on the well-being of specific individuals or groups, and the circumstances of these individuals were known in detail, it might be possible to reach political consensus on more "sophisticated" or "higher level" ethical criteria. However, such detailed information is generally difficult to obtain or develop, and policy decisions must be made under time and resource constraints. Economic appraisal techniques offer a framework for organizing available information in ways that are suggestive of the general direction of policy effects on human well-being, and thus can often increase decision makers' confidence in the likely appropriateness of a specific policy alternative.

The fact that the use of an economic criterion is practical and that its adoption would lead to "reasonable, pretty good" decisions most of the time does not, of course, mean that it will result in the best decision in a specific case. If a policy decision has far reaching, important implications, it may well demand a more careful examination than can be provided by a cost-benefit or solely economic framework. However, most policy decisions suffer from the opposite problem: potentially useful information from a sound cost-benefit analysis is never available to decision makers or the public.

Box 3.1 UNDP Social indicators/ Human Development Index

The Human Development Index (HDI) was developed by the United Nations Development Programme (UNDP [1993]). It measures "development" in terms of:

      a) longevity
      b) knowledge
      c) income

Longevity is measured by life expectancy at birth. Knowledge is measured as a weighted average of literacy (weight 2/3) and years of schooling (weight 1/3). Income is expressed in utility terms so that at higher income levels, increases in income are weighted less than increases at lower income levels.

The HDI is a deprivation index - it measures development relative to highest and lowest measures of each component worldwide. For example, for Singapore:

Highest Life Expectancy in World	= 78.6 years
Lowest Life Expectancy in World	= 42.0 years
Maximum educational attainment	= 3
Minimum educational attainment	= 0
Maximum (weighted) GDP/capita	= $5075
Minimum (weighted) GDP/capita	= $367
Singapore Life Expectancy	= 74 years
Singapore Adjusted GDP/capita	= $5043

gives:

$$\text{Singapore Life Expectancy Deprivation} = (L_{max} - L_s)/(L_{max} - L_{min})$$
$$= (78.6 - 74)/(78.6 - 42.0)$$
$$= 0.126$$

and similarly, educational deprivation = 0.320
              GDP deprivation = 0.007

These deprivation measures are then averaged to give

$$(0.126 + 0.320 + 0.007)/ 3 = 0.151$$

and the Singapore HDI is then $1 - 0.151 = 0.849$

The HDI for 1993 is shown over for selected countries:

HDI Rank	Country	1993 Index (for 1990)
1	Japan	0.983
2	Canada	0.982
3	Norway	0.979
4	Switzerland	0.978
5	Sweden	0.977
6	USA	0.976
7	Australia	0.972
8	France	0.971
9	Netherlands	0.970
10	UK	0.964
70	Brazil	0.730
85	South Africa	0.673
101	China	0.566
127	Kenya	0.369
142	Nigeria	0.246
168	Mali	0.082
173	Guinea	0.045

Box 3.2 Compensating and equivalent variation versus willingness to pay and willingness to accept measures of economic value

	Compensating Variation	Equivalent Variation
	Amount of money that can be taken away from an individual after a change while leaving him as well off as he or she was before it.	Amount of money that would need to be given to an individual if a change did **not** happen to make him as well off as if it did.
Increase in Human Well-being	$W_0(Y_0 - WTA, E_1)$ $= W_0(Y_0, E_0)$	$W_1(Y_0 + WTA, E_0)$ $= W_1(Y_0, E_1)$
	Amount individual would be willing to pay for the change from E_0 to E_1 (Finite amount: limited by income)	Amount individual would be willing to accept to forego the change from E_0 to E_1 (Could be infinite: not limited by income)
Decrease in Human Well-being	$W_0(Y_0 - WTA, E_1)$ $= W_0(Y_0, E_0)$	$W_1(Y_0 - WTP, E_0)$ $= W_1(Y_0, E_1)$
	Amount individual would be willing to accept as compensation for the change from E_0 to E_1 (Could be infinite: not limited by income)	Amount individual would be willing to pay to avert the change from E_0 to E_1 (Finite amount: limited by income)

Chapter 4

Decision Rules

Introduction

In the last chapter we examined the meaning of the criterion of "economic efficiency" in terms of how changes in states of the world affect a single individual's well-being. We also discussed four of the main limitations of this economic criterion for the analysis of policy options. In Chapters 6 - 10 we describe various "valuation techniques" for determining how environmental policy analysts can determine changes in individuals' well-being (or "willingness to pay"). In this chapter we assume that it is possible to determine how a project, policy, or regulation affects individuals' well-being; our focus here is on how this information--once it is available--can be used to aid policy choice.

We show how criteria other than economic efficiency (i.e., increased human well-being) can be introduced in a systematic way into policy evaluation. The need for additional criteria for policy choice arises for two kinds of reasons. The first is because decision makers may not feel the valuation techniques used to measure human well-being are adequate, and they may seek supplemental indicators. The second is because other, distinct criteria may also be relevant to policy choice.

Two types of decision rules for policy choice are discussed. The first--based on the concepts of dominance and noninferiority - does not require that information on changes in human well-being or other criteria be collapsed into a single measure. For example, if one policy is preferred by all the affected parties in all time periods on all relevant criteria, then aggregation is not necessary to identify the best alternative.

The second type of decision rule requires the explicit consideration of the "relative value" of policy effects in different time periods, to different affected parties, measured in terms of multiple criteria. These "relative values" are also termed "trade-off coefficients". When such comparisons are made across time periods, the trade-off coefficients are termed "discount factors". When comparisons are made across affected groups, the trade-off coefficients are termed "equity weights".

When comparisons are made across criteria, there is no consistent terminology used by different disciplines to refer to the trade-off coefficients; they are sometimes called "objective function weights". In all cases, however, these trade-off coefficients enable the analyst to aggregate across these categories in order to obtain summary measures of the attractiveness of policy alternatives. For this type of decision rule, three basic aggregation issues arise:
  (1) how to aggregate changes in well-being over different affected individuals or groups;
  (2) how to aggregate over different time periods; and
  (3) how to aggregate or compare different criteria (one of which is the focus of this manual: changes in human well-being).

The first raises the issue of how to handle equity concerns in policy analysis; the second of how to treat the time profile of costs and benefits. The third raises the question of how cost-benefit results can be used in conjunction with other policy-relevant information.

A conceptual framework for policy analysis (and a basic dilemma)

Suppose a policy maker (or a policy making body) must choose between three states of the world, S_0, S_1, and S_2. Each of these states of the world can be attained by the implementation of a different policy alternative, either A_0, A_1, and A_2 [2]. Let S_0 be the status quo, so this state of the world can be attained by the alternative (A_0) of simply letting things stay as they are (i.e., letting present trends continue without directly intervening).

The consequences of implementing Alternative A_1 can then be expressed as a movement from S_0 to S_1 and the consequences of Alternative A_2 as a movement from S_0 to S_2 [3]. If implemented, each of these two policy options would affect (i.e., change the well-being of) a group of individuals. (The groups of individuals affected by these two alternatives need not be the same.)

This situation is depicted in the alternatives-by-affected individuals (parties) decision matrix in Table 4.1, where the columns are the two policy alternatives (A_1 and A_2) that involve changing the status quo, and the rows are the individuals 1 ... N affected by these policy options. Each cell entry is a single individual's willingness to pay (or accept) to have one of the policy alternatives implemented (i.e., to have the change occur), and is thus measured in monetary units. If a policy alternative results in a movement from the status quo to a state of the world in which an individual's well-being is increased, the cell entry will be positive. If it decreases the individual's well-being, the cell entry will be negative. These cell entries can be thought of as the "building blocks" of a system of information designed to aid policy choice.

Table 4.1 Alternatives-by-affected-individuals decision matrix

Policy Alternatives

Affected Individuals	Alternative A_1 ($S_0 - S_1$)	Alternative A_2 ($S_0 - S_2$)
Individual 1		
Individual 2	[cell entry]	
:	willingness to pay of individual 2 for alternative 1	
:		
:		
Individual N		

This decision matrix can be expanded to include other criteria besides economic efficiency. For economists, the ethical criterion of maximizing individuals' preference satisfaction arises from abstract reasoning about the nature of the public interest, and they often tend to think of this criterion as all encompassing (or perhaps as competing with - or being traded off against - an "equity criterion"). But other disciplines are also engaged in abstract reasoning about the nature of the public interest and the characteristics of a "good society," and have proposed other broadly applicable criteria for consideration in public discussion and debate of policy options. For example, such additional criteria might include the achievement of goals or standards based on nonconsequencialist reasoning, moral rules, or environmental ethics independent of human well-being.

Also, analysts trained in disciplines other than economics often define criteria in terms of more specific problem descriptions and their understanding of the causal relationships that relate policy alternatives to outcomes. Such criteria tend to be less abstract, more explicit, and, for some people, easier to understand. For example, an ecologist might define a criterion of "acres of wetland maintained" or "number of 'critical' plant and animal species preserved," and evaluate the available policy options in terms of how well they achieved this criterion. In such a case the direct outcomes of a policy alternative are the criteria: outcomes do not need to be transformed into more abstract criteria such as individuals' willingness to pay [4]. One way to show this expanded decision matrix (alternatives-by-criteria-by-affected individuals) is presented in Table 4.2.

The decision matrix in Table 4.2 can be extended to yet another dimension: time. It can be useful for the analysis of policy options to think of Table 4.2 indexed over time periods. Suppose, for example, that we consider a time increment of one year. Then we could have a matrix such as shown in Table 4.2 *for each year* that the two policy options affect any of the N individuals. For example, in this case the cell entries associated with the criterion of human well-being (or economic efficiency) would measure a specific individual's willingness to pay in a given year for the change in well-being that would result from a specific policy option being in effect in that year.

We now have a four dimensional policy evaluation or decision matrix: policy alternatives x affected individuals x criteria x time. One can think of this four-dimensional policy evaluation matrix as consisting of a series of "spreadsheets." If a single spreadsheet depicted an alternative-by-criteria -by-affected individuals matrix as in Table 4.2, then one such spreadsheet would be required for each time period.

Imagine that we knew who all the individuals were that would be affected by the policy alternatives under consideration in terms of all the relevant criteria, and how these policy alternatives would affect each individual in terms of each criteria, i.e., that all the cell entries were known for the full four-dimensional matrix. If there were five policy alternatives (in addition to the status quo), 1000 affected individuals, 3 criteria, and 10 time periods, we would then have 150,000 cell entries. Here we face a dilemma: what can we do with all of this information? How could it be used to aid policy choice?

Clearly ways would need to be found to summarize this information in a manner useful for decision makers and for public debate and negotiation. If we want a *single number* that summarizes the attractiveness of each policy alternative, then we would need to undertake three distinct tasks:
(1) aggregate the consequences of each policy alternative in each time period in terms of each criteria for each affected individual;
(2) aggregate over the affected individuals to obtain a single measure of the attractiveness of the policy alternative to all affected parties ("society") for each criteria; and
(3) aggregate over the multiple criteria.

The sequence of these tasks could be varied, but these three fundamental calculations would still have to be done. The goal of providing expert advice to aid policy choice does not, however, necessarily require that all this information must be summarized or collapsed into a single number for each policy alternative. There is much middle ground between this extreme and simply presenting information on all cell entries.

Table 4.2 Alternatives-by-criteria-by-affected-individuals decision matrix

<u>Policy Alternatives</u>

CRITERION 1
(Increased Human Well-being)

<u>Affected Individuals</u>	Alternative A_1 $(S_0 - S_1)$	Alternative A_2 $(S_0 - S_2)$
Individual 1		
Individual 2	[cell entry]	
: :	willingness to pay of individual 2 for alternative A_1	
Individual N		

CRITERION 2

<u>Affected Individuals</u>	Alternative A_1 $(S_0 - S_1)$	Alternative A_2 $(S_0 - S_2)$
Individual 1		
Individual 2	[cell entry]	
: : :	effect of alternative A_1 on individual 2 in terms of criterion 2	
Individual N		

CRITERION M

<u>Affected Individuals</u>	Alternative A_1 $(S_0 - S_1)$	Alternative A_2 $(S_0 - S_2)$
Individual 1		
Individual 2	[cell entry]	
	effect of alternative A_1 on individual 2 in terms of criterion m	
Individual N		

Solving the decision matrix: Concepts of dominance and noninferiority

The first class of decision rules for "solving" the decision matrix does not require that cell entries be added together to create summary measures of the attractiveness of the policy alternatives. If one policy alternative is better than the other alternatives in some respects, and at least as good as each of the others in all respects, then it can be said to **dominate** the set of feasible policy alternatives. The decision rule is to always select a dominant alternative.

A policy alternative is said to be **noninferior** if there is no alternative that dominates it, i.e., the other alternatives that are better in some respects are worse in other respects. In this case there is no decision rule for selecting among noninferior alternatives. The only advice the policy analyst can offer is to choose from among the set of noninferior alternatives (i.e., avoid inferior alternatives).

When policy analysts use these concepts of dominance and noninferiority, they typically focus on one dimension of the four-dimensional decision matrix at a time. This focus on a single dimension yields three distinct cases.

i) Case 1: Affected individuals

If the focus is on affected individuals, then it is typically assumed that the other criteria and time dimensions are collapsed. Economists are generally most concerned with this case. Let us assume that the criterion of interest is increased human well-being. The analyst then searches for a policy alternative that makes some individuals better off and no one worse off. More formally, let WTP_i be the willingness to pay of individual i for the policy alternative.

Economists call the implementation of a policy alternative a **Pareto improvement** (relative to the status quo, if
$WTP_i > 0$ for some i, and
$WTP_i \geq 0$ for all i.

A Pareto optimal state is a state of the world from which no Pareto improvement is possible. A policy alternative that achieves a Pareto optimal state must either be a **dominant** or a **noninferior** alternative.

ii) Case 2: Multiple criteria

When applying the concepts of dominance and noninferiority to problems with multiple criteria, the analyst typically assumes that the dimensions of time and affected individuals have been collapsed so that each policy alternative has a single score for each of the multiple criteria. A policy alternative **dominates** all other alternatives if its score for each criterion is at least as high as that for all other alternatives, and its score for at least one criterion is better than all the other policy alternatives. A policy alternative is **noninferior** if it is not dominated by any of the other alternatives.

iii) Case 3: Multiple time periods

This case has received little attention in the policy analysis literature, largely because economists have been strong advocates of the use of discounting to collapse the time dimension of the decision matrix, and because critics of discounting have not generally applied the concepts of dominance and noninferiorty to the time dimension of policy problems. The concepts are, however, easily applied.

If the analyst collapses the criteria and affected individuals dimensions of the decision matrix, each policy alternative has a single score in each time period. In this case a policy alternative dominates all other alternatives if its score for each time period is at least as high as that for all other alternatives, and its score for at least one time period is better than all the other policy alternatives. Just as with case 2, a policy alternative is noninferior if it is not dominated by any of the other alternatives.

The concepts of dominance and noninferiority of policy alternatives could conceptually be applied to all three of these dimensions simultaneously. For a policy alternative to dominate all other alternatives, its score for each affected individual for each criteria for each time period would need to be at least as high as that for all other alternatives, and its score for at least one of these cells would be better than for all the other policy alternatives. This is a very stringent test; a policy alternative would very rarely dominate other alternatives in all three dimensions of the decision matrix. However, applying the notion of noninferiority might identify some inferior alternatives that could be excluded from consideration.

The notions of dominance and noninferiority can enable policy analysts to provide policy advice that appears objective and free of the anyone's value judgments. The decision rules based on these concepts - i.e., choose dominate alternatives and reject inferior alternatives - are thus typically compelling. However, policy makers and the public often want additional summarization of the cell entries. This requires aggregation over some dimensions of the decision matrix.

Solving the decision matrix: Aggregating the effects on individuals

If the consequences of implementing a policy alternative are widespread and affect large numbers of individuals, there will be many rows in the alternatives-by-affected-individuals decision matrix. Several means have been used to present this information in more succinct, compact form. To illustrate approaches for aggregating the cell entries for different individuals (or parties) for a single policy alternative, we will assume that there is only one criterion (economic efficiency) and one time period.

i) The issue of standing

The rows of the alternatives-by-affected-individuals matrix (Table 4.1) list the individuals affected by the policy alternatives. Before any attempt can be made to aggregate the cell entries for the affected individuals, the analyst must decide *who* the affected parties are that should be considered in the analysis, i.e., which individuals are to be counted and given **standing**. This issue of who is to count in the analysis is not as straight forward as it might first appear (Whittington and MacRae, [1986]). Society places moral or ethical bounds on the application of policy analysis by not granting standing to certain individuals or to the preferences of certain individuals in specific situations. For example, policy analysts are expected to evaluate alternatives assuming the existing system of property rights or entitlements is maintained. Illegal transfers of property are not deemed acceptable or permissible, and thus criminals would not be accorded standing in order to register their gains from stolen property in the decision matrix [5]. The usual assumption in policy analysis is that all persons within a country's national boundaries are to be included, provided that they have at least some rights of citizenship. This practice of equating standing with citizenship worked reasonably well in many early applications of cost-benefit analysis when the effects of a project rarely spilled over national boundaries. Environmental policies of an individual country can, however, have effects far beyond its borders. If a country is considering the implementation of an environmental policy that would improve the well-being of citizens of neighbouring countries, should an analysis of this policy alternative include the effects on its neighbours?

This question arose in a decision by the United States Nuclear Regulatory Commission on how stringent to make emission standards for release of radon gas from uranium mill tailings in the western part of the United States. Radon gas is an odourless, colourless gas that is emitted from both natural sources and the residue (tailings) of uranium mining operations and can be carried long distances in the air. It is known to increase the risk of lung cancer when inhaled. The adverse health effects of radon gas emissions from uranium mill tailings extend far beyond the borders of the United States. Adverse effects on citizens of Canada and Mexico were estimated to be 10 percent of the total forecast for the North American contingent. Increased cancer deaths in Continental Europe and Asia due to exposure to radon gas from the United States were estimated to be 25 percent of those in North America.

In its analysis of regulatory options, the U.S. Nuclear Regulatory Commission included the effects of radon emissions on Canadians and Mexicans--effectively granting them full standing in the analysis. Individuals in Europe, Asia, and the rest of the world were not, however, counted. In public comments on the Commission's environmental impact statement, representatives of the uranium industry objected to the equal treatment given to Canadians and Mexicans. In a subsequent analysis of this environmental problem, the U.S. Environmental Protection Agency did not grant standing to anyone outside of the borders of the United States.

Whether or not to give standing to citizens outside a nation's borders is largely an ethical and political decision. It may seem unconscionable to many people for the U.S. Environmental Protection Agency to ignore the consequences of its actions on citizens of other countries, but policy analysts have rarely argued that affected foreigners should be treated *equally* with citizens of their own country. If such a universalist position were applied to international questions of income equity or the welfare of the poor in developing countries, it would diverge widely from views of justice held by most citizens of rich countries, and neither policy makers nor the public would likely consider such analysis to be useful for policy choice.

The issue of standing arises in another context that is perhaps even more important for the analysis of many environmental policies: the treatment of future generations. Many environmental policies will have consequences far into the future, long after the individuals alive today are dead. These consequences will affect the well-being of members of future generations. Should the individuals in future generations be included in the rows of Table 4.1? Two different answers are commonly given to this question.

The first is to assume that future generations do not have standing; only individuals currently alive are to be included in the rows of the alternatives-by-affected-individuals decision matrix. In that case, the welfare of future generations would still affect the outcome of the policy analysis, but only indirectly. The welfare of future generation would count to the extent that it influenced the welfare of individuals alive today. In this reasoning, the well-being of an individual alive today might depend on how a policy alternative would affect the well-being of future generations, and this individual would be willing to pay something to increase the well-being of future generations. This increased willingness to pay for the well-being of future generations would be registered in the cell entry for that individual associated with the policy alternative. Although *measuring* how the well-being of future generations will be affected by the implementation of environmental policies today often poses great practical difficulties, we do not believe that there is any ethical basis for denying standing to future generations. We thus do not consider this first approach to be acceptable.

The second approach is to grant standing to future generations and include the members of future generations in the rows of the decision matrix. The effects of policy alternatives on the welfare of future generations are thus deemed to count directly in the evaluation of policy options, not indirectly through individuals alive today. (Whether future generations should be given *equal weight* in any summation of changes in well-being over affected individuals is another matter, discussed below.)

Decisions regarding standing are often difficult to resolve and involve ethical decisions outside the scope of traditional economics. Yet many times they lie at the heart of environmental policy debates. Such decisions must finally be made by the political process after public debate and discussion.

ii) Summarizing effects on individuals

Once the question of who has standing in the analysis has been resolved by the political process, the policy analyst can proceed to summarize the cell entries of the affected individuals in the matrix in order to offer either a client or the public choices that are easier to understand than the full alternatives-by-affected-parties decision matrix. Three basic approaches are available.

1. Unweighted summation of individuals' willingness to pay
(Potential pareto improvement criterion)

First, cost-benefit analysts have often advocated a simple summation of the cell entries associated with each policy alternative. In Table 4.1 this would involve summing the cell entries in each column to obtain an aggregate estimate of the total willingness to pay of the affected individuals for each policy alternative.

This unweighted summation procedure thus yields two summary measures--one for each policy alternative:

$$\text{Aggregate willingness to pay for policy alternative j} = \sum_{i=1}^{N} \text{WTP}_{ij} \qquad (4.1)$$

where WTP_{ij} = willingness to pay of individual i for the policy alternative j
(and is represented in the alternatives-by-affected-parties decision matrix as a single cell entry).

Economists often call these measures of aggregate WTP the "economic benefits" of the respective policy alternatives. The decision rule cost-benefit analysts propose is to choose the policy alternative with the largest positive net benefits. Economists thus argue that alternative 1 is more attractive economically (i.e., more efficient) than alternative 2 if the aggregate WTP for 1 minus the costs of alternative 1 is greater than the aggregate WTP for alternative 2 minus the costs of alternative 2.

If the net benefits of alternative 1 and 2 are positive, the implementation of either would result in a **potential Pareto improvement** relative to the status quo. This decision rule of selecting the policy alternative with the largest difference between the aggregate willing to pay of the individuals affected and the costs is referred to as the **potential Pareto improvement criterion**. It is the standard approach used in cost-benefit analysis for evaluating the attractiveness of policy alternatives that affect different individuals. However, as discussed in Chapter 3, it does not account for the fact that individuals' willingness to pay for the proposed policy alternative is likely to be influenced by the current income distribution, entitlements, and distribution of property rights in society.

2. Equity weighting schemes

In an attempt to correct this latter deficiency, some economists have suggested a second technique for aggregating estimates of individuals' WTP: the use of "equity weights". This involves two steps:
  (1) multiplying the WTP measure (cell entry) of an individual deemed particularly worthy or needy by an "equity weight" to increase the social significance in the summation of his or her change in well-being, and then

  (2) summing the adjusted (and any unadjusted) measures of WTP for the affected individuals to obtain a summary measure for the attractiveness of the policy alternative.

In other words an equity weighting procedure requires the following summation:

$$\text{Aggregate weighted willingness to pay for policy alternative j} = \sum_{i=1}^{N} v_i(WTP_{ij}) \qquad (4.2)$$

where v_i = equity weight assigned to individual i.

This procedure is used to weight gains to the poor more heavily than gains to the rich in an attempt to incorporate a concern for "equity" or "social justice" in the aggregate measure of the attractiveness of each policy alternative.

Equity weights are commonly expressed in terms of the "social value" of an extra unit of income accruing to individuals in specified groups or income classes. If an equity weight of zero were assigned to an individual, this would be equivalent to not giving him standing in the analysis. In practice, economists have generally proposed equity weighting schemes based on a functional relationship between an individual's utility (U) and his income (Y). Two commonly proposed functional forms are

$$dU/dY = Y^a, \text{ where } a < 0 \qquad (4.3)$$

and

$$dU/dY = e^{(Y/Y^0)} \qquad (4.4)$$

where Y^0 is the mean income of the population.

The derivative of the function evaluated at a particular income level is t :med the "equity weight". Since the units of the cell entries associated with the economic criterion of increased human well-being are money (willingness to pay), the equity weights themselves are simply unitless numbers. The multiplication of an individual's WTP measure by an equity weight does not change the unit of the cell entry (i.e., the product of this multiplication is still measured in money terms). For example, suppose a person below a certain income level is assigned an equity weight of 2 and his WTP for a policy alternative is $100. Using an equity weighting procedure, his adjusted WTP for the policy alternative would be $200.

If the analyst is uncertain what values to use for equity weights, one approach is to treat the weights as unknowns and solve for the values that would make one policy alternative just as attractive as another. For example, suppose that there are only two groups of affected individuals: the poor and everyone else.

An equity weight, v_{poor}, is required to increase the social value of benefits to the poor, and the weight for other groups is simply equal to one. Let the summation of the willingness to pay of poor individuals for policy j be:

$$WTP_{poor,j} = B_{poor,j} \qquad\qquad (4.5)$$

and the summation of the willingness to pay of everyone else for policy j be:

$$WTP_{nonpoor,j} = B_{nonpoor,j}. \qquad\qquad (4.6)$$

If policy alternatives 1 and 2 were equally attractive in terms of an economic efficiency criterion, this would imply that:

$$v_{poor}B_{poor,1} + B_{nonpoor,1} = v_{poor}B_{poor,2} + B_{nonpoor,2} \qquad\qquad (4.7)$$

Solving for v_{poor} yields:

$$v_{poor} = (B_{nonpoor,2} - B_{nonpoor,1}) \,/\, (B_{poor,1} - B_{poor,2}) \qquad\qquad (4.8)$$

If the values of $B_{poor,1}$, $B_{poor,2}$, $B_{nonpoor,1}$, and $B_{nonpoor,2}$ were known, then equation (4.8) could be solved for a value of v_{poor} that would make the two policy alternatives equally attractive. Depending on the values of $B_{poor,1}$, $B_{poor,2}$, $B_{nonpoor,1}$, and $B_{nonpoor,2}$, higher or lower values of v_{poor} would favour one policy alternative or the other. This type of "breakeven analysis" can be quite useful if the analyst is uncertain of the exact value of an equity weight, but is confident that it is above or below a certain value, or lies within a certain range.

Equity weighting schemes of various types have been proposed by some economists and policy analysts for over thirty years, but they have rarely been used in practice. Nor in our judgment is it likely that they will be used in the future. The reason for this lack of acceptance is not hard to discern: neither decision makers nor the public are interested in the aggregate measures that result from equity weighting procedures. This is in large part because there is no political consensus (in any society) on how such equity weights should be determined. More broadly, such equity weights rarely capture the ethical complexity of policy choices, and thus do not help policy makers or the public think carefully or creatively about the attractiveness of policy alternatives.

Thus, despite their prominence in the literature on cost-benefit analysis, we do not consider equity weighting schemes to be a useful (or interesting) approach to aggregating measures of individuals' willingness to pay (or, more generally, to incorporating equity concerns in policy analysis).

3. Partial (unweighted) aggregation

A third approach to summarizing the information in the cell entries does not attempt to come up with a single number for all the individuals affected by a policy alternative, but rather presents information on how different **groups** of individuals are affected. In fact, this is how much of the information that can be obtained from valuation techniques is available anyway. With this approach no attempt is made by the policy analyst to compare or aggregate WTP measures for these different groups: this information is simply presented to decision maker(s) or the public for reflection and debate. As with the equity weighting scheme approach, the distribution of costs and benefits among the affected groups is deemed to be relevant, important information for a choice among policy alternatives. However, unlike equity weighting schemes, analysts using this third approach do not believe that any further reduction in the number of rows of the matrix is useful.

This third approach will usually not reveal a dominant or Pareto superior policy alternative. Here, the policy analyst's role is not to find the best policy alternative, but is rather to present policy-relevant information that is useful to policy makers and the public and that can facilitate an informed choice. For example, suppose a policy was proposed to improve air quality by requiring all new automobiles to meet specified emission standards. Some of the affected groups might include employees and shareholders of automobile manufacturing companies, car owners, taxpayers, and asthmatics. This third approach would entail estimating the costs and benefits to each group (in terms of their willingness to pay for the proposed change), and then presenting these estimates in a summary table. Such a data summary would greatly reduce the number of rows in the matrix in Table 4.2, but would not collapse the N rows of the original matrix to a single row as would the first two approaches.

Solving the decision matrix: Aggregating effects over time

The time profile of policy effects on individuals can be an important consideration in the choice between policy options. If the consequences of policies occur over an extended period of time, however, a complete enumeration of these effects in each time period may involve the presentation of more information than policy makers or the public can easily understand or use. It is thus often useful to collapse the time dimension of a decision matrix by aggregating the cell entries over time periods. In other words, it may aid policy choice to reduce the number of time periods for which information is to be presented. For purposes of illustration, we will consider two cases. In the first we look at this issue from the perspective of *a single individual* affected by a policy alternative in different time periods. In the second we assume that we have *already* summed the willingness to pay of the affected individuals for the policy alternative for each time period. In this case we have a time profile of the aggregate willingness to pay of the affected individuals in each period.

i) The individual's perspective

Suppose that an individual i, would be willing to pay WTP_{ijt} for the change in his well-being that resulted in period t from the implementation of a specific policy alternative j. Assume that these WTP measures are positive in each period and extend from period 1 to period 10. The individual thus receives the following benefit stream from the implementation of the policy alternative:

$$WTP_{ij,t=1} , WTP_{ij,t=2}, \dots , WTP_{ij,t=10} \tag{4.9}$$

How could this time stream of benefits to the individual be summarized? Just as with the summation over different individuals' willingness-to-pay measures in the alternatives-by-affected-parties decision matrix, the WTP measures of a single individual in different time periods could simply be added together:

$$\text{Summary measure} = WTP_{t=1} + WTP_{t=2} + \dots + WTP_{t=10} \tag{4.10}$$

Such an unweighted summation of WTP measures in different time periods implies that the individual is indifferent between receiving an increase in well-being in the different time periods. For some kinds of experiences this would seem to be an accurate description or characterization.

For example, it would be considered a reasonable statement if an individual asserted that she wanted to ensure the long term survival of African rhinoceros, but that if the species was going to become extinct, it really did not matter to her whether this occurred five years from now or ten years from now. In other words, *when* the loss happened did not affect the *magnitude* of the loss *to this individual*. Or someone might reasonably assert that they wanted to spend two weeks observing birdlife in the Amazon rain forest sometime during their life, but he did not care when he had this experience.

The issue of assigning a monetary value to this experience, however, raises a related question of the possibility of *exchanging* this experience for money. If such an exchange actually occurred, and the individual had money in some future period instead of the experience, then the individual would be able to enter into additional exchanges in the financial markets. Borrowing and lending opportunities would then be available that would enable the individual to *shift when* he decided to consume the goods and services he exchanged for the original experience.

Suppose, for example, that this trip to the Amazon rain forest would cost the individual US$5000 today. Assume that he had this money now and was contemplating whether to take the trip. If the individual really valued the experience of visiting the rain forest the same today compared with five years from now, then he should consider the fact that he could put the US$5000 in the bank (or invest it elsewhere) and earn a return. Assuming the real cost of the trip had not changed and he was still alive, at the end of five years he would have the US$5000 for the trip plus the accrued interest. Thus, ignoring uncertainty (e.g., the rain forest might be gone, he might suffer accidental death or injury, the real cost of the trip might escalate), the individual should postpone his trip to take advantage of his access to financial markets. The benefits to the individual from trading in the financial markets derive from the fact that he is indifferent between using financial resources today and in the future, and other individuals are not: they prefer to use those resources now rather than wait.

If an individual can purchase the goods and services of concern with money and has borrowing and lending opportunities in financial markets, then it is possible to assign weights w_t to the individual's willingness-to-pay measures in different time periods so that a meaningful summation can be made.

The summary measure is then:

$$\text{Sum} = w_{t=1}\text{WTP}_{ij,t=1} + w_{t=2}\text{WTP}_{ij,t=2} + \ldots + w_{t=10}\text{WTP}_{ij,t=10} \qquad (4.11)$$

What should these weights, w_t, be?

If a person puts $\$x_0$ in a bank in period 0 at an interest rate r, after 1 period he has a sum of $\$x_0 (1+r)$, after two periods $x_0(1+r)^2$, and after N periods, $x_0(1+r)^N$. Ignoring risk and uncertainty, he would thus be indifferent between receiving $\$x_0$ in period 0 and $x_0(1+r)^N$ in period N. Let $x_N = x_0 (1+r)^N$, the sum received in period N. The ratio x_0/x_n is equal to $1/(1+r)^N$. These ratios $1/(1+r)^t$ are simply the weights to be used by the individual in a financial analysis to convert money in the future into equivalent amounts of money in a prior period.

For example, if the individual wanted to convert a stream of dollar values received over time into money in period 0, then the summation or aggregation over time periods would be:

$$\text{Sum} = [1/(1+r)^1] \text{WTP}_{ij,t=1} + [1/(1+r)^2] \text{WTP}_{ij,t=2} + \ldots + [1/(1+r)^{10}] \text{WTP}_{ij,t=10} \qquad (4.12)$$

This sum is termed the "present value" of the time stream of benefits. If the "benefits" in each period are net of costs, then this sum is the "net present value" of the policy alternative, and its calculation is analytically the same as the equity weighting schemes. The net present value to the individual can be calculated for each of the policy alternatives. The decision rule for comparing the policy alternatives is to select the policy alternative with the highest positive net present value. If neither of the two policy alternatives has a positive net present value, this means that the status quo is preferable to both.

ii) Society's perspective

In Chapter 12 we examine the question of what weight to assign benefits in different time periods from a social perspective: this is the issue of appropriate social rate of discount. Here we simply introduce the topic and show its relation to other weighting procedures for summarizing dimensions of the four-dimensional decision matrix.

Assume that the rows of the alternatives-by-affected-parties decision matrix have already been collapsed to a single row representing the aggregate WTP of all affected individuals for various policy alternatives. (This could be either an unweighted or weighted summation). For an unweighted summation we have the following time profile of summary effects for policy alternative j:

$$\sum_{i=1}^{N} WTP_{ij,t=1} , \quad \sum_{i=1}^{N} WTP_{ij,t=2} , \quad ..., \quad \sum_{i=1}^{N} WTP_{ij,t=10} \tag{4.13}$$

and to simplify the notation,

$$\text{let } \sum_{i=1}^{N} WTP_{ij,t} = B_{j,t} \tag{4.14}$$

Dropping the j subscript, we have a time profile of economic benefits from a single policy alternative of

$$B_1, \quad B_2, \quad ..., \quad B_{10} \tag{4.15}$$

A series of weights w_t is again necessary to sum or collapse this time stream of benefits into a single measure of present value:

$$\text{Present value} = w_1 B_1 + w_2 B_2 +, \quad ..., \quad + w_{10} B_{10} \tag{4.16}$$

In this case the weights describe how the value society places on aggregate WTP measures, declines over time. These "social weights" are related in an important way to both the interest rate used in the individual's financial analysis and the equity weights described above for aggregating over individuals. To see this relationship, suppose that the rate of decline in the weights in (4.16) is constant from period to period:

$$\frac{w_t - w_{t+1}}{w_{t+1}} = K \text{ (some constant rate)} \tag{4.17}$$

In the financial analysis the weights took the form
$$w_t = 1 / (1+r)^t$$
and this constant rate of decline in the weights, K, is equivalent to the interest rate r [6].

The "social rate of discount" or "social rate of time preference" is simply this constant rate K at which society's valuation of human well-being (or individuals' willingness to pay) declines if it is available in the future versus today. From a social point of view, why should society value the well-being of individuals today higher than the well-being of individuals in the future?

The ethical argument is precisely analogous to that proposed for the equity weighting schemes: that since individuals in the future will likely be better off (i.e., have higher well-being) than individuals today, an increase in their well-being should be given less weight. Individuals in the future are thought to be better off due to economic growth over the planning period. If this economic growth does not occur--or if economic growth does not result in increased human well-being--then this ethical rationale for discounting loses its force.

In the aggregation of policy effects over time, it is common to use weights of the form: $w_t = 1/(1+K)t$, where K is the social rate of discount. In equity weighting schemes an equity weight w_t is often conceptualized as a multiple of the average person's weight, rather than as a rate of decline. Analytically, however, the procedures are the same and are based on the same ethical reasoning.

Instead of solving equation (4.16) for the net present value of the time stream of benefits, an alternative approach to comparing policy alternatives is to set the present value of the time stream equal to zero, treat λ in equation (4.18) below as an unknown, and then solve for λ.

$$NPV = 0 = [1/(1+\lambda)^1] B_1 + [1/(1+\lambda)^2] B_2 +... + [1/(1+\lambda)^{10}] B_{10} \qquad (4.18)$$

In this case λ is defined as the "internal rate of return" of the project. The decision rule for selecting among policy alternatives is to select the alternative with the highest internal rate of return. The internal rate of return of an alternative must be greater than the prevailing interest rate r for the alternative to be better than the status quo.

Both the net present value and internal rate of return are thus measures of the attractiveness of a policy alternative that summarize a stream of net benefits over time. The units of the two measures are, however, different. The unit of the net present value measure is money in the initial period. The internal rate of return measure is simply a rate--a unitless number. It can only "stand for" or "correlate with" the criterion of human well-being.

A financial paradigm is often used to think about the appropriate value for the social rate of discount, rather then explicit equity considerations about the deservingness of future versus current generations. The financial analogy may seem particularly appropriate if a government agency is considering financing a public investment project with borrowed funds and if these funds displace investments in the private sector that would have yielded returns approximately equal to the interest rate on long term corporate debt. Both the United States Government and the World Bank, for example, use this reasoning in their justification of the use of a 10 percent real rate of discount for project appraisal.

The financial paradigm also pervades much thinking about the exchange and substitutability of environmental goods and services in different time periods, and in many cases it is appropriate. There are, however, environmental goods that cannot be easily substituted for other goods and services, and if they are lost there are not opportunities to increase human well-being by increasing the amount of other things (represented by money income). For example, if whales become extinct or the Madagascar rain forest is destroyed, there is no way to replace the experiences these environmental resources offer to some individuals. In such cases the attempt to summarize these effects by discounting them can be misleading. However, an *unweighted* aggregation of such effects is also misleading. The most sensible approach is to discount those effects for which other goods and services are good substitutes in terms of increasing human well-being (e.g., for which money can compensate for losses). For unique environmental assets we recommended that the analyst simply present the effects of the policy alternatives in the time period in which they occur, and not attempt to collapse the time dimension to a single number. This approach is analogous to the procedure for aggregating effects over some groups of specified individuals. In both cases the number of cell entries can be reduced. However, we do not always consider it advisable or informative to collapse the affected-individuals dimension or the time dimension to a single number for a given policy alternative.

Solving the decision matrix: Aggregating over multiple criteria

Using tradeoff coefficients to aggregate over multiple criteria in the decision matrix is analytically similar to the procedures used to aggregate over individuals and time periods. In this case the four-dimensional decision matrix has already been collapsed into the criteria-by-alternatives decision matrix depicted in Table 4.3. Here we have two criteria, Z_1 and Z_2, and two alternatives A_1 and A_2. Assume that the effects of each policy alternative on each criterion have already been determined so that we have two measures of the desirability or attractiveness of each alternative. Cell 1 measures A_1's score in terms of criterion Z_1; similarly, Cell 4 measures A_2's score in terms of criterion Z_2.

Note that the units of the cell entries in this criteria-by-alternatives matrix are different: cells 1 and 2 are measured in units of criterion Z_1, and cells 3 and 4 are measured in units of criterion Z_2. In our discussions of the alternatives-by-affected-individuals decision matrix and the time profile of benefits of each policy alternative, the units of all cell entries in the matrix were the same. The trade-off coefficients (equity weights and discount factors) were simply unitless numbers used to weight cell entries that were already measured in the same units. We thus had the option of determining an **unweighted** summation of the cells associated with a specific policy alternative and of calculating a single score for each alternative.

An unweighted summation of cell entries is not, however, meaningful for the criteria-by-alternatives decision matrix. In this case a tradeoff coefficient indicates the relative value of two criteria and is used to convert the scores for one criterion into scores for another. These tradeoff coefficients are termed "marginal rates of substitution" or simply "weights" in the multi-objective programming (i.e., operations research) literature (Cohon, [1978]). For example, suppose the benefits of A_i in terms of Z_j are denoted by $B_{zj}(A_i)$, and that we want to measure the attractiveness of each policy alternative in terms of a single number. Suppose we want to add $B_{z2}(A_1)$ to $B_{z1}(A_1)$ and $B_{z2}(A_2)$ to $B_{z1}(A_2)$.

We thus need to convert $B_{z2}(A_1)$ and $B_{z2}(A_2)$ into the same units as Z_1. This requires that we multiply both $B_{z2}(A_1)$ and $B_{z2}(A_2)$ by a weight w that indicates the number of units of Z_1 that a decision maker (or society) is willing to give up to obtain a unit of Z_2 (i.e., units of Z_1 per unit of Z_2). The summary measure of the attractiveness of A_1, measured in units of Z_1, is then given by $B_{z1}(A_1) + w\, B_{z2}(A_1)$, and the summary measure of A_2 measured in units of Z_1 is $B_{z1}(A_2) + w\, B_{z2}(A_2)$.

Just as with equity weighting schemes, the policy analyst may wish to calculate the "breakeven weight" that would make A_1 and A_2 equally attractive. This requires that we solve the following equation for w:

$$B_{z1}(A_1) + w\, B_{z2}(A_1) \;=\; B_{z1}(A_2) + w\, B_{z2}(A_2) \qquad\qquad (4.19)$$

$$w \;=\; \frac{B_{z1}(A_2) \;-\; B_{z1}(A_1)}{B_{z2}(A_1) \;-\; B_{z2}(A_2)} \qquad\qquad (4.20)$$

For criteria-by-alternatives decision matrices with more than two criteria, more than one weight will be needed to convert the cell entries into the units of a single criterion. In general, if there are m criteria, m-1 weights will be required.

Although the analytics of the criteria-by-alternatives matrix are straightforward, the rationale behind the sequence of decision-making steps being represented is perhaps less clear. If the policy analyst is going to collapse the scores of the policy alternatives in terms of multiple criteria into a single measure of the attractiveness of a policy alternative (i.e., a score on a single criterion for each alternative), why bother using multiple criteria at all? Why not simply decide first which criterion is of most policy interest and measure the physical consequences or outcomes of each alternative in terms of that criterion? For example, for many economists the criterion of overriding concern is "increased human well-being", measured in terms of individuals' willingness to pay for the policy alternative, and most other stated criteria are simply means to achieve this end.

There are two distinct advantages of introducing multiple criteria into the analysis of policy alternatives. First, one need not convert the scores in the criteria-by-alternatives matrix into the units of a single criterion; the cell entries can simply be displayed and used to promote policy dialogue and discourse. Often such presentations of policy effects in terms of multiple criteria are all that a decision maker wants to aid his or her choice.

Second, because many people conceptualize decisions in terms of multiple criteria, they may wish to see the scores associated with "intermediate criteria" (i.e., those criteria that are collapsed in the final summation) and to see the sensitivity analyses associated with multiple criteria analysis. The relative values depicted in the weights may not be known in advance to some decision makers, but may rather be "learned" as a result of thinking carefully about the nature of the trade-offs involved.

For many individuals the presentation of multiple criteria trade-offs may facilitate such learning about values.

Table 4.3 **Criteria-by-alternatives decision matrix**

<u>Policy Alternatives</u>

Criteria	Alternative A_1	Alternative A_2
Criterion Z_1	Cell 1 $[B_{z1}(A_1)]$	Cell 2 $[B_{z1}(A_2)]$
Criterion Z_2	Cell 3 $[B_{z2}(A_1)]$	Cell 4 $[B_{z2}(A_2)]$

Chapter 5

Shadow Pricing

The fundamentals of shadow pricing

Chapters 3 and 4 established that a policy, project or programme should be evaluated according to the **net benefits that it confers on society as a whole**. "Society" in this context relates to the aggregate of all individuals in that society, and benefits and costs are evaluated according to whether or not individuals' preferences are met or not. This general objective can be rephrased as saying that all inputs and outputs should be evaluated according to their contribution to the nation's well-being. From the nation's standpoint, inputs and outputs should be valued according to their **opportunity costs** - the value of production forgone by using particular inputs to produce a particular output. The opportunity cost of, say, consuming oil resources for domestic electricity production would then be the value of the oil as an export, since domestic consumption is at the expense of exports. The process of **shadow pricing** is essentially one of using opportunity costs to value inputs and outputs [7]. Ruling market prices may or may not reflect opportunity costs. If there are subsidies or taxes, they will not do so. If there are price and quantity controls, market prices will also not reflect opportunity costs. The divergence between market prices and opportunity costs will tend to be most marked in those countries where there are the most economic distortions. This is why the shadow pricing literature has concentrated on developing countries. But it should not be forgotten that developed countries also have many economic distortions. Shadow pricing then becomes just as relevant for them.

As a general rule we can write:

$$SP = MP. CF \qquad [5.1]$$

where SP = shadow price
       MP = ruling market price
       CF = "conversion factor".

A conversion factor is then an adjustment that permits us to convert ruling market prices into shadow prices which reflect the opportunity cost of the input or output. This is sometimes expressed by saying that shadow prices convert **financial values** into **economic values**.

This chapter is concerned mainly with the way in which these conversion factors can be estimated.

The problem of the numeraire

Shadow prices can be expressed in two ways. The shadow pricing literature of the 1970s was largely devoted to what appeared to be the competing claims of the **border price approach** and the **domestic price** approach [8] (Little and Mirrlees [1974]; UNIDO [1972]). But the approaches do not compete - they are alternative ways of saying the same thing. They use different **numeraires**. On the border price approach, opportunity costs are expressed in terms of foreign exchange units - this is the "unit of account". In the domestic price approach the unit of account is domestic prices. This means that the conversion factors that enable us to go from domestic prices to shadow prices will differ in the two approaches. But there will be a specific relationship between them. The best way to illustrate the numeraire issue is to use a simple example. Table 5.1 shows a hypothetical example in which the border price numeraire is applied to an export product and the domestic price method is applied to a product that substitutes for an import. In each case, however, the contribution to national well-being is the same.

Table 5.1 **Hypothetical example to illustrate domestic and border price numeraires**

Market Prices	Export Product: Border Price Numeraire	Import Substitute: Domestic Price Numeraire
Revenue $1000 x 15 =	15,000 Rs	15,000 Rs x 1.4 = 21,000 Rs
minus Traded Input $ 500 x 15 =	7,500 Rs	7,500 Rs x 1.4 = 10,500 Rs
minus Domestic Input 6000 Rs x 0.71 =	4,286 Rs	6,000 Rs
equals Net Revenue	3,214 Rs	4,500 Rs

Under the border price approach, the export product earns $1000 in foreign exchange. This is converted at the official exchange rate of 15 Rupees = $1 to give the domestic currency equivalent. An import of $500 of inputs is needed to produce the export, so this is deducted from the revenue obtained, again using the official exchange rate. A domestic input is also used and this is valued at 6000 rupees at domestic prices. But how much is this domestic input worth at border prices? In the example, it is assumed that there is a 40% tariff on all imports, so that domestic prices are on average 40% higher than border prices: i.e., DP/WP = 1.4. Then, border prices must be 1/1.4 times domestic prices, which gives a ratio of 0.71. So, to get the domestic input priced at border prices we must multiply the 6000 Rs cost by 0.71. Finally, we deduct the border price cost of the two inputs from the border price revenue to give the net revenue figure of 3214 Rs. Note that the border price method in this example expresses the amounts in domestic **currency**. This should not be confused with expressing amounts in domestic **prices**.

The approach under domestic prices, or the willingness to pay approach, is the same but the conversion factors are now different. The revenue from the import substitute is exactly the same as the revenue from the export at 15,000 Rs. But as we need to express this in domestic price terms, it needs to be raised by 40% to reflect the assumption about tariffs. One way of interpreting this is to say that the country in question is "willing to pay" 15,000 x 1.4 = 21000 Rs to avoid an import with a border price of 15,000 Rs. The imported input is treated in the same way - its price at the border is multiplied to 1.4 to express it in domestic price terms. The domestic input, however, is not adjusted. It costs 6000 Rs and this reflects the domestic willingness to pay for it. The same process of deducting costs from revenue produces a net revenue of 4500 Rs.

Does the difference between the two net revenues under the two approaches indicate that the import substitute is worth more than the export? Since they both yield 15,000 Rs this cannot be the case. In fact the final net revenues are the same: they are simply expressed in the two different units. To compare them, we can multiply 3,214 by 1.4 (the average ratio of domestic and border prices) to get

4,500. **Once the results are expressed in the same units the net contribution to the economy in this example is seen to be the same.**

The example in Table 5.1 is very simplified. It can be made more complicated by using particular conversion factors for particular inputs and outputs. For example, the domestic input might be labour. Hence we will require a conversion factor for labour. This may differ according to whether the labour is skilled or unskilled: there may be a lot of unskilled labour and a scarcity of skilled labour for example. Shadow pricing can therefore become quite complicated in practice. An example later in the chapter illustrates the kinds of adjustments that might be made.

The border price system

For any policy, project or programme we require that its **net present value** be greater than zero, or

$$NPV > 0 \qquad [5.2]$$

and where there are competing uses of funds we require that we choose those uses with the highest NPVs. We can decompose the NPV into its component parts, taking foreign exchange, labour, "non-traded goods" and transfers as our categories. A "non-traded good" is one that cannot be traded internationally: it does not mean that it does not have a market. The importance of the traded/non-traded distinction is clearly that a truly non-traded good does not have an opportunity cost in terms of forgone exports or imports. It does however have an opportunity cost since it uses up resources that could have been used for something else. In practice, non-traded goods can themselves be "decomposed" into traded good categories by looking at each of the inputs used to produce them. For example, electricity is often a non-traded good in many countries - it cannot be exported or imported. But electricity production uses up imported inputs and potentially exportable inputs and hence the value of the electricity may be decomposed into its tradeable parts.

We can rewrite the NPV rule as:

$$NPV = FE + NTG + LAB > 0 \qquad [5.3]$$

where FE   =   foreign exchange
          NTG =   non-traded goods
          LAB =   labour

each expressed in present value terms to avoid dealing explicitly with discounting problems for the moment.

It is commonplace to distinguish skilled and unskilled labour but we avoid that here to keep the example simple.

We now need to express the NPV rule in terms of the border price numeraire and this means applying conversion factors to each of the component parts as follows (dropping the notation that NPV needs to be positive, for convenience):

$$NPV_{bp} = CF_{fe}.FE + CF_{ntg}.NTG + CF_{lab}.LAB \qquad [5.4]$$

We now need to investigate the estimation of each of the conversion factors which, it will be recalled, must all convert market prices to shadow prices. CF_{fe} can quickly be dispensed with since the numeraire on the border price approach is foreign exchange. Hence $C_{fe} = 1$. Before looking at the other conversion factors we also need to note that NTG can be decomposed into tradeable inputs and outputs. If it can be completely decomposed NTG will disappear from the equation and its parts will be allocated to FE and LAB. In the simplest case, then, the NPV equation reduces to

$$NPV_{bp} = FE' + CF_{lab}.LAB' \qquad [5.5]$$

where FE' and LAB' now denote the fact that NTG has been reallocated to FE and LAB.

In practice, NTG is rarely totally decomposable in this fashion. So the analysis proceeds by allocating as much of NTG as possible.What is left over, the "residual" NTG, can be converted to shadow prices using an **average conversion factor** (ACF) or, the same thing, the **standard conversion factor**. The ACF is given by

$$ACF = OER/SER \qquad [5.6]$$

where OER is the official exchange rate and SER is the **shadow exchange rate**. How is the shadow exchange rate estimated? A typical expression for the SER is:

$$SER = (1 + WATR). OER \qquad [5.7]$$

which means that:

$$ACF = OER/SER = (1 + WATR) \qquad [5.8]$$

WATR is the "weighted average tariff and subsidy rate" [9]. Suppose the average tariff, weighted by the importance of each product in overall imports and exports is 25%, then $(1 + WATR) = 1.25$, and this is the average conversion factor. The shadow exchange rate is then simply 1.25 x the OER.

Equation [5.5] now becomes:

$$NPV_{bp} = FE' + CF_{lab}.LAB' + ACF. NTG' \qquad [5.9]$$

where FE', LAB' and NTG' denote each component after the decomposition of NTG. NTG' is then the "residual" after this process has been completed. Equation [5.9] can then be written also as:

$$NPV_{bp} = FE' + CF_{lab}.LAB' + OER/SER. NTG' \qquad [5.10]$$

or even as

$$NPV_{bp} = FE' + CF_{lab}.LAB' + (1 + WATR). NTG' \qquad [5.11]$$

We are now left only with the conversion factor for labour. This will be equal to:

$$CF_{lab} = SWR/MWR \qquad [5.12]$$

where SWR is the **shadow wage rate** and MWR is the market wage rate. It is usual to distinguish contexts in which there is excess supply of labour from contexts in which there is excess demand. For the excess supply context the expression for the shadow wage rate is:

$$SWR = \Sigma a_i.m_i.CF_i \qquad [5.13]$$

where:
a_i is the proportion of new workers coming from activity i;
m_i is the output forgone for workers coming from i, valued at domestic prices;
CF_i is the conversion factor for sector i, converting domestic to world prices.

As an example, suppose a project pays 5000 Rupees per person per year (MWR) and that it draws its workers from a low productivity export crop activity which generates incomes of 1000 Rs at domestic prices (m_i) and that the ratio of border to domestic prices is 1.4 (CF_i). Then the SWR is simply 1000 x 1.4 = 1400, and the CF for labour is 1400/5000 = 0.28.

Hence we can write [5.11] as:

$$NPV_{bp} = FE' + SWR/MWR.LAB' + (1 + WATR). NTG' \qquad [5.14]$$

This completes the outline analysis of the border price approach. In practice, computations are complex and other conversion factors are involved, especially where individual conversion factors are appropriate for individual inputs and products - see Curry and Weiss [1993] and Ward, Deren and D'Silva [1991].

The Domestic Price System

The domestic price system can be analysed in the same way as the border price system. The NPV formula is:

$$NPV_{dp} = cf_{fe}.FE' + cf_{ntg}.NTG' + cf_{lab}.LAB' \qquad [5.15]$$

where the lower case "cf" serves to remind us that the conversion factors under the domestic price system will differ from the conversion factors (the CFs) under the border price system. FE'. NTG' and LAB' remind us that NTG will once again be decomposed into component parts, leaving NTG' as the "residual" NTG. Once again, we can investigate the conversion factors.

Under this system, cf_{fe} will be equal to SER/OER, i.e., the inverse of the ACF. This is because all border prices are being converted to domestic prices.

cf_{ntg} will be equal to unity because NTG will already be expressed in domestic prices.

[5.15] then becomes:

$$NPV_{dp} = SER/OER.FE' + NTG' + cf_{lab}.LAB \qquad [5.16]$$

We are once again left with labour. As with the border price system the general equation is:

$$SWR_{dp} = \Sigma a_i.m_i.cf_i \qquad [5.17]$$

This is the same as equation [5.13] but the conversion factor is now in terms of domestic prices. Pursuing the example given under the border price system, we recall that MWR = 5000 Rupees, but that labour was drawn from a low productivity export activity producing 1000 Rs per worker. In the border price approach this was revalued at the ratio of border prices to domestic prices to give a SWR of 1400 Rs. For the domestic price version we need to multiply again by the ratio of SER to OER (or 1/ACF) to get the SWR in domestic price terms. Hence [5.16] becomes:

$$NPV_{dp} = SER/OER.FE' + NTG' + SWR_{dp}/MWR.LAB \qquad [5.18]$$

We now have the elements of shadow pricing expressed in both numeraires, border prices and domestic prices.

The discount rate

All the expressions in the equations used so far have been in present value terms. It is necessary now to look at the **discount rate** that should be applied in the border price and domestic price systems. Recall that the two numeraires are:

(a) domestic prices, which effectively uses **consumption** as the numeraire. In turn this means converting all benefits and costs into consumption units and valuing them at domestic market prices. This is the **UNIDO Guidelines Approach** (UNIDO [1972]). As noted, it is sometimes known also as **the willingness to pay** (WTP) approach because it focuses on what consumers are willing to pay for goods and services, but WTP approaches can be carried out at either domestic prices or border prices (the prices secured for exports or paid for imports). The UNIDO approach is an example of a WTP approach that uses domestic prices;

(b) by using foreign exchange or **investment** as the numeraire. The rationale for this is that $1 of consumption is not as valuable as $1 of investment, particularly in the developing country context where growth is likely to be closely related to investment. But the same argument is relevant to the developed economy context as well. Using investment as the numeraire, and valuing costs and benefits at "border prices" (i.e., the prices secured for exports or paid for imports - world prices in other words) is the hallmark of the Little-Mirrlees [1974] and Squire-van der Tak [1975] approaches. The Little-Mirrlees numeraire is also known as 'uncommitted income in the hands of the government', or 'social income' for short. A wider form of this approach uses **foreign exchange** as the numeraire and does not discriminate between who the recipients of the foreign exchange are -i.e., it does not regard foreign exchange in the hands of the government as being more important than foreign exchange in the hands of others (Gittinger [1982]). This is the approach we have used in this chapter.

Consider an investment of $1 that yields a return of $R in one year's time, i.e., the value of the investment in one year is $(1+R). Suppose the initial investment was obtained by reducing other investments by $a, and consumption by $(1-a). Further, out of the return, $b is reinvested and $(1-b) is consumed. Then, the present value of this investment is:

$$PV = -\{(1-a) + ak\} + (1+R)\{(1-b) + bk\}/(1+s) \qquad [5.19]$$

where k is the **shadow price** of the investment, i.e., the value of investment in terms of consumption, consumption being the numeraire; s is the rate of discount to be discussed shortly, and is known as the **consumption rate of interest**. The first expression on the right hand side of equation [5.19] is the cost of the investment, and the second expression is the benefit. In each case these costs and benefits have been "shadow priced" by the term k. Note that if k=1, the above expression simplifies to

$$PV = -1 + (1+R)/(1+s) \qquad [5.20]$$

which is the conventional formula for the discounted value of a $1 investment yielding R% and discounted at a rate s.

In practice, equation [5.19] is extremely difficult to estimate. The difficult items are the values of a, b and k. The values of a and b typically require some macroeconomic estimates of the sources of investment funds and the likely use of revenues. The estimate of k, the shadow price of capital, also involves fairly sophisticated exercises and there has been no agreement on likely values, although figures in the range 1-3 have been provided. In practice, therefore, it may not be possible to carry out cost-benefit appraisals that account accurately for different sources of funds and different allocations of the returns. In terms of this section, the focus of interest is on s, the consumption rate of interest.

On the investment approach it is necessary to convert all <u>consumption</u> gains and losses into investment terms. This can be done by using a ratio $Wc/Wg = 1/v$, where Wc is the value of consumption welfare and Wg is the value of welfare of government funds. Flows of investment will not need weighting in this way.

Equation [5.19] would then become:

$$PV = -\{(1-a)1/v + a\} + (1+R)\{(1-b)1/v + b\}/(1+ARI) \qquad [5.21]$$

Whereas the consumption approach involved applying a shadow price of capital to get back to consumption units, the investment approach involves revaluing all consumption flows back to investment units. Notice also that the discount rate has now changed. "ARI" is the **accounting rate of interest** and it is defined as the rate at which the value of government income falls over time, i.e:

$$ARI = (Wg_1 - Wg_0)/Wg_1 \qquad [5.22]$$

where subscripts 1 and 0 refer to time periods.

In fact the multiplication factor $1/v$ is not used and instead a **consumption conversion factor** (CCF) is used. CCF is the value of consumption at domestic prices if one more unit of foreign exchange is committed to consumption. Approximately, it is the value of (marginal) consumption at border prices divided by the value at domestic prices.

If we ignore the sources of funding and dispositions of returns, then the investment numeraire approach computes:

$$PV = -C_0 + B_0.CCF_0 + B_1.CCF_1/ (1 + ARI) \qquad [5.23]$$

for an investment of C_0 that yields an immediate consumption return of B_0 and a consumption return in year 1 of B1.

An estimate of CCF can be obtained from:

$$CCF = q/s.v \qquad [5.24]$$

where: q is the marginal product of capital in the public sector;
v is the value of government income relative to additional consumption at the average consumption level;
s is the consumption rate of interest.

The focus of interest in this section is on ARI, the accounting rate of interest. Essentially, on the domestic price approach we need to estimate CRI. On the border price approach we need to estimate ARI. Chapter 12 investigates the procedures for estimating them in detail.

PART III

VALUATION

Chapter 6

An Overview of Valuation Techniques

Introduction

In this third part of the book, we discuss the principal techniques for assigning economic values to non-market goods and services. There is both great interest and great scepticism in attempts to put monetary values on environmental goods and services - to quantify what many people believe is best left unquantified (Hanemann, [1992]). The interest in valuation techniques arises in part from concern that efforts to protect and improve the environment be cost effective. The scepticism has two somewhat different sources. First, some people feel that it would be useful to know the economic value of environmental goods and services, but do not believe that it is possible to measure it accurately. Second, others feel that it is possible to measure economic value, but do not believe that this is relevant information for making public decisions regarding the environment.

These differences in perspective result in the four categories depicted in Table 6.1. Individuals in cell A believe that it is possible to develop reasonable estimates of the economic value of environmental goods and services, and that such information is useful for policy making. We would throw our lot with individuals in this category. Individuals in cell B believe that estimates of economic value would be useful if they were available, but feel it is unlikely that current measurement techniques are sufficiently accurate and reliable to generate usable information for policy purposes. We are sympathetic with this perspective; many environmental valuation problems pose thorny methodological and theoretical difficulties. But in this third part of the book we hope to convince individuals in cell B that valuation techniques have advanced to the point where it is often worth the effort to try to estimate economic values. This part of the book is written for readers who fall in cells A and B and want to learn more about the available valuation techniques.

Individuals in cell C do not doubt that economists can assign values to environmental goods and services, but do not believe that this is relevant or useful information for setting environmental policy. Individuals in cell D do not believe economists can estimate economic values accurately, but they do not consider this much of a problem because, like individuals in cell C, they do not think this information is of much use. Perhaps we will be unable to convince anyone in cells C and D to change their mind about either the feasibility of environmental valuation techniques or the utility of information on economic values, but our intent is to try. It is important to reiterate that we do **not** believe that information on individuals' preference satisfaction is the only relevant information on which to base environmental policy decisions. But we do believe that human well-being matters and that people are usually the best judges of their own well-being. Given this, it makes sense to measure the criterion of preference satisfaction as best we can, and it is to this task that we now turn.

Types of valuation techniques

The valuation task is to determine how much better or worse off individuals are (or would be) as a result of a change in environmental quality. Economists define the value of a change in terms of how much of *something else* an individual is willing to give up to get this change (or how much they would accept in order to permit the change to occur), but conceptually, how can an analyst ever *know* what an individual would be willing to give up (or to pay) in order to have a specified change in environmental quality occur? There are **five** broad ways to try to address this question.

First, one could experiment. If an analyst wanted to know how much people value a potential new national park, the park could be created and an entrance fee could be charged. An analyst could then observe how many people *actually* used the park, in effect exchanging money for the recreation and aesthetic experience of visiting the park. Or if an analyst wanted to know how much people would be willing to pay to live in a city with improved air quality, an experiment could be conducted in which air quality standards and property taxes would be raised in some cities and not in others. The analyst could then see how many people found it worthwhile to move to cities with improved air quality and higher taxes. In practice, of course, such large scale experiments of this kind are exceedingly difficult to design and politically impossible to implement. Other ways must be used to determine how people value environmental goods and services.

A second approach is simply to ask people how much they would be willing to give up (i.e., how much they would be willing to pay) to have a specified environmental quality improvement happen. This is known as the "stated preferences", or "contingent valuation method", and is described in chapter 7. It is also termed the "direct approach" because people are directly asked to state or reveal their preferences. If people were able to understand clearly the change in environmental quality being offered, and answered truthfully, this direct approach would be ideal. It measures precisely what the analyst wants to know - the individual's strength of preference for the proposed change - and could be used not only for non-market goods and services, but market goods as well. Chapter 7 describes many practical difficulties with this stated preferences approach, but the central problem is whether the **intentions** people indicate *ex-ante* (before the change) will accurately describe their **behaviour** *ex-post* (after the change) when people face no penalty or cost associated with a discrepancy between the two.

Economists in particular have been very concerned that stated intentions will not correspond to behaviour, and have thus traditionally used a **third** approach for measuring the value of non-market goods: surrogate markets. To use this technique, economists try to find a good or service that is sold in markets and is related to or "bundled with" the non-market service. In this situation the individual may reveal his or her preferences for both the market and non-market service when he or she purchases the market good. For example, when making a decision on what house to buy or apartment to rent, an individual may consider many factors, such the size and age of the house, its proximity to schools, shopping, and place of employment - and perhaps the air quality in the neighbourhood. Chapter 8 describes how an estimate of the value of improved air quality can be "recovered" from a careful analysis of such transactions in the housing market. This surrogate market method is known as the "hedonic property value model". Chapter 8 also describes other surrogate market methods, such as the travel cost model, the hedonic wage model and avertive behaviour technique.

All of these surrogate market methods rely on the "behavioral trail" left by individuals as they make actual decisions that affect their lives. Individuals reveal their preferences through their actual behaviour. The estimates obtained of the value of non-market goods are based on information on what people actually did and on a set of maintained assumptions about *why* they did them - not what people said they would do under a set of hypothetical conditions.

This third approach is not, however, without disadvantages. For example, it is not feasible to use surrogate market methods to estimate the value of a new good or service, or of a change in environmental quality outside of current experience because no situations exist where people have been offered this new level of environmental quality and have revealed their preferences for it. Even if the non-market good or service has been available, there may never have been any significant variation in its quality, so that everyone in a particular area must "consume" the same amount (level) of it. In such a case, it is impossible to infer how people in the area would respond to a change in quality. Finally, as will be discussed in Chapter 8, to implement any of the surrogate market methods, the analyst must impose a theoretical framework in order to interpret the information on individuals' decisions within a valuation context. The estimates of value derived will thus depend upon a series of assumptions that remain largely untested.

A **fourth** approach is available. For changes in environmental quality that reduce individuals' well-being, an analyst can attempt to determine the **damages** an individual will suffer. A deterioration in environmental quality could cause a loss of productive assets or loss in earning power. An individual could be "made well" or restored to their initial state of well-being by being compensated in money or other goods or services by the amount of the loss. This is termed the "damage function" approach and is described in Chapter 9.

The damage function and surrogate market techniques are termed "indirect" valuation approaches because neither relies on people's *direct* answers to questions about how much they would be willing to pay (or accept) to have a change in environmental quality occur.

The **fifth** approach to obtaining estimates of the value of environmental goods and services takes a somewhat different tack. Rather than developing new estimates of value for the environmental good or service of interest, the analyst finds estimates of value for the same or similar good or service in other locations, and then *transfers* these estimates - perhaps after some adjustment to the location of interest. The analyst can transfer estimates of value developed using any of the other approaches described above. This "benefit transfer" approach is discussed in Chapter 10.

An overview of the literature on valuation techniques

Tables 6.2-6.7 list some of the existing valuation studies by area of application and location, for different valuation techniques. In presenting these tables, our intent is not to be comprehensive. There are many valuation studies not listed, and those that are listed were not selected randomly. In some cases the categorization of studies by area of application was somewhat arbitrary. Our purpose here is simply to show some general trends.

A brief examination of the tables reveals several things. **First**, the non-market valuation techniques described in this third part of the book are not untested: several have been used in both industrialized and developing countries in a wide variety of sectors and areas of application. **Second**, much of the valuation literature is very recent. For all of the valuation techniques, in all areas of application, and in all parts of the world, the majority of the work has been done since 1980.

This recent surge of interest in valuation work throughout the world is due to several factors. In the United States in 1981 President Ronald Reagan signed Executive Order 12291, which required that all "major" federal regulations pass a cost-benefit test (Smith, 1984). U.S. government agencies responsible for the management and protection of the environment and natural resources found that they needed non-market valuation techniques to estimate the benefits of regulations designed to improve environmental quality.

Perhaps even more important than Executive Order 12291, in 1980 the U.S. Congress passed the

Comprehensive Environmental Response, Compensation, and Liability Act (CERCLA). This legislation established that "potentially responsible parties" could be liable for the costs of cleanup **and** the damages caused by their spill or release of hazardous or toxic substances. The federal and state governments were designated as the "trustees" of the nation's natural resources and could sue corporations or individuals who damaged such resources. The U.S. federal government was charged with developing regulations to determine how the magnitude of these damages should be assessed (Hanemann, [1992]; Kopp and Smith, [1991]). The regulations and procedures were slow in coming, but after they were finally promulgated, they were quickly subject to legal challenge.

The most famous of the natural resources damage assessments to end up in court has been the federal and state suits against Exxon for its role in the Prince William's Sound oil spill in Alaska, but there have been many other cases. The litigation process surrounding natural resource damage assessment in the United States has focused attention on the strengths and weaknesses of non-market valuation techniques in a manner largely unprecedented in "normal" academic debate. In the Exxon-Valdez case in particular, parties to the litigation sponsored large research projects on non-market valuation in order to support or discredit the estimates of environmental damage prepared by other parties.

The result of these two developments has been a period of major innovation and research in the United States during the 1980s on the theory and methods of non-market valuation. In Europe heightened awareness of the importance of environmental issues has sparked a renewed interested in policy instruments that can be used to improve environmental quality. Valuation techniques are central to this effort. As the tables show, work on valuation applications in Europe began even more recently than in the United States, but now appears to be increasing rapidly. To date the majority of applications in Europe have been in Norway, Sweden, and England, but research and applications are accelerating throughout both eastern and western Europe. Most of the applications in developing countries are even more recent than in Europe.

Third, the majority of applications of all of the valuation techniques have been carried out in the United States and Canada, followed by Europe. Not surprisingly, the fewest applications have been done in developing countries. However, interest in valuation work in developing countries is growing rapidly in Africa, Latin America, and Southeast Asia because both development banks and national governments seek to incorporate environmental concerns into policy and project appraisals.

Fourth, comparing the number of applications of the different valuation techniques, there are a surprisingly large number of applications of the contingent valuation method. This is in part because the contingent valuation method is flexible in terms of data requirements and can be applied to many different kinds of valuation problems. There are in fact large numbers of studies in the United States using the travel cost model to estimate the value of recreational sites and activities and the value of water quality improvements. Studies using hedonic property value models have largely focused on measuring the value of air and water quality improvements and the value of urban amenities. But these surrogate market methods have been largely used in the United States and Canada; applications in developing countries are still rare.

Fifth, for all the valuation techniques the major areas of application in the United States have been air and water quality, recreation (including fishing, hunting, parks, wildlife preservation), health risks, and water supply (including groundwater protection). With a couple of exceptions, European applications have followed a similar pattern. In Europe there seem to be more applications of valuation techniques, in relative terms, in the areas of forestry and transport than in the United States. In developing countries the applications to date have been largely restricted to two sectors: (1) water and sanitation, and (2) recreation (tourism, national parks). This is principally due to the interest and commitment of the World Bank in these areas.

Choice among valuation techniques

All of the valuation techniques described in the following chapters have strengths and weaknesses, and the decision on which valuation technique to use for a particular application requires experience and judgment on the part of the analyst. The advantages and disadvantages of the techniques available will be considered in the following chapters. There are, however, some general points to consider when making this choice. **First**, it is often possible to use more than one valuation technique and compare the results. The estimates of value obtained from all the methods described will be somewhat uncertain. If the analyst has multiple estimates, he or she will have greater confidence in the magnitude of the value of the proposed change.

Several of the valuation techniques typically use data from a household survey (e.g., contingent valuation, travel cost model, and hedonic property value model). When the implementation of a valuation technique requires that **primary data** be collected with a household survey, it is often possible to design the survey to obtain the data necessary to undertake more than one valuation method. Particularly in developing countries, secondary data are rarely available for carrying out valuation work, and household surveys are required. Such surveys need to be designed with the goal of developing value estimates with multiple methods.

Second, different valuation techniques may measure different things. In this sense they should be considered complimentary, not competing tools. For example, the contingent valuation method is the only available technique for measuring nonuse (or passive use) values. Suppose that estimates of use value of a national park and wildlife reserve were obtained using a travel cost model and estimates of nonuse value were obtained from a contingent valuation survey. These value estimates are not substitutes for one another; both are useful for policy makers.

Similarly, revealed preference methods measure the *perceived* benefits to individuals; they do not capture the value of effects of which people are unaware. For example, if individuals do not know that a cancer-causing substance is in their drinking water, they obviously will not take action to avoid this risk. There will thus be no "behavioural trail" that an analyst can follow to determine how much they would be willing to pay to avoid such a risk. However, using the damage function approach, an analyst could estimate the reduced cancer deaths that would result if the carcinogenic substance was removed from the water supply.

Third, it is important to consider the needs of the user(s) of valuation studies. In some cases clients have preferences for the use of one valuation technique over another. For example, estimates obtained from travel cost or hedonic property value models may be considered too theoretical or too complex. A particular client may feel that contingent valuation estimates are too subjective and unreliable to support policy debate and discussion. The analyst carrying out policy work must be sensitive to such concerns.

Fourth, the analyst should consider not only the client's needs, but also the needs of the public. Information elicited on people's values for environmental improvement is often of great interest to a wide variety of groups in society. In choosing a valuation technique, thought should be given to how the information obtained will be received by the public and interested parties other than the immediate client. Information from valuation studies need not, of course, contribute to democratic dialogue or a participatory political process; it could easily be used in a "top-down" hierarchical planning process. However, the use of a technique such as contingent valuation often bears a resemblance to a referendum or voting process. The final decision on a policy or project may not be determined by an election, but the process of eliciting information on people's preferences involves a certain degree of participant involvement in the decision making. Analysts need to be sensitive to the political implications and consultative nature of the valuation task, and choose techniques that inform and facilitate public debate. One useful step is often to hold public hearings or meetings with local community leaders to explain the findings of valuation studies.

Fifth, the cost of carrying out a valuation study or set of studies must be weighed against the value of the information in helping to make a better policy or project decision. Clearly more money could be spent on a valuation study than a policy decision warrants. But it is also important to keep in mind that many policies and projects have large-scale environmental implications that extend far into the future. In this case there is a substantial risk that *too little* money will be spent on the use of valuation techniques.

Table 6.1 **Perspectives on measuring economic values of environmental goods and services, and the usefulness of such information for policy making**

Economic Values of Environmental Goods and Services

	Can be Measured Accurately and Reliably	Cannot be Measured Accurately and Reliably
Economic Values of Environmental Goods and Services are		
Useful for Policy Making	Cell A	Cell B
Not Useful for Policy Making	Cell C	Cell D

Table 6.2 - **An Overview of the Contingent Valuation Studies (Stated Preferences) by Area of Application and Location**

Valuation Technique: Stated Preferences Area of Application	United States and Canada	Europe	Developing Countries
Agriculture	Bergstrom et al [1985] Lant [1988] Purvis et al [1989] Syme et al [1990]	Aakkula [1991] Drake [1993] Hanley [1986, 1989]	
Air Quality	Ahearn [1984] Balson et al [1990a,b] Blank et al [1978] Brookshire et al [1979a] Carson et al [1990c, 1991c] Chestnut and Rowe [1990, 1991] Dickie and Gerking [1989b, 1991b] Hoehn and Fishelson [1987] Katz and Sterner [1990] Levy [1991] McClelland et al [1991] Loehman [1984] Loehman and Boldt [1988] Mitchell and Carson [1988d] Mitchell et al [1989] Rae [1982, 1983, 1984] Rahmatian [1979] Randall [1979] Randall et al [1985] Rowe and Chestnut [1986] Rudd [1986] Schulze et al [1979, 1981a, 1983a] Shechter [1989] Shechter and Zeidner [1991] Tolley et al [1985] Zeidner and Shechter [1988]	Aakerman [1988] Hylland and Strand [1983] Johansson and Kristrom [1988] Navrud [1988b] Schulz [1985] Strand [1985] Shechter [1988]	
Climate Change		Bateman [1990]	
Energy	Braden et al [1992] Doane et al [1988] Meta Systems [1986] RCG/Hagler [1986, 1988, 1989a,b,c,d, 1990a,b, 1991a,b] Sanghvi [1990] Woo & Pupp [1992]	Carlsen [1987]	Liu [1989]
Fishing: Commercial	Bishop et al [1987] Dragun [1991] Hoehn [1987] Milon [1986]	Carlsen [1985] Strand [1981a]	
Fishing: Recreational	Anderson and Devereaux [1986] Bergstrom et al [1989] Bergstrom et al [1990] Binkley and Hannemann [1978] Boyle and Bishop [1979] Brooks [1991] Carson et al [1990b] Duffield [1988] Huppert [1989] Mathews and Brown [1970] Meyer [1978, 1979, 1980, 1987] Olsen et al [1991]	Amundsen [1987] Bonnieux et al [1991] Navrud [1988a] Silvander [1991] Strand [1981]	

Forestry	Crocker [1985] Freimund [1990] Loomis et al [1993] Sorg and Loomis [1984] Walsh et al [1990] Walsh [1991]	Bojo [1985] Crocker [1984] Everett [1979] Ewers [1986] Hanley and Common [1987a,b] Hoen and Winther [1991] Johannesson et al [1992] Johannesson and Jonsson [1991a] Linden and Oosterhuis [1988] Kristrom [1988] Loyland et al [1991] Navrud et al [1990] Nielson [1992] Ovaskainen et al [1991]	
Health Risks	Acton [1973] Berger et al [1987] Birkan et al [1992] Chestnut et al [1988, 1992] Eom [1992] Hammit [1986] Hill [1988] Muller and Reutzel [1984] Smith and Eom [1992] Thompson [1986] van Ravenswaay and Hoehn [1991] Vicusi et al [1989]	Wind [1991] Willis and Garrod [1991]	
Recreational Hunting	Brookshire et al [1983] Davis [1964] Donnelly [1986] Duffield and Neher [1991] Hay [1988a] Loomis and Cooper [1988] Loomis et al [1988] Loomis et al [1989] Miller [1980] Sorg and Nelson [1986] Stoll [1980] Young [1987]	Sydal [1989]	
Parks, Nature, Reserves and Wildlife	Adams et al [1989] Bennet [1984] Bishop and Boyle [1985, 1986, 1987] Boyle et al [1990] Brookshire et al [1978, 1983] Cocheba and Lanford [1978] Duffield [1991b,c] Gilbert et al [1991] Halstead et al [1991] King et al [1987] King and Flynn 1989 Loomis [1987b] McKillop [1992] Michalson and Smathers [1985] Rubin et al [1991] Samples and Hollyer [1990] Schulze et al [1981b] Smith, N.E. [1980] Stevens [1991] Walsh and Gilliam [1982] Whitehead [1990]	Bateman [1992] Dahle et al [1987] FHRC [1989] Green et al [1990b] Hanley and Common [1987a,b] Hanley [1989a] Hanley et al [1987a, 1987b] Harley and Graig [1991] Navrud [1991d] Willis [1990] Willis and Garrod [1991]	Abala [1987] Grandstaff, Dixon and Eutriak [1986] Enis and Shechter [1972] Mitchell [1982] Shechter [1974]
Roads/Transport	Natchman [1983]	Bateman [1991] Bristow et al [1990] Riera [1991]	

Water Quality	Carson et al [1991,b,] Bockstael et al [1989] Caudill and Hoehn [1992] D'Arge and Shogen [1985] Harris [1984] Hayes [1987] Hoehn and Walker [1988] Kaoru [1991] Lant and Mullins [1991] Mitchell and Carson [1981, 1986b] O'Neil [1985] Oster [1977] Ribaudo [1983] Smith and Desvousges [1986] Smith et al [1983] Whittington et al [1993c]	Dalgard [1989] Green and Tunstall [1991] Heiberg and Hem [1987] Magnussen [1992a,b] Matymaa [1991] Navrud [1989, 1991b,c] Signorello [1992] Silvander [1991] Turner and Brooke [1988] WRC/FHRC [1989]	McConnell and Ducci [1989] Oliveira [1992] Whittington et al [1993b]
Water Supply and Sanitation (including Ground Water Protection)	Carson [1989,] Carson et al [1991a,d] Howe and Smith [1991] Lazo and Schulze [1992] Loomis [1987a] McClelland et al [1992] Mitchell and Carson [1986b, 1987] Musser et al [1992] Poe and Bishop [1992] Powell [1991] Rowe et al [1985] Schultze [1992] Sutherland and Walsh [1985] Thomas and Syme [1988] Walker and Hoehn [1989]	Hervik et al [1987] Strand and Wenstrop [1991]	Altaf [1992] Aedo [1992] Boadu [1992] Briscoe et al [1990] Bohm et al [1993] CONSPLAN [1992] Lauria et al [1993] ODA [1990] Singh [1993] Robinson [1988] Strasa Inversion y Desarrollo S.A. [1992] Whittington et al [1988 1990, 1991a,b, 1992a, 1993a,d,e]

Table 6.3 An Overview of the Hedonic Property Value Studies by Area of Application and Location

Valuation Technique: Surrogate Markets (Hedonic Property Value Models) by sector	United States	Europe	Developing Countries
Agriculture	Palmquist and Danielson [1989]		
Air Quality	Many applications: e.g.,: Anderson and Crocker [1971] Cobb [1977] Deyak and Smith [1974] Freeman [1971, 1974a,b] Harrison and Rubinfeld [1978] Kneese [1984] Murdoch and Thayer [1988] Nelson [1978] O'Byrne [1985] Palmquist [1983] Peckham [1970] Polinsky and Shavell [1975, 1976] Ridker and Henning [1967] Small [1975] Smith and Dyak [1975] Spore [1972] Steele [1972] Wieand [1973]	Hoffman [1984] Larsen [1985] Starkie and Johnson [1973]	
Health Risks	Michaels and Smith [1990] Nelson [1981]		
Hunting (Recreational)	Brookshire et al [1983]		
Noise	Li and Brown [1980] McMillan et al [1980] Nelson [1979, 1982]	Hoffman [1984] Larsen [1985] Oosterhuis and van der Pligt [1985] Pennington et al [1990]	
Parks, Nature Reserves and Wildlife	Abelson [1979] Bartik [1988a,b] Blomquist and Worley [1981] David [1968] Diamond [1980b, 1982] Grieson and White [1989] Stoll and Johnson [1984] Walsh, Loomis and Gillman [1984]	Garrod and Willis [1991] Green et al [1988, 1989] Harley and Hanley [1989] Willis and Benson [1988]	
Water Quality	Devousges et al [1983] Smith and Desvousges [1986]		
Water Supply and Sanitation (including groundwater protection)	Edwards [1988]	Green et al [1987, 1988]	Follain and Jimenez [1985] North and Griffin [1993] Malpezzi and Mayo [1985]

Table 6.4 An Overview of Hedonic Wage Risk Studies and Averting Behaviour Studies

Hedonic Wage Risk Studies		
United States	Europe	Developing Countries
Smith (R) [1974] Thaler/Rosen [1976] Smith (R) [1976] Viscusi [1978] Dillingham [1979] Brown [1980] Viscusi [1980] Viscusi [1981] Olson [1981] Arnould et al. [1983] Butler [1983] Low/McPheters [1983] Dorsey/Walzer [1983] Smith (V) [1983] Dickens [1984] Leigh/Folsom [1984] Smith and Gilbert [1984] Dillingham [1985] Gegax et al [1985] Leigh [1987] Herzog and Schlottman [1987] Viscusi/Moore [1987] Garen [1988] Cousineau et al. [1988] Moore/Viscusi [1988a,b] Viscusi/Moore [1989] Moore/Viscusi [1990a,b] Kniesner and Leeth [1991]	Melinek [1974] Veljanovski [1978] Needleman [1979] Marin et al. [1982] Georgiou [1992]	
Avertive Behaviour Studies		
Blomquist [1979] Courant and Porter [1981] Dardis [1980] Dickie and Gerking [1991a,] Harford [1984] Ippolito and Ippolito [1984]		

Table 6.5 An Overview of Travel Cost Studies by Area of Application and Location

Valuation Technique: Surrogate Markets (Travel Cost Models) by sector	United States	Europe	Developing Countries
Fishing: Recreational	Many applications (some listed under "Parks") Donnely et al [1985]	Hjalte et al [1982] Navrud [1984, 1988a,] Rolfsen [1990] Scancke [1984] Silvander [1991] Singas [1991] Strand [1981b] Ulleberg [1988]	
Parks, Nature, Reserves and Wildlife	Many Applications: e.g., Clawson [1959, 1966] Smith and Karou [1990]	Benson and Garrod [1989] Willis and Garrod [1991]	Grandstaff and Dixon [1986] Whittington et al [1990]
Water Quality	Many applications, e.g., Smith and Devousges [1985] Smith et al [1989] Bockstael et al [1987a,b]		Luken [1987]
Water Supply and Sanitation (including groundwater protection)		Willis et al [1990] Willis and Garrod [1990]	

Table 6.6 An Overview of Damage Function Studies by Area of Application and Location

Valuation Technique: Damage Function (by sector)	United States	Europe	Developing Countries
Agriculture	Adams and Crocker [1989] Adams, Crocker and Thanavibulchai [1982] Adams and McCarl [1985] Howitt, Gossard and Adams [1984]	van der Erden [1987] van der Erden [1988] ECOTEC [1988] AED [1991]	Bojo [1987] Kim and Dixon [1987] Wiggins and Palma [1980]
Air Quality		SPCA [1991]	
Fishing (Commercial)		Ewers and Schulz [1982] Ramussen et al [1991	
Forestry		Ewers et al [1986] IIASA Forest Study [1991] Linden and Oosterhuis [1988] Nilsson [1991] NNM [1988]	Anderson [1987] Dixon et al [1986, 1988]
Health Risks		Opschoor [1987]	
Materials Damage	Fink et al [1971] Freeman [1982] Gillette [1975] Horst et al [1986] Horst et al [1990] Lipfert [1987]	Feenstra [1984] Glomsrod and Rosland [1988] Heinz [1980] Jansen et al [1974] Jansen and Olsthorn [1982] Lanting and Morree [1984]	
Water Quality	Baan [1983]		Phantumvanit [1982]
Water Supply and Sanitation (including groundwater protection)		Winge et al [1991]	Briones [1986]

Table 6.7 An Overview of Benefit Transfer Studies by Area of Application and Location

Valuaion Technique: Benefit Transfer, Area of Application	United Sates and Canada	Europe	Developing Countries
Forestry	Sorg and Loomis [1984]		
Recreation	Forster [1989] Smith and Karou [1990] Vaughn and Russell [1982] Walsh, Johnson, and McKean [1988, 1990 1992] U.S. Water Resources Council [1983]		
Water Quality	Desvousges et al [1983, 1992d] Luken et al [1992] Naughton and Desvousges [1986]		

Chapter 7

Stated Preferences

Introduction

The contingent valuation method (CVM) is a survey technique that attempts to elicit information about individuals' (or households') preferences for a good or service. Respondents in the survey are asked a question or a series of questions about how much they value a good or service. The technique is termed "contingent" because the good or service is not, in fact, necessarily going to be provided by the enumerator or research analyst: the situation the respondent is asked to value is hypothetical. The CVM can be used to obtain values of private goods, goods with both private and public characteristics (such as various kinds of infrastructure), and "pure" public goods. Often it is used to assess preferences for goods or services for which a conventional market does not exist.

At first glance the contingent valuation method appears similar to public opinion polling and market research techniques, and although there are indeed important similarities, there are also significant differences. The contingent valuation technique seeks to obtain a monetary measure of the change in well-being an individual would obtain from the provision of a particular good or service. Public opinion polls on the other hand do not seek information in order to derive measures of welfare change or require an individual to carefully consider his or her budget constraints. Public opinion polls are typically concerned with people's attitudes and opinions, not the translation of these into monetary valuations.

Market researchers, on the other hand, want to know whether people will purchase various goods if they were offered at specified prices, but these goods or services are typically private in nature. There is convincing evidence that the answers people give to hypothetical questions about their willingness to pay for private goods contain information about what they would purchase if confronted with an actual choice. Contingent valuation research, however, typically focuses on individuals' preferences for public or mixed private-public goods. Here the kinds of hypothetical situations that must be described to respondents in the questionnaire are often more complex and difficult for people to understand.

Over the last decade the contingent valuation method has attracted an increasing amount of attention in the environmental economics profession and in the broader environmental policy community. In the United States it has been acknowledged by the courts as a recognized, legitimate procedure for valuing environmental benefits (State of Ohio v. Department of Interior, 880 F. 2d 432, D.C. Cir. 1989). There are several reasons for this widespread interest in the contingent valuation method--some good and some not. First, **the CVM is the only practical means of estimating some kinds of environmental benefits**. For example, if policy makers want to know people's existence values for a unique natural habitat or wilderness area, the contingent valuation method is the only available benefit estimation procedure.

Second, the evidence available from the United States and Europe suggests that estimates of environmental benefits obtained from well-designed, properly executed contingent valuation surveys appear to be as good as estimates obtained with other valuation methods (Cummings, Brookshire and Schulze, [1986]; Mitchell and Carson, [1989]; Arrow et. al, [1993]). Third, the ability to design and carry out large scale surveys and to rigorously analyze and interpret the information obtained has been greatly enhanced by advances in scientific sampling theory, the economic theory of benefit estimation, computerized data management, and public opinion polling.

On the negative side some naive analysts are attracted to the contingent valuation method because it appears on the surface to be so easy to do: just ask people a few questions and tabulate their answers. Over the last few decades survey researchers involved with public opinion polling have learned a great deal about the "art of asking questions," and their conclusions should give newcomers to the contingent valuation method reason for caution (Schuman and Presser, [1981]). Public opinion pollsters have found that the task of obtaining accurate assessments of people's reasoned judgments is much more complicated that many initially believed. Respondents often give seemingly contradictory, inconsistent answers to questions; they sometimes fail to give truthful answers to survey questions; they have a tendency to give an opinion even when they do not have a real point of view on a subject; and their answers may change depending on the precise wording of a question. Survey researchers and public opinion pollsters have learned that reliable information can often be obtained, but only with carefully designed, well-executed studies (Dillman, [1978]).

Types of interviews used in contingent valuation surveys

The interviews for a CV study can be conducted by mail, telephone, or in-person--or some combination of these. Each type of interview can be appropriate under certain conditions. In-person interviews are generally considered to provide the highest quality data if the resources are available to properly train and supervise the enumerators (Arrow et. al., [1993]). The major disadvantages of in-person interviews are their expense and the possible biases introduced by different enumerators asking the same question in different ways. In developing countries in-person interviews are typically the only option because a substantial portion of the population may not have a telephone or may not be able to read (or return) a mail questionnaire.

In industrialized countries where almost everyone has a telephone, telephone interviews offer several advantages. First, they are relatively inexpensive and can be carried out in a short time. Second, random-digit dialing methods can be used to obtain a relatively representative sample frame. Third, response rates in well-conducted telephone surveys are quite high--approximately 75 percent in the United States. Fourth, as with an in-person interview, the interview is interactive: the respondent can ask the enumerator questions if something is unclear or requires clarification.

There are two main disadvantages of a telephone survey. First, it is difficult to convey much information about the hypothetical scenario over the telephone. For example, it is not possible to show the respondent pictures, diagrams, or lists of items to consider. Second, the amount of time respondents are generally willing to spend on a telephone interview is quite limited (about 10-15 minutes in the United States).

In industrialized countries mail surveys have often been used to carry out CV interviews. Mail surveys are less expensive than in-person interviews, and avoid the problem with in-person interviews introduced by differences among enumerators. Responses rates in properly designed, well-executed mail surveys are generally high, and can be increased further if respondents are compensated for completing the questionnaire. However, the sequence in which the respondent reads the questions in a mail survey cannot be controlled, and this precludes the use of many of the types of questions that

CV researchers would like to ask. Also, mail surveys obviously cannot be completed by illiterate respondents.

These three types of interviews can be combined in different ways in an attempt to minimize the disadvantages of each approach. For example, a respondent may be asked to complete and return a mail questionnaire; this may be followed up by a telephone interview. Other possibilities include a telephone-mail-telephone sequence and a mail-in-person sequence.

Components of a contingent valuation questionnaire

Whatever type of interview is selected, most CV survey instruments have three basic parts. **First**, a hypothetical description of the terms under which the good or service is to be offered is presented to the respondent. This description seeks to present sufficient information for the respondent to consider carefully the value of the proposed good or service. In mail or in-person interviews pictures or diagrams are often used to convey information to the respondent. In general, the description of the good or service to be valued should include information on such things as:
* when the service will be available;
* how the respondent will be expected to pay for it;
* how much others will be expected to pay;
* what institutions will be responsible for delivery of the service; and
* the quality and reliability of the service.
Survey designers face a trade-off between providing respondents with sufficient information to make a reasoned decision and overloading respondents with too much information, so they may become distracted, bored, or confused. An example of a description for an improved sanitation system used in a CV study in Kumasi, Ghana is presented in Box 7.1.

Second, the respondent is asked one or more questions that try to determine how much he or she would value a good or service if actually confronted with the opportunity to obtain it under the specified terms or conditions. In a **contingent valuation study** such questions may take the form of asking how much an individual is willing to pay for the service, or how much he is willing to accept in compensation to forgo a loss. Respondents are sometimes asked how they would change their behaviour in response to a hypothetical change in a good or service. Their responses are then used in econometric models to **infer** their willingness to pay for the described change.

Respondents may also be asked how they would **vote** on a proposal to provide a public good at a specified price. This may appear to be simply a public opinion polling type of question, but by varying the price offered to different respondents (i.e., using multiple versions of the questionnaire), respondents' willingness to pay can be estimated with the use of econometric techniques[10].

Third, CV survey instruments usually include a series of questions about the socioeconomic and demographic characteristics of the respondent and his or her family. These data are obtained in order to relate the answers respondents give to the valuation questions to the other characteristics of the respondent. Information may also be collected on respondents' knowledge, attitudes, and practices regarding goods or services similar or related to what is being offered in the hypothetical market scenario. The actual sequence of these parts in the questionnaire depends on the particular cultural and social environment.

Elicitation procedures

The parts of the survey instrument that are unique to the contingent valuation method are the description of the hypothetical market and the valuation questions. There are several ways that a respondent can indicate his or her choice or preferences. One is simply to answer a question as to whether or not he would want to purchase the service if it cost a specified amount. We refer to this as a **YES/NO question**. Another possibility is to ask the respondent a direct question about the most he or she would be willing to pay for the good or service; we refer to this as a **direct or open-ended question**.

These two types of questions can be combined in a CV questionnaire to create different ways of eliciting the valuation information (Whittington and Swarna, [1993a]). As detailed in Table 7.1, each has distinct advantages and disadvantages, and the appropriate choice for a specific problem is a matter of judgment on the part of the analyst. However, the options in which a respondent is offered the good or service at a specified price and is then requested to give a YES/NO answer are generally preferred to the option of starting with a direct, open-ended question or options that depend upon a long sequence of responses to YES/NO questions.

In addition to the valuation question structures described in Table 7.1, respondents may be shown a list of possible answers in the form of a "payment" card, and asked to indicate their selection from the list. This approach cannot easily be used in telephone interviews or in countries with high illiteracy rates. It also requires a careful determination of the range of possible answers to be presented on the payment card. Another approach called **contingent ranking** is to ask the respondents to rank different projects or policies in terms of their desirability or priority.

Types of errors and biases in contingent valuation studies

There are three basic categories of errors (or sources of problems) involved in contingent valuation studies. First, at the level of the individual, there are a variety of reasons why a respondent may not reveal his or her "true" value of the good or service. Second, an individual may offer an accurate answer to a question he or she thought they heard, but this is not in fact the question the enumerator thought he or she asked. Third, even if each individual were to reveal his or her "true" preferences, problems can arise when analysts attempt to aggregate individual valuation responses to the level of a group or community.

i) Individuals answer CV questions inaccurately

Many people--but particularly economists--are deeply sceptical about the validity and reliability of respondents' answers to hypothetical WTP questions. Two main kinds of concerns are at issue. The first is whether respondents will answer WTP questions honestly and accurately. The second is whether WTP responses are reliable measures of value. In this context reliability can be viewed either as the variance of a sample of WTP responses around the "true" mean WTP, or as the probability that a respondent's answer to a WTP question would be the same if he or she could be repeatedly tested (or asked the WTP question many times). If the reliability of WTP responses is poor, answers to WTP questions may be of little value, even though respondents did not intentionally give inaccurate answers.

Economists have long worried that if individuals actually had to pay their reported WTP values, then they would be tempted to understate their true preferences for public goods in hopes of a "free ride" while others pay for the provision of the good or service (Samuelson 1954). Alternatively, if the price to be charged for the public good is not tied to an individual's WTP response, but the provision of the public good is, the respondent may over-report WTP in order to ensure the provision of the good. In both cases the bid would be systematically different from the respondent's "true" willingness to pay. Literature on the contingent valuation method has termed this difference "strategic bias."

Systematic (that is, nonrandom) differences between respondents' answers to WTP questions and their true willingness to pay can arise for other reasons. Respondents in a particular cultural context may feel it inappropriate to answer some kinds of questions in specific ways or may attempt to give answers that they think will please the enumerator. This "compliance bias" can result in substantial differences between reported and true WTP values.

The reliability of respondents' answers to WTP questions may be weakened in a number of ways. A respondent who does not know his willingness to pay and does not wish to exert the mental energy to think about his preferences may simply guess at an answer to a WTP question. If this is simply a random guess, such behaviour would increase the variance of WTP bids in a sample of respondents without changing the expected value of the mean or "true" WTP. If there is a pattern to these guesses, perhaps derived from cultural norms or customs, such "hypothetical bias" may be introducing systematic errors into the WTP bids.

Despite these potential pitfalls, recent assessments of contingent valuation studies suggest that self-reported preferences from WTP questions for goods and services with *use value* (such as water and sanitation services) are generally much more reliable than economists have traditionally thought (Mitchell and Carson, [1989]). In particular, research findings from a number of studies in industrialized countries fail to support the hypothesis that respondents will act strategically when answering WTP questions. Recent contingent valuation studies in developing countries have similarly demonstrated that respondents in both urban and rural locations give apparently reasonable answers to WTP questions about improved water services and that these answers are systematically related to their socioeconomic characteristics (Whittington, Briscoe, Mu, and Barron, [1990]; Briscoe, de Castro, Griffin, North, and Olsen, [1990]; Whittington, Smith, Okorafor, Ókore, Lui, and McPhail, [1992b]; Altaf, Whittington, Jamal, and Smith, [1993]). There is little evidence yet, however, that such conclusions about the absence of strategic bias can be generalized to other developing countries or to different cultures.

ii) Miscommunication between the enumerator and the respondent

If a survey is not well designed, it is easy for the enumerator to ask a question that he or she thinks is clear, but for the respondent to interpret it differently than was intended. In such cases, the respondent may answer the question he heard honestly (accurately), but this answer is not to the question that the enumerator thought he or she asked. These kinds of problems arise in part because certain words mean different things to different people, and because survey researchers tend to impose their own conceptual framework on problems and situations that respondents understand quite differently. Such risks of miscommunication are especially acute in cross-cultural surveys.

There is considerable evidence from public opinion polls that people have particular problems understanding certain kinds of questions that depend on insight into their own feelings or their memory of events or feelings. Contingent valuation questions related to environmental policy are very susceptible to such problems because attitudes toward such issues as environmental degradation and the preservation of species evoke deeply held moral, philosophical, and religious beliefs.

One particular aspect of this problem has been of central concern to CV researchers. In some cases respondents may interpret the hypothetical offer of a specific good or service to be indicative of an offer for a broader set of similar goods and services. For example, if a respondent was asked for her willingness to pay for improved water quality in a specific river, she might misinterpret this question to mean her willingness to pay for cleaning up *all rivers* in a region or country. In this case her answer(s) to the willingness-to-pay question(s) would not reveal the value sought by the enumerator. This is referred to as the "embedding problem" because the value of the good or service the CV researcher is seeking is embedded in the value of the more encompassing set of goods or services reported by the respondent.

To illustrate the nature of this problem, consider the CV scenario depicted in Box 7.2. The respondent in an industrialized country is asked to indicate whether he or she would be willing to pay higher taxes in order to compensate developing countries for the establishment of five major wildlife and rainforest reserves. Suppose policy makers wanted to know whether compensation was feasible; in this case it would be important for the CV study to determine how much individuals value the **five** proposed reserves. But would respondents really think about **five** reserves (as opposed to **ten** or **twenty** reserves)? They may simply feel that they are being asked to value the preservation of rain forests and the protection of wildlife in the tropics. In the latter case their answers may reflect not the value of five specific rainforest reserves, but rather a program to preserve all rain forests -- or they may want to make an ideological or moral statement about the general subject.

This example is indicative of another, even broader problem with obtaining accurate answers to CV questions regarding public goods. People in industrialized countries are constantly being asked to contribute to one worthy cause or another. Many people do in fact contribute to some of these causes, but almost no one can make substantial contributions to them all: there are simply too many. It is likely that many individuals do not contemplate a comprehensive set of choices in light of their total budget constraint, and then take a reasoned decision on which causes deserve contributions. Instead, incremental decisions are often made as requests for donations appear. Some individuals probably pick a few causes to contribute to and then stop, feeling that they have "given enough" for now. This is not an unreasonable donation strategy if there are many causes of roughly similar value to the individual.

The problem this decision process poses for CV studies is that respondents may not compare the hypothetical good or service with other possible donations. In the context of this example, a respondent might indicate that he would be willing to pay US$500 to contribute toward the establishment of five rainforest and wildlife reserves. But what does this assume about his other "environmental giving"? What if another CV researcher asked him how much he would be willing to pay for preserving blue whales, and another how much he would be willing to pay for cleaner air? At the margin, if no one else asked the respondent how much he would pay (or how much he would contribute) for any other environmental good, the valuation information he provided for the wildlife and rainforest reserves might be accurate, but does this process provide the kind of information necessary for sound societal environmental decision making?

The problem is not simply that the respondent may not think carefully about his total willingness to pay for environmental goods and services, but that the CV researcher may not have specified the most policy-relevant hypothetical scenario for the respondent to value. It may be true that the respondent would be willing to pay $US500 per year for the five wildlife and rainforest reserves, assuming all his other contributions to environmental causes are known, or fixed. However, the policy maker often wants to know the answer to a different question: how much would people be willing to pay in total for improved environmental goods and services, and how would individuals set priorities among competing environmental concerns?

For a single individual, the total amount he or she would be willing to pay for improved environmental goods and services may be determined by the **composition** or **components** of the total set of environmental projects and policies to be funded. But this information is not likely to be obtained from the aggregation of values based on a set of CV studies designed to measure individuals' preferences for narrowly defined environmental goods. In some situations respondents may be able to accurately value local environmental amenities at the margin, considering their real budget constraints. At the other extreme, CV studies that attempt to determine existence values for global environmental goods would need to carefully inform respondents about other environmental services or programs that could be made available and help respondents understand the trade-offs implicit in their choices.

iii) Problems involved with aggregation of individuals' responses to CV questions

Most analysts working in the contingent valuation field have been worried about the accuracy and reliability of responses to CV questions at the level of the individual, but problems of aggregating individuals' responses may in some circumstances be equally or even more important. Analysts often wish to (1) summarize respondents' answers to valuation questions in terms of the mean willingness to pay for the good or service, or (2) develop an aggregate benefit estimate for a community or region. Even if all respondents answered the valuation questions truthfully, such attempts to summarize information from a sample of respondents can suffer from two types of problems: sampling errors and insufficient sample size. Although these problems are not unique to CV surveys, they are often overlooked by analysts primarily concerned with potential biases that may arise at the individual level.

Non-random samples

There are numerous kinds of sampling errors that can arise in the implementation of CV surveys. For example, a non-random sample of the general population may be inadvertently selected, making accurate extrapolation of results from the sample problematic. This is a particular risk in developing countries where good sample frames are typically nonexistent. Second, a non-random sample may result from non-responses to the questions. Non-responses are a particularly acute problem in contingent valuation studies because it is likely that individuals who refuse to answer valuation questions are not randomly distributed in the population. For example, they could be the most educated or the highest income individuals[11].

Insufficient sample size

Even if the analyst obtains a random sample, if the size of the sample is small, there is a "substantial" risk that the characteristics of the sample will not be representative of the general population. In the past many contingent valuation studies have been based on very small samples, and as a result their findings are typically subject to wide confidence intervals. Box 7.3 illustrates how the likely value of the mean willingness to pay of respondents in a CV study changes with changes in sample sizes.

Testing for biases and errors in contingent valuation studies

There are two ways of minimizing the risk of some of the errors and biases described above. First, contingent valuation researchers have devised ways of minimizing the **occurrence** of some types of errors and biases. Second, even if the probability of the occurrence of certain types of errors and biases cannot be reduced, the cost of being misled by poor quality estimates can be reduced by finding out whether or not a particular bias exists. In some cases, the magnitude of the bias can be estimated and the estimates of respondents' willingness to pay can be corrected to remove this bias.

For example, suppose a CV researcher is worried about the possibility of strategic behaviour on the part of respondents. The first approach would suggest that the analyst construct a hypothetical market scenario that would make it difficult for a respondent to determine how to behave strategically, or would encourage him not to behave strategically. A statement such as the following might achieve this objective:

> It is important that you answer these questions as carefully and honestly as possible. If you say an amount higher than you can really afford to pay, then if the good [service] is provided and such a price is charged, then you would not be able to afford it. On the other hand, if you give a price lower than you are willing to pay, then maybe the good [service] may not be provided and you will have to continue with the existing situation. So, please tell the truth.

Of course, it would not be plausible to include this kind of statement in many settings because it assumes that the CV study is being conducted under the auspices of an institution that can actually control an investment or policy. Nevertheless, it serves to illustrate the point that respondents can be encouraged to avoid strategic behaviour.

One of the principal criterion for selecting an elicitation procedure is, in fact, whether it provides an opportunity or creates an incentive for a respondent to act strategically. Economists term a CV question or elicitation procedure "incentive-compatible" if it does not induce a respondent to answer strategically. One of the main reasons many CV researchers prefer the referendum question format is that it is incentive-compatible: a respondent can do no better than reveal his or her true willingness to pay for the good or service.

There are several procedures for implementing the second approach. Experimental design procedures can and should be used to detect whether subgroups of the overall sample respond to changes in the survey instrument in the way one would expect. For example, one could divide the sample of respondents into two groups and present one group with a statement that **encourages** strategic behaviour, and present the second group with a statement designed to minimize or reduce strategic behaviour. If such a test uncovers strategic behaviour in the first group, then the analyst can adjust the estimates to remove the bias.

In general, many kinds of experiments can be designed for CV surveys in which different "split samples" of respondents are given different questionnaires so that analysts can check to see whether such "treatments"--or variations in the questionnaire--result in different willingness-to-pay responses. Comparisons of means or multivariate analyses are commonly used to test whether the effect of the treatment is statistically significant. Such tests may include checks for:

(1) **starting point bias**, i.e., different subsamples are given the same elicitation procedure but with different initial amounts specified in, for example, a bidding game (see Table 7.1).
(2) the effect of **different elicitation procedures**, i.e., different subsamples are given different elicitation procedures (e.g., different options described in Table 7.1). For example, some respondents may receive a single, direct open-ended question and other respondents may receive a bidding game with three YES/NO questions.
(3) the effects of **"time to think"** - i.e., some respondents may be given a day or more to reflect upon their answers to willingness-to-pay questions, while others may be asked to

answer the questions immediately (Whittington et. al., [1992b]).

(4) the effects of **question order**--if respondents are asked to value two or more goods or services, then the order of the valuation questions can be changed for different subsamples of respondents. In general, the order of the questions would not be expected to influence respondents' valuation information. If it did, this would suggest a problem with the CV results.

(5) the effects of providing more or less **information about the good or service** - i.e., respondents' valuation of the good or service may depend on how much they know about it.

One of the most powerful ways of checking the reliability of the valuation information is to carry out **multivariate analyses** of the determinants of the valuation responses (Mitchell and Carson, [1989]). In order words, the analyst examines how respondents' willingness to pay varies with changes in the socioeconomic variables suggested by demand theory, such as income, education, family composition, housing conditions, etc. If such multivariate analyses indicate that:

(a) variation in individuals' responses to valuation questions cannot, at least in part, be explained by the models; and

(b) the main socioeconomic variables do not affect individuals' willingness to pay as hypothesized;

then the CV researcher must be concerned about the quality of the valuation information obtained.

The use of split-samples to test for accuracy and reliability of WTP responses can be quite tricky and requires considerable care in survey design. It is often a much more subjective process than many analysts would like to admit. For example, several early studies in the contingent valuation literature introduced variations in the method of payment for the good or service offered. The assumption was that respondents would be indifferent about modes of payment. When the surveys revealed that individuals were in fact *not* indifferent, the analysts claimed to have discovered a "payment bias" in responses to contingent valuation questions. On further reflection, most researchers concluded that this was not in fact a "bias" but rather a legitimate preference regarding the way people wanted to pay for a good or service.

Another approach that can be used to increase the analysts' confidence in the quality of the CV data is to compare the CV estimates with estimates obtained from other, indirect valuation techniques (such as those described in subsequent chapters). Unfortunately, this is often not feasible due to data limitations and other difficulties. Whenever possible, such comparisons should be attempted, but they should not be interpreted as simply a "check" on the CV estimates. Indirect estimates are themselves susceptible to a variety of errors and biases, and should not be used as a standard or benchmark against which to judge CV estimates. If a comparison of CV estimates and estimates obtained with an indirect valuation techniques indicates that the two valuation methods provide roughly similar answers, then the analyst can place more confidence in the accuracy of **both** (Cummings, Brookshire and Schulze [1986]). On the other hand, if the estimates obtained with the two approaches are different, then the analyst is required to make a more complex judgment as to which one is likely to be more accurate.

Analysis of willingness-to-pay responses

The information obtained from contingent valuation surveys is typically analyzed in three, increasingly sophisticated ways. First, analysts examine the frequency distribution of the responses to the valuation questions. Second, analysts look at cross-tabulations between WTP responses and such variables as socioeconomic characteristics of the respondent and attitudes toward the environment. Third, analysts use multivariate statistical techniques to estimate a valuation function that relates the respondent's answer to the socioeconomic characteristics of the respondent and attitudes toward the environment. The types of statistical procedures utilized are dependent on whether the respondent answered a direct, open-ended valuation question or a YES/NO question. The purpose of all three types of analyses is twofold: (i) to see whether respondents' answers are consistent with theory and common sense (this increases one's confidence in the accuracy and reliability of the information); and (ii) to establish statistical relationships or models that can be used in the aggregation of sample responses to the overall population under study, or for developing forecasts of benefits under alternative future scenarios.

Before any of these analyses can be undertaken, the data must be "cleaned" by removing "protest responses" given by individuals who for one reason or another reject the hypothetical scenario and refuse to give meaningful answers. In this section of the chapter we review very briefly some of the issues involved in the data analysis of valuation responses. Anyone who actually plans to undertake such analyses should refer to the large and rapidly growing technical literature on this subject.

i) Treatment of protest responses

In any contingent valuation study there will generally be some small percentage of the respondents who will give implausible answers to the valuation question. These responses are commonly termed "protest bids" because the respondent may be "protesting" the nature of the interview or scenario offered, rather than revealing anything about his or her value of the good or service. Protest bids can be either zero bids or very high bids, depending on the context of the valuation question. In a given data set one may find **both** high and low protest bids.

The task of the analyst is to remove protest bids from the data set because this information will bias the conclusions one may draw about the sample respondents' willingness to pay. Of course, not all zero bids or "very high" bids can be considered protest bids: some respondents may legitimately place no value on the good or service offered and others may value it very much. Since there is no independent criterion against which an analyst can judge the plausibility of a particular respondent's answer, the appropriate treatment of protest bids requires skill and judgement on the part of the analyst. A variety of strategies and "rules of thumb" have been used to "filter" or "sift" out protest bids from a contingent valuation data set.

For example, one strategy would be to set an upper limit on how much higher a respondent's bid could be above the mean bid of the sample. For example, an analyst could decide to consider any bid two standard deviations above the mean bid to be a protest bid. Another strategy would be to see whether respondents bidding very high or very low have the socioeconomic characteristics one would expect to be associated with such a response. For example, it is more plausible that a respondent with a very high income would offer a high WTP bid than a respondent with a low income. The analyst might decide that WTP bids from respondents in the lowest income decile that were one standard deviation above the mean WTP bid of the sample should be considered protest bids. Judgements of this kind are obviously arbitrary and should only be made after careful consideration of field conditions, first-hand experience with the interviews, and a thorough analysis of a data set.

When telephone or in-person interviews are used, the kinds of statistical procedures described above to identify protest bids can be supplemented with more qualitative information obtained from the person conducting the interview. The enumerator may be asked to rate the quality of the interview and provide an assessment of whether the respondent tried to answer the valuation question truthfully. One strategy would be to simply eliminate all interviews that enumerators judged to be of "low quality" or those that enumerators felt the respondent did not try to answer truthfully. Such a procedure could, however, inject a variety of other biases into the data. A better alternative is to use **both** the quantitative and qualitative information to identify protest bids. For example, the analyst could create a rule that any bid two standard deviations above the mean bid **and** that the enumerator judged to be of poor quality would be considered a protest bid and would be discarded from the data set.

For purposes of illustration, consider a situation in which the potential protest bids in a particular contingent valuation data set are all zero bids, and the analyst must decide which ones to remove from the data and which ones are legitimate values. The appropriate treatment of potential protest bids must lie somewhere between two extremes. On the one hand, the analyst could simply discard all zero bids. This strategy would probably remove some valid zero bids and as a result the analyst would conclude that the willingness to pay of the sample is **higher** than it really is. On the other hand, the analyst could take the conservative position that **all** zero bids were legitimate values; this would **lower** estimates of the sample's willingness to pay. Strategies for deleting some of the zero bids because they were judged to be protest bids would lead to conclusions somewhere between these two extremes. In such a case the analyst should conduct his or her data analyses with at least three data sets: (1) one in which all the zero bids were included in the data set, (2) one in which all the zero bids were out of the data set, and (3) one in which some of the zero bids have been deleted because they were judged to be protest bids. This approach will show the sensitivity of the final results to assumptions about how protest bids are treated.

ii) Frequency distributions of WTP responses

1. Answers to direct, open-ended questions, or multiple YES/NO questions

Respondents' answers to direct, open-ended valuation questions yield a data set of "point estimates" of individuals' willing to pay (i.e., we have a specific WTP value for each respondent). Answers to multiple YES/NO questions (i.e., a bidding game) place each respondent's willingness to pay in an interval defined by the *last* value accepted and the *last* value rejected. If these intervals are "tight", the analyst may feel that not much information is lost by making the assumption that each respondent's willingness to pay can be estimated by the mid-point of this interval. In this case these mid-points also provide a set of point estimates of individuals' willingness to pay.

Descriptive statistics such as the mean, median, and frequency distributions can easily be prepared for data sets of point estimates of WTP, and are often of particular value for policy purposes because that are easy for the noneconomist to understand and interpret. Figure 7.1 presents a frequency distribution of answers to an open-ended question that followed an abbreviated bidding game[12]. Two kinds of insights are often sought from such summary data. First, mean estimates of WTP or the frequency distribution of WTP can be used to develop preliminary estimates of the total value of the good or service, i.e., the total economic benefits. Second, the frequency distributions can be used to estimate the percent of the population that would choose to purchase the good or service if it were offered at a specific price (see Box 7.4).

Figure 7.1 **Frequency Distribution of WTP for KVIP**

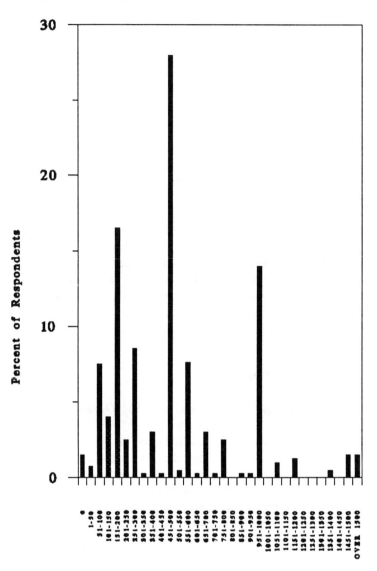

KVIP   WTP   (cedis/month)

Note: 350 cedis = US$1.00

Source: Whittington D., D. Lauria, A. Wright, K. Choe, J. Hughes and V. Swarna, [1993e].

2. Answers to a single YES/NO question (referendum model)

The answers to a single referendum valuation question can be summarized in a manner that provides similar information to the frequency distribution of point estimates described above. Recall that the implementation of the referendum model requires that respondents in different split-samples be asked how they would vote on a proposal that would provide a good or service at a specified price, and that respondents in different spilt-samples are offered the good or service at different prices. It is a straight forward calculation to determine the percentage of respondents in each split-sample that agreed to pay the stated price (i.e., that voted for the proposal).

The relationship between these percentages and the price of the good or service can be graphed, as shown in Figure 7.2. This figure shows the percentage of respondents in ten different split-samples that agreed to pay five different monthly tariffs for two levels of improved sanitation service: (1) a connection to a sewer line that collected wastewater and discharged it untreated into a nearby Lake, and (2) a connection to a sewer line that collected wastewater and treated it at a wastewater treatment plant before discharging it to the Lake. The study was conducted in Calamba, Philippines, a town of about 170,000 people. In this study each split-sample included 30-40 respondents. When the sizes of the spilt-samples are sufficiently large and the respondents are randomly selected, the analyst can be confident that such a relationship between the percentage of the population that agree to pay and the price of the good or service will hold for the entire sample.

iii) Cross-tabulations of WTP responses with socioeconomic characteristics of the respondent and attitudes toward the environment

1. Answers to direct, open-ended questions or multiple YES/NO questions

The next step in the analysis of contingent valuation data is to determine whether different groups of people in the sample gave different responses to the valuation question(s). These analyses begin to address the questions of **who** is willing to pay the most (and the least) for the good or service, and **why**. The answers to these questions are relevant both for an assessment of the accuracy and reliability of the WTP responses, and for policy inferences that may be drawn from the data.

When point estimates of willingness to pay are available for respondents, the analyst can calculate the mean WTP bid for different groups of respondents. As an example of such an analysis, Table 7.2 presents the mean monthly WTP bids of respondents in two regions of the Punjab, Pakistan (sweetwater zone and brackish groundwater zone), for a private water connection. Respondents are broken down into groups by both the education of the most educated member of the household, and the estimated value of their house (a proxy for wealth or income). As shown, respondents living in households in which the most educated member had 0-8 years of schooling had a lower willingness to pay for a water connection than respondents in households whose most educated members had more schooling. Also, as the value of a respondent's house increased, his willingness to pay for a water connection increased. These effects of education and income on willingness to pay were consistent in both the sweetwater and brackish water zones, and make sense in terms of prior expectations. Similarly, the mean willingness to pay of groups with different attitudes toward the environment, or different levels of existing services could be compared. When these kind of cross-tabulations of willingness-to-pay bids and socioeconomic or attitudinal information reveal the effects one would hypothesize based on demand theory and common sense, then the analyst has greater confidence in the quality of the data and greater insight into the factors that may determine an individual's willingness to pay.

Figure 7.2 **Percent of Respondents Who Gave Positive Answers
to Referendum Question (Calamba, Philippines)**

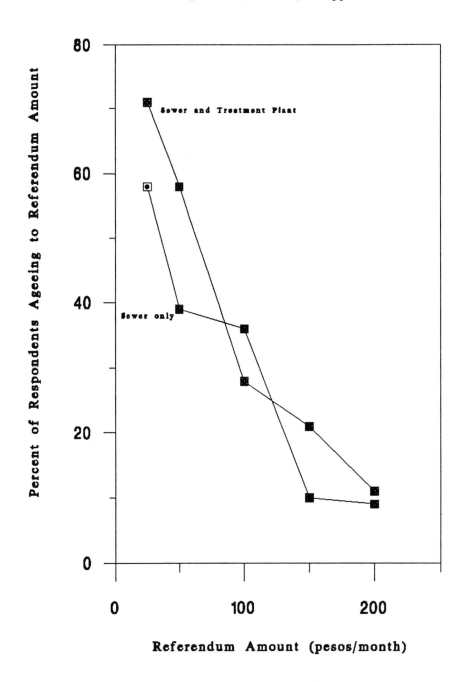

Source: Lauria, D.T., D. Whittington and K. Choe, [1993]

2. Answers to a single YES/NO question (referendum model)

It is possible to prepare cross-tabulations of answers to referendum questions, and socioeconomic and attitudinal information based on split samples, but this requires very large sample sizes. For example, consider an experimental design in which 1000 households were interviewed and asked how they would vote on a specific proposal if it were offered at a set of specified prices. Suppose that five different prices were offered to five split-samples so that 200 households received the first price, 200 households received the second price, and so on. For each split-sample one would calculate the percentage of respondents that voted for the proposal.

Now, it would be possible to take one of these split samples and divide these 200 households into two or more groups based on socioeconomic or attitudinal variables, and then calculate the percentage of respondents in each of these groups that voted for the proposal. This procedure could be repeated for each of the four remaining original split-samples to see if the effect of the groups on the percentage of affirmative responses was consistent in each of the five groups. The problem with this procedure is that many contingent valuation studies that use the referendum model include experimental designs with other treatments. As a result the size of the groups of respondents based on the socioeconomic classification is so small that it is difficult to discern anything except very large effects. There are simply not enough independent observations or degrees of freedom to carry out tests of differences between groups that have much statistical power.

For example, in the results presented in Figure 7.2, approximately 35 respondents answered a valuation question for each sanitation service level for each price. Preparing a cross-tabulation of the percentage of affirmative responses by, say, just two groups (e.g., low and high income) would require that 35 observations be split in two. If the income classification split the "cell entries" in half, there would just be 17 in one and 18 in the other. Obviously one could easily end up with some very small numbers in each income group, and it would be very difficult to tell whether the percentage of affirmative answers was affected by income. More powerful multivariate statistical techniques are required to sort out such influences (these are described below).

iv) Multivariate analyses of the determinants of WTP responses

1. Answers to direct, open-ended questions

The use of multivariate analysis can provide better information and greater insight into the factors that affect the WTP responses than simple cross-tabulations. The general approach is to estimate a **valuation function** that relates the hypothesized determinants with the WTP responses. The decision on what determinants of WTP should be included in the valuation function is typically based on consumer demand theory. Socioeconomic and demographic characteristics of the household (SE), and prices and availability of substitute goods and services (Ps) are commonly used. The valuation function thus takes the form ...

$$WTP_i = f(SE_i, Ps_i) \qquad (7.1)$$

where i is an index of households in the sample.

Since the answers respondents give to open-ended questions provide a continuous measure of willingness to pay for the good or service, in this case ordinary least squares (OLS) models can generally be used to explain the variations in the dependent variable (WTP bids). OLS techniques have the advantages of being widely used, and the parameter estimates are easy to interpret. OLS requires of course, that the determinants of the WTP responses be exogenous in order for the parameter estimates to be unbiased and consistent. This may be a questionable assumption for some attitudinal variables. For example, WTP for environmental quality improvements, and the responsibility one feels for environmental cleanup may be jointly determined.

Table 7.3 presents the results of an OLS valuation function for a contingent valuation data set from rural Haiti. In this study households were asked for their WTP for a private water connection. Their responses were hypothesized to be determined by the following variables: a proxy for household wealth, whether they received income from relatives abroad, whether they were a farmer or not, education level, the distance of their house from an existing water source, the perceived quality of water from an existing source, and the sex of the respondent. Economic theory (and common sense) would suggest that households with greater wealth should be willing to pay more, that households farther away from their existing source should pay more, and that households that perceive the quality of water from their existing source to be poor should be willing to pay more. As shown by the parameter estimates and t-statistics in Table 7.3, all of these hypotheses are supported by the analysis.

Such valuation functions often have relatively little explanatory power; the adjusted R^2 value of 0.34 in Table 7.3 is relatively high for such OLS models of the determinants of WTP responses. The generally low R^2 values for such valuation functions indicate that there is considerable "noise" in the estimates of WTP values, and that much of the variation in WTP values is not explained by the hypothesized determinants. Results such as presented in Table 7.3 clearly indicate, however, that the WTP values are not random, but rather are systematically related to the variables suggested by economic theory. If R^2 values for such a valuation function fall below 0.15, Mitchell and Carson [1989] suggest that the credibility of the values should be called into question: such results may simply be random responses.

2. Answers to a single YES/NO question (referendum model)

Since in this case the response to the valuation question is a not a continuous variable, but rather a discrete response, OLS techniques are not appropriate for the estimation of the valuation function. Instead, analysts utilize a variety of discrete choice models to attempt to explain the probability that a respondent will give a yes response to the valuation question. In this case the valuation model attempts to explain the respondent's answer to the referendum question as a function of the same kind of independent variables used in the OLS models described above:

$$
\left.\begin{array}{l} Yes = 1 \\ \\ No = 0 \end{array}\right\} \quad f\,(SEi,\ Psi) \qquad\qquad (7.2)
$$

Either a logit or a probit model can be used to estimate this relationship. The results of such discrete choice models can be used to derive estimates of the economic value of the good or service offered in the contingent valuation scenario. How this can be done is outside the scope of this chapter (see Hanemann, [1984]; Cameron, [1988]; McConnell, [1990]).

Such discrete choice models can also be used to derive estimates of the relationship (presented in Figure 7.2) between the percentage of respondents agreeing to pay and the price offered that control for socioeconomic characteristics of the respondents and other factors. Figure 7.3 presents such a relationship prepared in connection with a large contingent valuation study of the Exxon-Valdez oil spill in Prince Williams Sound, Alaska (Carson et. al..,[1992]). Respondents in a national survey were asked whether they would be willing to pay a specified amount to prevent a similar oil spill in the future. Respondents were the asked a second yes/no question depending on the answer they gave to the first question. The results presented in Figure 7.3 show the percent of respondents that would agree to pay different amounts as a one-time fee to prevent a similar accident, after controlling for socioeconomic characteristics and attitudes of the respondent; also shown are the 95 percent confidence intervals around this estimate. (This relationship is estimated using a maximum likelihood technique and assuming the distribution of WTP responses follows a Weibull distribution.).

Figure 7.3 **95 Percent Confidence Intervals for National Willinness to Pay Survival Curve**

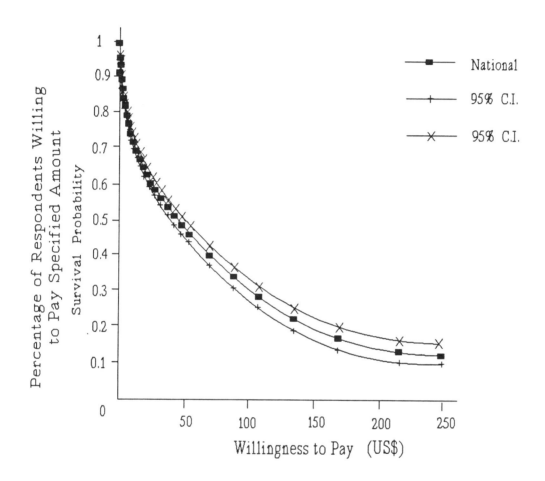

Source: Carson et al, [1992]

Concluding remarks: Should a contingent valuation study be undertaken?

If it were easy to elicit accurate responses to valuation questions about hypothetical situations, then there would be little reason for policy analysts to even bother with any other valuation technique. This is of course not the case: it can be quite difficult to get accurate, reliable answers to CV questions. In a report to the United States National Oceanic and Atmospheric Administration, Kenneth Arrow et. al. [1993] have offered a set of rigorous guidelines that they believe contingent valuation researchers should follow in order to ensure that CV studies provide accurate, reliable information (Box 7.5). After reviewing such guidelines some analysts may conclude that contingent valuation surveys are simply too complicated to be of practical use in environmental policy analysis. This is too simplistic an answer to the difficult question of when the contingent valuation method should be used.

An analyst contemplating undertaking a contingent valuation study has two related questions to answer: (1) whether to undertake the study, and (2) if the study is undertaken, how much effort should be devoted to assessing the reliability and accuracy of the results. As shown in Table 7.4, the analyst has three basic options: (1) to undertake the study and not spend much energy assessing the reliability and accuracy of the CV responses; (2) to undertake the study and carry out tests to determine whether or not the CV responses are "good" measures of individuals' preferences; and (3) to not carry out a CV study. Whichever of the three options is selected, the CV study may yield either reliable or unreliable results, and it is difficult to know before the study is done which of these two outcomes will occur. The three options coupled with the possibility of either reliable or unreliable results yields six possible outcomes.

If the analyst decides to carry out the study and test for the reliability of the results, and the CV study yields reliable answers (Case 1), then "good" results were obtained for policy purposes, but resources were spent "unnecessarily" testing for reliability. Still the final outcome must be considered "good" from the analyst's point of view. If the analyst carries out the CV study and tests for reliability, but the study yields unreliable responses (Case 2), then the money spent on the study was wasted, but the analyst at least knows not to use the poor estimates of benefits for policy analysis. This is not a good outcome from the analyst's point of view, but it could be much worse.

If the CV study is undertaken but no attempt is made to test for the reliability of the answers, and the results turn out to be reliable (Case 3), ex-post this is the best outcome. "Good" results are obtained for policy purposes, and no money is wasted on tests for reliability. On the other hand, if the CV study is done, tests of reliability are not made, and the results are unreliable (Case 4), we are faced with the worst case: the CV study results in poor information, but the analyst does not know it. This is the risk that is run by not conducting tests for the accuracy and reliability of the CV responses.

Finally, if the analyst decides not to carry out the CV study, but it would have yielded reliable results (Case 5), an opportunity has been missed. If the analyst does not carry out a CV study and it would have yielded unreliable results (Case 6), a good decision was made: resources were not wasted on a futile exercise.

The appropriate decision on whether or not to conduct a CV study, and if so whether to test for the reliability of the responses, depends primarily on four judgments:
>   (1) how likely one is to obtain reliable as opposed to unreliable information;
>   (2) the cost of testing the reliability and accuracy of the CV responses;
>   (3) the degree to which such testing increases one's confidence that the responses are reliable
>   (or unreliable) measures of individuals' preferences; and

(4) the value of "good" information in the policy process.

Most critics of the contingent valuation method believe that (1) the probability that unreliable results will be obtained is high, and (2) tests for reliability are themselves unreliable and are expensive. A state-of-the-art contingent valuation study can cost more than one million US dollars and take two years to complete. Ignoring the potential value of the information, they conclude that CV studies are never worth doing.

Advocates of CVM, on the other hand, expect to obtain reliable results most of the time. From their perspective testing for reliability is expensive and unnecessary. They thus propose the use of simple CV studies without associated efforts to check the reliability and accuracy of the CV responses.

From our perspective, a middle position between these two extremes is more appropriate. We believe that the contingent valuation method is an important, often useful approach to measuring individuals' willingness to pay for goods and services that are difficult to value with other approaches. However, analysts should use it with a measure of scepticism, keeping in mind that for a variety of reasons the method may not work as anticipated in a particular context or situation. If the information potentially available from a contingent valuation study is valuable for policy purposes, it is usually worth the time and resources necessary to do a careful job. Not only is this strategy likely to enhance the quality of the information that is collected, but it will also reduce the risk that poor information will be obtained and the analyst will not be aware of this.

Table 7.1 **Six options for asking contingent valuation questions**

Respondent is asked a single question

Option 1: Direct, open-ended question

Example:

What is the most your household would be willing to pay (WTP) per month for a connection to a sewer line?

Maximum WTP _____

Advantages:
a. Respondent is not given any clues regarding an expected or reasonable answer.

Disadvantages:
a. Respondents may be reluctant or unable to think carefully about the concept of the **most** or the **maximum** they would be willing to pay. Evidence suggests that many respondents give zero or unrealistically high amounts for an answer.

b. Difficult to use effectively for valuing public goods because respondents want to know what others in the community are going to pay before committing themselves to an answer. Respondents may not want to pay more than their "fair share," even if they have stronger preferences for the public good than other people.

Option 2: A single YES/NO question to an individual respondent, but assign different prices to randomly-selected individuals in the sample. (referendum model)

Example:

If the monthly cost to the household of obtaining a connection to a sewer line was US$ [**2, 4, 6, 8, 10, or 12**], would your household choose to connect or continue to use your existing sanitation system?

YES / NO

Advantages:
a. Evidence suggests respondents can think clearly about such a concrete choice.
b. Can be framed as a referendum on a vote for the provision of public goods where respondents may be reluctant to pay more than their "fair share" because the scenario description can specify that all members of the community will be required to purchase the public good at the specified price.

Disadvantages:
a. Since each respondent only answers one YES/NO question, the sample size must be increased to obtain "sufficiently accurate" information (approximately 66 percent larger compared to the open-ended question; (see Carson et. al., [1991]).
b. YES/NO responses are more difficult to interpret. Multivariate analysis of the determinants of the YES/NO responses requires sophisticated econometric techniques and assumptions about the form of the utility or expenditure function (See McConnell, [1990]; Cameron, [1987]).

c. In some cultural or social settings where bargaining is common or expected, a single YES/NO question may be considered somewhat abrupt or rude, and respondents may reveal little about their "true" willingness to pay in response to any initial question.

d. Some information on the likely distribution of respondents' willingness to pay is needed in order to select the set of prices to offer individuals. If the set of prices selected does not span the range of WTP, the required information will not be collected efficiently.

Respondent is asked two questions

Option 3 : A Single YES/NO Question, followed by a direct, open-ended question
(referendum model with open-ended follow-up)

Example:

(1) If the monthly cost to the household of obtaining a connection to a sewer line was US$ [**2, 4, 6, 8, 10, or 12**], would your household choose to connect or continue to use your existing sanitation system?

YES / NO

(2) What is the most your household would be willing to pay (WTP) per month for a connection to a sewer line?

Maximum WTP _____

Advantages:
a. Same as Option 2 above with the advantage of the extra information obtained from the second, open-ended question.

Disadvantages:
a. Same as Option 2 above (with possibility that (c) will be less of a problem).
b. Answers to the open-ended question may be influenced by the initial value the respondent received in the YES/NO question. [The analyst can test for the existence of such an effect by examining the determinants of respondents' answers to the open-ended question. One of the determinants would be the value the respondent received in the YES/NO question.]

Option 4 : Two YES/NO Questions (Abbreviated Bidding game)

Example:

A common procedure with this format would be to split the sample into two groups, and start one group at a low price and then for those respondents who answered YES, increase the amount to a higher price. For the other group, the good or service is first offered at a high price, and then, for those respondents who answer NO, the amount is decreased to the lower price.

For half the sample:

(1) If the monthly cost to the household of obtaining a connection to a sewer line was US$5, would your household choose to connect or continue to use your existing sanitation system?

```
                                              YES  -- GO TO (2)
                                              NO   -- STOP
```

(2) Suppose instead that the monthly cost to the household of obtaining a connection to a sewer line was **US$10**, would your household choose to connect or continue to use your existing sanitation system?

```
                                              YES  NO
```

For the other half of the sample:

(1) If the monthly cost to the household of obtaining a connection to a sewer line was US$10, would your household choose to connect or continue to use your existing sanitation system?

```
                                              YES  -- STOP
                                              NO   -- GO TO (2)
```

(2) Suppose instead that the monthly cost to the household of obtaining a connection to a sewer line was **US$5**, would your household choose to connect or continue to use your existing sanitation system?

```
                                              YES  NO
```

Advantages :
(a) Same as option 2
(b) Respondents' in both of the two groups fall into the same three categories of willingness to pay (in the example, the three categories are: $\leq$ US$10, US$5-9, and < US$5). This means that the responses of the two groups can be merged.

Disadvantages:
(a) Respondents who answer a second question may be influenced by the amount specified in the first question. Particularly if they said YES to the lower amount, their response may be "anchored" at this first amount. (Splitting the sample into two groups allows the analyst to test for the existence of this effect).
(b) Respondents' willingness to pay falls into one of three categories. For some purposes this may not provide enough discrimination among individuals or sufficient accuracy for policy purposes.
(c) The two specified amounts must be carefully selected in order to cover the range of individuals' willingness to pay. This requires knowledge of the frequency distribution of individuals' willingness to pay.

Table 7.1 (cont.) **Six options for asking contingent valuation questions**

<u>Respondent is asked three questions</u>

Option 5 : Two YES/NO Questions followed by an open-ended question
                (Abbreviated Bidding game with follow-up)

Example:

(1) If the monthly cost to the household of obtaining a connection to a sewer line was US$5, would your household choose to connect or continue to use your existing sanitation system?

> YES -- GO TO (2)
> NO -- STOP

(2) Suppose instead that the monthly cost to the household of obtaining a connection to a sewer line was US$10, would your household choose to connect or continue to use your existing sanitation system?

> YES NO

(3) What is the most your household would be willing to pay (WTP) per month for a connection to a sewer line?

> Maximum WTP _____

Advantages:
(a) All the advantages of option 4 with the added benefit of any information collected by the open-ended follow-up question.

Disadvantages:
(a) All the disadvantages of option 4 with the added difficulty that the responses to the open-ended follow-up question may be influenced by the sequence of previous YES/NO questions.

Option 6 : Three YES/NO Questions (Full Bidding Game)

Example: There are two basic formats for the full bidding game with three YES/NO questions.

Option 6a:

If the full sample receives the same questionnaire, the structure of the questions is as follows:

(1) If the monthly cost to the household of obtaining a connection to a sewer line was US$5, would your household choose to connect or continue to use your existing sanitation system?

> YES -- GO TO (2)
> NO   -- GO TO (5)

(2) Suppose instead that the monthly cost to the household of obtaining a connection to a sewer line was US$**7.50**, would your household choose to connect or continue to use your existing sanitation system?

YES -- GO TO (3)
NO -- GO TO (4)

(3) Suppose instead that the monthly cost to the household of obtaining a connection to a sewer line was US$**10.00**, would your household choose to connect or continue to use your existing sanitation system?

YES -- STOP
NO -- STOP

(4) Suppose instead that the monthly cost to the household of obtaining a connection to a sewer line was US$**6.25**, would your household choose to connect or continue to use your existing sanitation system?

YES -- STOP
NO -- STOP

(5) Suppose instead that the monthly cost to the household of obtaining a connection to a sewer line was US$**2.50**, would your household choose to connect or continue to use your existing sanitation system?

YES -- GO TO (6)
NO -- GO TO (7)

(6) Suppose instead that the monthly cost to the household of obtaining a connection to a sewer line was US$**3.75**, would your household choose to connect or continue to use your existing sanitation system?

YES -- STOP
NO -- STOP

(7) Suppose instead that the monthly cost to the household of obtaining a connection to a sewer line was US$**1.25**, would your household choose to connect or continue to use your existing sanitation system?

YES -- STOP
NO -- STOP

Advantages:
(a) This three-question bidding game produces a great deal of discrimination among respondents' willingness to pay.
(b) The bargaining nature of the repeated questioning may be appropriate in some cultural or social contexts.

Disadvantages:
(a) It is not possible to test to see whether respondents' answers to the second (and third) questions are influenced by their answer to the first (and second) questions.

Option 6b :

An alternative approach that uses three YES/NO questions is to split the sample into two groups, and start one group at a low price and then continue to raise it as long as the respondent agrees to pay the specified amount. Start the other group at a high price and continue to lower it as long as the respondent refuses to pay the specified amount.

For half the sample: (Ascending)

Example:

(1) If the monthly cost to the household of obtaining a connection to a sewer line was US$3, would your household choose to connect or continue to use your existing sanitation system?

$$\text{YES -- GO TO (2)}$$
$$\text{NO -- STOP}$$

(2) Suppose instead that the monthly cost to the household of obtaining a connection to a sewer line was US$6.00, would your household choose to connect or continue to use your existing sanitation system?

$$\text{YES -- GO TO (3)}$$
$$\text{NO -- STOP}$$

(3) Suppose instead that the monthly cost to the household of obtaining a connection to a sewer line was US$9.00, would your household choose to connect or continue to use your existing sanitation system?

$$\text{YES -- STOP}$$
$$\text{NO -- STOP}$$

For half the sample: (Descending)

Example:

(1) If the monthly cost to the household of obtaining a connection to a sewer line was US$9.00, would your household choose to connect or continue to use your existing sanitation system?

$$\text{YES -- STOP}$$
$$\text{NO -- GO TO (2)}$$

(2) Suppose instead that the monthly cost to the household of obtaining a connection to a sewer line was US$6.00, would your household choose to connect or continue to use your existing sanitation system?

$$\text{YES -- STOP}$$
$$\text{NO -- GO TO (3)}$$

(3) Suppose instead that the monthly cost to the household of obtaining a connection to a sewer line was US$3.00, would your household choose to connect or continue to use your existing sanitation system?

$$\text{YES -- STOP}$$
$$\text{NO -- STOP}$$

Advantages:
(a) Same as option 6a (although the discrimination among respondents is not as detailed).
(b) Permits the analyst to test whether the order of the three YES/NO questions (i.e., ascending or descending) affects respondents' final willingness to pay.

Disadvantages:
(a) Same as option 6a
(b) Respondents may be more likely to be anchored at YES answers in the ascending bidding game than at NO answers in the descending bidding game. If anchoring at the specified amounts (starting point bias) is strong, it is difficult to assess the accuracy of the willingness to pay information.

Table 7.2 Example of Cross-Tabulation of Households' Willingness-to-pay Bids and Socioeconomic Characteristics of the Household (Punjab, Pakistan)

Socioeconomic Characteristics	Sweetwater Zone		Brackish Water Zone	
	Percentage of Sample	Mean WTP Bid, Rs/Month	Percentage of Sample	Mean WTP Bid, Rs/Month
Years of education of most educated member of household:				
0-8	44	15	38	36
9-12	41	21	41	40
>12	15	33	21	47
Construction value of house (Rs.)				
0-49,000	38	14	9	33
50,000-99,000	40	20	22	36
100,000-149,000	10	21	19	38
≥150,000	12	35	50	44
Overall Mean		21		40

WTP bids are for a connection to a piped water system.

Source: Atlaf, M.A., D. Whittington, H. Jamal and V.K. Smith. "Rethinking Rural Water Supply Policy in the Punjab, Pakistan." Water Resources Research. Forthcoming, 1993.

Table 7.3 Example of Valuation Function Estimated with Ordinary Least Squares (Laurent, Haiti)

Dependent <u>variable</u>:

Household willingness to pay for private water connection (gourdes*/month)

Independent <u>variable</u>:	Coefficient	<u>t</u>
Intercept	-1.468	-0.32
Household wealth index (WLTH)	1.280	4.73
Household with foreign income (FINC, =1 if yes)	-0.654	-0.42
Occupation index (IOCP = 1 if primary occupation is farmer)	-2.463	-1.69
Household education level (HHED)	0.986	3.83
Distance from existing source (DIST)	0.003	2.24
Quality index of existing source (QULT = 1 if respondent is enthusiastic about the quality of the water)	-0.664	-2.79
Sex of the respondent (RSEX, =1 if male)	0.307	0.25
Adjusted R^2	0.34	
F Value	10.25	
Degrees of freedom	120	

* 5 gourdes = US $1

Source: Whittington, D., J. Briscoe, and X. Mu [1987], *Willingness to Pay for Water in Rural Areas: Methodological Approaches and An Application in Haiti*, WASH Technical Report No. 213, U.S. Agency for International Development, Washington, DC.

Table 7.4 **Should a contingent valuation study be undertaken? Six cases.**

	A Contingent Valuation Study May Yield ...	
	Reliable Results	Unreliable Results
Analyst's Options:		
1. Carry out CV Study & Test for Reliability and Accuracy of the Results	Case 1	Case 2
2. Carry out CV Study & do not test for Reliability and Accuracy of the Results	Case 3	Case 4
3. Do Not Carry out CV Study	Case 5	Case 6

Review of six cases:

Case 1: Analyst obtains good estimates of respondents' preferences, but resources are spent "unnecessarily" testing for the reliability and accuracy of the survey results.

Case 2: Analyst wastes resources conducting the CV study, but is not misled about the quality of the estimates. The use of poor estimates in a policy analysis is avoided.

Case 3: Analyst obtains good estimates, and resources are not spent unnecessarily testing for reliability and accuracy of the results.

Case 4: Analyst obtains poor quality estimates, but is unaware of this fact. Estimates may lead to misguided policy.

Case 5: Analyst misses an opportunity to obtain good quality estimates with CVM.

Case 6: Analyst does not waste resources on a futile exercise.

Box 7.1 **Example of a description of a hypothetical market scenario for a contingent valuation study of household demand for improved sanitation in Kumasi, Ghana**

I would like to ask you some questions about how much your household would be willing to pay for an improved sanitation system.

[Show Respondent Photograph]

The first type of improved sanitation system is called a KVIP latrine, which is a ventilated pit latrine. This KVIP latrine would be private and each toilet room would have two holes (only one of which is in use at a time). It does not use water, but it could be built inside the house (on the ground floor). It can be entered from inside the house. The excrement falls into one of two adjacent pits. When one pit is full, you switch to the other. You wait to empty the pit until the excreta is turned into manure which is safe to use in a garden. This takes about two years. The pit can then be emptied from outside of the house.

This kind of latrine is specially designed so that if it is kept clean, it will not smell. It has a vent pipe to eliminate odours, and a fly screen to eliminate flies. The KVIP--a ventilated improved pit latrine--is not like an ordinary pit latrine. It is a permanent facility. What makes it permanent is that the two pits are lined with brick or masonry and can easily be emptied and reused. Because the KVIP latrine has two pits, it does not have to be emptied very often and is thus very inexpensive to operate. It is a safe, sanitary means of excreta disposal.

I would now like to answer any questions you have about the KVIP latrine.

Suppose that it was possible to purchase a KVIP latrine for this house by making payments on a monthly basis. There would be no initial charge or fee to have the KVIP latrine installed, only the monthly payment. You would have to pay this amount monthly for 10 years.

Box 7.2 A Contingent valuation scenario designed to value rainforest and wildlife reserves in developing countries

Contingent valuation scenario

Suppose that the United Nations Environment Programme has proposed that 5 major wildlife and rainforest reserves be established in several developing countries. The locations of these reserves would be determined by an international commission of experts in tropical ecology and forestry. The commission members would be instructed by UNEP to select sites that are most threatened and that contain the most valuable biological resources. Each reserve would be approximately 1 million hectares in size --large enough to be a viable, sustainable ecological system.

The UNEP plan calls for the major industrialized nations to compensate each of the five developing countries involved for the development opportunities foregone by the creation of the wildlife and rainforest reserve within its borders. The share each industrialized country is asked to contribute to this compensation fund is to be determined by the country's population and per capita income.

Suppose that a national referendum were held in your country on whether or not to participate in this UNEP scheme for saving selected areas of tropical rainforest. The referendum would call for all households to pay an annual income-tax surcharge. This surcharge would be progressive: the higher the household income, the higher the surcharge. Your country's participation would be conditional on the participation of "almost all" of the other industrialized countries. The industrialized countries would agree to pay the annual compensation for 20 years--assuming the reserves were established and managed as agreed--at which time the terms of arrangement could be renegotiated.

Suppose that the annual income-tax surcharge for your houschold would be US$250.

Valuation questions:

(a) Would you vote in favour of this UNEP proposal and agree to pay US$250 per year as an income-tax surcharge?

> YES --- GO TO (b)
> NO --- GO TO (c)

(b) How high would the income-tax surcharge have to be before you would decide **not** to vote for the UNEP proposal?

> Amount _____ STOP

(c) What is the highest income tax surcharge you would agree to pay and support the UNEP proposal?

> Amount _____ STOP

Box 7.3 The effect of sample size on the statistical inferences of OLS estimation: A case study using Monte Carlo Simulations[13]

The use of random sampling procedures is one way to ensure that the answers obtained from a contingent valuation study reflect the nature of the population being studied. Sample size and choice of sampling design influence the types and degrees of estimation errors and the accuracy of findings in multivariate analyses of the determinants of respondents' answers to willingness-to-pay questions. Though statistical theory provides a way of predicting the size of estimation errors as sample size changes, little attention has been paid to how much the efficiency of statistical inferences changes by varying the number of selected sample units in a two-stage, stratified sampling strategy.

Choosing an effective sampling design for a contingent valuation study requires achieving a balance between research costs (including time) and the desired level of precision in the results. A larger sample will be more expensive, but yield more precise estimates. The results of a Monte Carlo simulation using a real data set suggest that increasing second-stage sample size within a limited number of enumeration areas selected at the first stage of sampling will result in a much faster positive marginal return in statistical and sampling design efficiency, as compared to increasing the number of enumeration areas with a limited second-stage sample size.

The data used in this study were drawn from a 1989 Contingent Valuation survey of households, in Kumasi, Ghana (see Whittington, Lauria, Choe, Hughes, Swarna and Wright, [1993d] and [1993e]). This study used a two-stage stratified sampling procedure to select a random sample of households to interview. The 373 enumeration areas (EAs) in Kumasi were first stratified according to household density per building (very low, low, medium, high), and 26 EAs were selected for inclusion in the sample. From these, about 1600 households were selected to be interviewed. For the Monte Carlo simulations presented here, a subsample of 769 households was used. These households were found in 23 of the 26 EAs: 7 EAs from the high-density, 9 from the medium-density, 6 from the low-density, and 1 from the very-low-density stratification.

To analyze what factors explain the variances in households' willingness-to-pay (WTP) bids for improved sanitation services, we selected 10 exogenous variables. We regressed households' WTP bids for KVIPs (a type of improved on-site sanitation system) against these 10 exogenous variables in order to provide "baseline" estimates. The OLS estimates of the coefficients, standard errors, and t-ratios for each variable are reported in Table 7.3.A. Note that for most of the "baseline" estimates (except for the variables TIMETT and TRADER, see the last column of Table 7.3.A), the null hypothesis of $\beta = 0$ can be rejected, at a level of statistical significance of 5 percent. We use the parameter estimates from this model as a baseline for the comparison with the results from the Monte Carlo experiments.

The Monte Carlo experiments used four different sample sizes: 600, 400, 200 and 50 observations. For each size sample, we replicated the OLS model estimation 40 times by drawing random samples of households, estimating the OLS model with data for these households, and averaging the resulting estimates for each sample size. Table 7.3.B reports the means of standard errors of coefficients, SE($\hat{\beta}$), the means of estimated t-statistics, and the percentages of cases rejecting the null hypothesis, $\hat{\beta} = 0$, out of the 40 replications.

As would be expected, the mean of SE($\hat{\beta}$) increases as the sample size is reduced. Table 7.3.B shows that--while keeping the number of enumeration areas at 23 at the first stage --the mean of SE($\hat{\beta}$) increases more than four times the "baseline" SE(β) when sample sizes are reduced to 50. With a sample size 200, the mean of SE($\hat{\beta}$) is almost twice as large as the "baseline" SE(β).

Since t-statistics are calculated as $\hat{\beta}$ divided by $SE(\hat{\beta})$, it is clear that reducing the sample size (n) results in smaller t-statistics. Estimates based on small sample sizes (n = 50 or 200) could easily result in a situation where analysts might make incorrect interpretations regarding the significance of key variables. Rejection of the null hypothesis, $\hat{\beta} = 0$, is generally less than 50 percent for sample sizes 50 and 200. This pattern is clearly shown in Figure 7.3.A. Especially when the sample size was limited to 50, most variables had a low percentage of rejection rates in terms of the values of t-statistics. This means that, when sample size was fixed at 50, analysts might be misled and incorrectly conclude that an exogenous variable is not related to the WTP bids.

These findings indicate that the gains in statistical efficiency attained by increasing the number of enumerator areas at the first stage are small compared to the gains achieved by increasing sample size in the second-stage of the sampling design.

Table 7.3.A. **Description of the exogenous variables and the "baseline" estimates from the entire sample (769 households)**

Type of Variable Name	Variable Description	Coefficients (β)	Standard Errors (SE(β))	t-ratio
INTERC	intercept	198.57	32.96	6.02**
Questionnaire Design				
START	1 = If bidding game used high starting point, 0 = low starting point	53.35	18.99	2.81**
TIMETT	1 = if respondent was given time to think about WTP, 0 = no time to think	-9.43	26.73	-0.35
Household Socio-Economic Characteristics				
INCOMER	monthly household income in 10,000 cedis	43.74	5.85	7.48**
YRSEDUC	years of education of respondent	4.17	1.96	2.14*
TRADER	1 = if primary worker's occupation is trader, 0 = otherwise	-19.65	20.26	-0.97
STORY	1 = if house is multi-story building, 0 = otherwise	-83.87	26.68	-3.14**
LANDLORD	1 = if landlord lives in the house, 0 = otherwise	42.09	19.32	2.17*
Water and Sanitation Practices				
WATERTAP	1 = if private water tap is primary water source, 0 = otherwise	97.11	22.79	4.26**
SANEXPNR	monthly sanitation expenditure per household (in 100 cedis)	26.87	3.05	8.80**
SATISFY	1 = if respondent was very satisfied with current sanitation system, 0 = otherwise	-111.72	49.68	-2.24*

* Significant at .05.
** Significant at .01.

125

Table 7.3.B Sampling Distribution of Estimated Standard Errors and T-Ratio: {EA=23, S=n}
(Varying the No. of Obs. While Holding the No. of EA=23)

SAMPLE ID	INTERC	START	TIMETT	INCOMER	YRSEDUC	TRADER	STORY	LANDLORD	WATERTAP	SANEXPNR	SATISFY
Baseline Values: SE(beta)	32.96	18.99	26.73	5.85	1.96	20.26	26.68	19.32	22.79	3.05	49.68
Baseline Values: t-ratio	6.02	2.81	-0.35	7.48	2.14	-0.97	-3.14	2.17	4.26	8.80	-2.24
No. of Obs. = 600											
Avg. of estimated SE(beta)	35.48	20.42	28.71	6.31	2.10	21.82	28.67	20.76	24.55	3.26	53.97
Efficiency Ratio	1.08	1.08	1.07	1.08	1.07	1.08	1.07	1.07	1.08	1.07	1.09
Avg. of estimated t-ratio	6.06	2.52	-0.24	6.64	1.83	-0.76	-2.62	1.90	3.64	8.03	-1.82
% rejected Ho***	100%	80%	8%	100%	53%	28%	80%	63%	100%	100%	55%
No. of Obs. = 400											
Avg. of estimated SE(beta)	44.00	25.20	35.83	7.78	2.60	26.95	35.69	25.68	30.40	4.07	66.37
Efficiency Ratio	1.34	1.33	1.34	1.33	1.33	1.33	1.34	1.33	1.33	1.33	1.34
Avg. of estimated t-ratio	5.13	2.36	-0.32	5.51	1.21	-1.03	-2.08	1.15	2.91	6.27	-1.52
% rejected Ho***	100%	68%	5%	100%	33%	25%	68%	25%	93%	100%	40%
No. of Obs. = 200											
Avg. of estimated SE(beta)	63.12	36.54	51.69	11.34	3.79	39.16	51.84	37.17	43.92	5.91	97.86
Efficiency Ratio	1.92	1.92	1.93	1.94	1.94	1.93	1.94	1.92	1.93	1.94	1.97
Avg. of estimated t-ratio	3.45	1.42	-0.19	3.53	1.03	-0.48	-1.60	1.28	2.37	4.30	-1.16
% rejected Ho***	95%	38%	20%	100%	30%	10%	53%	28%	73%	100%	38%
No. of Obs. = 50											
Avg. of estimated SE(beta)	138.79	79.73	114.68	24.87	8.35	83.93	111.17	80.79	95.85	12.76	215.31
Efficiency Ratio	4.21	4.20	4.29	4.25	4.27	4.14	4.17	4.18	4.21	4.18	4.33
Avg. of estimated t-ratio	1.16	0.67	-0.03	2.01	0.84	-0.34	-1.07	0.82	0.99	2.38	-0.41
% rejected Ho***	30%	12%	9%	61%	21%	9%	24%	15%	12%	76%	3%

*** The number of replications in which the estimated t-ratio was rejected at 10% significance level divided by the total number of replications in each experimental design.

* Out of 40, only 33 replications resulted in full rank, and were used for analyzing sampling distribution properties of the OLS estimator.

Figure 7.3.A **Percentage of the Replications in Which the Null Hypothesis,**
b=0, Were Rejected: {EA = 23, S = n}

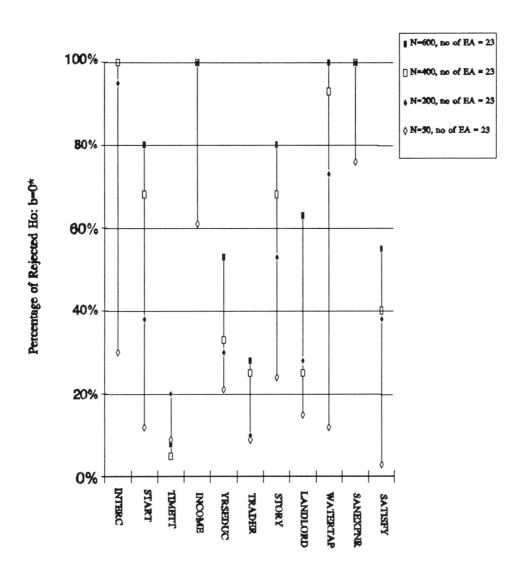

In 1987 many citizens of Onitsha, Nigeria purchased water from tanker truck vendors for about US$2 per cubic meter, or from water kiosks at even higher prices. Most people used about 20 litres per capita per day. The water utility was considering charging households about US$0.25 per cubic meter for water from a private connection from a new water distribution system. After the new water distribution system was installed, it was estimated that households with a connection would use about 130 litres per capita per day.

In the summer of 1987 a USAID and World Bank consultant team supervised a contingent valuation survey of 235 households in Onitsha, Nigeria, to determine whether households would connect to a water distribution system if different prices of water were charged. (see Whittington, Lauria, and Mu 1991, for a more detailed presentation). Each interview focused on estimating the household's willingness to pay for a private connection to a new, improved water distribution system being constructed for the city. The enumerator read each respondent a carefully worded statement that described the terms under which water would be provided, and then conducted a bidding game with the respondent (there was no open-ended follow-up question). The contingent valuation questions were designed to determine whether the respondent would choose to have a private, metered connection if the price of water were a specified amount.

For example, the enumerator first asked the respondent whether he or she would like to have a metered connection to the new water scheme if the price of water was 1 naira per drum (the volume of a drum was about 45 imperial gallons; in 1987 US$1 = 4.3 naira). If the respondent answered yes to that price, the enumerator raised the price to 2 naira per drum. If the respondent answered no to the opening price of 1 naira per drum, the price was lowered and the procedure continued. In Onitsha it made sense to respondents to pose the questions in terms of a price per unit of water, because almost everyone in the city was buying water from vendors and was thus familiar with prices based on volume.

Each household could be classified into one of seven groups on the basis of how much the respondent indicated that his or her household was willing to pay:

0.00 - 0.24 naira per drum	(0.00 - US$0.28 per cubic meter)
0.25 - 0.49 naira per drum	(US$0.29 - US$0.56 per cubic meter)
0.50 - 0.99 naira per drum	(US$0.57 - US$1.14 per cubic meter)
1.00 - 1.49 naira per drum	(US$1.15 - US$1.71 per cubic meter)
1.50 - 1.99 naira per drum	(US$1.72 - US$2.29 per cubic meter)
≥ 2.00 naira per drum.	(≥ US$2.29)

Figure 7.4.A presents a frequency distribution of the households' WTP bids (after converting the units of the bids from naira per drum to US$ per cubic meter), from which one can calculate the percentage of sample households that stated a willingness to be connected to the water system at a given price of water. Figure 7.4.B presents the percentages of households that would choose to connect at different prices.

At a price of about US$0.20 per cubic meter, almost everyone in the sample indicated that their households would choose to connect. At a price of US$0.40 per cubic meter, 86 percent would connect. The percentage falls dramatically as the price of water increases from US$0.40 to US$1.00 per cubic meter. When the price of water is increased above US$1.30, the proportion of households wanting connections would fall only slightly--an indication that above this price the demand for connections is much more inelastic.

These two ways of presenting the frequency distribution of WTP bids provide important, easily interpretable information for the managers of the water utility. The price of water charged by the water utility in Onitsha will affect the economic benefits to households in two ways: (1) it will determine the number of households that connect to the new system; and (2) it will influence the amount of water those households purchase. These two effects of the price charged determine the quantity of water sold by the utility, its costs of production, and the total economic benefits obtained by households.

An important objective of a water utility is to pursue projects with high economic returns, but the frequency distribution of WTP bids can shed light on other objectives. One of these is financial viability: to raise sufficient revenues to cover its costs and provide high-quality service to its customers. The total revenues that the water utility will receive from households in Onitsha can be roughly estimated as follows:

Annual revenues =   proportion of the population that decides to connect to the new water system times the population of Onitsha; times the price charged by the water utility; times annual per capita water use for individuals connected to the system.

One difficulty with this calculation, however, is that annual per capita water use cannot be determined independently of the price of water. A demand function for water is required to relate the quantity of water demanded by a household to the price of water charged.

As with most cities in developing countries, no research exists on the household demand function for water in Onitsha. Figure 7.4.C presents the relationship between the price of water and annual revenues for three assumed demand functions. At first, as the price of water increases, revenues increase. But if the price of water is increased above US$0.40 - 0.60 per cubic meter (depending upon the assumed demand function), total revenues actually decrease, because the number of households that connect to the system decreases rapidly. The maximum attainable revenue is in the range of US$5 million to US$11 million depending on the demand function assumed. This level of revenue can be obtained when the price of water is about US$0.50 per cubic meter. If the price were lowered to US$0.20 per cubic meter, annual revenues would fall to approximately US$5 million for all three demand functions. Similarly, if the price were increased to US$1.90 per cubic meter, annual revenues would decrease to about US$1.5 million. Comparing Figures 7.4.C and 7.4.D, note that over the range of prices from US$0.00 to about US$0.50 per cubic meter, as prices increase, revenues are increasing, but economic benefits fall. At prices higher than US$0.50, both revenues and economic benefits fall as price increases.

The water utility also has a social objective: to provide safe, reliable, high-quality water to as many people as possible. (Typically this objective will correspond closely to the economic efficiency criterion.) The trade-off between financial and social objectives that the Onitsha water utility faces is depicted in Figure 7.4.E. For example, assuming a linear demand function, annual revenues of about US$1.7 million can be achieved if about 10 percent of the households in Onitsha are connected (point A); if 100 percent connect, revenues will rise to about US$6 million (point E). From a social point of view, it is clearly preferable to have a larger percentage of the population served and to have higher revenues. Similarly, point D (about 85 percent connected; revenues of about US$9 million) is preferable to point B (about US$4 million, but only about 20 percent connected). Moving from point A to point C, both revenue and the percentage of households desiring connections increase. Assuming a linear demand function, this means that the prices should not be set higher than a level that would result in connected households falling below 60 percent. Choosing between points on the downward-sloping portion of the curve, CE, is more difficult, because in these cases revenues can only be increased by reducing the number of households connected to the system. This "northeast" portion of the curve in Figure 7.4.E characterizes the trade-offs between the utility's financial and social objectives and presents the management of the water utility with a hard set of choices. Note that the shape of this portion of the curve depends on the assumed water demand function. For exponential and log-linear functional forms, it would not make sense for the percentage of the population with connections to fall below about 85 percent.

Although highly stylized, this example serves to illustrate how a simple frequency distribution of households' willingness-to-pay bids for improved water services, obtained from a contingent valuation survey, can be used to support management decision making.

Figure 7.4.A **Frequency Distribution of Willingness To Pay Bids For a Private, Metered Water Connection (Onitsha, Nigeria)**

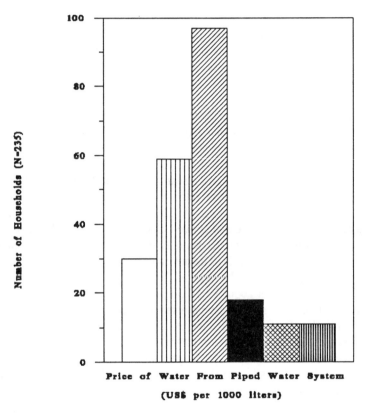

Figure 7.4.B **Price of Water vs. Percentage of Households Subscribing to Private, Metered Water Connection (Onitsha, Nigeria)**

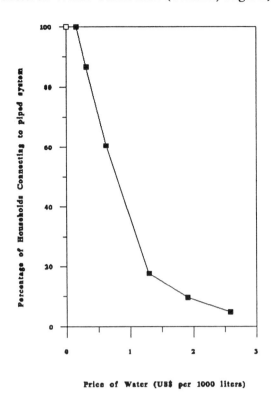

Figure 7.4.C **Hypothetical Water Demand Functions for Private, Metered Water Connections (Onitsha, Nigeria)**

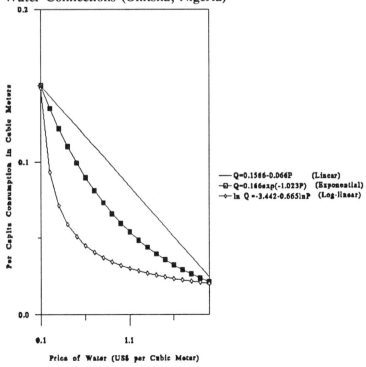

Figure 7.4.D **Price of Water vs. Annual Revenues to Water Utility From Private Water Connections (Onitsha, Nigeria)**

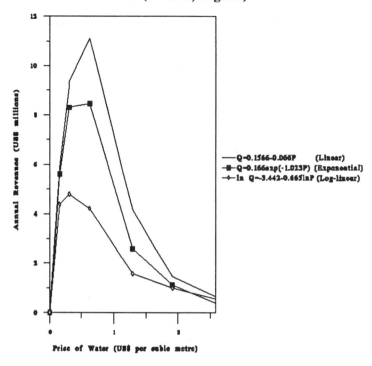

Figure 7.4.E **Percentage of Households With Private, Metered Connection vs. Annual Revenues of Water utility (Onitsha, Nigeria)**

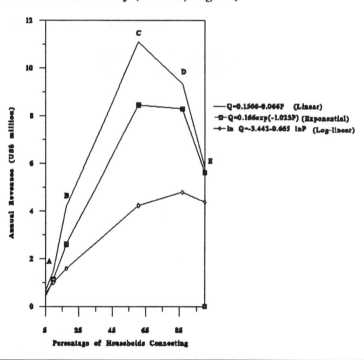

Box 7.5 **Guidelines for conducting contingent valuation studies**
(Adapted from the report of the National Oceanic and Atmospheric Administration Panel on the Contingent Valuation Method, Arrow et. al., [1993])

General Guidelines

1. Sample Type and Size: Probability sampling is essential. The choice of sample specific design and size is a difficult, technical question that requires the guidance of a professional sampling statistician.

2. Minimize Non-responses: High nonresponse rates would make CV survey results unreliable.

3. Personal Interview: It is unlikely that reliable estimates of values can be elicited with mail surveys. Face-to-face interviews are usually preferable, although telephone interviews have some advantages in terms of cost and centralized supervision.

4. Pretesting for Interviewer Effects: An important respect in which CV surveys differ from actual referendum is the presence of an interviewer (except in the case of mail surveys). It is possible that interviewers contribute to "social desirability" bias, since preserving the environment is widely viewed as something positive. In order to test this possibility, major CV studies should incorporate experiments that assess interviewer effects.

5. Reporting: Every report of a CV study should make clear the definition of the population sampled, the sampling frame used, the sample size, the overall sample non-response rate and its components (e.g., refusals), and item non-response on all important questions. The report should also reproduce the exact wording and sequence of the questionnaire and of other communications to respondents (e.g., advance letters). All data from the study should be archived and made available to interested parties.

6. Careful Pretesting of a CV questionnaire: Respondents in a CV survey are ordinarily presented with a good deal of new and often technical information, well beyond what is typical in most surveys. This requires very careful pilot work and pretesting, plus evidence from the final survey that respondents understood and accepted the description of the good or service offered and the questioning reasonably well.

Guidelines for Value Elicitation Surveys

7. Conservative design: When aspects of the survey design and the analysis of the responses are ambiguous, the option that tends to underestimate willingness to pay is generally preferred. A conservative design increases the reliability of the estimate by eliminating extreme responses that can enlarge estimated values wildly and implausibly.

8. Elicitation Format: The willingness-to-pay format should be used instead of compensation required because the former is the conservative choice.

9. Referendum Format: The valuation question generally should be posed as a vote on a referendum.

10. Accurate Description of the Program or Policy: Adequate information must be provided to respondents about the environmental program that is offered.

11. Pretesting of Photographs: The effects of photographs on subjects must be carefully explored.

12. Reminder of Substitute Commodities: Respondents must be reminded of substitute commodities.

This reminder should be introduced forcefully and directly prior to the main valuation to assure that the respondents have the alternatives clearly in mind.

13. <u>Temporal Averaging</u>: Time dependent measurement noise should be reduced by averaging across independently drawn samples taken at different points in time. A clear and substantial time trend in the responses would cast doubt on the "reliability" of the value information obtained from a CV survey.

14. <u>"No-answer" Option</u>: A "non-answer" option should be explicitly allowed in the addition to the "yes" and "no" vote options on the main valuation (referendum) question. Respondents who choose the "no-answer" option should be asked to explain their choice.

15. <u>Yes/No Follow-ups</u>: Yes and no responses should be followed up by the open-ended question: "Why did you vote yes/no?"

16. <u>Cross-tabulations</u>: The survey should include a variety of other questions that help interpret the responses to the primary valuation question. The final report should include summaries of willingness to pay broken down by these categories (e.g., income, education, attitudes toward the environment).

17. <u>Checks on Understanding and Acceptance</u>: The survey instrument should not be so complex that it poses tasks that are beyond the ability or interest level of many participants.

Chapter 8

Surrogate Markets

Introduction

Surrogate Market techniques are an indirect approach to monetary valuation of environmental benefits, which aim to measure individuals' preferences for better levels of environmental quality, usually by looking at observed market behaviour and choices. Surrogate markets look at markets for some other good or service related to the environmental benefits and costs of concern. The goods or factors of production bought and sold in these surrogate markets will often have as **complements** (or attributes) the environmental benefits and costs in question and these will influence the decision to buy or sell. As an example neighbourhood air quality is an attribute of houses, which are bought and sold in markets and so a surrogate market for air quality is housing. The techniques we shall look at in this chapter are, the **Travel Cost** method, **Hedonic Pricing**, and **Wage Risk** methods. These techniques are best suited to valuing sites and services and for urban pollution problems. They have the advantage that they are based on real rather than the hypothetical choices discussed in the previous chapter and are known as **Revealed Preference** techniques. Values found are therefore more likely to be acceptable to policy and decision makers. We shall also look at the **Avertive Behaviour** method, which looks at markets for **substitutes** of the environmental good or service. For example, noise insulation is a substitute for a reduction in noise at source. The avertive behaviour technique can use either real or hypothetical choices.

All the techniques can only be used when people are aware of environmental effects, and, they often require large amounts of data and statistical sophistication, as well as imposing restrictive assumptions to the extent that their use in developing countries may be limited. Benefit valuations obtained from these techniques are more or less "Ball Park" estimates, their accuracy depending to a large extent on the quality of the data used. Furthermore, the techniques can only measure **use values**, with the other constituent parts of **total economic value** being ignored.

In this chapter we first consider the general case of measuring environmental benefits from market data when the output resulting from the use of an environmental resource is not directly measurable, and then go on to consider each of the above techniques in detail.

Benefit measurement

As was discussed in Chapter 3, economic benefits or well-being are measured by the area under the compensated demand curve for the **Compensating** and **Equivalent Variation** definition of benefits. In general this is approximated by the area under an ordinary demand curve also known as **Consumer Surplus**. Our problem is that this cannot be estimated from any direct observations of transactions in environmental goods and services since no market exists for them. Revealed Preference approaches look at the relationship between private marketed goods (the surrogate good) and environmental goods in order to derive inferences about the unknown environmental demand. To exploit the information we have on the private marketed good we need to make some a priori assumptions regarding the relationship between the environmental good and the private good. We first examine the case where the two goods are **weak complements**, by which it is meant that when the demand for the private

135

marketable commodity is zero, then the value of the environmental good is also zero. In other words the value of the environmental good is entirely due to its use alongside the private good. To make this clear consider the diagram below.

Assume that for a given level of the environmental good, the demand curve for the associated private good has been estimated and is given by the curve BC. The current price of the private good is given by Px', at which demand for the private good equals X'. The consumer surplus at this price is given by ABC. Now, availability of the environmental good increases such that there is also an increase in the demand for the private good (since they are complements) leading to a shift in the demand curve to ED.

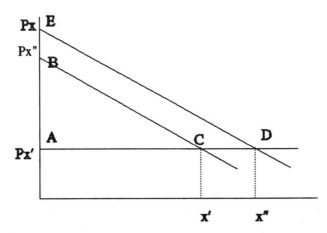

The benefit associated with this change is as follows: For the demand curve BC, if price increases to a level where demand equals zero, Px'', then for the individual to be as well off as before he must be compensated by the amount ABC. Environmental resource availability increases such that the demand curve shifts to ED. Due to the weak complementarity assumption, the welfare of the individual is not affected since the consumption of the private good is zero. Now if the price falls back to its initial level, Px', then the individual is better off by the area ADE. The net effect therefore of the change in the environmental good is a gain to the individual of the area BCDE (= ADE - ABC).

The assumption of weak complementarity therefore allows the estimation of environmental resource values from information on the change in demand for a private marketable good. This is the fundamental idea through which the Travel Cost approach works. The Travel Cost method estimates the demand function for recreational facilities and finds how visitation to a site changes - how the demand curve will shift - if an environmental resource in the area changes. The value of the resource change is given by the area between the two demand curves as above.

Furthermore, if weak complementarity is assumed and the supply of the private marketable good is fixed, then a change in environmental resource availability will be capitalised in market prices of the private good and so it is possible to estimate the value of changes in the environmental resource by looking at these market prices.

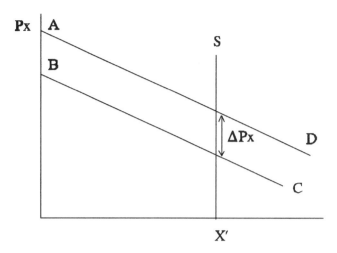

The demand curve for the marketable good is given by BC, and its intersection with supply determines price. The environmental resource is increased and so the demand for the private good shifts to AD (again due to complementarity). Assuming AD is parallel to BC, then price will have increased by ΔPx, and the gain in consumer surplus is given by $\Delta Px.X'$. The value of the change in the resource is therefore given by the price change. This is the basis of the Hedonic Pricing approach, with land being the factor assumed to have fixed supply.

Weak complementarity therefore allows us to estimate environmental resource values, but requires private goods demand or price response functions to be estimated, necessitating the use of large amounts of data.

The following sections look at the techniques based on the weak complementarity assumption and how they are carried out, in more detail.

The Travel Cost method

The Travel Cost method has been widely used to measure the demand and benefits of recreation site facilities and characteristics as well as for the general valuation of time, for example in the benefits of improved fuelwood supply or water collection in developing countries.

The basic idea behind the technique is that information on **money** and **time** spent by people in getting to a site is used to estimate **willingness to pay** for a site's facilities or characteristics. The problem here is that some recreation sites charge a zero or negligible price which means that it is not possible to estimate demand in the usual way. However, by looking at how different people respond to differences in money travel cost we can infer how they respond to changes in entry price, since one acts as a surrogate price for the other and variation in these prices results in variation in consumption.

The Travel Cost demand function is interpreted as the **derived** demand for a site's services and depends on the ability of a site to provide the recreation activity. Only **Use** Values are therefore considered, with **Existence** and **Option** values being ignored. Since the recreation activity takes place at specific sites that have observable characteristics and measurable travel costs then recreational service flows are described as **site specific**. The approach can therefore provide us with estimates of the value of the site itself and, by observing how visitation rates to a site change as the environmental quality of the site changes, provide us with values for environmental quality itself. The estimation of demand and the derivation of these values requires observations on the variation in prices, consumption and the quality characteristics of the site.

The procedural steps involved in a Travel Cost study are as follows:

1. For the site in question, the area around it is divided into concentric circles (called **Zones**), such that the travel cost of getting to the site and back from each zone is measurable. The travel cost includes any site entrance fee, the direct money costs of getting there (petrol, etc), as well as time costs involved in getting to the site and at the site (see later).
2. Visitors to the site are sampled using a questionnaire to determine their:
    Zone of origin and other demographic/attitudinal information.
    Frequency of visits to the site in question.
    Frequency of visits to substitute sites.
    Trip information e.g., length of trip, nights stayed in motel etc, travel paths, meals at restaurants, etc.
3. **Visitation rates** are then found for each zone of origin using above information (to get visitor days per capita).
4. A measure of travel costs to and from the site is found using above information.
5. Statistical techniques such as multiple regression are used to test the hypothesis that visitation rates depend on travel cost i.e., visitation rates are regressed on travel costs and other socioeconomic variables such as income, education, etc, as well as the prices and distances of competing sites.
    e.g., $V_i = a + b.TC_i + c.INC_i + d.ED_i + \ldots\ldots + f.STC_i$
    where V is the number of visits to the site, TC is the total travel cost to the site, INC is the individuals income, ED is their education, STC is total travel cost to substitute sites, the subscript i denotes the respondent, and a,b,c,d,f, are the coefficients to be estimated. The coefficient b gives the change in number of visits for a change in travel cost (admission price).
6. The observed total visitation for the site from all zones represents one point on the demand curve for the site.
7. Assuming that any increase in travel cost has the same effect on visitation as an equivalent increase of a hypothetical admission fee, then other points on the demand curve are found by using the estimated visitation rate equation to compute visitation rates and total visits for all travel cost zones for a given increase in admission price (or rather its surrogate, travel cost). This is repeated for successive increases in admission price such that the full demand curve is found. The benefits (consumer surplus) of the site are then found from the area under the demand curve.

Box 8.1 contains an example of a travel cost study used to value a rainforest reserve in a developing country.

Time costs

Since the cost of visiting a site consists of the transportation costs plus the costs of the time taken to get to the site and the time spent at the site, the role of **Time** is critical to the estimation of travel costs. It may be asked why time costs are included at all? The answer is that time has an **opportunity cost** i.e., there is some alternative usage of that time available, for example, one could work instead. We need to know what elements of time are to be included in the travel costs, what money values to use for these time costs, and how their inclusion will affect the demand and benefit estimates.

If time costs are ignored then benefits and demand will be biased (since for example we could have different zones having equal money travel costs but requiring substantially different times to get to the site. Unless time costs are included, visitation rates may appear to be equal for the two zones and willingness to pay for the site will be equal). The effects of both time costs and money travel costs on visitation rates therefore need to be estimated separately, but since the two may be highly correlated and so separate estimation difficult, time costs are given a money value using some **shadow price of time** and lumped together with the transportation costs. It was mentioned that time at the site should also be included in travel costs. This is relevant because time spent at the site may not be independent of the distance travelled. The shadow price of time at the site and time getting to the site may however be different. Any difference will be due to individuals deriving pleasure from the journey to the site, e.g., by taking a scenic route. If no pleasure or displeasure is forthcoming then the shadow prices are the same.

For our purposes we need to know what an appropriate shadow price of time is. One popular choice has been to use the **marginal Wage Rate**, since this reflects the opportunity cost of time between working and not working. However this trade-off may be distorted by institutional constraints such as maximum working hours, taxation etc; or, using the wage rate may be inappropriate for certain groups such as the unemployed. Previous empirical work has therefore suggested that the shadow price of time may be substantially less than the wage rate and lie somewhere between 1/4 and 1/2 of the wage rate with a value of **1/3 of the wage rate** being appropriate (Cesario [1976]).

Exclusion of time costs in general, will result in a more elastic (flatter) demand curve and bias the benefit estimates downwards. Exclusion of **on-site** time costs, if they are not independent of distance travelled and vary inversely with it, will result in a less elastic demand curve and an overestimate of benefits.

Environmental quality improvements

In order for a value to be placed on the benefits of environmental improvements at the site further work has to be done. If there is an improvement in a site's facilities, for example, water quality has improved, then to find individuals willingness to pay for the improvement we need to find how the demand curve for the site shifts as facilities improve. Benefits will then be approximated by the shaded area in the diagram below.

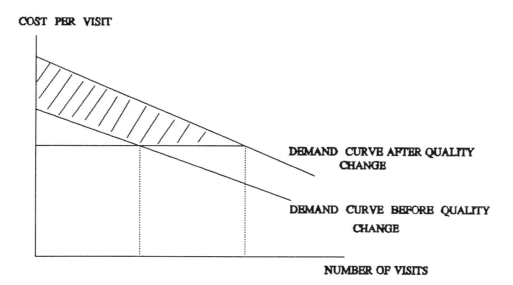

For practical purposes this means that we need to include variables for the quality of the site facilities of concern, in the regression used to find the visitation rate equation. However, if this is estimated at a single point in time then there will obviously be no variation in the site quality for a given site. We could instead try to look at the variation in quality across sites, but again for a single point in time, the set of quality variables for all sites together will not vary. The procedure we follow therefore is to estimate the visitation rate equation for each site separately, without including the quality variables and then try to explain the difference in the coefficients on the travel cost (price) terms by regressing them on the quality variables, Q, etc; i.e., the coefficient b in the visitation rate equation shown earlier is regressed as follows for each site denoted by the subscript j.

$$b_j = x + y.Q_j + ... + \text{other quality variables}$$

The coefficient, y, shows how the demand curve shifts as quality of the site changes and so can be used to estimate the benefits of the change.

This approach is called the **Varying Parameter Model**. Smith and Desvousges [1986] use this procedure to estimate the benefits of water quality improvements to a sample of U.S. Army Corps of Engineers water based recreation sites. They regressed the Travel Cost coefficient (shown as b in the equation above) against the following site characteristics: total shore miles at site during the peak visitation period; the number of multipurpose recreational and developed access areas at the site; size of the water pool surface relative to total site size; dissolved oxygen (percent saturation); variance in dissolved oxygen levels during the recreational season of the survey.

The Travel Cost technique as was mentioned earlier, can also be used to estimate points on the demand curve for commodities such as **fuelwood** and **water**, which is of particular interest for developing countries. Although there may be no money charge for these commodities, consumers will have to spend time collecting them and this may take a considerable amount of their available time. This time has an opportunity cost which gives the **implicit price** of the commodity. The value of improving supply of these commodities can hence be found in terms of the time savings involved.

Specification and estimation issues

We now turn to the data requirements of the approach, specification of the demand relationships and other estimation issues.

1. Data requirements
Obviously, the data requirements of the approach are fairly substantial. A survey must be carried out to establish the number of visitors to a site, their place of origin, socioeconomic characteristics, the duration of the journey and time spent at the site, direct travel expenses, values placed on time by the respondent (see earlier discussion), the total population in each zone, purpose of the visit other than visiting the site (multi-purpose visits raise problems for the technique), and a whole range of environmental quality attributes for the site and substitute sites. All of this data collection will be expensive and time consuming to carry out.

The socioeconomic characteristics will include things like income, age, a measure of education, and perhaps some measure of the subjective strength of preference for the particular type of recreation being offered.

The environmental quality attributes should include variables such as land area, shore miles, the number of recreation areas on the site, etc; as well as data on water quality such as temperature, pH, dissolved oxygen levels and turbidity; air quality such as particulate matter, sulphur dioxide levels, etc. We must be able to **quantify** the levels of environmental quality and so in practice the quality variables will often be a proxy for a variety of parameters that can be affected by pollution. One important question here is whether **objective** measures such as dissolved oxygen should be used, or whether **subjective** (perceived) measures are more appropriate. There may be wide differences between the two. For welfare analysis it is individuals' preferences and perceptions which are important. However, the importance of individuals' perceptions of quality in explaining recreational choices has not been proven. Furthermore, perceptions of quality even if they do govern recreational choices may not be analogous to objective measures actually used in studies, and so policy induced changes in environmental quality which will depend on objective quality measures will not be relating to recreation behaviour which depends on perceptions. It is best to try to choose measures which are consistent with what is believed to matter to recreationists, which help to actually predict demand, and which are objective in that similar values will be found by different individuals for similar levels of quality.

Some studies use **gross indicators** of quality such as nitrogen or phosphorus, but this may mean that no quality variation is observed across individuals at any one site. If an **aggregated index** of quality measures is used then we need to consider what weights are applied.

Uncertainty is also a problem for quality measurement. **Expected values** should be used, but since expected values and actual values may differ, the difference needs to be taken into account.

Correlation among variables, especially price, is inherent in cross sectional observations on recreational activity and so care must be taken to avoid this problem.

2. Specification of the demand relationship
By this we mean what functional form should be used for the visitation rate (demand) function. The problem here is that the specification of the demand relationship is crucial to the benefit estimates obtained. The statistical techniques will in general not be able to discriminate in favour of one specification or another. In practice the choice of functional form needs to be determined empirically on an individual study basis. However a number of studies have found that the visitation rate equation is best estimated using a **semi-log** form i.e., the logarithm of the number of visits to the site is regressed against travel cost, etc. Generally, it has been found that log-linear and semi-log specifications increase valuations relative to results found using a semi-log for the explanatory variables (Smith and Kaoru [1990]).

3. Other estimation issues
An issue of serious importance is the fact that in any data set, we will have information on people who actually have visited the site, but not on non-participants. Non-users need to be included to see what determines participation. This problem is known as **Truncation Bias** and results in the estimated demand curve being flatter than the true one. If there are systematic influences on the participation decision then what is called a sample selection problem exists. The bias can be corrected but requires more sophisticated statistical ability.

4. Multiple sites
When individuals are faced with the choice of many sites at various distances and with different quality characteristics, it may be better to use **Discrete Choice** models of behaviour. These include the **Logit** model, which looks at the probability that a particular site will be visited, depending on the attributes of that site and other sites, and on the households' characteristics. Since individuals will make no visits to some of the sites then there will be some zero values for the visitation rate variable in the multiple regression technique described earlier. Using this technique therefore, implies that a change in the quality of a site will have an effect on visitation rates, even if the site is not visited. Clearly this is incorrect and so the logit model is used instead. In this, the benefit per visit of an improvement in site quality can be estimated from the logit equation if a measure of travel cost is included. An increase in quality will increase the probability of visiting a site. The benefit per visit is then found by calculating the compensating increase in travel cost that would leave the probability of visiting the site unchanged. This requires total differentiation of the logit equation.

Meta-Analysis

Meta-Analysis involves the statistical analysis of different empirical studies of environmental values in an attempt to explain the variation in the results of those studies. For example, if there are numerous travel cost studies, a meta-analysis would treat the demand equation from each study as a datum and would pool the equations. Econometric analysis would then be applied to the new pool of data in order to find the most important factors determining recreation demand and, to explain the variation in the factors of importance across the different studies. Two studies of recreational demand meta-analysis exist, by Smith and Kaoru [1990] and by Walsh, Johnson and McKean [1989].

The Smith and Kaoru studies involved an analysis of 200 individual recreational demand studies prepared from 1970 to 1986. Various functional forms were applied to test the link between the dependent variable - visitor-days - and the independent variables: type of survey, type of recreation activity, type of recreation site, price of substitute site, a measure of opportunity cost (e.g., value of time), specification of the demand function, the year of the estimate, and the type of statistical estimator used. Note that the method of study enters the analysis, as well as factors directly influencing recreational demand. A mean of $25.2 per trip or per activity day was found. Analysis of the "t" statistics for the preferred model shows that the nature of the site is significant, as are the substitute price, opportunity cost of time, model specification and some specific econometric attributes of the original studies.

Walsh, Johnson and McKean [1989] report a meta-analysis of 287 estimates of the net value of a recreation day based on 156 TCM estimates, 129 CVM estimates and 2 hedonic price estimates over the period 1968 to 1988. In 1987$ the mean value of a recreation day was $34 and the median (which they prefer) is $27. The highest values are reported for hunting, fishing, boating, hiking and winter sports. The study did not, however, seek to explain the variation in benefit estimates. Site quality was found to be significant as an explanatory variable, as were regional factors, mixed public and private sites, the role of open-ended questions and the existence of hunting and saltwater fishing.

Application of Travel Cost to developing countries

Applications are numerous in developed countries where motor cars enable easy access to sites, and where time has significant opportunity costs. This will not often be the case for developing countries. Recreation areas will often be close to urban areas (due to limited transportation and low incomes) and so travel costs will be very small. Valuation of non-work time is also more crucial since there will be more people who are non-producers than in developed countries. Also, visitors will often use a recreation area to seek a break from work. Access to sites may be subject to constraints and so observed travel costs may not accurately reflect actual willingness to pay.

However, with the growth in tourism the approach may still have an important role to play in valuing recreation areas such as national parks as well as its established contribution to valuing commodities such as fuelwood and water.

In conclusion, we can say the Travel cost approach is an important method of evaluating the demand for recreational facilities. The techniques used have improved considerably since the earliest studies were carried out both from an empirical and theoretical point of view. There are reservations as to its use, particularly concerning the large amounts of data required which are expensive to collect and process. Furthermore difficulties remain with the estimation and data analysis techniques and so the method is likely to work best when applied to the valuation of a single site, its characteristics and those of other sites remaining constant.

Hedonic Pricing

The Hedonic Pricing method has been used extensively in developed countries to place values on environmental benefits and costs relevant to air and noise pollution. The approach looks at finding a market in some good or service for which the environmental good or service of concern is an **attribute**, in order to infer individuals' preferences for environmental quality. An example of this is the property market, in which one of the attributes of housing which influences an individual's decision to buy or sell may be the level of environmental quality, such as air pollution in the surrounding neighbourhood.

Given that different locations of property will have different levels of environmental attributes and that these attributes affect the stream of benefits from the property, then the variation in attributes will result in differences in **property values** (since property values are related to the stream of benefits). The hedonic pricing approach looks for any systematic differences in property values between locations and tries to separate out the effect of environmental quality on these values. Since there are many factors which influence property values, these must all be separated out using statistical techniques such as multiple regression so that we can identify how much of a **property differential** is due to any difference between environmental attributes at the properties. The hedonic approach then goes on to infer how much individuals are willing to pay for an improvement in environmental quality, i.e., estimate the demand for it.

Identifying a property price effect for environmental quality involves the following steps:
1. Define the market commodity (in this case property) and the environmental good or service of concern which is an attribute of the market commodity (e.g., air pollution).
2. A functional relationship is specified between the market price and all the relevant attributes of the market commodity. This is called a **Hedonic Price function**. The relevant attributes will in the case of property, include the structural characteristics of housing, the neighbourhood characteristics and the environmental attribute of concern (for the purposes of example we use air pollution).

    $P = P(S, N, E)$, where P = property price, S = structural characteristics of housing, N = neighbourhood characteristics,

    E = air quality at the property (see later for full details on specification).

3. Cross-sectional data (covering a large number of properties at one point in time) or time series data (covering a smaller number of similar properties over a number of years) is collected for property values and the associated characteristics above. The house price data could come from estimates by real estate agents.
4. Calculate the coefficient on air quality at the property, i.e., $\Delta P/\Delta E$ using techniques such as multiple regression analysis. This coefficient is known as the **marginal implicit price** of the air quality and gives the additional amount of money that must be paid by an individual to move to an identical property but with a higher level air quality. What we are in fact trying to identify is the curve AB in the diagram below which shows the relationship between the level of air quality and the price of the property. Further work must be carried out in order to get the demand curve for air quality improvements. We come back to this later.

143

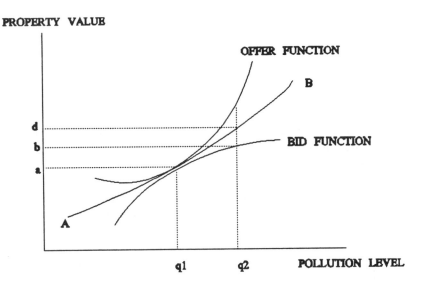

The curve AB in the diagram represents the result of a market **equilibrium** in which individuals buy property at some level of air quality and suppliers (owners or property developers) sell property with various air quality levels. The pollution level axis shows increasing levels of air quality. Individuals will buy property at some level of air quality according to their **bid curves** and suppliers supply property with this air quality level according to their **offer curves**, with points of tangency between the bid and offer curves giving equilibrium points on the **hedonic price curve**.

In benefit estimation we are interested in individuals' willingness to pay for better air quality. How does this relate to the previous diagram. Well, say the level of air quality changes from q_1 to q_2, then individuals' willingness to pay for this change is given by the distance ab in the diagram. However, the estimated hedonic price function would tell us that the willingness to pay for the change would be the distance ad, and so gives an overestimate of the benefits of the change. To correct for this bias and so estimate the true inverse demand (willingness to pay) curve, a second stage to the procedure is used. This involves a further statistical regression in which the marginal implicit price of air quality is regressed against the socioeconomic characteristics of individuals (including income) to estimate the bid function.

This second stage of the analysis raises a whole series of estimation problems, and although the procedure can be carried out, advanced techniques beyond the scope of this chapter are needed. In any case benefits can be approximated from the hedonic price function and so we therefore leave this second stage out of any further discussion.

Benefit approximation from the Hedonic Price function

First of all, we can say that if all individuals are identical in all respects such as income, preferences, etc, then the **implicit price function** over the range of air quality (which is the slope of the hedonic price function over the air quality range - see earlier discussion on implicit price) will give the **inverse demand function** since the implicit price function shows the locus of points on individuals' inverse demand curves which will all coincide since individuals have the same preferences, income, etc. Although this assumption allows easy benefit estimation from just the hedonic price function (see below) it is obviously a fairly unrealistic case.

We can show the benefits from an improvement in air quality with the aid of the following diagram from Freeman [1979].

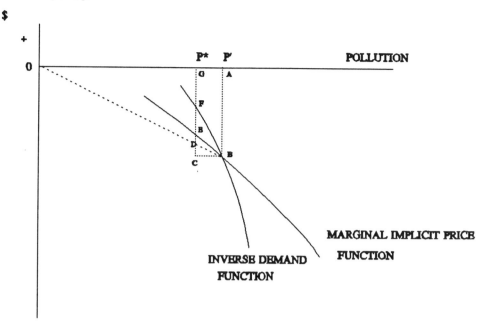

This shows the implicit price function over the range of air quality. Also shown is the inverse demand curve for air quality for an individual, which is the slope of the bid function over the pollution range. From the estimation procedure earlier we know one point on each individuals inverse demand functions but not their entire functions. These points are given by the implicit price curve.

Now, if the entire inverse demand functions were known then the benefit of a fall in the level of air pollution from level P° to P' would be given by the area ABFG. Since we do not know the entire function, but only the implicit price for pollution then we have to make an assumption regarding the shape of the demand function. If we assume that marginal willingness to pay is constant so that the demand function is horizontal, then benefits of the air quality improvement are given by the area ABCG (which equals the marginal implicit price of air quality multiplied by the observed air quality change).

Alternatively if we assume the inverse demand curve is linear from the estimated observed point back to the origin, then benefits are given by the area ABDG.

Finally as was mentioned earlier, if all individuals have the same income and preferences then the implicit price function and demand curve coincide and so benefits are given by the area ABEG.

Specification and estimation issues

1. Choice of functional form

The choice of functional form will have a significant impact on benefit estimates even if statistical tests find all the choices of form acceptable. In order for a preference to be made between functional forms, two questions should be asked about what properties the hedonic price function should possess. These are, whether the marginal implicit price of pollution is independent of the levels of the other attributes of housing and, whether the marginal implicit price depends on the pollution level itself and if so how? With regards to the first question only the Log, and Box-Cox forms (see below) impose dependence on the levels of other attributes. The second question relates to the slope of the implicit price function and whether this is linear or not. In practice it is found that non-linear functional forms give better fits for the data, especially the log and semi-log variety. However, use could be made of the Box-Cox transformation which allows the data to determine the precise form. Whichever functional form is used, care must be taken when transforming the estimated coefficients back to their original form (e.g., from log back to antilog) since biases can result. Alternative functional forms for hedonic price functions are shown in annex 2.

2. Data requirements

The data requirements of the approach are substantial. Data from a wide range of different properties is required with information on all features that influence the properties' value such as structural characteristics (number of rooms, size, etc), neighbourhood characteristics ("prestige", closeness to business and amenity areas, etc), and environmental characteristics (air quality, noise levels, etc), as well as on the property values themselves. Socioeconomic data on individuals (such as income, age, education, etc) is also required if the second stage estimation procedure is to be carried out.

Sufficient data of this variety to enable reliable estimation may be difficult to come by, especially in areas and countries containing a large amount of public sector housing.

The data on property values should come from actual market data but since only a small percentage of the total owner-occupied housing stock may be sold per year, then collection of a large enough sample of data may be difficult. Care must be taken to account for the effects of property taxation on property values otherwise their use will result in an overestimation of benefits. A further problem is that property prices may be influenced by expected future changes in the property and so the characteristics at the time of a sale may not adequately explain the selling price. Rental price data could be used to overcome this and is in any case the theoretically correct measure to use. However the rental market may be even less perfect than the property market in some countries. As an alternative Real Estate agent valuations could be used.

In general then, as many variables as is possible should be included. Omission of variables can bias the coefficient estimates. However, including too many variables can lead to **correlation bias**. Measurement errors in the variables can result in extreme changes in the environmental quality coefficients.

Turning now to the data on environmental quality attributes we need to know which pollutants are of interest and whether or not measures exist for them. Threshold levels may mean difficulty in measurement, or that pollution effects take a long time to show up. Temporal variations in concentrations may mean that it is best to use annual averages. We also face the same problems regarding objective and subjective measures of quality as we did for the Travel cost approach. Subjective measures are what people's behaviour is based on and so are important for benefit estimation. Objective measures however are more extensively monitored for many pollutants. Will these objective measures coincide with people's perceptions? For measures such as suspended particulates which are readily perceptible and their effects apparent in terms of visibility, etc, there should be no problems. Sulphate pollution level measures are also thought to coincide with perceptions.

When a single pollution variable is used, problems may arise with the pollution coefficient which may include the effects of omitted but collinear pollution variables. An aggregate index of pollution could instead be used. In practice it is best to try a number of measures and choose the best.

3. Other issues

The whole approach relies on the assumption of a **freely functioning** and **efficient** property market in which individuals have perfect information and mobility such that they can buy the exact property and associated characteristics that they desire and so reveal their demand for environmental quality. In reality the housing market is unlikely to be so. As was mentioned earlier a large part of the housing stock may be in the public sector and so allocated subject to price controls. Furthermore **market segmentation** may exist whereby mobility between housing areas is restricted. To get around this problem separate hedonic price functions should be estimated for each segmented area.

Finally, the possibility that **mitigating or averting behaviour** by individuals may take place to avoid the effects of pollution, such as installing pollution filters, needs to be looked at (see later). If this behaviour is unrelated to the characteristics of the property then it will reduce the value of the property and need not be measured separately. If changes do occur to the property then the value of the property will increase and so such changes need to be included in the hedonic equation.

Box 8.2 shows an example of a Hedonic Pricing Study.

Applicability to developing countries

Developing countries are less likely to have freely functioning and efficient property markets, and, housing mobility and choices will be more constrained by income, institutional, cultural and ethnic factors. Use of the technique should be made with great care, therefore, even without considering the fact that there will be less information and data available.

Although markets may exist in developing countries, prices are not likely to be market clearing due to the imposition of rent controls and state intervention. Housing shortages will mean there is also little choice of residence. However, simple versions of the technique may be useful (indeed have been) in establishing the effects on property values of improvements in neighbourhood amenities such as water supply, rubbish collection, street lighting, etc, providing there is data on property values before and after the changes, and so give rough estimates of benefits. Some examples of the technique in developing countries are shown in Box 8.3.

In conclusion we can say that the Hedonic Price Technique has been widely and effectively used to estimate the impacts of environmental factors, particularly air and noise pollution, on property values. The approach does not measure non-use values and is confined to cases where property owners are aware of environmental factors and act because of them. Applications to developing countries have been few due to problems of data availability and the nature of markets in these countries. The technique is not very suitable where markets are not functioning efficiently, and will work poorly if the environmental effects are unclear to the affected individuals and cannot be suitably measured. Despite the many problems of the approach, the model when applied carefully and in the right situation is capable of a level of accuracy consistent with the results of other approaches.

Wage Risk

The Wage Risk approach to valuation is used to place a value on the benefits of environmental improvement to **human health**. These improvements will consist of reduced **mortality** and **morbidity**. Benefit estimation requires that we place a monetary value on the benefits of changes in the risk of death, injury and illness. In order to measure these benefits it is assumed that an individual can substitute between income and health. In other words, they can make **trade-offs** between income and health, with the trade-off being measured by willingness to pay and so revealing the value of health.

The approach utilises the same basic idea as the hedonic property price approach, except that the market now being looked at is not property but the labour market. In the same way that supply and demand in the property market is influenced by the attributes of the property, the labour market looks at the supply and demand for a set of job characteristics or attributes which taken together define the job. The wage rate is now the "price" of the job. A comprehensive description of any particular job requires specifying not only the wage rates and tasks involved, but also other job characteristics such as working conditions, location and accident risk.

Now if the labour market functions freely then the mixture of job characteristics will adjust to clear markets for each type of labour, such that each type of job will have its own equilibrium mixture of job characteristics. Other things being equal, it is expected that jobs with a higher risk of accidents will have to pay a higher wage than otherwise. Furthermore, if firms incur expenditures in reducing the risks of accidents then it is expected that they will want to pay lower wages than otherwise. We therefore have the potential for a trade to be made between the two such that a price for safety will emerge. This price is the **"Hedonic Wage"**.

In the same way as for the property market, the wage risk approach seeks to find any systematic differences in the wage rates of jobs and tries to separate out the influence of safety on the wage. All of the attributes and characteristics of the job must be separated out using the same techniques as for property prices. We can then identify what part of the **wage differential** is due to differences in the safety risks of the job and from this infer what the benefits of safety improvements are.

A Wage Risk study will involve the following steps:

1. Specify a functional relationship between the wage rate and all the relevant attributes and characteristics that influence the wage. This is called an **earnings function**. The attributes and characteristics that influence earnings will include various job related characteristics (such as occupation, unionisation, working conditions, number of weeks worked in the year, location, etc), the socioeconomic characteristics of individuals (such as income, age, education, job experience, etc,) as well as the risk of accidents.
   $W = W(J, S, R)$, where W is the wage of the individual, J is the job related characteristics, S is the socioeconomic characteristics of the individual, and R is the accident (death or injury) risk for the job.
2. Cross-sectional data is collected for wage rates and the other associated characteristics above. This may involve matching accident risk rates from one data source, with the data on wages and other characteristics from another source. This is done using **Standard Class Industry (SIC) Codes** since accident risk data is often categorised by these codes which are then matched to the industry code of the individual.
3. Multiple regression analysis is used to calculate the coefficient on accident risk, i.e., $\Delta W/\Delta R$. This coefficient gives the **implicit value** of the risk of an accident. Wage risk theory suggests that we should expect to find risk of accidents entering as a positive coefficient into the earnings equation.
4. The purpose of wage risk studies is to place a value on the benefits of reducing the risk of damage to human health in terms of death and injuries. These benefits are found in terms of placing a Value on Life and Limb. The **"Value of Life"** is actually a misleading term since what we are actually looking at, is reducing the risk of death to statistical lives i.e., reducing risk of death from say 1 in 10000 to 1 in 20000. Now, we know that the risk term measures risk in terms of accidents (deaths or injuries) per 100,000, per year. Now the coefficient on the risk term gives the amount £X per year that must be paid to a worker to accept a job with an extra 1 in 100,000 chance of an accident occurring. For a group of 100,000 workers each with an increase of 1 in 100,000 in the risk of an accident, there would statistically be one extra death on average. £X was paid to each of the 100,000 workers to accept the statistical death of one person and so the Value of this Statistical Life is £100,000.X

So, **Value of Life = 100,000 . $\Delta W/\Delta R$**

where $\Delta W/\Delta R$ is the coefficient on risk.

A common functional form (see later) looks at the logarithm of earnings as a function of explanatory factors. In this case the Value of Life is given by

$$VOL = 100,000 \cdot \text{average wage} \cdot \Delta\ln W/\Delta R$$

with ($\Delta\ln W/\Delta R$) now being the coefficient on risk.

Specification and estimation issues

1. Choice of functional form

The same issues regarding choice arise here as did for the property pricing technique. Studies in the past have tended to use the logarithm or semi-log functional forms since these give the best fit over the distribution of earnings.

2. Data requirements

Again the data requirements of this approach are very large and so considerable expense in terms of time and money may be incurred in such an estimation.

Data will first of all be required on the risks to which workers are exposed. We are again faced by the question of whether to use objective or subjective measures of risk. It is workers' perceptions of risk which are important in order for an implicit price of risk (or **risk premium**) to emerge. Workers must in fact perceive differences in risks between jobs rather than in the absolute level of risk. If objective measures of risk are used and these are imperfectly related to workers' subjective assessments of risk then, if the risk variables are distributed randomly around their true value, empirical estimates will be biased downwards. How much of a problem this is in practice is debateable, with past studies giving similar results regardless of whether objective or subjective measures are used.

Most developed countries will have data on risk in terms of risk of death, risk of injuries, risk of accidents etc, according to the occupational group that a worker is in. These risks will be expressed as either the probability of death, etc (e.g., 1 in 100,000), or, as the number of deaths, etc, per year (and so must be divided by the number of workers in that occupational group to get a probability). The risk variable must consider risk of death, etc, at work, rather than being a general risk variable for death, otherwise there will be measurement errors (since the reason for the death may have been contracted elsewhere rather than at work).

Both risk of death and risk of injury should be included in the specification, otherwise, overestimates of the coefficient on the single risk variable will occur. However, there is a fundamental difference between deaths and injuries which has implications for their valuation. This is that injuries vary in their severity, whereas death does not. Injuries therefore need to be characterised by some meaningful scales of impairment. Inclusion of the various injury severities as explanatory variables in the earnings function will give rise to collinearity problems. Most studies have therefore tended to carry out valuations for deaths.

Risk data often comes in the form of risk according to occupation or risk by industry. If one believes that the risk to an occupation is similar for that occupation no matter what particular industry it is in, then **occupational** risk data should be used. If on the other hand risks are thought more similar for jobs within an industry then **industrially** classified data should be used. Empirically this question has not been settled and it may be that some combination of industry and occupation specific data is needed.

Data is furthermore required on the job related characteristics as well as socioeconomic variables of the individuals. Again, as for property values, as many explanatory variables as is possible need to be included, otherwise, biased estimates will occur. Sufficient quantities of data to enable reliable estimation is also needed and this may raise problems if the labour market is controlled e.g., through wage and incomes policies. In developed countries data sets containing the relevant information are

149

likely to exist. Obviously in developing countries this may be a problem as also will be the problem of finding accurate risk data.

Data on the level of unionisation should also be included since the presence of trade unions may result in the labour market not functioning freely. Wage premia for risk may still exist but may be influenced by the power of trade union bargaining. The effect of this needs to be separated out and so unionisation is included in the earnings equation. This could be in terms of whether the individual is a member of the union or not, or the percentage of unionised labour in the individuals' occupational group.

3. Other issues

The approach relies on the free functioning and efficiency of the labour market such that individuals have perfect information and mobility. This will obviously be fairly untrue in many countries due to unionisation, monopsony power of firms, barriers to entry and other institutional considerations. Furthermore labour market segmentation may also exist such that different earnings equations are needed for the separate segments.

The implicit price for risk obtained from wage risk studies is found from information on **voluntary incurred risk**. Individuals are being asked what they are willing to accept to incur a voluntary increase in risk (rather than what they are willing to pay). Using the values obtained from this approach in areas where risk has been imposed may lead to underestimates of damage since compensation required for involuntarily accepted risk is many times greater than for voluntarily accepted risk.

Box 8.4 gives an example of a Wage Risk study. Table 8.1 below gives estimates of Values of Life found in Hedonic Wage Risk studies.

Application to developing countries

Labour markets in developing countries are likely to be highly imperfect, often having an excess supply of labour. People may even disregard risk in the search for a job and income if they are poor. Furthermore risk perceptions are unlikely to be high, and the returns to a job may depend on caste, class, etc. Data requirements make the approach prohibitively expensive and so few uses in developing countries are envisaged.

To conclude, wage risk studies, like hedonic property pricing and travel cost studies have the advantage of being based on real rather than hypothetical choices. The reliability of estimates depends firstly on the quality of the multiple regression analysis and avoidance of statistical errors, secondly on the nature and quality of workers' perceptions of job risk and thirdly on the labour market operating freely and being in equilibrium. The approach has been widely used to place monetary values on life and gives results similar to those found using other methods.

Avertive Behaviour

The above three approaches all looked at the case where the relationship between a private marketed good and the environmental good of concern was complementary. The **Avertive Behaviour** technique to valuation, instead assumes that the marketed good and the environmental good are **substitutes** for one another. Households will often spend money and/or time to avoid or mitigate the effects of environmental hazards. For example, purchase of noise insulation materials, or risk reducing expenditures on smoke detectors, safety belts and water filters.

Substitutes

If we assume that there is a private good, X, and an environmental good or service, Q, which together produce some output, Y, and that the two goods are perfect substitutes such that the rate that X substitutes for Q in the production of Y is given by a constant, k, as shown below.

$$Y = X + kQ$$

Now, if the environmental good is reduced by one unit, then for the output Y to remain the same, the private good must be increased by k times X. If the price of the private good is given by P_x, then the value of the reduction in the environmental good is given by k times P_x. The constant k, is known as the substitution ratio between the two goods.

In order to apply this approach the averting behaviour must be between two perfect substitutes otherwise an underestimation of the benefits of the environmental good will occur. Averting behaviours are never likely to involve perfect substitutes and even when they do, bias in the estimation of benefits can still occur. Further problems with the approach include the fact that individuals may undertake more than one form of averting behaviour to any one environmental change, and, that the averting behaviour may prevent the adverse effects of reducing the environmental good but may also have other beneficial effects which are not considered explicitly, e.g., sound insulation may also reduce heat loss from a home. Furthermore, averting behaviour is often not a continuous decision but rather a discrete one - a smoke alarm is either purchased or not, etc. In this case the technique will again give an underestimate of benefits. (Discrete choice models for averting behaviour are available to deal with this problem but they are beyond the scope of this chapter.)

Estimation

To undertake such an estimation, data on the environmental change and its associated substitution effects is required. Fairly crude approximations can be found simply by looking at the change in expenditure on the substitute good arising as a result of some change in the environmental commodity of interest. Alternatively, if the substitution ratio between the environmental commodity and the private good, which can be found from known or observed technical consumption data, is multiplied by the price of the substitute, then the value per unit change of the environmental good can be found.

As has already been mentioned, even when perfect substitution possibilities occur, benefit measures from this approach can still be imperfect. If for example, there is an increase in environmental quality, the benefit of this change is given by the reduction in spending on the substitute market good required to keep the individual on their original level of welfare. However when the quality change takes place the individual will not reduce spending so as to stay on the original welfare level. There will have been an income effect as well as a substitution effect between environmental quality and the substitute good. Expenditure will therefore be reallocated among all goods with a positive income elasticity of demand and so the reduction in spending on the substitute for environmental quality will not capture all of the benefits of the increase in quality.

So, simple avertive behaviour models although having relatively modest data requirements may give incorrect estimates if they fail to incorporate the technical and behavioural alternatives to individuals responses to quality changes.

An example of the approach which uses survey data to look at the effects of stratospheric ozone depletion on skin damage is given in Box 8.5.

Other examples of the approach include, looking at expenditure on improved ventilation in order to reduce the exposure to radon in houses. Examples in developing countries include valuing the costs of siltation from upstream erosion by looking at the expenses that farmers incur when installing protection structures, and, valuing health hazards from river water by looking at willingness to pay for bottled water, filtration devices and private well installation.

Table 8.1 **Empirical Estimates of Statistical Life Valuation**

		Year	£(1991) million
UK	Melinek	74	0.5
UK	Veljanovski	78	5.0-7.0
UK	Needleman	79	0.2
UK	Marin et al.	82	2.2-2.5
UK	Georgiou	92	8.0
			———
	average UK wage-risk		3.4
			———
US	Smith (R)	74	7.4-14.0
US	Thaler/Rosen	76	0.6
US	Smith (R)	76	3.5
US	Viscusi	78	1.2-3.6
US	Dillingham	79	0.4-1.3
US	Brown	80	1.7
US	Viscusi	80	2.5-6.9
US	Viscusi	81	3.4-6.0
US	Olson	81	7.2
US	Arnould et al.	83	0.6
US	Butler	83	0.75
US	Low/McPheters	83	0.6
US	Dorsey/Walzer	83	5.5
US	Smith (V)	83	1.6-4.9
US	Dickens	84	1.6-1.9
US	Leigh/Folsom	84	4.6-6.0
US	Smith and Gilbert	84	0.4
US	Dillingham	85	1.4-4.0
US	Gegax	85	1.1-1.4
US	Leigh	87	3.7-7.0
US	Herzog and Schlottman	87	4.5
US	Viscusi/Moore	87	0.9-1.1
US	Garen	88	3.5
US	Cousineau	88	0.7-2.2
US	Moore/Viscusi	88a	1.0-4.8
US	Moore/Viscusi	88b	4.8
US	Viscusi/Moore	89	4.5
US	Moore/Viscusi	90a	9.0
US	Moore/Viscusi	90b	9.0
US	Kniesner and Leeth	91	0.35
			———
	average US wage-risk		3.5
			———

Box 8.1 **The domestic consumer surplus from visits to a rainforest reserve in Costa Rica**

The value of domestic eco-tourism at a tropical rainforest site was found using the travel cost method. The site looked at is the privately owned Monteverde Cloud Forest Biological Reserve. This consists of a large area of mainly virgin rainforest, to which tourism has been increasing over the last two decades.

Visitation Rates were assumed to be a function of travel cost (DISTANCE), population density (DENSITY) and the illiteracy rate (ILLITERACY).

Data was obtained from a sample of domestic visitors to the site, who left their addresses whilst entering a competition. Visitation rates were calculated by dividing the number of trips to the site by census populations, for each of the districts (cantons) in Costa Rica. As well as population, the census provided information on densities and illiteracy rates for each district. The distances from the main population area of each district and the site along the main route were found. Travel costs, including the value of travel time, were estimated at US$ 0.15 per km.

Because the visitation rate from many of the districts was zero, the semilog functional form could not be used and so a linear demand function was estimated as below using multiple regression.
VISITATION RATE = α + β DISTANCE + Δ DENSITY + δ ILLITERACY

Information on other socioeconomic variables was unavailable.

It was found that all the coefficients had the expected sign. The coefficient on price (DISTANCE) was negative and statistically significant and resulted in a maximum price per visit (were visits become zero) of between US$ 49-52 (depending on the precise specification and assuming travel costs are US$ 0.15 per km).

Since consumer surplus for each of the districts is equal to the area under the demand curve for the site, between the actual price for the site and the maximum price, then summing across all districts yields a consumer surplus of US$ 97,500-116,200 p.a. or about US$ 35 per visitor.

Foreign visitors to the site were not included in the study (despite the fact that they outnumber domestic visitors by four to one) and so if their consumer surplus is included at the lower bound value of US$ 35 (it is likely to be greater than this for foreign visitors due to their higher income and lack of nearby substitutes) then this results in a net present value of US$ 1250 per hectare (recreational values only). Since the price of acquiring new land near the reserve is between US$ 30-100 per hectare then expansion of the protected area is justified.

Source: Tobias and Mendelsohn, [1991]

Box 8.2 Example of a Hedonic Pricing study

The Value of Noise Reduction in the Netherlands

In the study by Oosterhuis and Van der Pligt [1991], the value of noise reduction in the Netherlands was estimated using a simplified version of the hedonic property approach.

The formula used to assess the benefits of noise reduction was
    dTV = N.C.dG.V
where, dTV is the change in total market value of houses due to the noise reduction; N is the number of houses affected by the reduction, dependent on the threshold value of noise in dB(A); dG is the change in noise level in dB(A); C is the noise depreciation sensitivity index (NDSI), which gives the percentage increase in house price due to a one percent decrease in noise level in dB(A); V is the market value of the house.

Due to uncertainties three different values for the threshold level of noise (65, 60, and 55 dB(A)), and three values for noise depreciation sensitivity index (0.1, 0.4, 1.0 %) were used. Furthermore three values were used for property values (Dfl. 50,000; 100,000; 150,000). The NDSI values were found from previous American studies.

It was found that the expected increase in house values due to a decrease in noise levels by 1 dB(A) range from Dfl. 50 to Dfl. 1500 with a most likely value of Dfl. 400.

The NDSI values were found from previous American studies. Table 8.2.A below shows the results of some such studies. The relationship between noise levels and house prices is presented in terms of a "price elasticity"- i.e., for each unit change in the noise level, measured in standard noise units, the percentage change in property price is shown. For aircraft noise the estimates suggest that for every unit change in NEF (noise exposure forecast) property prices might change by around 1%, and for every unit change in NNI (noise and number index) the change is around 0.5%. For traffic noise, measured in Leq, a one unit change again produces property price depreciation of 0.5-1.0%. Clearly, using property price changes to measure preferences for reducing noise nuisance does not encompass all the benefits of noise reduction. High and continuous levels of noise are probably associated with health impairment through stress, for example. It is unlikely that individuals will be sufficiently aware of health risks to "capture" their value in the form of house location choice. None the less, the hedonic property price approach offers a reasonable approach to the valuation of the dominant benefit of noise reduction - reduced irritation and nuisance.

Table 8.2.A The Value of Reducing Noise Nuisance

Study:	Impact of 1 Unit Change in	
	NEF	NNI
Aircraft Noise		
USA		
Los Angeles		0.8
Englewood		0.8
New York	1.6-2.0	
Minneapolis	0.6	
San Francisco	0.5	
Boston	0.8	
Washington DC	1.0	
Dallas	0.6-0.8	
Rochester	0.6-0.7	
Canada		
Toronto		0.2-0.6
Edmonton	0.1-1.6	
UK		
Heathrow		0.2-0.3
Manchester		0.0
Australia		
Sydney	0.0-0.4	
Switzerland		
Basel		0.2
Netherlands		
Amsterdam	0.3-0.5	
Norway		
Bode	1.0 (per dB)	
Average:	0.6-1.3	0.2-0.5

Traffic Noise	Impact of one unit Change in Leq
USA:	
N.Virginia	0.1
Tidewater	0.1
N.Springfield	0.2-0.5
Towson	0.5
Washington DC	0.9
Kingsgate	0.5
North King County	0.3
Spokane	0.1
Chicago	0.7
Canada:	
Toronto	1.0
Switzerland	
Basel	1.3
Norway	
Oslo	0.8 (against 1000 average daily traffic flow)
Average:	0.5

Sources: OECD, [1989], *Environmental Policy Benefits: Monetary Valuation*, Paris: OECD; Nelson, J., [1980], "Airports and Property Values: a Survey of Recent Evidence", *Journal of Transport Economics and Policy*, XIV, 37-52; Nelson, J., [1982], "Highway Noise and Property Values: a Survey of Recent Evidence", *Journal of Transport Economics and Policy*, XVI, 117-130; Navrud, S., [1992], "Norway", Ch.5 of J.P Barde and D.W.Pearce, *Valuing the Environment*, Earthscan.

Box 8.3 Examples of Hedonic Pricing in developing countries

The Determination of Land Values in an African City: The Case of Accra, Ghana

The factors that influence the value of urban land in a developing country were examined in order to assess the formulation and implementation of land related policies. The hedonic model estimated the effects on property prices of various variables such as, distance of the land from the sea, whether the land is located in an ethnically heterogeneous or homogeneous area, and size of the plot of land. Surprisingly it was found that land prices were positively related to the distance from the sea, due to the fact that in many developing countries beaches are left unattended, therefore allowing erosion, corrosion and pollution.

Consumer Demand for Rice Grain Quality

The implicit prices of rice grain quality characteristics in Thailand, Indonesia and the Philippines are estimated using the HPM model. The quality characteristics include physical characteristics such as shape and chalkiness, and chemical characteristics such as fragrance and gel consistency. The implicit prices are used to look at consumer preferences for grain characteristics and whether they differ between the countries.

Sources: Asabere [1981], Unnevehr [1986].

Box 8.4 Example of a Wage Risk study

The Marin and Psacharopoulos Study on Value of Life

This study looked at data on deaths classified by occupation for the period 1970-1972. The risk variable used is the excess death rate due to accidents.

An earnings function is estimated using data on household information combined with the risk data. The earnings function has the general form,

$$\ln(Y) = f(S, EX, EX^2, \ln(WEEKS), RISK, UNION, OCC, UNIONxRISK)$$

where, ln refers to logarithms; Y is annual earnings; S is a measure of education; EX is years of experience in the labour force (the square of EX is to take account of non-linearity); WEEKS is the number of weeks worked in the year; RISK is the risk variable above; UNION is a measure of the degree of unionisation; OCC is a measure of the desirability of the occupation; UNIONxRISK indicates any possible interaction between unionisation and risk.

Linear multiple regression is used to estimate the coefficients of the equation.

The estimated equation was found to be:

$$\ln(Y) = 1.95 + 0.058[S] + 0.046[EX] - 0.0008[EX^2] + 1.13[\ln(WEEKS)]$$
$$+ 0.229[RISK] + 0.002[UNION] + 0.008[OCC]$$

The coefficient on UNIONxRISK was dropped from the equation because it was found to be insignificant. The other coefficients were all significant.

Risk of death is expressed as X per 1000 workers. Now if a sum of £Z per worker is required to compensate for an increased risk of death of 1 in 1000 then the value of life is £1000.Z for the 1000 workers affected. Now Z is given by the change in earnings for a given change in risk ($\Delta Y/\Delta RISK$). Now since $\Delta Y = Y(\Delta \ln(Y))$, then the value of life is
$$VOL = 1000.Y.(\Delta \ln(Y)/\Delta RISK)$$

But since the term in brackets is the coefficient on RISK in the estimated equation (= 0.229) then the value of life can be found if we know average income.

This study found that the value of life was in fact £681,000 (1975 prices) for the above estimated equation.

Source: Marin and Psacharopoulos [1982]

Box 8.5 The effects of stratospheric ozone depletion on skin damage

The averting behaviour technique was used to value reductions in the risk of skin cancer using survey data. Individuals were questioned as to what they thought the chances of getting skin cancer were (by being shown a picture of a ladder with twenty steps on it and being asked to state their chance according to which step they thought they were on, each step reflecting the number of chances in twenty of getting skin cancer). The individuals were then told what the actual chances of the average person were. They were then asked questions relating to various factors which would alter their risks of contracting skin cancer, such as the amount of time that they spent in the sun. Following this they were again asked to state their perceived chance of getting cancer by referring to the ladder. Respondents were then asked for their willingness to pay for a hypothetical product (skin cream) which would reduce the risk of skin cancer, and, to estimate the risk reduction (in terms of the ladder) that they thought the product would give them.

Using regression techniques, willingness to pay for a one percent reduction in perceived skin cancer risk was found to be between $7.950 and $3.386 depending on the discount rate used.

Source: Dickie et al [1991a]

Chapter 9

Damage Functions

Introduction

The Damage Function approach to economic measurement of environmental benefits does not aim to measure individuals' preferences for better levels of environmental quality directly. Rather, it looks at establishing a **dose-response** relationship between environmental damage (response) and some cause of this damage such as pollution (the dose). Only then are individuals' preferences for the damage applied by valuing the response using unit valuations from market prices, or revealed/inferred prices if no markets exist.

Damage actually done is found using a "**damage function**" which relates physical/biological changes in the ambient environment to the level of the cause of the change. The damage function is then multiplied by the unit "price" or value per unit of physical damage to give a "**monetary damage function**". The procedural steps involved in finding a measure of the monetary benefits of some environmental effect are as follows:

1. Estimate a physical damage function, $R=R(P$, other variables), where R is physical damage (response), and P is the cause of the damage (dose). For the purposes of illustration we shall use pollution as being the cause of damage.
2. Calculate the coefficient of R on P, i.e $\Delta R/\Delta P$, using statistical techniques such as multiple regression analysis.
3. Calculate the actual change in pollution due to the environmental policy change, i.e., ΔP.
4. Calculate $V.\Delta P.(\Delta R/\Delta P) = V.\Delta R = \Delta D$, where ΔD is "damage avoided". In other words the response to the actual change in pollution (ΔR) is found and is multiplied by the monetary value per unit of physical damage (V) to give the "damage avoided" or benefit of the environmental effect.

The damage function approach is used extensively where dose-response relationships between some cause of damage such as pollution, and output/impacts are known. For example, it has been used to look at the effect of pollution on health, physical depreciation of material assets such as metal and buildings, aquatic ecosystems, vegetation and soil erosion. The approach is mainly applicable to environmental changes that have impacts on marketable goods and so it is unsuitable for valuing non-use benefits. If these values are important then the use of the method will underestimate benefits.

There are two main reasons why the approach is used. Firstly, in situations where people are unaware of the effects that pollution causes, valuations based on revealed and stated preferences will be biased. Secondly, direct methods of elicitation may not be possible due to a lack of data or market sophistication, especially in developing countries where price and expenditure data are poor, and where Contingent Valuation Methods have their own set of problems (see Chapter 7).

Valuing marginal damages derived from a Dose-Response function

The damage function technique in its most basic form looks at environmental resources which lead to a marginal change in the output of a good sold on a competitive market and values the impact directly in terms of output changes valued at market prices. More formally suppose the production function for a single output y is given by: $y = F(X, Z)$

where X is a set of inputs and Z is the input of the unpriced environmental resource. Assume that we can measure the output y and that this output is sold on a market at price s. The price of inputs X is given by the price vector P. Now, if prices are not expected to change when supply of the environmental resource changes, then the economic value of the change in the supply of the resource is the value of the production change accompanying the change in resource availability at constant inputs of the other factors.

If the change in resource supply is large, but leaves prices unchanged, then the value of the resource supply change must be measured as the difference between the profit after the change and before the change, taking all changes in factor use into consideration (see Annex 3).

If on the other hand output price does change, then there is still a change in producer's surplus or profit, but now there will also be an effect on consumer's surplus due to the price change. Consider some environmental degradation which reduces output of a marketable good and increases its price. In the diagram below, DD' is the demand curve for the marketed good, and MC is its marginal cost curve before the environmental degradation. Initially the equilibrium price of the good is P, but after the degradation this increases to P' since the marginal cost curve increases to MC'.

Initial producer surplus equals the area abc. After the change this equals xyz. The loss in producer's surplus is then $\Delta PS = ABC - XYZ$. Producers may be better or worse off, depending on whether the percentage reduction in quantity is greater or less than the percentage increase in price. Consumers face an increased price and so face a loss in consumer's surplus of $\Delta CS = CBYZ$. So, the total loss from the environmental degradation is equal to:

$$\Delta TV = CBYZ + ABC - XYZ.$$

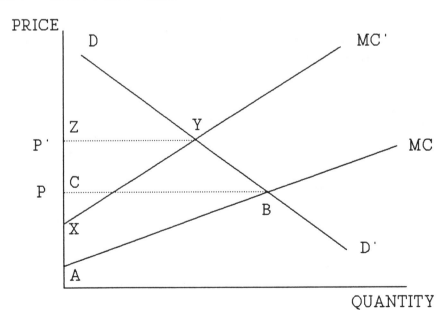

If prices change therefore, the new price level needs to be predicted. Such prediction of market responses is complicated. Individuals will often change their behaviour and take action to protect themselves against any effects (**averting behaviour**), for example, by switching to crop varieties whose yields are resistant to a particular form of air pollution in the region, or they may alter the use of other inputs such as calcium carbonate which mitigates the pollution impact. Also corrosion of materials can be countered by painting the material, switching to substitute materials which are corrosion resistant, or simply replacing the materials more often. Such behaviour implies expenditures which can be used as a measure of willingness to pay. Dose-response estimates may need to be linked to a behavioural model of the demand for the products that are affected otherwise biases will result. The changes in profits and welfare that accompany these behavioral responses are indications of their effects on the welfare of producers and consumers. Changes in producer behaviour at different levels of air quality are modelled with the assumption that the producer is a maximiser of expected profits, taking the prices of all inputs and outputs as given. The supply curves for each of the varieties of crops produced in a region can then be derived, given the production technology and the yield response relationship. Supply curves have been estimated on the assumption of profit maximisation and appear to fit well to the actual data. The supply relationships specify the amount that will be supplied of each crop as a function of the prices of all the crops, the prices of the variable inputs, the quantities of the fixed inputs, and the level of air pollution. Hence, if the pollution levels were to fall, the supply of products that were adversely affected by that pollution would be expected to increase and the output of those products whose yields were pollution resistant to decrease. The impact of these supply changes on the prices of the commodities will depend on the market structure that is prevalent. If prices are market determined, they will adjust to bring supply and demand into balance, and the magnitude of the price change will depend upon how many producers are affected by the pollution and how responsive supply and demand are to price changes. If on the other hand, the prices are administratively set, then there is no direct price effect to consider. However, the prices of related commodities that are market determined may be affected.

In order to assess the impact of a change, a model of the markets for the products affected is required, in which specific account is taken of the yield response relationship on the supply side and of the impact of prices on the demand side. Given such a model one can calculate the pre- and post-pollution change prices and quantities for each commodity. The change in the sum of the consumer surpluses plus the change in the profits of the producers, less any increase in government subsidies, is then regarded as an approximation to the economic benefits of the change in pollution levels. Modelling such an interrelated system of markets is an open ended activity and can be extremely sophisticated or fairly simple. The simpler models can provide useful estimates provided their shortcomings are recognized[15].

Furthermore, other price distortions can mean that the use of actual prices gives a misleading picture (for example, where monopoly, price controls or protection exist). Prices should therefore be adjusted to market clearing/competitive levels by shadow pricing.

The following components are then typically employed to value damage.

1. Scientific studies are employed to specify the dose-response relationships i.e., the physical damage resulting to output as a function of specific pollutants. These studies also characterize the different permutations that environmental change presents in terms of production and consumption opportunities. Statistical relationships are used to estimate the physical relationship between inputs and outputs for the varying levels of environmental effects.

2. The response of input/output market prices to these relative changes in output is determined (demand).

3. The adaptations that affected agents can make so as to maximise gains or minimise losses from the changes in opportunities and prices are identified (supply).

4. Once the parameters of the market demand and supply equation have been estimated the system is simultaneously solved by a market clearing identity which equates quantity supplied with quantity demanded.

Specification and estimation of the Dose-Response relationship

The physical damage or dose-response function is estimated using regression analysis and aggregated over the affected population. Clinicians, epidemiologists and economists alike have constructed dose response functions in an ongoing attempt to relate certain types of health damages to changes in specific air pollutant levels. However, each profession has adopted a different approach as indicated below:

(a) Toxicological Studies

These are largely the domain of the clinician in which animal subjects are exposed to acute (ie. short term, high concentrations) levels of pollutants in control-led experiments. The results from such experiments can be useful in indicating likely human exposure response.

(b) Micro epidemiological Studies

Clinicians and epidemiologists have also been involved in controlled studies on human subjects. These studies focus on the exposure of individuals to single (or combinations of) pollutants in controlled conditions over a period of time. The types of responses studied are typically limited to those that are short term and reversible due to obvious moral imperatives. A further limitation of highly controlled micro studies is that they cannot capture the effects of averting behaviour that is likely to occur in real life situations.

(c) Macro epidemiological Studies

Epidemiologists and economists have been involved in such broader based studies. Macro studies employ large data bases relating ill health and mortality to various factors including pollutant levels and socio-economic variables. Such studies are clearly distinguishable from micro studies which seek to control as many factors as possible.

Dose-response functions can be summarised by some **coefficient** or **elasticity**.
    Let Impact/Damage $= I = F(P,V)$
where P is pollution or other degradation, and V is a set of other relevant variables.
If our functional form is of the type, $I = \alpha P + \beta V$ etc, then $\alpha = dI/dP =$ the coefficient, or if the form is, $\ln I = \alpha_1 \ln p + \alpha_2 \ln V$ etc, then $\alpha_1 = (dI/I) / (dP/P) = dI.P/dP.I =$ the elasticity $=$ the percentage increase in damage caused by each percentage point increase in pollution. The elasticity is of relevance to pollution policy since this is often expressed in terms of target percentage reductions in emissions or concentrations.

Where there is more than one cause at work then elasticity is given by
    $dI.P_i/dP_i.I + dI.P_j/dP_j.I$
The coefficient, dI/dP, can then be multiplied by the monetary value per unit of physical damage (V) to give the total monetary damage for the increase in pollution.

V. dI/dP

Dose-response functions incorporating elasticities are illustrated in Box 9.1.

The specification of the dose-response relationship is crucial to the accuracy of the approach. All possible variables affected need to be identified and included. Often there may be subtle but significant forms of damage e.g., in vegetation studies the dose-response functions will typically relate pollution levels to physical deterioration such as leaf drop or discolouring. However, effects such as reduced plant vigour, lower rates and less resilience to pests may arise. If there is a problem with measuring some of these variables and/or difficulty getting consistent data for them, then other measurable factors which attempt to account for the unmeasurable factors can be used. Often the relationship between a pollutant and effect is not well established. Some effects will be easier to quantify than others and forging links between cause and effect may require making assumptions and transferring data on relationships and sources established elsewhere.

There is a further difficulty with isolating the effects of one cause from that of others in determining the impact on a receptor (e.g., Synergistic effects where several pollutants or sources exist), and also isolating other factors such as climate which may vary by area. The problem of determining the marginal impact of man-made pollution when both man-made and natural sources combine towards ambient pollution levels. Attributing all damage to man-made sources may overstate the situation and, even if the proportion of emissions attributable to man are known, damage estimates may still be difficult to find if the dose-response function or monetary damage function is non-linear.

Identification of damage threshold levels may be important in the specification of the dose-response relationship as shown in Figure 9.1. The long term effects of low to medium levels of pollution may be unidentifiable, especially in the case of ecosystem behaviour. Discontinuities in the dose-response function may also exist. These problems must be taken account of or incorporated in the analysis

Figure 9.1 **Damage thresholds**

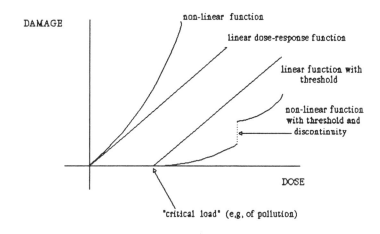

163

Figure 9.1 (cont) **Damage thresholds**

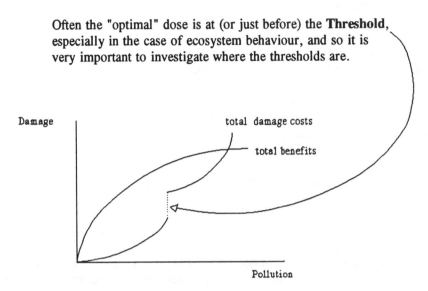

Often the "optimal" dose is at (or just before) the **Threshold**, especially in the case of ecosystem behaviour, and so it is very important to investigate where the thresholds are.

Despite their problems, dose-response relationships can provide first approximations to the true economic value measures. If the relationships are poor then this should be stated explicitly and a range of estimates given. Where some effects cannot be measured or valued then these should be listed.

Examples of dose-response functions are given in Box 9.1 and in Annex 4 and 5.
Some qualitative illustrations of dose-response relationships for pollutants and health are shown below.

Figure 9.2 **Dose-Response curve for the combined effects of SO2 and SPM**

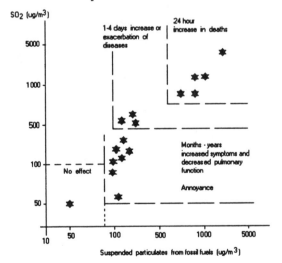

Source: Wilson et al [1980]

Figure 9.2(cont) **An ozone health damage function for the E.C.**

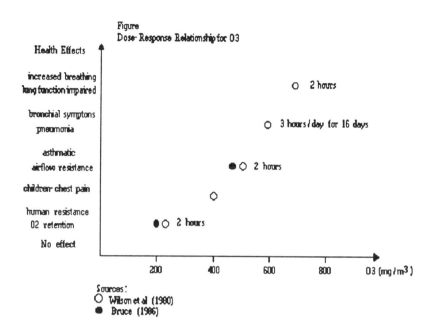

Figure
Dose- Response Relationship for O3

Sources:
○ Wilson et al (1980)
● Bruce (1986)

Marginal damages versus total or average damage

In order to be of use in a policy making context, marginal damage valuations are needed. Dose-response relationships are likely to be non-linear with damage rising proportionately more as pollution increases. Even if physical damage increases proportionately, monetary valuation per unit damage may still be non-linear. Valuations therefore based on average physical damage and average valuations will underestimate damage values at high pollution levels and overestimate them at low levels. Damages from each incremental unit of ambient pollution concentration need to be found and linked to changes in pollutant emissions such that we have marginal damages per unit of emissions.

Unit values of monetary damage

Since dose-response functions are defined in per unit terms then knowledge of the actual quantity of material exposed to pollution is required. This problem is compounded by the trouble mentioned earlier which was that valuing marketable goods involves taking account of the impact of supply changes caused by pollution on price, and whether or not producers' responses, production methods and costs are affected. If they are, then any appraisal not taking this into account will overestimate the value of effects. If on the other hand an appraisal is carried out after adaptive responses have taken place, then the impact on producer and consumer surplus will be underestimated. Allowance must also be made for distortions in the price level due to market interventions and imperfections, e.g., E.C. CAP guaranteed agricultural prices.

Non-marketed goods require the use of values from close marketed substitutes or, for subsistence production "border prices" can be used. Revealed/stated preference study estimates, such as Value of Life figures found from Compensating Wage Differentials studies are used when other values are not available. This raises the issue of **Benefits Transfer** (see Chapter 10). Benefits transfer refers to the possibility of using the results of existing studies to derive the relevant prices, V, to apply to dose-response functions. For example, if other studies reveal a cluster of values around an average value, Va, it is possible that Va could be applied to a new context. If so, considerable effort could be saved through this "borrowing" procedure. The transferability of valuation estimates is not well understood and work is at an early stage on this issue. The basic procedure is to engage in **"Meta-Analysis"** (see Chapter 8) whereby existing studies are assembled and their results are compared using regression techniques. The aim is to explain the variability of the price estimates. That is, some central value, Va, might be found by averaging the results of the various studies, but the statistical analysis shows how variations about Va are explained. For a given context it may be observed that the value clusters around Va-v, i.e., is less than Va. If the new context is similar to the analysed context, the value Va-v could be used. If the new context is thought to be broadly representative of the average, then Va could be used. The use of borrowed estimates in this way assumes that analysis has been done of the existing empirical work. While there is a growing literature on "meta analysis" it is still not developed enough to provide a rigorous justification for using borrowed values. Nonetheless, where resources are limited, some kind of averaging of existing findings may be justified.

Aggregation of damage estimates

Since valuations are usually carried out at local level, they have to be generalised to other areas to give aggregate figures. However, since conditions such as climate can vary substantially between regions then simply scaling up by some factor may result in significant errors. Furthermore, it must be remembered that the dose-response approach only gives use-value estimates and even then doesn't include all of these. A lower bound figure of benefits is therefore found.

Dose-Response and developing countries

Environmental benefit estimation in developing countries is usually of the dose-response type, especially in the field of agriculture. The approach is well suited to this area since it relies on observed market behaviour, it is readily intelligible to decision makers and looks at outputs normally included in national accounts.

An example of the approach as applied to developing countries is shown in Box 9.2 and a further example looking at soil erosion is in Annex 4.

The approach is not without its problems when applied to developing countries though. Markets for the output affected may not exist or be underdeveloped, for example, in subsistence economies. The use of other valuation techniques or of strong assumptions regarding comparable products may be necessary. Furthermore the use of dose-response relationships established in industrialised nations may be inapplicable to developing countries. For example, the relationship between pollution and materials damage has mainly been found for developed countries and so the relevance to tropical and humid climates is limited. Even then there are likely to be a different range of materials at risk in developing countries.

Another problem lies in the fact that output changes in one good may cause its substitution for another, which itself may replace a third good (see the Nepal Hill Forest Development Project in Box 9.2).

To conclude then, the Dose-Response approach is a technique that can be used where the physical and ecological relationships between pollution and output or impact are known. The approach cannot estimate non-use values. The approach is theoretically sound, with any uncertainty residing mainly in the errors of the dose-response relationship, e.g., are there threshold levels before damage occurs, or discontinuities in the dose damage function. It is necessary to allow for the fact that the behaviour individuals may change in response to changes in the environment. If this is not possible, but the direction of any bias resulting is known then this should be stated. The Dose-Response approach has perhaps the greatest potential for valuation in the developing country context where other approaches suffer a number of problems. However, the approach may be costly to undertake if large databases need to be manipulated in order to establish the relationships. If the dose-response functions already exist though, the method can be very inexpensive and with low time demands. Examples of the application of the technique are shown in Annex 6.

Box 9.1 **Morbidity and air pollution**

Ostro [1983], uses data from the Health Interview Survey of the US National Center for Health Statistics, a database covering 50,000 households. The health data is then matched to pollution data and other information from other sources. Morbidity was measured by days off work - "work loss days " (WLD) - and "restricted activity days" (RAD), i.e., days in which activity was restricted because of ill-health. Then WLD and RAD are regressed on various variables: indicators of chronic disease, race, marriage, temperature, population density, rainfall, cigarette consumption and work status. There were no variables for air pollution other than sulphur oxides and suspended particulates, nor anything for water quality or diet. The results, showing just the estimates for the two air pollution variables, were:

$$RAD = -0.83 + 0.00282 \text{ TSP} - 0.00008 \text{ SULF} + \ldots$$

and $$WLD = -0.47 + 00.00145 \text{ TSP} - 0.001 \text{ SULF} + \ldots$$

In the equations, the sulphur coefficients were not significant which means that sulphur concentrations are not implicated in morbidity. This bears out some earlier studies. The coefficients for TSP were significant and can be translated into "elasticities", showing the percentage increase in morbidity for each percentage point increase in air pollution. The coefficients were 0.45 for WLD and 0.39 for RAD when expressed as elasticities. Thus, a 1% improvement in air quality would reduce working days lost by 0.45%.

Source: Ostro, [1983].

Box 9.2 Valuing the benefits of a Nepal hill forest development project

Several market values are adopted to value the effects of the project. The project was concerned with improved land-use planning, the improvement of 7000 hectares of timber stand, management of 16,000 hectares of scrubland, additional fencing to stop livestock damage, and 4000 hectares of afforestation for fodder, fuelwood and fencing timber. Its "outputs" were increased fuelwood and fodder, higher land productivity and reduced soil erosion. To find the incremental productivity arising from the management programme it was necessary first to estimate the value of output from land without the project. As an example, grazing land produces two products, milk and animal dung which is used as fertilizer. Each animal produces 15 kg of nitrogen-equivalent and 2 kg of phosphorus-equivalent per year. Nitrogen is valued at 6 rupees/kg and phosphorus at 18 Rs/kg, so that one animal produces:

$((15\times6) + (2\times18))$ Rs of fertilizer per year = 126 Rs. One hectare supports 0.0857 of an animal, so fertilizer production per hectare is 0.0857 x 126 = 11 Rs/hectare.

Table 9.1

Output for Total Land Area (Rs million)

		With Project	Without Project	With - Without
Year	1	12.5	7.5	5
	2	5.3	7.2	-1.9
	3	10.8	6.9	3.9
	4	5.8	6.6	-0.8
	5	9.9	6.4	3.5
etc				
	40	21.7	1.6	20.1

The forest management project involved changes in land use. Hence the need was to value the output from each land use, and then to see what changes arose from (a) differences in value due to differences in land use, and (b) increased productivity on a given land use. The discounted value of the net benefit streams shown above was then compared to the discounted value of costs. The result was expressed as an internal rate of return of 8.5%.

Source: Dixon et al. [1988].

Scrubland and unmanaged forest produce fertilizer, milk and fuelwood. Fuelwood was valued three different ways. First, it is sold on the market and the market price net of collection costs was 280 Rs per cubic metre. Second, the substitute for fuelwood would be animal dung. Dung could in turn be valued in several different ways, but the method chosen was to look at crop responses. Thus, 1 cubic metre of wood = 0.6 tons of dried manure ·= 2.4 tons of fresh manure. Maize yields were estimated to rise by 15% because of applications of. 6 tons p.a. of fresh manure to a 0.5 hectare plot. Productivity of 1.53 tons of maize per hectare would rise to 1.8 tons/hectare, and maize output is worth 1200 Rs/ton, so the productivity gain is (1200 x (1.80 - 1.53)) = 324 Rs. Hence the value of a cubic metre of wood is: (324 Rs x 0.5 hectares)/6tons = 27 Rs/hectare for fresh manure = (27 x 2.4) Rs per cubic metre = 65 Rs/cubic metre. The third way fuelwood can be valued is at the time taken to collect it. Each family collects 7.92 cubic metres per year and spends 132 days doing this. At 5 Rs per day as the alternative income from other activity, each cubic metre of wood costs: (132

169

x 5)/7.92 = 83 Rs/cubic metre.

So by looking at each type of land, output can be calculated. When project interventions are envisaged, it is necessary to estimate output with the changed land use under the project, and compare it with output without the project.

Chapter 10

Transferring Benefit Estimates

Introduction: What is "Benefit Transfer"?

In the previous chapters that describe different economic valuation techniques, we have implicitly assumed that when a policy analyst wants to know the economic value of the consequences resulting from a project, policy, or regulation, that he or she would initiate a new study in the project area to determine how the well-being of the individuals potentially affected would change if such an action were undertaken. This is not, however, the only possible benefit estimation approach. An alternative procedure would be to obtain an estimate of the economic value of the consequences of a *similar* project or policy that had been implemented in a different location and then to *assume* that this existing estimate of economic value could be used (perhaps after some adjustment) as an approximation of the economic value of the proposed project or policy.

For example, suppose that a development project would result in the destruction of a certain number of hectares of wetlands, and an analyst wished to estimate the economic value of the environmental losses associated with this proposed project. Rather than attempt to undertake a new study at the site of the proposed development, the analyst could identify previous studies that had estimated the economic value of wetlands, and then assume that the loss of a hectare of wetland at the proposed development site would be the same as (or similar to) this previous estimate. Such an approach has been termed "benefit transfer" because the estimates of economic benefits are "transferred" from a site where a study has already been done to the site of policy interest. The site of the previous research has been called the "study site" (Desvousges et. al., [1992d]); for convenience we also call it site A. The site where the new benefit estimate is needed is termed the "policy site"; we call this site B. The benefits transferred from the study site could have been measured using either direct (e.g., contingent valuation) or indirect (e.g., travel cost or hedonic property value) valuation techniques.

More formally, suppose the willingness to pay (compensating variation) of household i for a change from an initial environmental quality Q_0 to an improved environmental quality Q_1 is given by
$$\text{WTPi} = f\ (Q_1 - Q_0,\ P_{own,i},\ P_{sub,i},\ SE_i) \qquad (10.1)$$
where
P_{own} price of using the environmental resource ("own price")
P_{sub} price of substitutes for use of the environmental resource
SE_i socioeconomic characteristics of household i

Benefit transfer requires three steps. First, the analyst must find (1) an existing study where this demand relationship has been estimated for the study site, and (2) values for Q_1, P_{own}, P_{sub}, and SE at the policy site. The second step is to determine the "extent of the market" at the policy site, i.e., the geographic area over which households will benefit from the change in environmental quality. Third, the analyst must substitute the values of the independent variables for the households (or classes of households) at the policy site into (10.1) to calculate the benefits to household i at the policy site. Then the analyst must aggregate these estimates for all households affected in order to obtain the aggregate benefits at the policy site.

It is not necessary that an analyst be restricted to the use of just one site A as the source of information to be transferred to a site B. Information could be obtained from several site A's and summarized for transfer to a site B. For instance, in the example above the analyst could take the average estimate of the value of a hectare of wetland from existing studies at study sites "similar" to the policy site. A more sophisticated approach would attempt to explain the determinants in the variation in estimates from existing study sites, and then use this model and values of the independent variables (the determinants of the variation) from the policy site to estimate the benefits (value) at the policy site. For example, a regional, multisite travel cost model which incorporates variations in the quality of different sites (A) could be used to estimate the benefits of recreation at a policy site B that is different from any of the study sites. (It is simply necessary that the quality of site B be some linear combination of the characteristics of the study sites.)

Benefit transfer methods can be thought of as a *historical approach* to the valuation problem because they make use of information analysts have learned from past experience about households' willingness to pay for goods and services. The term "benefit transfer" has arisen in the field of *nonmarket* valuation, but conceptually the approach of using values from one location in another context is actually a common practice in standard cost-benefit analysis when analysts must estimate shadow prices for goods traded in markets. It is not unusual, for example, to assume that demand elasticities for a good or service estimated with one set of data can be used to approximate the demand for the output of a specific project or policy.

Most of the existing applications of benefit transfer methods in nonmarket valuation have attempted to estimate the recreational benefits of new projects or opportunities. This focus on recreation benefits has been largely due to the demands of policy makers in the United States for such information; there is no reason benefit transfer methods cannot be more widely used to address other kinds of environmental valuation problems.

Advantages of a Benefit Transfer approach

There are two principal potential advantages of using a benefit transfer procedure for estimating the economic value of a policy, project, or regulation. The **first** is that an estimate of economic benefits can often be obtained more quickly by using a benefit transfer approach than by undertaking a new valuation study at the policy site. New valuation studies normally require primary data collection and often take several months (or even years) to complete. Benefit transfer methods hold out the hope that estimates of economic value can be obtained in much less time.

Second, a benefit transfer study will typically be less expensive to carry out. This is due both to the reduced time required by the analyst to conduct such a study and to the fact that primary data collection is not necessary. Both of these advantages are obviously appealing when government decision makers want answers quickly and cheaply. In practice, government agencies often do not have the patience (or financial resources) to sponsor the research efforts necessary for original valuation research specific to a particular problem.

There is a tendency on the part of academic researchers to bemoan the fact that a benefit transfer approach is "less than ideal," but in practice almost all valuation efforts are less than ideal in the sense that better estimates could be obtained if more time and money were made available. Analysts must constantly judge how to provide policy advice in a timely manner, subject to the resource constraints they face. If resource constraints are realistically considered, there are likely to be many cases in which benefit transfer methods can actually yield *better* estimates of economic values than can be obtained from studies specifically tailored to estimate the value of proposed changes at the policy site. This situation is most likely to arise when:
  (1) the study site is very similar to the policy site;
  (2) the policy change or project at the study site is very similar to that proposed at the policy site;
  (3) the valuation procedures used at the study site were analytically sound and carefully

conducted;

(4) time, financial resources, and (or) personnel available for analysis at the policy site are not sufficient to undertake a high-quality study.

Also, benefit transfer methods may be particularly useful in policy contexts where rough or crude estimates of economic benefits may be sufficient to make a judgment regarding the advisability of a policy or project. In this case a benefit transfer approach could be viewed as a "screening device" for reviewing projects. For example, an estimate of economic benefits from a benefit transfer application might indicate that the benefits from a project were many times greater than the costs: in this case more refined estimates of economic value would not be necessary.

Three approaches to Benefit Transfer

i) *Transferring mean unit values*

The easiest approach to transferring benefits from one site or location to another is to simply assume that the change in well-being experienced by an average person at the study site (A) is the same as that which will be experienced by the average individual at the policy site (B). For the past few decades such a procedure has often been used in the United States to estimate the recreational benefits associated with proposed multipurpose reservoir developments. The calculation requires three steps. **First**, the analyst must determine the kinds of recreational activities that would occur at the policy site (B) if the reservoir were built, and then forecast the levels of such activities (i.e., the number of person-days of fishing, picnicking, swimming, etc. that would occur at the reservoir). **Second**, the analyst must find a previously completed study that estimates the consumer surplus, or average willingness to pay, of individuals engaged in such recreational activities, or use available published estimates of such "unit values" (e.g., U.S. Water Resources Council, [1983]). **Third**, these unit values of a day spent by a person in a specific type of recreational activity in the study site (A) must be multiplied by the number of days of such activity forecast to occur at policy site B to obtain an estimate of the aggregate economic benefits from this recreational activity at site B.

Numerous summaries of such "unit values" have been compiled from previously completed research studies on recreation benefits in the United States. Table 10.1 presents a summary of unit values of days spent in various recreational activities obtained from 287 such studies (Walsh et. al., [1992]). These units values are the estimated amounts that individuals would be willing to pay over and above their current expenditures in order to ensure the continued availability of the resource for recreational use. Both travel cost models and the contingent valuation method were used to obtain these estimates.

As shown, the mean economic value (consumer surplus) of a recreational day, averaged across the various types of activities is about $34. The unit values for some activities are consistently much higher than for others. For example, the mean value of a day spent salt water fishing is $72; for anadromous species (e.g., trout, salmon) the mean value of a fishing day is $54. The value of a day spent sailing or canoeing ("boating, nonmotorized") is $49. On the other hand, the estimated value of a day spent in organized camps, cabins, or resorts is only $12.

Table 10.1 Net economic values per recreation day reported by TCM and CVM demand studies from 1968 to 1988, United States (third quarter 1987 dollars):

ACTIVITY	NUMBER OF ESTIMATES	MEAN	STANDARD ERROR OF THE MEAN	MEDIAN	95% CONFIDENCE INTERVAL	RANGE
Total	287	$33.95	$27.02	$1.67	$30.68-37.22	$3.91-219.65
Camping	18	19.50	18.92	2.03	15.52-23.48	8.26-34.89
Picnicking	7	17.33	12.82	5.08	7.37-27.29	7.05-46.69
Swimming	11	22.97	18.60	3.79	15.54-30.40	7.05-42.94
Sightseeing and off-road driving	6	20.29	19.72	3.73	12.98-27.60	10.33-31.84
Boating, Motorized	5	31.56	25.67	10.36	11.25-51.87	8.27-68.65
Boating, nonmotorized	11	48.68	25.36	15.85	17.61-79.75	10.26-183.36
Hiking	6	29.08	23.62	5.82	17.67 10.49	15.71-55.81
Wintersports	12	28.50	24.39	4.48	19.72-37.28	11.27 66.69
Resorts, cabins, and organized camps[a]	2	12.48				3.91-19.93
Big game hunting	56	45.47	37.87	3.47	38.67-52.27	19.81-142.40
Small game hunting	10	30.82	27.48	3.51	23.94-37.70	18.72-52.04
Migratory waterfowl hunting	17	35.64	25.27	5.87	24.13-47.15	16.58-102.88
Cold water fishing	39	30.62	28.49	3.24	24.27-36.97	10.07-118.12
Anadromous fishing[b]	9	54.01	46.24	11.01	32.43-75.59	16.85-127.26
Warm water fishing	23	23.55	22.50	2.46	18.73-28.87	8.13-59.42
Salt water fishing	17	72.49	53.35	14.05	44.95-100.03	18.69-219.65
Nonconsumptive fish and wildlife	14	22.20	20.49	2.30	17.69-26.71	5.27-38.06
Wilderness	15	24.58	19.26	6.10	12.62-36.54	8.72-106.26
Other recreation activities	9	18.82	16.06	3.65	11.67-25.97	6.81-43.39

[a] Resorts were 1.83% valued at $19.93 per day; seasonal and year-around cabins were 3.06% valued at $3.91 per day; and organized camps were 1.79% valued the same as camping.
[b] Anadromous fishing estimates included in cold water fishing. Estimated as roughly 5%.

SOURCE:

Walsh, R.G., D.M. Johnson, and J.R. McKean, [1992], "Benefit Transfer of Outdoor Recreation Demand Studies, 1968-1988", *Water Resources Research*, Vol. 28, No. 3, March, [Special Section: Problems and Issues in the Validity of Benefit Transfer Methodologies.]

To illustrate this benefit transfer procedure, suppose the following forecasts were available of the anticipated annual recreational use of a proposed reservoir and associated park:

1. Boating, motorized — - 5,000 days per year
2. Boating, nonmotorized — - 1,500 days per year
3. Camping — - 2,000 days per year
4. Picnicking — - 10,000 days per year
5. Swimming — - 3,000 days per year
6. Hiking — - 800 days per year

Using the mean unit values of these activities from Table 10.1, the total recreational benefits estimated using this simple "unit-value" benefit transfer procedure would be:

1. Boating, motorized -   5,000 days per year x $32 / day = $160,000
2. Boating, non motorized -   1,500 days per year x $49 / day = $73,500
3. Camping -   2,000 days per year x $20 / day = $40,000
4. Picnicking-   10,000 days per year x $17 / day = $170,000
5. Swimming-   3,000 days per year x $23 / day = $69,000
6. Hiking-   800 days per year   x $29 / day = $23,200

                                                         Total $535,700 per year

The obvious problem with this "unadjusted unit value" approach is that individuals in the policy site B may not value recreational activities at the proposed reservoir the same as the average individual at the study sites on which the unit values are based. There are two principal reasons why such differences might exist. **First**, people at the policy site B might be different than individuals at the study sites in terms of income, education, religion, ethnic group, or other socioeconomic characteristics that affect their demand for recreation. **Second**, even if individuals' preferences for recreation in the policy site and study sites are the same, the recreational opportunities may not be. For example, if individuals at the policy site (B) already have many other places nearby where they can go for water-based recreation activities, the economic value of the recreational opportunities at the proposed reservoir would be less than at study sites where fewer alternative opportunities exist.

ii) Transferring adjusted unit values

A more sophisticated benefit transfer approach would be to attempt to "adjust" a mean unit value for location A *before* transferring it to location B. Conceptually there are two different types of adjustments that can be made. **First**, the analyst may judge the unit value available from site A to be biased, or estimated inaccurately. In this case the unit value may need to be "adjusted" or "corrected" before it is transferred to site B.

Second, even if the unit value available from site A is judged to be "accurate" for the location where it was developed, it may need to be adjusted in order to better reflect conditions at the policy site. This second kind of adjustment should ideally address three potential differences between the study site and the policy site:
(1)   differences in the socioeconomic characteristics between households in the policy site and study site(s);
(2)   differences in the policy, project, or regulation at the policy site and the study site(s); and
(3)   differences in the availability of substitute goods and services at the policy site and study site(s);

In a recent study Walsh, Johnson, and McKean [1992] show one way such an adjustment in unit values can be made. They analyzed the determinants of variations in 287 separate estimates of mean unit values obtained from 120 studies of recreational benefits--based on both the travel cost method (TCM) and the contingent valuation method (CVM). They found that variations in mean unit values in the different studies could be partly explained by several types of independent variables: (1) quality of the sites, (2) benefit estimation technique used (either contingent valuation or travel cost method), and (3) type of recreational activity, and (4) region of the United States where the study was conducted.

The two variables with the largest effects on unit values in their analysis were (1) a qualitative variable which indicated whether the site where the recreation occurred was of very high quality (in the top 15% of all sites in the sample studies), and (2) whether the recreation activity was salt water fishing, anadromous fishing, or big game hunting. For example, the mean unit value of a recreation day at a site of "low" or "average" quality estimated with the travel cost model was about $33; if the site was of "very high" quality, the unit value increased to $72. If the recreational activity was salt water or anadromous fishing, the mean unit value increased by about $43.

Recreational activities in the southern region of the United States were less valuable than in other parts of the country. The authors interpret this regional variable as a proxy for socioeconomic characteristics of the population. Residents of the southern United States have lower average incomes than elsewhere, and thus lower willingness to pay for recreational activities. In general the CVM estimates were 20-25% *lower* than estimates from the TCM. For the travel cost models, if the travel time cost was omitted from the model specification, the unit value estimate was about 40% lower. Household surveys yielded higher estimates of unit values than on-site surveys.

Their regression equations explaining variations in unit values of recreation activity could be used in the following manner to estimate the unit value at a policy site (B). Suppose a unit value was desired for a policy site. The analyst would collect data on the values of the independent variables in the model that described the policy site, such as the region of the country, the quality of the site, and the type of recreational activity to be valued. Values of independent variables that described the estimation method, model specification, or type of data could be set by the analyst to reflect his or her judgments with respect to the best available practices or procedures. Values of other independent variables could be set at their mean values for the study site(s). With these data and assumptions for the independent variables, the analyst can use the regression equation to calculate an adjusted unit value for a recreation day. Once this adjustment in unit values for the policy site is made, the rest of the benefit transfer procedure is the same as in the unadjusted, unit value calculation described above.

In a similar type of study, Smith and Kaoru [1990] also analyzed the variations in recreation benefit estimates in 77 studies conducted using the travel cost method. They examined how variables describing site characteristics, the recreation activities undertaken at each site, behavioural assumptions, and modelling specifications affected estimates of consumer surplus per unit from the different studies. As in the Walsh et. al. study, Smith and Kaoru found that some of the variation in benefit estimates can be explained by variables suggested by consumer demand theory. For example, benefit estimates were clearly higher for recreation experiences at unique, high quality national parks than for recreation at more developed or state parks.

However, other aspects of Smith and Kaoru's findings should give analysts using benefit transfer methods considerable pause. They found a systematic relationship between the benefit estimates and the features of the empirical models used. In other words, the estimates of consumer surplus per unit (either per person-day or per person-trip) obtained were quite sensitive to such modelling strategies as the choice of functional form of the demand equation, how the analyst treated the opportunity cost of travel time in the demand equation, how the price of substitute sites was handled (if at all), and the estimation method. For example, their model suggests that the assumption made regarding the opportunity cost of travel time (as a portion of average wage rate) could lead to as much as a 50%

difference in consumer surplus per unit. Benefit transfer applications that fail to pay close attention to the appropriateness of both modelling strategies and the judgments and assumptions made by the analyst in the course of the empirical work may be subject to considerable variability. Indeed, Smith and Kaoru caution against using their type of model for benefit transfers in actual policy applications.

iii) Transferring the demand function

Instead of transferring adjusted or unadjusted unit values, the analyst could transfer the entire demand function estimated at a study site(s) to the policy site. Such an approach is conceptually more appealing because more information is effectively transferred. The demand relationship to be transferred from the study site(s) to the policy site could again be estimated using either direct or indirect approaches. For example, for a zonal travel cost model, the demand function might be of the form (Loomis, [1992]) :

$$X_{ij}/POP_i = b_0 - b_1 C_{ij} + b_2 \, Time_{ij} + b_3 \, Psub_{ik} + b_4 \, I_i + b_5 \, Q_j \qquad (10.2)$$
where
X_{ij} number of trips from origin i to site j
POP_i population of origin i
C_{ij} travel costs from origin i to site j
$Psub_{ik}$ a measure of the cost and quality of substitute site k to people in origin i
I_i average income in origin i
Q_j quality of site j for recreational uses.

To implement the third benefit transfer approach using this zonal travel cost model, the analyst would find a study in the existing literature with estimates of the parameters b_0, b_1, b_2, b_3, b_4, and b_5. Then the analyst would collect data on (1) population of zones "around" the policy site j, (2) travel costs from these zones to the policy site, (3) the cost and quality of the alternative recreational sites available to people living in the zones designated to be around the policy site, (4) the average income of people in these zones, and (5) a measure of the quality of the policy site for recreational uses. The values of these independent variables from the policy site and the estimates of b_0, b_1, b_2, b_3, b_4, and b_5 from the study site would be replaced in the travel cost model (10.2), and this new equation could then be used to estimate both the number of trips from the designated zones to the policy site and the average household willingness to pay for a visit to the policy site (see Cicchetti, Fisher, and Smith, [1976], for an early example). Using this zonal travel cost model, an analyst can take account of both the size and spatial distribution of the population around the policy site in a straightforward manner. Data on population and distance from governmental units (e.g., counties) or census tracts are usually readily available.

There are several reasons to expect that transferring the demand (or benefit) function would be more accurate than transferring a mean unit value (Loomis, [1992]). **First**, because the total benefits depend upon both the benefit per unit (e.g., per visit or per user-day) and the level of use (e.g., the total number of visits or visitor-days), it is important that the assumptions underlying unit value and usage be consistent. When benefit transfers are based on average unit values, it is easy for the underlying assumptions and data for value and use to be different. Transferring the demand function ensures that the estimate of total benefits is based on estimates of use and value derived from the same data set.

Second, even if households in the study and policy sites have similar preferences and the project or policy change in the two locations is very similar, the total benefits at the policy site may be affected by the *distribution* of population around the policy site. Thus, even if the average unit values are the same at the study and policy sites, the implementation of a benefit transfer approach based on unit values may yield a different estimate of total benefits than an approach based on transferring the entire demand function because the latter can take account of the socioeconomic characteristics of the population in different zones or living different distances from the policy site.

Loomis [1992] investigated the magnitude of the difference between estimates of recreation benefits at 10 rivers in Oregon, United States, obtained by transferring a demand function and by transferring a unit value for a trip to the river. All ten rivers were used for fishing for steelhead trout. He first estimated a multisite travel cost model (see Chapter 8) that included all ten rivers as possible destinations. He then deleted one of the rivers and re-estimated the model for the remaining nine rivers. Loomis used this estimate of the demand function from the nine rivers to calculate the benefits of a trip to the river left out of the nine-river model. This procedure was carried out ten times so that each of the ten rivers was deleted from the multisite model once. The results of Loomis's calculations are presented in Table 10.2.

The average per-trip benefit for all of the 10 rivers based on the full, ten-river, multisite model was $66.42. Given that all of these ten rivers were in the same state and used for the same type of recreational activity, one could hardly imagine a more advantageous situation for the application of the average unit value approach. However, if we assume that the "correct" value of a trip to a specific river is given by the estimate for that river from the full, 10-river model, Loomis's results suggest that transferring the demand equation from a nine-river model to the river of interest is a better benefit transfer procedure.

The last two columns in Table 10.2, for each of the ten rivers, show the percentage difference between the estimate of the value of a trip to the river based on the full, ten-river model and (1) the estimate from the nine-river model, and (2) the average value at the ten rivers (based on the full, ten-river model). The estimate obtained by transferring the nine-river model is closer than the average value in seven of the ten cases. In several cases the differences were surprisingly large. For example, for the Coquille River, the "best estimate" of the value of a trip from the ten-river model was $47.76. The estimate for the Coquille obtained by transferring the nine-river model (that omitted the Coquille River) was $48.21 per trip--about a 1% difference. The ten-river average value of $66.42 per trip was 39% higher. Loomis concluded that transferring the fishing demand equation from a multisite model within a very homogenous region yielded differences in total recreation benefits in the range of 5-15%. However, using an average unit-value benefit approach resulted in percentage differences of 5-40%.

Difficulties with the implementation of Benefit Transfer methods

i)   Availability and quality of existing studies

Benefit transfer methods require existing, high-quality studies that can be "transferred" to a policy site. In many areas of likely application the stock of available literature is limited, particularly in developing countries. Even when high-quality studies exist, they are often inaccessible or poorly documented for use in benefit transfer applications[16]. In the long run the successful and widespread use of benefit transfer methods requires a well-documented, easily accessible library of high-quality valuation studies. Academic journals serve this purpose to a limited extent, but many details of valuation studies important for benefit transfer are often not discussed in journal articles. Also, analysts may need the original data sets in order to correct errors in existing work or to do further analysis in order to obtain more appropriate demand equations for a benefit transfer exercise (OECD, [1992]).

Boyle and Bergstrom [1992] have thus suggested the establishment of a "nonmarket valuation library". The long-run cost savings from such a library are likely to be large, particularly as serious environmental valuation efforts become part of standard project appraisal and policy analysis procedures in developing countries. An analyst working in a developing country will have great difficulty in accessing the applications of valuation techniques to similar problems *in other developing countries*. The establishment of a library of existing valuation studies and documented data sets should be the responsibility of the likely users of such information. In the international field the multilateral development agencies such as the World Bank and the Organization for Economic Cooperation and Development would be logical candidates to house such a library of valuation studies.

ii) Valuation of new policies or projects

Benefit transfer methods can only be used to value the outcomes of projects, policies, or regulations that have already been implemented elsewhere. They are of little use in estimating the value of innovative or new policies that have not been tried before. This is simply because in such cases there are no study sites from which to transfer information.

Benefit transfer methods must be used with caution when the expected change resulting from a policy is outside the range of previous experience. For example, suppose a policy was under consideration to impose regulations to improve air quality that were more stringent than any that had previously existed. Even if there were existing studies that indicated the value of air quality improvements from past regulatory efforts, it might not be justified to extrapolate these findings to the air quality improvement under consideration. This is because the relationship between air quality and benefits is likely to be nonlinear. Also, ex-ante preferences for goods and services with which individuals are not familiar may not be the same as ex-post preferences (see Chapter 3).

iii) Differences in the study site(s) and policy site

Any of the benefit transfer approaches could be invalid if there are significant differences between the study site(s) and the policy site that are not accounted for and these differences affect households' preferences for the policy change. When using the unit-value approach to benefit transfer, the analyst attempts to control for differences between the study site(s) and policy site by selecting sites that are "very similar". Because the stock of existing benefit studies is limited, this approach is not always possible. Both the adjusted unit-value, and the demand function approaches to benefit transfer can explicitly account for some differences between the study and policy sites (such as household income, quality of the environmental resource, and price of using the resource). However, the study site(s) and policy site may differ in other ways that render benefit transfer problematic or impossible. For example, there may be unique cultural or religious factors at the policy site that do not exist at any of the study sites, even though the locations are similar in other respects.

Table 10.2 In-state transfer of multisite TCM demand equation

River	Full Model	Transferred n-1 River Model	% Difference Between Models	% Difference From Average Benefits
Alsea				
Total benefits	$419.705	$404,871	-3.53	
Per-trip benefits	$56.49	$58.87	-4.21	-17.58
Clackamas				
Total benefits	$2,767,452	$2,884,168	4.22	
Per-trip benefits	$58.63	$60.06	-2.43	-13.29
Coquille				
Total benefits	$242,226	$223,884	-7.57	
Per-trip benefits	$47.76	$48.21	-0.93	-39.07
Deschutes				
Total benefits	$2,023,773	$1,914,721	-5.39	
Per-trip benefits	$88.66	$87.66	1.14	25.08
Hood				
Total benefits	$952,126	$1,049,273	10.20	
Per-trip benefits	$48.54	$45.95	5.35	-36.83
John Day				
Total benefits	$243,043	$203.339	-16.34	
Per-trip benefits	$89.19	$86.33	3.21	25.53
Rogue				
Total benefits	$2,865,059	$3,366,678	17.51	
Per-trip benefits	$64.17	$70.11	-9.27	-3.51
Siletz				
Total benefits	$1,989,578	$2,282,046	14.70	
Per-trip benefits	$85.76	$90.08	-5.04	22.54
Umpqua				
Total benefits	$2.434,101	$2,294,523	-5.73	
Per-trip benefits	$64.13	$68.81	-7.31	-3.58
Wilson				
Total benefits	$2,707,982	$2,522,463	-6.85	
Per-trip benefits	$60.90	$50.20	17.58	-9.07
10-river average	$66.42			

SOURCE:

Loomis, J. B., [1992], "The Evolution of a More Rigorous Approach to Benefit Transfer: Benefit Transfer Function", *Water Resources Research*, Vol. 28, No. 3, March.
[Special Section: Problems and Issues in the Validity of Benefit Transfer Methodologies.]

iv) Determination of the "extent of the market"

Conceptually, the determination of the area around the policy site in which households are affected by the change in the policy under consideration (i.e., the extent of the market) should be an empirical question. For example, if a new recreational site is to be constructed, it may be of no value to any households farther than 100 kilometres away. In this case the extent of the market would be a range from 0 to 100 kilometres from the policy site. Alternatively, a few people may travel from all over the world to reach some unique wildlife reserves or archaeological ruins. For such policy sites the extent of the market is global.

The determination of the extent of the market may, however, depend in large measure on an analyst's judgment. Some demand models offer evidence of how far people will travel to a new recreation site, or the probability that a household in a given location would travel to a new site, but rather arbitrary assumptions are often made about the shape of such distributions as one gets farther and farther from the policy site. In practice, the analyst must often make an educated guess as to whom will be affected by the proposed policy change or how far the effects of the policy will reach. There has not yet been much scrutiny of how such judgments are made. Smith [1992] has shown that estimates of aggregate benefits can be quite sensitive to analysts' assumptions about the extent of the market.

Conclusions

The use of benefit transfers in policy applications involving nonmarket goods and services is still in its infancy. To date there has only been one legal proceeding in the United States in which contingent valuation estimates from one study were used to estimate values at another location, and in this case the court refused to accept the "transferred values" as legitimate evidence (State of Idaho versus Southern Refrigerated Transport, Inc., cited in Brookshire and Neill, [1992]). This lack of support from the legal system is, however, likely to change as research accumulates on the accuracy and reliability of various benefit transfer approaches. As the demand for valuation studies increases, benefit transfers will become much more common in both industrialized and developing countries.

Because the application of benefit transfer methods to the valuation of nonmarket goods is relatively new, procedures for dealing with questions and problems common to most studies have not been standardized. This is in part because much of the existing literature is unpublished and difficult to access, and thus it has been difficult for analysts using benefit transfer techniques to learn from the work and innovations of others. Smith [1992] has called for the development of a standard protocol or guidelines for conducting benefit transfer studies. Such a protocol would describe the issues to be considered in determining the extent of the market, choosing study site(s), judging the quality of existing empirical work, using demand models to develop aggregate benefit estimates, and balancing the risks of making different types of errors. It would also offer guidance on how such tasks should best be accomplished.

Such protocols are needed for applications of benefit transfer methods to a wide variety of environmental valuation problems. However, it is unlikely that a single protocol will be useful for a wide range of applications. Because most of the existing benefit transfer studies have focused on recreation benefits from new projects or environmental quality improvements, there has been a tendency for researchers in the benefit transfer field to restrict their attention to these issues. Since experience in the use of benefit transfer methods to value other environmental goods and services is extremely limited, researchers attempting to apply benefit transfer methods to new problems will naturally look for guidance and insight from the existing work on recreation benefits. But the potential usefulness of benefit transfer techniques extends far beyond the valuation of recreation benefits.

Acknowledgments

This chapter draws heavily on the insights of the authors of a special issue of *Water Resources Research* on benefit transfer methods. We would like especially to acknowledge the work of V. Kerry Smith, David Brookshire, Ted McConnell, William Desvousges, and John Loomis.

Chapter 11

National Accounts and the Environment

Chapter 2 investigated environmental information systems. It was shown there that environmental information can be fully integrated into economic information systems at a national level through a set of monetised national income accounts. National accountants are not wholly agreed on the right way in which to adjust national income account for the monetised value of environmental changes. We set out below one logically consistent approach.

Natural resources may be thought of as part of the **capital stock** of a nation or the world as a whole. In this way, the natural world can be seen as part of the productive capacity of an economy. Any diminution of this base, in the absence of technological improvements, obviously leads to a loss in productive capacity. Yet, the current system of economic national accounts fails, in almost all cases, to treat natural assets in this way. Because of this, major efforts are under way to adjust the system of national accounts (SNA) to reflect better the natural capital assets in an economy and their flows of economic services. One obvious adjustment is to the treatment of mineral resources. More interestingly, the basic framework involved can be extended to other forms of natural capital and perhaps even more ambitiously, to the natural world in its widest sense.

National accounts classify the transactions of an economy in a systematic manner. In this way, information concerning the economic activity within the sphere of an economic system is captured by the accounting framework. The extent of this framework will be determined by the relevant questions that society wishes to ask and by the particular institutional structure, in addition to practical limitations. Any framework should hence be amenable to change in the light of changes in these questions. Policy makers have tended to base decisions on two aggregate flows - **Gross Domestic Product** (GDP) and **Gross National Product** (GNP)[17]. With the emergence of **sustainability** as an increasingly important issue in the management of economies and of the world economy, emphasis has shifted to net concepts - **Net Domestic Product** (NDP) and **Net National Product** (NNP). The various definitions of these will be outlined below.

This shift from gross to net concepts is a result of interest in national product after the netting out of "capital" used up in the production of final output in the accounting period. Conventionally defined capital constitutes such fixed assets as machinery, buildings and roads (referred to here as **reproducible capital** or **man-made capital**. The challenge that has now been taken up is to expand this definition of capital - to take a more comprehensive view of what constitutes the productive base of the economy. A corollary of this is, how much of this base is used up in production processes?

First, we illustrate the current treatment of reproducible capital in national accounts. GNP can be defined as the sum of consumption (C) and investment (I) to yield the identity:

$$GNP = C + I \qquad (11.1)$$

But this identity involves some double-counting since it includes both capital and the goods produced by it during the course of its productive life. Some capital will inevitably be used up in the process of production in any accounting year. In the case of reproducible capital this takes the form of wear

183

and tear etc. This must be subtracted from GNP to arrive at NNP (defined as **capital consumption** in the United Nations System of National Accounts).

Broadly, capital constitutes any asset capable of yielding a flow of services over time. As such, the concept of capital goes much wider than the emphasis on reproducible capital (important though it remains). This is exactly what the extension of analysis into the productive capacity of the natural world sets out to achieve.

While it remains the case that there exists no one underlying model for measuring the flows of natural capital, significant consensus has been achieved to this end, as shown by the progress made in the construction of SNA satellite accounts by United Nations Statistical Office (UNSO).

Recall that an alternative measure to GNP was NNP which conventionally measured is,

$$NNP = GNP - dK \qquad\qquad (11.2)$$

where dK represents deterioration (d) of the reproducible capital stock (K), (we do not consider valuation of this depreciation here). What we require is an expanded definition of this NNP that encompasses concerns with respect to the use of the natural world in economic processes. Economic theory can provide some answers as to how these magnitudes are to be netted out (Hartwick, 1990). Firstly, it is convenient to distinguish three components of the stock of natural capital:
  (i)   **Non-renewable resources**, comprising of the stock of mineral assets and fossil fuels;
  (ii)   **Renewable resources**, such as forests, fisheries and soil;
  (iii)   **Environmental capital**, such as airsheds and watersheds.

We deal with each in turn.

  (i)   **Nonrenewables**: here it can be shown that,

$$NNP = GNP - dK - [P-MC].[N-D] \qquad\qquad (11.3)$$

where P is the market price of resource, say oil, MC is the marginal cost of its extraction (i.e., the cost of extracting <u>one additional unit</u> of that resource), N is output and D is new discoveries. Note the importance of incorporating discoveries in a context where **rent** (shown here as P - MC) is a measure of resource scarcity: any positive level of D in an accounting period decreases what should be netted out in the absence of such discoveries.

(ii) **Renewables** are treated in a similar fashion, but the allowance to be subtracted is for **any overuse of this resource** -i.e. a rate of harvest over the rate of growth. This can be represented as:

$$NNP = GNP - dK + [P-MC].[g(R)-R] \qquad\qquad (11.4)$$

where g(R) is the growth of the renewable resource (which, in the case of forestry, say, can be thought of as the mean annual increment) and R the rate of harvest. This makes the implications of over-use clear - i.e where g(R) < R there is clearly the potential for resource exhaustion or extinction.

(iii) **Environmental Capital**: the relevant flows here are pollution abatement expenditure (E) and pollution damage (X). Then:

$$NNP = GNP - dK - [P - MC].[E - X] \qquad\qquad (11.5)$$

In practice, monetary valuation is often difficult. In particular, marginal cost information is largely unavailable, so that empirical studies have typically used data on average costs (AC) as a proxy (see for example, Repetto [1989]). This will only be consistent with the above where MC = AC. In practice we will often expect MC > AC. Hence the true economic rent (that portion of receipts to be reinvested) is overstated and true NNP will therefore be understated.

So far we have been concerned with flows (i.e., GNP, NNP, rates of loss of biodiversity, deforestation etc.). Concentration on this has been to the neglect of stocks presented in the balance sheets of national accounts. Balance sheets can be in either physical or monetary form. They present an opening stock (V_0) at the beginning of period 1 and the closing stock (V_1) at the end of the period. Crudely then, it can be seen that the difference, $V_1 - V_0$, is the corresponding flow that links opening and closing stocks. This is the link to satellite accounting. Some adjustments have to be made to this such as for volume changes (discoveries, damage, etc.) and revaluation at closing period prices to take account of price fluctuations during the period. For any assets, if either balance sheets (or flow accounts) are to be undertaken on a regular (yearly) basis, prices and quantities need to re-estimated in each period. This may place a burden on data collection.

PART IV

RISK AND TIME

Chapter 12

Discounting and Time

Introduction

Chapter 3 established that projects, programmes and policies can be evaluated, from the standpoint of the individual, according to the impact they have on that individual's **well-being**. Changes in individual well-being are measured by the individual's **willingness to pay** (WTP) to secure the benefit in question (or to forgo a cost), or the individual's **willingness to accept** compensation (WTA) to forgo the benefit (or accept a cost).

Chapter 3 set out the conditions under which it is legitimate to aggregate individual preferences, expressed through WTP and WTA, so as to secure a **social decision rule**.

The basic value judgement at both the individual and aggregate (social) level is that individual preferences should count. This value judgement affects resource allocation in various ways:

(a) using WTP and WTA to measure economic value means that resources are allocated to the production of those goods and services which maximise aggregate economic value;

(b) since WTP and WTA are affected by income levels (see Chapter 3), use of these measures of value will allocate goods to people in proportion to their purchasing power. Whether this is desirable or not depends on the view taken about the distribution of income and wealth before and after the project;

(c) since individuals have preferences for <u>when in time</u> benefits and costs occur, the use of WTP and WTA will also determine the **intertemporal allocation** of goods and resources.

This chapter is concerned with the way in which preferences affect intertemporal allocation. Once the value judgement that "preferences count" is accepted, it appears logical to accept its implications for the intertemporal allocation of resources. Since individuals are typically impatient - they prefer benefits now rather than later, and costs later rather than now - the result of extending the basic value judgement to the timing of resource allocation is that **discounting** will be justified. Discounting means that costs and benefits are given lower weights the further into the future they occur.

However, there is at least one important way in which the basic value judgement that preferences count comes into conflict with other value judgements once time is introduced. The issue centres round **whose preferences** are to count. Generations to come appear to have no power to influence resource allocation decisions made now but the consequences of which may be borne by those future generations. They have no apparent vote. Using the "preferences count" value judgement, then, may conflict with the interests of future generations. Just as intratemporal resource allocation based on WTP and WTA may conflict with some notion of **social justice**, so intertemporal resource allocation based on WTP and WTA may conflict with some notion of **intergenerational justice.** In both cases there can be a dispute about the moral superiority of conflicting value judgements (Box 12.1).

Another way of stating this issue is that societies typically have **multiple objectives** when taking decisions about the allocation of resources. Those objectives include **economic efficiency** and **intratemporal equity**. In recent years a great deal of attention has also been given to **intertemporal equity**, i.e., the distribution of resources through time. These three objectives may well conflict: achieving one may mean sacrificing an element of the other. The nature of the trade-off between these multiple objectives will vary from country to country, but it is likely to be especially marked between rich and poor countries. In rich countries there is likely to be a more marked concern for the nature of the intertemporal allocations than in poor countries where the focus is likely to be more on the immediate needs of the poor. To this extent, concern for the "sustainability" of development might attract a lower weight in poor countries than in rich countries. Since discounting appears to conflict with sustainability, we might expect a social discount rate to be higher in poor countries than in rich countries. However, sustainability must not be thought of as a luxury: something that can only be afforded when people are better off. Sustainability remains an important consideration in the developing world since, without it, the benefits of aid flows and domestic investments will be short-lived and the chance for development to "take off" will be missed. The choice of discount rate thus remains problematic in all economies, rich and poor.

In many contexts, the individual responsible for appraising projects and policies will not have to estimate a social discount rate. It will be "given" as a standard number, usually with a range of variation to allow for sensitivity analysis. In such circumstances the details of this chapter will not be an issue of concern. However, because the social desirability of a project or policy often is sensitive to the choice of discount rate it is important to have some idea of the arguments that can influence the use of one rate rather than another.

The basic analytics of discounting

Accepting the basic value judgement that justifies discounting means that any benefit (B) or cost (C) should be given a lower weight the further it is into the future. This means that we cannot simply add benefits and costs as they accrue over time. Chapter 3 showed that we have to obtain some <u>weighted sum</u> :

$$w_t.(B_t - C_t)$$

where the weight in any period can be written:

$$w_t = 1/(1 + r)^t$$

r is then the **discount rate** and the whole expression above is the **discount factor**.

There are varying views about how r is to be determined. These may be conveniently discussed in the following categories:

(a)   **social rate of time preference, or consumption rate of interest**
(b)   **the accounting rate of interest**
(c)   **the consumer discount rate**
(d)   **the producer discount rate**
(e)   **"synthetic" rates.**

The social rate of time preference

There are two concepts that may be subject to discounting:
(a) future **consumption** may be discounted because of some judgement that it will generate less "well-being" (or utility) than current consumption. This is **consumption discounting**;
(b) future **well-being or utility** may be discounted because people simply prefer their

pleasures (benefits) now and their costs later.

It can be shown that a **social time preference rate** can be derived which incorporates both elements of discounting with the result that (Markandya and Pearce [1988], see Annex 8):

$$s = p + u.g \qquad\qquad [12.1]$$

where   s = social time preference rate of discount;
             p = "pure time preference", i.e the rate at which <u>utility</u> is discounted;
             u = elasticity of the marginal utility of consumption schedule, i.e., the rate at which marginal utility declines as consumption increases;
             g = the expected growth rate of consumption per capita in the economy.

s is also frequently referred to as the **consumption rate of interest** (CRI). Strictly, the CRI is the rate at which <u>individuals</u> discount the future, whereas the social time preference rate (STPR), which has the same formula, is the rate at which <u>society</u> discounts future consumption. The difference between CRI and STPR is that social valuations need not be the same as individuals' valuations. If they are, then STPR = CRI. Note that the CRI or STPR combines consumption discounting and utility discounting (pure time preference). Many analysts have judged utility discounting to be illicit because it is based solely upon "impatience" which itself may be inconsistent with maximising lifetime well-being for an individual. If so, then, p in equation [12.1] is zero. Jevons, Bohm-Bawerk and Pigou all considered pure time discounting to be irrational and myopic.

To estimate the CRI including pure time preference requires estimates of p, u and g.

Estimates of p tend to be arbitrary. Ray [1984] reports "common practice" of adding 2-5% for pure time preference. Highly growth - oriented countries could legitimately argue that p is very low, perhaps zero, since the higher is p the less is growth favoured. A study of the UK (Scott [1977]) suggested a p of 0.5%, which was then increased to 1.5% to reflect the risk of "total destruction of society". Others have suggested that the threat of extinction is the only rationale for positive pure time preference. Following earlier work by Eckstein, Kula estimated pure time preference rates for several countries based on risks of mortality. For consumption one year ahead, the time preference rate is the probability of not surviving that year. For longer periods it is the geometric average of annual mortality rates. Using this approach for Trinidad and Tobago, Kula [1986] found pure time preference rates of 1.1-1.9% for the period 1946-1975; a similar study (Kula [1987]) suggests rates of 1.2% for the UK and 1% for Canada and for the USA.

Values of u, the elasticity of the marginal utility of consumption, have also been estimated, although they are the subject of controversy. Stern [1977] uses the British tax system to identify government attitudes to redistribution. He derived a value of u = 2 on this basis. Scott [1977] suggests a value of u = 1.5 for the UK.

Box 12.2 illustrates some results for various regions of the world using past rates of consumption growth as a guide to expected growth rates, together with differing assumptions about the value of u.

The accounting rate of interest

The accounting rate of interest measures the rate at which the value of "public income" - in the developing country context this is effectively foreign exchange (see Chapter 5) - declines over time. While the actual formula for estimating ARI can quickly become complex, a convenient approximation is given by:

$$ARI = m.q + (1 - m)s \qquad\qquad [12.2]$$

(See Markandya and Pearce [1988].) This equation holds provided the values of m are small. Equation [12.2] says that the ARI is a weighted average of the marginal product of capital in the public sector (q) and the CRI, with the weights being the proportions of marginal public income that is reinvested (m) and consumed (1-m).

To obtain estimates of m it is necessary to look at past data on government expenditure. If the proportion of government investment expenditure is available separately, then a regression of this on total government expenditure should enable an estimate to be made of the extra investment expenditure from a given increment in government expenditure (basically, this would be the coefficient x in the regression $M = a + xE$, where M is investment expenditure and E is total government expenditure). As examples, m was found to be 0.52 for Pakistan for 1972-78, and 0.27 for 1978-1984 in two separate studies.

To obtain values of q, various approaches are possible. Those that have been used are:

(a) the rate at which a country borrows abroad. The argument here is that this is the relevant rate because a country can always use its funds to retire foreign borrowings. If capital is truly this "fungible", then the argument is valid. Often it is not this fungible in developing economies;

(b) the rate of return to private and public sector investments, including equity and debt. Thus, if the rate of return to debt is d% and the return to equity is e%, then q might be approximated by:
$$q = w_1.d\% + w_2.e\%$$
where w_1 and w_2 are the proportions of debt and equity in the financing of government projects. The result must be converted to investment units by adjusting for the shadow exchange rate and the shadow wage rate;

(c) a macroeconomic approach based on the formula:
$$q = [dQ/dK - dQ/dL.dL/dK]. SPP/KCF \qquad [12.3]$$
where

dQ/dK is the incremental output-capital ratio, which in turn is the inverse of the more familiar incremental capital-output ratio (ICOR) and can be estimated from national accounting data;

dQ/dL is the marginal product of labour, in turn often approximated by the average product of labour which may be estimated by dividing the wage bill by employment;

dL/dK is the marginal labour-capital ratio, which can be measured as dQ/dK (above) divided by the average productivity of labour (which in turn approximates dQ/dL), i.e., $(dQ/dK)/(dQ/dL) = dL/dK$;

SPP is the shadow price of net income and is approximated by $(1+z)SCF - zSWR$ where z is the average employment cost divided by value added in the economy, SCF is the standard conversion factor, and SWR is the shadow wage rate;

KCF is the capital conversion factor, and is estimated as for the CCF but for capital goods only.

Clearly, if microeconomic evidence is available on the size of q, estimating the ARI need not be too complex. Use of the macroeconomic approach may often be unavoidable if the only reliable data are those for national accounts, e.g. where banking and financial institutions are not developed.

The consumer discount rate

The consumer discount rate is simply the rate at which consumers can lend and borrow in the market place. Provided capital markets are perfect, this rate will give rise to a **discount factor** equal to the **consumer's marginal rate of substitution** between income in different time periods, i.e., the income they require in the future to compensate for surrendering a unit of income today. That is, the discount factor is $1/(1+i)$ where i is the consumer discount rate.

Estimating i from market data is not straightforward. One approach is to look at the real rate of return on government bonds which, by their nature, are risk free in the developed country context. Technically, it is the after-tax return that needs to be computed. In the United Kingdom such rates have probably been in the range of 2-3%. Such a rate is likely to be a lower limit since not all individuals are net savers. Some are borrowers and at high rates of interest.

Clearly, the consumer discount rate is akin to the CRI when the CRI is construed to reflect individuals' time preference rather than some "social" perspective.

The producer discount rate

The producer discount rate, r, gives rise to a **discount factor** that is formally equal to the **producer's marginal rate of transformation**. This rate of transformation is the inverse of the marginal rate of capital productivity. Thus, if an input of $1 today yields r% tomorrow, the marginal rate of transformation is $1/(1+r)$. In this case, r is similar to q in the previous discussion, i.e., it is the marginal product of capital. However, cost-benefit appraisals often relate to public sector investments and public decision-making. The value of r could then be the marginal product of capital in the public sector, but it is more typically the marginal rate of return in the **private sector**. The rationale for using a private sector rate of return to discount public sector costs and benefits is that public investment is likely to be at the expense of the quantity of investment in the private sector. This usually reflects a judgement about the effects of "crowding out" private sector investments. r is then the **marginal opportunity cost** of investing in the public sector.

How might r be estimated ? The discussion on estimating q in the formula for the ARI (above) is relevant here since r is effectively the private sector interpretation of q which, it will be recalled, is the public sector marginal rate of return. The value of r might thus be estimated as the weighted average of returns to debt and equity in the private sector. Debt could be represented by government bonds where relevant, or by interest rates on bank loans and advances. Rates of return in the private sector will be higher than the public sector due to the fact that the private sector has to pay tax. Thus, to pay i% to shareholders, the private sector must earn $i(1-t)\% = r\%$ where t is the tax rate. This "tax wedge" puts private rates of return above the rate of return to government bonds. In the United Kingdom, for example, it is suggested that the difference is between 3-4% on government borrowing and 4-6% for the marginal rate of return in the private sector.

As a general rule, then, r can be approximated by the weighted average of the returns to equity and the returns to debt. The former can be calculated by looking at the historical evidence on dividend yields and adding capital growth to it. This might then be adjusted for any judgemental change in expected yields and capital growth. The return to debt can be obtained by looking at government bonds ("gilts") or bank loan interest rates.

Synthetic discount rates

Synthetic discount rates seek to obtain social discount rates by using both the social time preference rate and the marginal opportunity cost rate based on private sector rates of return. The ARI discussed above is a form of synthetic discount rate based on the proportions of benefit that are consumed and reinvested. A very general form of the synthetic discount rate is given by Harberger [1976] as:

$$w = h_1.s + h_2.r$$

where h_1 and h_2 are the fractions of government expenditure displacing private investment and private consumption. Very approximate measures of h_1 and h_2 are the shares of investment and consumption in the national income. Such approximations might be used if there is limited data to estimate the marginal displacement effects of public expenditure.

Some conclusions on choosing discount rates

Even without considering environmental issues, it is evident that the choice of social discount rate is problematic. The general candidates appear to be:

The Consumption Rate of Interest.
The Accounting Rate of Interest.
The marginal rate of return to private sector investment.
Some synthetic rate, reflecting both the CRI and the marginal rate of return on private sector investment.

The chart below summarises the outcomes.

CRI = s = p + u.g	s = u.g if disregard p u is strictly non-observable
ARI = m.q + (1 - m)s	if m = 1 (i.e., all benefits are reinvested) then ARI=q q is public sector return
SDR1 = r	r is private sector return
SDR2 = h1.s + h2.r	h1 and h2 are coefficients of displacement of private consumption and investment

To illustrate. In the United Kingdom, ignoring "pure" time preference and selecting a value of u = 1 gives a CRI of 2.6%. The value of r is probably some 7%. The share of investment in the national income is 0.18 and the share of consumption is 0.82. The value of SDR2 is therefore some 3.4%. If the real long term government borrowing rate is used to estimate consumer discount rates then a rate of 3-4% would emerge. All this suggests that rates of discount might range from 2.6% to 7%. This is a wide range, and the different rates would have different implications for the environmental impacts of projects and policies the issue to which we turn very shortly.

Can there be negative discount rates?

Discounting at positive rates is consistent with the **sequencing** of events in which the best occur first and the worst last. The rationale for discounting is that costs are postponed, benefits are desired early on. But there is evidence to suggest that, in some cases at least, people leave the best to last and they prefer the worst to occur first. In such a context the result is **negative time preference**. The idea of preferring the worst first arises from the "dread" phenomenon, i.e., getting it over with. The idea of preferring benefits last is the "savouring" phenomenon, i.e., wanting things to "end on a good note".

The implication is that, when viewed in isolation individuals make decisions that are consistent with positive time preference. When viewing decisions as a **sequence**, however, they may sometimes exhibit negative time preference (Lowenstein [1987]). If relevant at all, negative time preference is likely to be more relevant to richer, developed economies.

Discounting and the environment

From an environmental standpoint, the choice of a discount rate works in two opposite directions. With a high discount rate, fewer investments are undertaken, particularly investments with long-term payoffs and large initial costs. These include items such as water management projects, including hydroelectric projects. This means that the preservation of certain natural areas is more likely to be achieved at higher discount rates. On the other hand, higher discount rates imply a more rapid development of non-renewable resources and shorter rotation periods and smaller stocks of renewable resources (see Box 12.3). For non-renewable resources this leads to the conservationist's fear that stocks will be depleted "too fast", perhaps with respect to the availability of substitute fuels for the next generation. For renewable resources, the implications of smaller stocks for environmental preservation are obvious. In addition, investment projects in forestry are unlikely to be justifiable, because of the long gestation periods involved in the investments (particularly slow growing species).

In addition to the considerations discussed above, environmental factors are affected in two other ways by the choice of the discount rate. One is the fact that projects with **potentially catastrophic consequences** do not get a fair "hearing" with positive discounting. For example, suppose that a particular programme involves a significant probability of a major catastrophe through soil contamination in a hundred years time. The cost of this contamination is estimated, in today's prices, to be $100 million and the probability that it would occur is 0.5. Then the expected cost in 2092 is $50 million. Discounted at 10% per annum this amounts to $36, at 5% it amounts to $3802 and at 2% it amounts to $69,016. Although the discount rate makes a considerable difference to the discounted present value of the cost, none of these figures is likely to sway the decision on the justifiability of the project. Hence there is a genuine concern that, with discounting, catastrophic future costs are not given their true importance.

The other environmental impact of concern is **irreversibility**. Some investments may result in the permanent destruction of certain species and habitat and the loss of irreplaceable environmental facilities. Should this irreversible loss receive a special weight? If so, how is it to be calculated? And does it have any implications for the discount rate to be used? The overall conclusion is that the issue of irreversibility, as well as those of environmental catastrophe and renewable resource depletion, is generally better dealt with by making other adjustments to the cost-benefit analysis rather than by adjusting discount rates. Thus, all these features underline the importance of **proper valuation**, the correct choice of **time horizons** (e.g., for irreversible losses the time horizon is infinite), and, where necessary the superimposition of some other constraints on the cost benefit analysis.

There is no unique relationship between high discount rates and environmental deterioration as is often supposed. Thus, high rates may well shift cost burdens forward to later generations, but, if the discount rate is allowed to determine the level of investment, they will also slow down the general pace of development through the depressing effect on investment. Since natural resources are required for investment, the demand for natural resources may be less with high discount rates than with low ones. High rates will also discourage development projects that compete with existing environmentally benign land uses - e.g., watershed development as opposed to an existing wilderness use. Exactly how the choice of discount rate impacts on the overall profile of natural resource and environment use in any country is thus ambiguous. This point is important since it reduces considerably the force of arguments to the effect that conventionally determined discount rates should be lowered (or raised, depending on the view taken) to accommodate environmental considerations.

Objections to discounting

Nonetheless, concern for the environmental dimension of development policy has led to a questioning of the basic rationale for discounting. We outline below some of the points that have been raised.

(a) Pure time preference

Pure time preference dictates positive discount rates. As a fact of human nature no-one appears to deny that impatience exists (but see the discussion on negative discount rates above). The objections to permitting pure time preference to influence social discount rates are as follows. First, individual time preference is not necessarily consistent with individual lifetime welfare maximisation (Strotz [1956]). This is a variant of the more general view that time discounting, because of impatience, is generally irrational (Pigou [1931]). Second, what individuals want carries no necessary implications for public policy. This amounts, of course, to a rejection of the underlying value judgement of cost-benefit comparisons. Third, the underlying value judgement is improperly expressed. A society that elevates want-satisfaction to high status should recognise that it is the satisfaction of wants <u>as they arise</u> that matters. But this means that tomorrow's satisfaction matters, not today's assessment of tomorrow's satisfaction. Fourth, if the "risk of death argument" is used, it is illegitimate to derive implications for potentially immortal societies from risks faced by mortal individuals.

What view is taken on the normative relevance of pure time preference depends on the acceptability of one or more of these objections. Overturning the basic value judgement underlying the cost-benefit style appraisal requires good reason: i.e., the rationale for paternalism should be a strong one. Such arguments do exist, but, in the context of developing countries, one has to weigh carefully the contrasting forces of meeting basic needs and diverting resources to long-term development potential: the former might favour accepting pure time preference, the latter might not. Philosophically, the argument that the value judgement needs re-expressing in line with the third observation above is impressive. In practical terms, however, the immediacy of wants in many developing countries where environmental problems are serious might favour the retention of the usual formulation of the basic judgement.

(b) Risk and uncertainty

It is widely argued that a benefit or cost is valued less the more uncertain is its occurrence. Since uncertainty is usually expected to increase with time from the present, this declining value becomes a function of time and hence is formally expressible in the form of a discount rate for risk and uncertainty.

The types of uncertainty that are generally regarded as being of relevance are:

(i)   uncertainty about the presence of the individual at some future date (the "risk of death" argument)

(ii)   uncertainty about the preferences of the individual even when his existence can be regarded as certain

(iii) uncertainty about the availability of the benefit or the existence of the cost.

The objections to using uncertainty to justify positive discount rates are several.

First, uncertainty arising from not being sure that the individual will be present to receive a distant benefit - the "risk of death" argument - ignores the argument about the "immortality" of society in contrast to the mortality of the individual. Indeed, a number of attempts have been made to measure time preference rates using survival probabilities (Eckstein [1961], Kula [1984, 1985, 1986]).

Second, uncertainty about preferences is clearly relevant if we are talking about certain goods and perhaps even aspects of environmental conservation, but hardly seems relevant if we are considering projects or policies whose output is food, shelter, water and energy, as is often the case in the developing country context. If anything, we can be more sure of future preferences for these goods (Barry [1977]).

Third, uncertainty about the presence or scale of benefits and costs may be unrelated to time, and certainly appears unlikely to be related in such a way that the scale of risk obeys an exponential function as is implied in the use of a single rate in the discount factor:

$$e^{-rt}, \text{ or } 1/(1 + r)^t$$

Uncertainty and risk are not irrelevant to the <u>decision-guiding rule</u>, but their presence should not be handled by adjustments to the discount rate. For such adjustments imply a particular behaviour for the risk premium which it is hard to justify.

If uncertainty does not take on a form consistent with exponential increase, the suggestion is that risk and uncertainty are better handled by other means - i.e., via adjustments to cost and benefit streams, leaving the underlying discount rate unadjusted for risk. This argument seems to be correct. It is worth noting, however, that adding a premium to the discount rate for risk <u>is</u> widely recommended.

(c) Diminishing marginal utility of consumption

Critics question the μg component of the CRI formula, suggesting either that it is irrelevant because μ is not an observable or measurable entity, or that it could take any value, including negative ones, since g could be greater or less than zero. Objection to assuming $\mu > 0$ are:

Many economists dispute whether there is any meaningful way of measuring μ. Empirical estimates of μ do exist - e.g., Stern [1977]. Others dispute the possibility of empirically measuring the entity. Further objections arise because the measure implies interpersonal comparisons of utility if a person is regarded as being a different entity in different time periods.

Second, and especially relevant for developing country appraisals, there can be no guarantee that g will be positive (see Box 12.2).

If it is legitimate to include pure time preference rates in the estimate of s, it is likely that they will result in high discount rates in poor developing economies. Many would argue that is justified because the mere presence of poverty itself induces high discount rates as concern is focused on food security over the next year or even few months rather than the long term. Proponents of the mortality-based time preference rates would argue that risk of mortality is also higher the poorer is the country, so that component will also be high on these arguments.

There is, however, a problem with inferring high time preference rates from the observation of poverty, particularly so in the context of environmental problems. High discount rates are a <u>cause</u> of much environmental degradation as individuals opt for (totally understandable) short-term measures designed to satisfy immediate wants, and at the expense of sustainable practices. But, in turn, poor prospects arising from environmental degradation actually assist in generating the poverty that "causes" high discount rates. The apparently high values of p are not independent of the environmental conditions. To use those rates to <u>evaluate</u> environmentally oriented investment (e.g., soil conservation measure, afforestation, water harvesting, etc.) is erroneous.

If high personal time preference rates are allowed to influence the value of i, the implication may therefore be that the discount rate unjustly reflects constrained activity, a situation where individuals are unable to act in a normal economic and environmental framework. This raises questions about the validity of such rates, perhaps abandoning the search for a social time preference rate altogether, or modifying the choice of rate to reflect the constraints on behaviour. The problem then is that there are no clear rules for choosing a discount rate. Essentially, g and p in the social time preference rate formula are not independent: the lower are the expected values of g the higher p will be. At the very least, then advocacy of the use of social time preference rates requires some downward adjustment of p in contexts where the environment-poverty linkage is a strong one.

(d) Opportunity cost of capital

The position taken by many economists is that the "proper" social rate of discount is the rate of return on the marginal project displaced by the investment in question (see Chapter 3). The arguments relating to which rate this might be have already been examined, and it was observed that investments may well displace a "mix" of investment and consumption, leading to weighted or "synthetic" rates of discount. In this section we are concerned only with any additional arguments which might be held to cast doubt on the use of opportunity cost rates of discount.

It has to be recalled that, from a government or donor agency's point of view, the function of the discount rate is to assist in the process of allocating capital funds. This offers a prima facie bias in favour of rates reflecting returns on displaced investment. Additionally, social time preference rates are very unlikely to be equal to marginal rates of return on displaced investment for all the reasons given earlier. The last preliminary remark is that, even in a world where consumer interest rates are broadly equal to opportunity cost of capital rates, we still have the presumption that social time preference rates of discount, expressing inter-temporal preferences when the individual sees himself as part of a collective community, will be lower than any observed market rates - the "isolation paradox" (Sen [1967, 1982]).

The environmental literature has made some limited attempts to discredit discounting due to opportunity cost arguments (Parfit [1983], Goodwin [1986]). This literature is, however, confusing since most of the objections arise because the implication of opportunity cost discounting is that some rate greater than zero emerges and this is then held to be inconsistent with a concept of intergenerational justice. There do, however, appear to be two criticisms which are generally, but not wholly, independent of this wider concern.

The first arises because the discount factor arising from a constant discount rate takes on a specific exponential form. This is because discounting is simply the reciprocal of compound interest. In turn, compound interest implies that if we invest £100 today it will compound forward at a particular rate, provided we keep not just the original £100 invested but also reinvest the profits. Now suppose the profits are consumed rather than reinvested. The critics suggest that this means that those consumption flows have no opportunity cost. What, they say, is the relevance of a discount rate based on assumed reinvested profits if in fact the profits are not reinvested but consumed.

If the argument is correct it provides a reason for not using a particular rate - the opportunity cost rate - for discounting streams of consumption flows as opposed to streams of profits which are always reinvested. But, in that context, it would not provide a reason for rejecting discounting altogether, since consumption flows should be discounted at a social time preference rate (or, "consumption rate of interest"). That is, the critics have not seen that a future holiday is worth less than a current holiday if we admit any of the arguments for a social time preference rate.

The second argument relates to intertemporal compensation. Consider an investment which has an expected environmental damage of £X in some future time period T. Should £X be discounted to a present value? The argument for doing so on opportunity cost grounds is presumably something like the following. If we debit the investment with a social cost <u>now</u> of £X/ (1+r), then that sum can be invested at r% now and it will grow to be £X in year T and can then be used to compensate the future sufferers of the environmental damage. Parfit [1983] argues that this argument has confused two issues. The first is whether the future damage matters less than current damage of a similar scale. The second is whether we can devise schemes to compensate for future damage. The answer to the first question, he argues, is that it does not matter less than current damage, or if it does, it matters less only because we are <u>able</u> to compensate the future as shown. If we are not able to make the compensation, the argument for being less concerned, and hence the argument for discounting, becomes irrelevant.

Part of the problem here is that actual and "potential" compensation are being confused. As typically interpreted, cost-benefit rules require only that we could, hypothetically, compensate losers, not that we actually do. In this case, the resource cost to the current generation of hypothetically compensating a future generation is, quite correctly, the discounted value of the compensation. Really what Parfit is objecting to is the absence of built-in <u>actual</u> compensation mechanisms in cost-benefit appraisals. It is possible to have considerable sympathy with that view, but it is <u>not</u> relevant to the issue of how to choose a discount rate.

These particular arguments against opportunity cost related discounting are not persuasive.

Discounting and natural resources

One set of effects of positive discounting relates to the repercussions of the discount rate on the management of natural resources. The choice of the discount rate has a particular effect on the rate of exploitation of natural resources. The basic decision with regard to such resources is how much to consume now and how much to hold in store for future consumption. It is intuitively clear that this decision is going to be influenced by the price of present versus future consumption - i.e., the discount rate. The main point to note with regard to non-renewable resources is that the higher the discount rate, the faster is the rate of depletion of the resource in the earlier years and the shorter is the interval before which the resource is exhausted. With a higher discount rate, a lower value is placed on future consumption relative to present consumption. Hence it is fairly clear that an optimal depletion policy, which seeks to maximise the discounted net benefits from a given stock of the resource, will prefer present consumption as the discount rate rises.

With renewable resources, the discount rate determines the rate of harvesting. The higher this rate is, the more intense is the harvesting effort and so the smaller is the stock which will exist. In general the "optimal" consumption of the resource requires a sustainable rate of use of the resource. This means that in the long-run the rate of harvesting must equal the rate of regeneration. However, it is possible, if the discount rate rises above the maximum biological growth rate of the stock, that, under certain conditions, the resource will be depleted and extinguished altogether: the phenomenon of "optimal extinction".

These features of optimal natural resource use have several implications for resource management policy. The first is that investments in resource exploiting activity need to pay special attention to the effects of a chosen discount rate on the time profile of benefits and costs. The discount rate and the cost-benefit stream are no longer independent as in the other cases so far considered. For example, if one is evaluating two projects, one of which exhausts a resource in 10 years and the other does so over 25 years, then the higher the discount rate, the more likely one is to favour the former to the latter. Such a discount rate could be chosen on "capital rationing" grounds. However, its implication is a more rapid exhaustion of a resource.

For renewable resources, a high discount rate can result in the resource being exhausted. For example, commercial logging operations evaluated at high discount rates could prove justified without replanting provisions (indeed this is more likely to be the case, given the normal time horizon over which such appraisals are made). As with exhaustible resources this implies that the planning process can involve discount rates that do not pay adequate attention to the longer term objectives of resource management.

Apart from public investment appraisal, the exploitation of natural resources is also affected by the difference between the private rate of discount and the social rate. If the former is believed to be much higher than the latter then resources in private hands will be overexploited. In general, however, correcting this over-exploitation does not involve changing the private discount rate. The reasons for this rate being too high are pervasive in the whole economy and the rate itself is not easily manipulated. However, resource conservation can be achieved by the appropriate use of resource taxes, so that the government can "capture" more of the economic rent arising from the resource development. Apart from slowing down this development where desirable, it also had the advantage of mobilising resources for government use in a particularly efficient way.

Overall, the choice of discount rate is of particular importance with regard to natural resource management. High discount rates can result in policies that are not desirable from an intertemporal point of view. The question that follows then is should one use a lower discount rate in appraising these projects or not? And if not, then what other policies are available? In our view, the use of a lower discount rate is not the best policy to follow. To begin with, there is the question of which project should qualify. Inevitably there will be grey areas and this would cause further problems. Second, there are a number of situations in which private decisions are central to the resource exploitation problem, and discount rate changes for these groups are not a practicable or efficient policy. Third, even if one used lower discount rates, there is no guarantee that some serious resource degradation might not occur.

Discounting and future generations

The question arises as to why market rates of discount are thought to be inappropriate in a context where the interests and rights of future generations are accepted as legitimate factors in the selection of a social rate.

As we have seen, the higher the rate of discount the greater will be the discrimination against future generations. First, projects with social costs that occur well into the future and net social benefits that occur in the near-term will be likely to pass the standard cost-benefit test the higher is the discount rate. Thus future generations may bear a disproportionate share of the costs of the project. Second, projects with social benefits well into the future are less likely to be favoured by the cost-benefit rule if discount rates are high. Thus future generations are denied a higher share of project benefits. Third, the higher the discount rate the lower will be the overall level of investment, depending on the availability of capital, and hence the lower the capital stock "inherited" by future generations. The expectation must be, then, that future generations will suffer from rates of discount determined in the market place since such rates are based on current generation preferences and/or capital productivity which is not associated with the general existence of future markets.

It might be thought, however, that existing preferences do take account of future generations' interests. The way in which this might occur is through "overlapping utility functions". What this means is that my welfare (utility) today includes as one of the factors determining it the welfare of my children and perhaps my grandchildren. Thus, if i is the current generation, j the next generation and k the third generation, we may have:

$$U_i = U_i\,(C_i,\ U_j,\ U_k)$$

where U is utility and C is consumption. In this way, we could argue that the "future generations problem" is automatically taken account of in current preferences. Notice that what is being evaluated in this process is the current generation's judgement about what the future generation will think is important. It is not therefore a discount rate reflecting some broader principle of the rights of future generations. The essential distinction is between generation i judging what generation j wants (the overlapping utility function argument) and generation i engaging in resource investment so as to leave generation j with the maximum scope for choosing what it wants.

The issue is whether such an argument can be used to substantiate the idea that current, market-determined rates reflect future generations' interests. The basic reason for supposing that the argument does not hold is that market rates are determined by the behaviour of many individuals behaving in their own interest. If future generations enter into the calculus, they do so in contexts when the individual behaves in his or her "public role". The idea here is that individuals make decisions in two contexts - "private" decisions reflecting our own interests, and "public" decisions in which we act with responsibility for our fellow beings and for future generations. Market discount rates reflect the former context, whereas social discount rates should reflect the public context. This is what Sen [1982] calls the "dual role" rationale for social discount rates being below the market rates because of the future generations issue. It is also similar to the "assurance" argument, namely that people will behave differently if they can be assured that their own action will be accompanied by similar actions by others. Thus, each person might be willing to make transfers to future generations, but only if each individual is assured that others will do the same. The "assured" discount rate arising from collective action is lower than the "unassured" discount rate.

There are other arguments that are used to justify the idea that market rates will be "too high" in the context of future generations' interests. The first is what Sen [1982] calls "super-responsibility" argument. Market discount rates arise from the behaviour of individuals, but the State is a separate entity with the responsibility of guarding collective welfare and the welfare of future generations as well. Thus, the rate of discount relevant to State investments will not be the same as the market discount rate, and since, high rates discriminate against future generations, we would expect the State discount rate to be lower than the market discount rate.

The final argument used to justify the inequality of the market and social rate of discount is the "isolation paradox" (Sen [1961, 1967]). This is often confused with the assurance problem (see above), but the isolation paradox says that individuals will not make transfers even if assurance exists. Demonstrating the difference between market and social discount rates in this context is not straightforward. Here we present the results. (For proofs, see Sen [1967]). Pursuing the argument above that individuals will place some weight on the consumption of future generations, especially on consumption of direct descendants, assume that the following weights are placed on consumption:

> own consumption $= 1$
> others' consumption in current generation $= b$
> consumption of descendants $= c$
> consumption of others in future generation $= a$

If $1 of saving today yields a return that is shared in the proportions h and 1-h between descendants and others in the future generation, then the market rate of discount is:

$$\pi = \frac{1}{ch + (1-h)a} - 1$$

Now suppose that individuals agree to make a collective saving contract for $1 of additional saving by all persons in the current generation, and that the return is enjoyed by descendants and others in the ratio 1 to n-1. Then the social rate of discount is:

$$p = \frac{1 + (n-1)b}{c + (n-1)a} - 1$$

The possibility exists that π and p are the same, but as long as the current individual fails to capture the entire investment returns for his or her descendants (h < 1), or as long as the individual's selfishness vis-à-vis others today is stronger than concern for his descendants vis-à-vis others in the future generation (c < a/b), then p is less than π.

Any positive social rate of discount will discriminate against future generations' interests. This suggests that the social discount rate is to be determined in the context of collective decision-making rather than some aggregation of individuals' decisions. This might mean looking at individuals' "public role" behaviour, leaving the choice of discount rate to the State, or trying to select a discount rate based on a collective savings contract. None of these options offers a theory of how to determine a discount rate in quantitative terms. What they do suggest is that market rates will not be proper guides to discount rates once future generations' interests are incorporated into the social decision rule. The view taken here is that these arguments can be used to justify rejecting the market rate of interest as a social discount rate <u>if it is thought that the burden of accounting for future generations' interests should fall on the discount rate</u>. However, this is unnecessarily complex. It is better to define the rights of future generations and use these to circumscribe the overall cost-benefit rule, leaving the choice of discount rate to fairly conventional current-generation oriented considerations. It is preferable to adjust other aspects of the investment appraisal to account for future generations' interests. A telling reason for this is that lowering rates will encourage more investment overall, and this will increase the demand for resources and environmental services. A lowering of rates across the board could thus have counter-productive results if the aim is to accommodate environmental concerns. One alternative, of course, is to lower discount rates for "environmental" projects, but not for other projects. In practice this is likely to be impossible to do because of the problems of deciding which is an environmental project and which is not. Is any rural development investment, for example, an environmental project? Since most projects will have an environmental dimension - they will all impact positively or negatively on the environment - the analyst would have to have some idea of the <u>scale</u> of the environmental dimension before deciding which discount rate to choose. Then a cut-off point would be needed in order to decide which projects qualify for the lower rate and which for the higher one. Altogether, the procedure has large arbitrary features.

While there are legitimate concerns in the future generations' argument, they may either backfire in the sense of not accommodating the concerns that motivate a reduced discount rate, or they will result in largely impractical procedures.

General considerations in dealing with the intergenerational problem

Assume that the future has at least some claim on the present simply because they have an <u>interest</u> in the present. This interest, arising from the fact that we do not know who future people will be, confers rights on future generations. Then a case for intergenerational justice exists, and the process of discounting appears to discriminate against it.

How might these future rights be protected in practice? Certain minimum requirements emerge with respect to any investment appraisal. Above all, it is essential that any investment appraisal should check on the resource and environmental consequences of the investment. This much has been recommended as standard procedure by OECD (OECD [1986]).

A second requirement is that efforts should be made to <u>measure</u> environmental damage. To some extent, this might be guaranteed by the use of <u>environmental impact assessment</u> procedures, but we would go further and suggest that attempts be made to identify the monetary cost of resource and receiving environmental damage. The rationale here is to demonstrate the economic importance of natural environments and natural resources.

The procedures identified above are, of course, essential whether the environmental considerations are located in the current or the future. The interests of the future require something more, however, and this is captured to some extent in the idea of **sustainability**. The basic idea is simple in the context of natural resources (excluding non-renewable resources) and receiving environments: the use made of these inputs to the development process should be sustainable through time. Unless there are good reasons to the contrary, the time horizon in question is an infinite one. The problem is how to attach meaning to this general concept.

If we now apply the idea to resources, sustainability might mean that a given stock of resources - trees, soil quality, water, etc. - should not decline. The way in which it can be preserved is by harvesting only the **sustainable yield** of that resource. In turn, the sustainable yield may vary with the stock size and, more importantly, with the management regime. For example, forest yields obviously vary with the size of the forest, and yields are noticeably higher in managed forests than in "virgin" forest. This all suggests that one should have some idea of the optimum stock of the resource to begin with. This is notoriously difficult to determine, even in reasonably well-defined conditions. In a great many developing countries, however, the complexity is reduced because of the fact that stocks are known to be well below any optimum. A reasonably simple indicator of this can be found by comparing resource demands with measures of **carrying capacity**. Carrying capacity is a measure of the maximum population sustainable for a given resource endowment, assuming some basic level of human consumption of the resource. Optimal stocks are virtually certain to be below carrying capacity levels. If actual use exceeds the carrying capacity rate of use, then, self-evidently, actual use exceeds optimal use. It follows, then, that for these economies, no project should reduce the stock of the resource unless there is some compensating increase elsewhere, either in the resource itself or in a substitute.

The sequence of argument then is as follows:
 i   the sustainable use of resources and environments serves two interests:
      a) current generations over their lifetimes;
      b) future generations since they inherit no smaller a stock than their predecessors;
 ii   sustainable use requires harvesting, or using, only the sustainable yield of the resource;
 iii ideally, the relevant sustainable yield is the one at the optimal stock, but there are obvious problems in measuring the optimal stock;
 iv   in practical terms, then, resource-using projects should use only the sustainable yield, or should include as a cost in the project the regeneration of any stock that is otherwise permanently removed.

Obviously, these requirements may turn out to be quite formidable for some projects since it is likely to be the second implication - the cost of regeneration - that will be relevant. Some projects may cease to be profitable and others may well have their "apparent" rate of return reduced. But really what is happening is that the project is being debited with the "true" cost of resource depletion. If it cannot meet that cost then it is not a project that is consistent with the sustainability requirement.

The implications for the discount rate are interesting. For what it suggests is that we do not need to adjust the discount rate for the interests of future generations. They are met by the sustainable use constraint and hence the changed cost profile for the project. The discount rate that is used can then be the opportunity cost of capital, adjusted if necessary for any consumption displacement effects. Moreover, it is in keeping with the arguments made earlier that adjusting the discount rate for future generations' interests is both clumsy and inefficient.

Clearly, if it was applied to each individual policy or project, the sustainability requirement as interpreted above would face major difficulties. The problem is that the sustainability requirement could, if applied to each and every investment, amount to <u>actual</u> compensating investments for every externality arising from the project. This could readily become stultifying and inoperable. The way around this problem is to ensure that in any <u>portfolio</u> of investments there are compensating investments in resource regeneration. This would mean a procedure something like the following:

i   engage in the "normal" investment activity, but with careful checks for environmental repercussions as discussed,

ii   where resource demands are significant, debit the project with the cost of regenerating the resource loss and include the regeneration project in the overall project,

iii   where resource demands are small or too difficult to accommodate by "in project" compensation, check the resource demands of the whole portfolio of investments and adjust the portfolio so that it includes specifically resource-generating investments. In this way, it is the whole portfolio of investments that bears the cost of the sustainability requirement, by having the marginal project removed and replaced with the environment improvement project.

Strictly, the environmental compensation project will not require assessment by standard cost-benefit procedures: it is designed to honour the sustainability constraint and is itself not to be evaluated by the conventional criteria. Nonetheless, such an appraisal should be carried out to check the price of the sustainability requirement. For example, if the compensating investment turns out to be one with a negative rate of return, this will indicate the sum of the sustainability costs omitted from the other projects.

The concept of the environmentally compensating investment is a practical one and reflects the wider concerns of sustainability or "permanent livability". It needs to be stressed that such pressure is <u>not</u> a blind "replace a tree for every tree removed" requirement. This would make investment and policy inoperable in practical terms, even if it could be regarded as having a rationale. Rather it is an attempt to accommodate the interest of future generations in a practical way by debiting projects or programmes with the costs of resource losses. At the very least it forces an environmental/resource assessment of investment and policy activity.

Box 12.1 **Alternative decision rules in temporal contexts**

	Efficiency	Equity
Intratemporal	Max. Unweighted Benefits - Costs	Max. Weighted Benefits - Costs
Intertemporal	Max. Unweighted, Present Value of Benefits - Costs	Max. Unweighted Benefits - Costs subject to a Sustainability Rule

Two objectives may be sought - economic efficiency and some notion of justice (equity). While some philosophers regard justice as being "morally prior" to efficiency - its interests should be served first (Rawls [1971]) - many see these objectives as being of equal importance. Most economists differentiate the contexts in which they should be addressed. Project investment, for example, may be an inefficient way of serving equity interests. This is usually better done through lump sum and other transfers at the macroeconomic level.

The two contexts for the rules are those of intratemporal and intertemporal allocation. Ignoring time, the difference between benefits and costs should be maximised. Intratemporal equity can, in principle, then be served by weighting the gains and losses by some indicator of income utility, or cruder measures such as the ratio of average income to the actual income of the affected groups. Measures of this kind have been used (e.g., Squire and van der Tak [1975]). Intertemporal decisions require the use of discount rates if efficiency is to be honoured. If intertemporal equity is of concern, it may be possible to weight costs and benefits more equally through time (e.g., by using a low discount rate or even a zero discount rate). An alternative is to seek a sustainability constraint which has to be honoured first (e.g., leaving the total stock of capital resources intact) and within which constraint it is then possible to maximise the present value of net benefits in the normal way (Page [1977], Pearce et al.[1989]).

Box 12.2 **Differing values for the consumption rate of interest**

	China India	Other Low Inc.	Low Mid Inc.	Upper Mid Inc.	High Inc.
Growth of Cons. = g	6.5	2.2	2.4	3.2	3.1
Growth of Popn. = n	1.5	2.6	2.0	1.8	0.6
g - n	4.0	-0.4	0.4	1.4	2.5
u = 1	4.0	-0.4	0.4	1.4	2.5
u = 2	8.0	-0.8	0.8	2.8	5.0

The table shows past growth rates on real consumption 1980-1989 for various regions of the world, and expected population growth for 1989-2000. The difference between the two is the expected growth in real consumption per capita, assuming past consumption trends are guides to future trends. Estimates of the elasticity of marginal utility of consumption are applied to these estimates to give the final two rows which show estimates of the CRI on the assumption that pure time preference is zero. In the rapidly growing economies of India and China, the effect is to produce CRIs of 4-8%. But in the other low income economies, negative CRIs emerge.

Box 12.3 **The effects of discounting on the rate of use of a non-renewable resource**

Under competitive conditions it is possible to write the price of a non-renewable resource as consisting of two components: the cost of extraction, C, and the royalty, R. Chapter 11 establishes that R in any period can be written:

$$R_t = [P_B - C][1 + r]^{-t}$$

where P_B is the price of the "backstop" technology that eventually substitutes for the non-renewable resource.

So, the price of a resource in the current period (t=0) is

$$P_0 = C + [P_B - C][1 + r]^{-t}$$

To see how price varies with a change in the rate of discount rate, take the example of a one period change (so that t = 1) and differentiate P_0 with respect to r to obtain:

$$\delta P_0/\delta r = [C - P_B][1 + r]^{-2}$$

Since r > 0 and, by assumption, P_B > C, this expression is negative. That is, as the rate of interest goes up so the price in the current period goes down. But if price goes down, quantity goes up. Hence the quantity extracted in the first period will increase because of the rise of the discount rate. Hence higher discount rates encourage "early" extraction.

Chapter 13

Risk and Uncertainty

The nature of risk and uncertainty

Risk and uncertainty are facts of life, and nowhere is this more true than in the environmental context. We often do not know what the environmental consequences will be of undertaking a particular policy or project. In large part this uncertainty arises because we do not fully understand how ecological systems function, and because we do not know how man-made substances - or increased quantities of "natural" substances - will interact with the environment. If we did know, then chlorofluorocarbons (CFCs) would probably not have been introduced. We know now that CFCs damage the ozone layer, and that the ozone layer serves valuable protective functions for life on earth. Uncertainties of this kind are pervasive. We cannot be sure what is happening with the increasing release of micro-pollutants into the environment, for example. Sometimes the consequences of undertaking action without knowing for certain what will happen is that we create **irreversible consequences** such as the elimination of a species. Once gone, we cannot recreate them. In turn, we cannot be sure what will happen if continued species elimination occurs. It may not matter much (from the human standpoint, that is) if species are lost, but we cannot tell. The scale of outcome could be large, or small. So, the context of much environmental policy is characterised by:

- uncertainty about the effect
- irreversibility of some effects
- uncertainty about the scale of the effect.

In the context of the chain events giving rise to pollution, for example, there may be uncertainty about the sources of emissions and their scale; there may be uncertainty about transformation processes in ecosystems and uncertainty about ecosystem response. In the context of renewable natural resource such as forests and fisheries, information on resource stocks may be deficient, while the understanding of the relevant population dynamics and the impacts of different harvesting regimes may not be known. In agricultural systems, natural events may be unforeseen - e.g., precipitation, pests, diseases. In industrial installations it is often not possible to predict breakdowns and accidents giving rise to the release of pollutants. The extent of irreversibility is often not known because the relevant thresholds have not been identified. While it is tempting to think that small changes in doses of pollutants should be accompanied by small changes in ecosystem reaction, this is often not the case.

One purpose of economic valuation is to **reduce uncertainty** about the importance of an effect since valuation provides one indicator of importance - the measure of human preference. More generally, economic appraisal also aims to improve the information on which decisions are based, thus reducing uncertainty. However, valuation techniques are themselves subject to error so that the reduction in uncertainty about whether an impact is "big" or "small" may be offset somewhat by uncertainty about whether the resulting economic value is, in some sense, the "right" one.

How do we handle risk and uncertainty? It turns out that there is no easy answer.

The terms "risk" and "uncertainty" are often used interchangeably. It is a matter of choice, but it is often helpful to distinguish risk from uncertainty in the following way. **Risk relates to a situation** where we have at least some idea of the probabilities of the effect occurring. For example, we might know that there is a 1/10,000 chance of being in an accident when crossing the road. The 1/10,000 is a probability, often written as a probability of 10^{-4}. Being able to assign a probability is therefore one feature of risk. The **magnitude** of the effect is the other dimension. Thus any risk should be definable in terms of a probability and a magnitude. Flood risk, for example, may be measured as the probability of a particular size flood multiplied by the value of the damage that is estimated to be caused. Flood height is a random (or "stochastic") variable, dependent upon rainfall patters. Of special interest in many environmental contexts are risks where the probability is very small and the magnitude of damage very large. These are the so-called "zero-infinity" problems.

Often we do not know the probability at all. This is true uncertainty. Climate change probably typifies the context of uncertainty - we cannot (yet, anyway) assign probabilities to climate change having particular effects. So, the basic distinction between risk and uncertainty is that, with risk, we have some idea of the probabilities of outcomes, while with uncertainty we do not. Some contexts will be characterised by a mix of risk and uncertainty: we may know the upper and lower bounds, for example, but have no idea of probabilities within the two bounds. Where probabilities cannot be assigned it is important to engage in **sensitivity analysis**. A sensitivity analysis shows the effects on the main indicators of project or programme performance (e.g., the net present value) of adopting the lower bound estimates and the upper bound estimates. It might also embody a "best guess" at a central estimate even though the probabilities of the bounds or central estimate cannot be stated.

Risk assessment

Much research is devoted to finding out just what the probabilities of adverse effects are and what the size of effect is. This process of **risk assessment** aims to determine the relationship between, say, the concentration of a pollutant in the environment and its effects on human health. We can therefore think of risk assessment as involving an analysis of the "dose" (the level of pollution) and the "response" (the human health effect). In this way, risk assessment tries to convert an uncertainty context into a risk context. Probabilities based on scientific observation and estimation are described as **objective probabilities**. Often, probabilities are based on the best guesses of experts and decision-makers. These are known as **subjective probabilities**.

Any risk assessment, then, should result in the identification of probabilities and some indicator of the severity of the risk. While risk assessment strictly relates to probabilistic contexts, much the same approach is required even if probabilities cannot be assigned.

Economic assessments of risk involve:
- an analysis of the initiating events and pathways of effect;
- specifying the probability distribution surrounding each type of damage effect;
- estimating the economic value of each impact;
- computing a probability distribution of the net benefits.

In industrial contexts, pathways of effect, together with probabilities of accidental damage, can be represented by **fault trees**. Box 13.1 provides an example of fault tree analysis. Natural systems are often subject to random influences, e.g., climatic factors. Predicting the impacts of, say, pollution in such a context can therefore quickly become complex. It may be necessary to simulate the effects using computer models, but this can be involved and expensive. It also requires substantial informational inputs which will often not be available.

Special attention needs to be paid to **cumulative effects** of pollutants. Cumulation may involve looking at the whole **life cycle** of an activity. For example, looking at the effects of increasing coal burning for electricity generation will mean that there will also be additional impacts from coal mining, coal transportation etc. These additional impacts may occur at quite some distance from the activity originally under consideration. Some pollutants also accumulate in the environment itself: nitrates accumulate in groundwater; trace metals accumulate in various environmental "sinks" and in biota.

Box 13.2 gives an example of risk assessment in terms of the relationship between numbers of people dying in the USA from particular environmental risks. The procedure involves first assessing what the risk of a particular hazard is, measured in terms of fatalities. To standardise the estimates, the fatalities are then expressed "per million" people, which is the same thing as a probability. So, a risk of 63,000 in 1 million is the same as a probability of 0.063 (63,000/1,000,000) for example. Box 13.2 also shows the costs of the legislation aimed at reducing these risks, divided by the number of lives saved. The result is a "cost per life saved" or "cost per death avoided". The information reveals some interesting results. For example, it suggests that the United States can save lives at a cost of $200,000 per life by reducing trihalomethane in drinking water, compared to $19 billion for one life saved from improving landfill site quality. If the landfill legislation did not exist its cost would be saved and could have been allocated to the drinking water legislation, saving many more lives in the process. This is an example of **cost-effectiveness analysis** and shows how we can maximise the number of lives saved for a given budget. Since environmental budgets are not infinite, nor could they ever be, it makes eminent sense to look at the cost per life saved. But there are other complex factors at work to do with the way in which the public **perceives** risk, an issue we address below.

Unfortunately, the kind of information in Box 13.2 is hard to come by for many risks. Governments rarely keep statistics in a form that permits this kind of cost-effectiveness analysis. Often, the cost of a policy is simply not known, while "dose-response" functions tend to be known only imperfectly and, sometimes, not at all.

In many risk assessments, information about the probabilities may be presented in terms of **expected values**. The idea is very simple. The context is one of risk so we assume we know the probabilities attached to outcomes. Consider an investment project with benefits that are known subject to certain probabilities. Suppose there is a 20% chance of the benefit being minus 5 (for the moment the units do not matter); a 50% chance of it being plus 15; and a 30% chance of it being plus 20. We can calculate the **expected value** of the benefits as:

$$(0.2 x-5) + (0.5 x 15) + (0.3 x 20) = 12.5$$

We could compare this expected value with the cost of undertaking the action. If it is less than 12.5, then the project looks worth undertaking.

Expected value is best applied in contexts where there is no reason to expect any strong **risk aversion** to the outcomes, that is in contexts where, say, the minus 5 outcome is not regarded as being dramatically bad. In an agricultural project, for example, there may be various possibilities with respect to the level of salinisation. Each level will have an associated value of damage, and each level may also have an attached probability. Then, the expected value approach is acceptable provided none of the outcomes has a dramatic consequence (e.g., total loss of output).

Risk management

If it is possible to assign probabilities, then, once a risk assessment is completed, the next stage is **risk management**. This is the whole process of bringing various disciplines to bear on two decisions: (a) how much risk is **acceptable** - which is sometimes known as **risk appraisal**, and (b) how unacceptable risks should be reduced - the **response to risk**.

Risk appraisal involves looking at the way society values risky outcomes. Expected value is now no longer applicable since, as noted above, it fails to account for differing social attitudes to the individual outcomes. Pursuing the previous hypothetical example, we may note that the investment might be undertaken and the loss of 5 might occur. In that case we will have invested money for nothing. Somehow, the expected value idea does not seem to capture the relevant concerns about the outcomes of the project. In particular, expected value seems not to capture our likely concerns about the extremes of the outcomes. People tend to be averse to bad outcomes such as the minus 5 in the example. Expected value approaches do not capture this **risk aversion**[18].

It seems more likely that the individual will attach some weights to the outcomes. The result is the **expected utility** approach rather than the expected value approach. Expected utility then has the same formula as the expected value approach but this time utilities rather than values are substituted. So, if we are very averse to the loss we might weight it more heavily, say by a factor of 5. Now the calculation will be:

$$(0.2x \ [-5x5]) + (0.5x15) + (0.3x20) = 8.5$$

The effect is to make the project much less attractive than it was previously[19].

The expected utility approach also seems able to handle the problem of disastrous outcomes. In our example, the minus 5 can be thought of as a potential "disaster". In the expected utility approach, then, we would attach a large utility value (or "disutility" value if it is a loss) to the outcomes we most like or dislike. Some attempts have been made to estimate "disaster aversion" measures. How, then, does the public perceive accidents?

Everyone is familiar with news items about road accidents in which multiple vehicles are involved and the deaths are several or many. This is the phenomenon of the "group accident". It partly explains why aeroplane crashes, boat sinkings, gas explosions, nuclear accidents and natural disasters such as hurricanes and tornados are news. Yet the deaths from such events rarely exceed 25 people and the events themselves are not very common. Compare that to the more than 5000 people who die every year in road accidents in the UK. What it suggests is that individuals perceive group accidents differently to accidents in which one person dies. Put another way, if 10 people die in one accident this is seen as being somehow far more serious than if 1 person dies in each of 10 accidents. There is what is known as **disaster aversion**. Allowing for disaster aversion in assessing environmental risks is perfectly legitimate if the requirement is that individuals' preferences should count. Moreover, disaster aversion is consistent with the economic theory of risk aversion. To see why we investigate briefly the nature of this theory. But we shall then discover that other aspects of human behaviour toward risk are not consistent with that theory. Box 13.3 shows some suggested rules taken from contexts in which safety investments have to be decided upon.

Summarising the rules so far, then, we have:

(a) **expected value approach**:
    compare costs with expected value of benefits where the expected value of benefits is equal to:

$p_1.B_1 + p_2.B_2 + p_3.B_3$ etc, or$\Sigma p_i.B_i$.

where p is probability and B is benefit measured in non-utility terms.

We can now see that the expected value approach is acceptable if we have reason to suppose that society is **risk neutral**, i.e., if it is indifferent between two outcomes with the same expected value, even though the **variance** about those expected values is different. But as soon as **risk aversion** is relevant, the expected value approach is not appropriate. Then the expected utility approach appears more applicable.

(b) **expected utility approach**:
compare costs with the expected utility of the benefits, i.e., with

$$p_1.U_1 + p_2.U_2 + p_3.U_3 \text{ etc, or } \Sigma p_i.U_i$$

In this case the value of the 'U's should enable the decision-maker to capture society's aversion to particular risks.

Why expected utility may not apply

The expected utility model is attractive, but extensive research suggests that it does not describe how people actually behave. Recall that if individual preferences count, then actual behaviour must be studied to see what people actually care about and why they behave as they do. This can be contrasted with the view that ignores how people actually behave and builds up an approach based on how they <u>ought</u> to behave if they are to be judged "rational" or "consistent". It is not always easy to keep this distinction in mind. After all, the very purpose of analysing decisions is to make them better. Better decisions could be ones that always obey the axiom that what people want is best. But we know that societies have always abrogated some individual sovereignty to the state in order to override individual preferences.

In practice, psychologists and economists have uncovered many kinds of behaviour which is inconsistent with expected utility theory. Just a few are listed below:

(a) people seem regularly to confuse probability with plausibility. The more they think it could happen ("it seems reasonable") the higher the probability they attach to it occurring. This **conjunction fallacy** is especially important if the event in question is described in some detail -e.g., the effects of a nuclear accident, islands disappearing under rising sea levels etc. This often happens in association with events that are easy to imagine (explosions, flooding) while events that are hard to imagine tend to attract low subjective probabilities (the issue of **availability**);

(b) people often suffer from the "it can't happen to me syndrome". Because it hasn't yet happened, people think it won't happen. This is the **fallacy of optimism**;

(c) experiments show that people do not correctly perceive low probabilities. Many seem to ignore them altogether, and much depends on how the risk is described (see Box 13.2). In many other cases, people exaggerate the low probabilities, believing some accidents to be more likely than, say, the risk of fatality in a road accident. This is the **under or over-weighting of low probabilities** issue;

(d) people seem "anchored" to wherever they are at the point in time they are asked to make a decision. This is their "reference" point, and people value risks with reference to that point rather than in abstract in the way the expected utility approach assumes. They also value losses from the standpoint of the reference point more highly than equivalent gains (the phenomenon of "loss aversion"), whereas economics has traditionally taught that there will be little difference in these values. This helps explain the difference between **willingness to accept** and **willingness to pay** in economic valuation (see Chapter 3). People also tend to make the risk problem simpler than it really is, as if they cannot cope with a more complex issue. These features of decision-making, together with the distortion of low probability perception, define **prospect theory**. Prospect theory seeks to explain how individuals behave with respect to risk in light of the apparent failure of expected utility theory to explain that behaviour;

(e) prospect theory also suggests that people put the various contexts for valuing risk into separate mental boxes, or **"mental accounts"**. They then have little difficulty in weighing up costs and benefits within each account, but find it difficult to make comparisons <u>across</u> mental accounts. If this is true then it goes some to explaining how people can seemingly entertain contradictory notions at the same time. For example, benefits might be in one "account" and costs in another. This does not invalidate cost-benefit thinking since the idea of cost-benefit is to <u>prescribe</u> actions. But it raises again the awkward problem of when individuals' actions can be regarded as "rational" and when they cannot;

f) much also depends on the context of risk. A risk of being injured or catching a disease is regarded as being very different if it is **involuntarily borne** as opposed to being **voluntary**. So, the risk of dying from lung cancer through smoking (a voluntary process, at least initially) is often seen as being less than the risk of cancer through exposure to nuclear radiation (involuntary), even though the former probability is substantially greater than the latter. The context issue can be complicated. Risks in the future are usually thought to be less important than risks now (the phenomenon of "discounting"), but recent research suggests that people often tend to value future risks more highly than present risks, and future benefits more highly than present benefits. This is because they sometimes like to "leave the best to the last" (in the case of benefits), or dread being vulnerable when they are older and perhaps less capable of looking after themselves (in the case of risks).

All in all, the issue of how people actually behave in the presence of uncertainty and risk turns out to be complex. It seems fairly clear that neither expected value nor expected utility are adequate to explain that behaviour, even if expected utility can accommodate many issues, such as disaster aversion. Other theories of risk-taking - such as prospect theory - have been developed to account for the inadequacies of expected utility. They tend to suggest that the context of the risk is important, and that we cannot advocate a single rule to deal with all risk and uncertainty contexts. The phenomenon of loss aversion is important for the environmental context because it is often the case that we are dealing with environmental losses rather than gains. Loss aversion means that those losses may be valued very highly by society. The issue of risk context means that we cannot analyse low probability, high damage events in the same way as we value "everyday" risk. Somehow we have to account for perceptions of low probability events. Finally, new theories of uncertainty suggest all kinds of ways in which people can be encouraged to deal with risk. As just one example, in some countries it is fairly usual to compensate people if a project perceived as risky is located in their vicinity. This might be a nuclear power station or even a waste landfill site. Compensation may work as a means of getting a more "rational" appraisal of risk not just because bearing the risk is itself compensated, but because the compensation creates a new context of sharing in risk compared to the uncompensated case in which the owner of the landfill site, or the nuclear power station is seen to be "imposing" the facility.

Risk and risk perception

The risk data in Box 13.2 are <u>objective</u> in the sense that the deaths per million are either based on actual past data, or on <u>expert</u> assessment of future risks. But the <u>public</u> often perceives risk in very different ways to experts. This disparity between public and expert risk assessment is absolutely fundamental to the problem of coping with risk and uncertainty. Recall that the cost-benefit way of thinking involves us in a process of recording <u>individuals' preferences</u> for or against some change. We tended not to ask where the preferences came from, or whether they were "good or bad" (subject to the law, that is). This is because cost-benefit approaches try to be "democratic" by using individuals' preferences rather than some expert's view.

When it comes to assessing risks, however, there is a problem. Suppose the expert assessment of risk is that some dreaded event, say a core meltdown in a nuclear power station, can only happen with a probability of 1 in a million reactor-years (10^{-6}). That is, the chance of an accident of this kind would only occur once in 1 million years of producing electricity from one nuclear reactor, or, once in 1000 years if there are 1000 nuclear reactors. This is an extremely small probability. And it is one that tends to be used when designing modern reactors in the developed world. Most people would agree that such a risk is so small it is not worth worrying about. Yet the fear of a nuclear accident is so great that in the United States no nuclear power station of any significance has been commissioned for the last twenty years. Clearly, there seems to be a marked disparity between what the public worries about and what the experts think is important. And this disparity has major implications for many projects and policies, e.g., the development of certain energy sources and the siting of allegedly hazardous facilities. Indeed, it generates the "NIMBY" syndrome ("not in my back yard") whereby people oppose the siting of such things as waste disposal sites, incinerators, and power stations in their area. They do this despite the expert evidence that the risks to health from such facilities are very small.

Box 13.4 shows the contrast between expert and public opinion. The expert information is for the USA but the public's opinion can be gleaned from surveys in the USA and the UK. It can be seen that what concerns the public is fairly similar in the two countries, and most of the exceptions are readily explained. For example, the US has debated the risks from exposure to radon (naturally occurring radioactivity) in domestic dwellings for quite some time and it has been a regular feature of media programmes. This concern is somewhat more recent in the UK and hence did not figure prominently in the 1989 public opinion polls. There have been similar investigations into indoor air pollution generally in the USA but, to date, very little has been said about this in the UK. Perhaps of more interest are the items that the US experts implied did not matter very much, but which the public thinks do matter. These are very much in a general category of "accidents" - nuclear, industrial, oil spills, underground storage tanks in the USA and problems with the nuclear fuel cycle. The only exception is bathing water which has been a specific problem in the UK because of a Directive from the European Community on the matter. The issue of "group accidents" was analysed above.

The Precautionary Principle

If individuals are very averse to environmental risk, it suggests a sound basis for the **precautionary principle**. This principle may take several forms, but strictly interpreted it suggests that no action should be taken if there is any likelihood at all, however small, that significant environmental damages could occur. This likelihood may be independent on the scientific evidence. That is, unless there is certainty that there are <u>no</u> detrimental effects, actions should not be taken which release harmful pollutants into the environment. Construed in this way, the precautionary principle can be thought of as one approach to the "zero-infinity" problems in which the probability of damage is small or unknown, but the consequences are potentially very large. As such, the precautionary principle can be held to apply to both risk and uncertainty contexts.

A second interpretation requires that there be a **presumption** in favour of not harming the environment unless the opportunity costs of that action are, in some sense, very high. Put another way, no significant deterioration of the environment should occur unless the benefits associated with that deterioration heavily outweigh the costs of the deterioration. Effectively, this **safe minimum standards** approach says that the benefit-cost ratio of any project or programme which incidentally damages the environment should be high. While this formulation is somewhat vague, it can be contrasted with the typical cost-benefit rule to the effect that the benefit cost ratio should be greater than unity.

The precautionary principle is embodied in some national environmental legislation, is espoused generally in European Community environmental legislation[20], and in some international agreements[21]. Clearly, adoption of the precautionary principle can be expensive. If the benefits forgone are substantial and new information reveals that the measure turns out not to have been warranted, then there will be a high net cost to precaution. On the other hand, if new information reveals that precaution was justified, nothing is lost. This suggests that some balancing of costs and benefits still must play a role even in contexts where the precautionary principle is thought to apply.

Annex 10 sets out some basic principles of analysis of risky contexts.

Dealing with uncertainty

As noted above, the very least that should be done when there is uncertainty but lower and upper bounds are known is to engage in **sensitivity analysis**. Sensitivity is usually performed with respect to:

- estimates of benefits: especially to allow for "optimism" and in-built tendencies to exaggerate benefits;
- estimates of costs: especially to allow for in-built optimism about the costs of projects (cost over-runs being more usual than underspends);
- estimates of discount rates and other important parameters.

It often helps to draw up a **payoff matrix'** in which the outcomes from various combinations of actions (decisions) and "states of nature" are portrayed. Box 13.5 gives an example of such a matrix. Note that drawing the matrix assists decision-making only by presenting the information in a comprehensible manner. The matrix itself does not offer guidance on what action to choose. Various decision rules have been devised to deal with the choice problem, each one corresponding to the "personality" of the decision-maker: e.g., optimists, pessimists, those concerned to minimise future regret, and so on.

Delaying decisions

It often pays to delay decisions while further information is brought to bear on the issue. The cost of delay then has to be compared to the benefits of delay. Annex 10 explores the analytics of this decision in more detail.

Integrating risk and uncertainty in decision-making

The previous analysis suggests that there are no simple or comprehensive rules for integrating risk and uncertainty into decision-making. But addressing the problem of risk and uncertainty should be an integral part of programme and project design and management. Certain steps in the procedure can be set out:

(1) potential sources of risk and uncertainty need to be identified at the outset, including the physical attributes and mechanisms of environmental systems likely to be affected. Systems simulation models are often a useful means of understanding the relevant natural processes;

(2) the quality of information needs to be assessed. For some effects very little will be known or predictable. For others, information may be available for upper and lower bounds. In still other cases it may be possible to fit a probability distribution to the pattern of effects;

(3) risk information can be portrayed in probability distributions and can be "reduced" to single numbers as expected values (if risk neutrality seems appropriate) or expected utility (if risk aversion seems appropriate). But the use of expected utility as a model is open to question. If cost-benefit analysis is meant to obey the value judgement that individuals' preferences count, then the observation that people often fail to obey the axioms of expected utility is problematic. If, on the other hand, cost benefit analysis is supposed to reflect some representative "rational" decision-making, it may be legitimate to adopt the expected utility model;

216

(4) Where probabilities are small but impacts are very large (the "zero infinity" dilemma) recourse may be had to the precautionary principle or safe minimum standards, but some reference to the opportunity costs of adopting these principles is required;

(5) uncertainty information can be portrayed in payoff matrices, but the matrices themselves do not enable a choice to be made. This requires some choice rule based in turn on the outlook and disposition of the decision-maker;

(6) the issue of delaying a decision needs to be investigated. This will be especially true where the issue is one of pollution prevention or remediation. The costs and benefits of delaying the action need to be compared with the costs and benefits of acting now.

Box 13.1 Fault tree analysis

Fault tree analysis is widely used to assess the risks of accidents, especially in nuclear plants. The technique involves calculating the probability of an accident or failure at each stage of a sequence of decisions or connecting links in an industrial process. The diagram over shows a simplified fault tree analysis for a "loss of coolant" accident (LOCA) in a nuclear power station. The initiating event is a pipe break, and subsequent failures involve the emergency core cooling system (ECCS), fission product removal and the containment of radioactive material.

The probability of an environment effect is then a conditional probability and is equal to the product of the probabilities of all the events required, in sequence, to create the effect. Since the probability of each event occurring is small, the probability of an environmental effect is even smaller - small probabilities are multiplied by small probabilities. This is why many fault tree studies conclude that risks of nuclear accidents are very small. But individual branches of the fault tree may not be independent of each other: accidents in which emergency procedures are hindered, for example, could be more serious than is implied by fault tree analysis. The method is useful, but needs to be used cautiously.

Fault-Tree Analysis as an Example of Risk Methodology

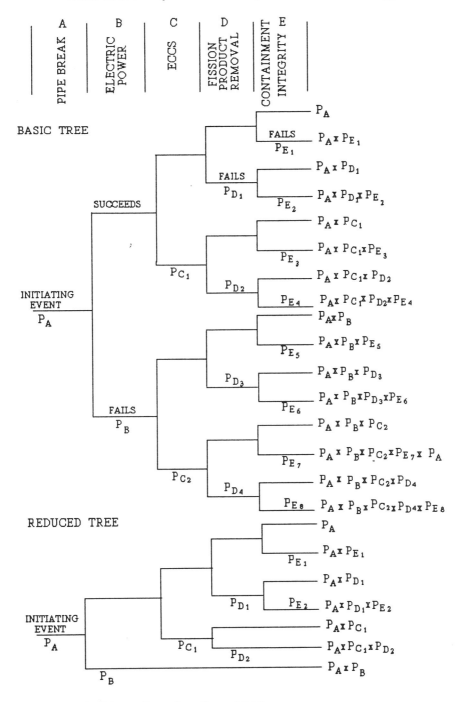

Simplified Event Trees for a Large LOCA

Source: Reactor Safety Study, Wash-1400, U.S. Atomic Energy Commission
August, 1974 (Draft)

	Deaths per 1 million people exposed	Cost to Avoid 1 death ($ mill)
Trihalomethane in Drinking Water	420	0.2
Radionuclides in Uranium Mines	6300	3.4
Benzene Fugitive Emissions	1470	3.4
Benzene Occupational Exposure	39600	8.9
Asbestos Occupational Exposure	3015	8.3
Arsenic/Copper Exposure	63000	23.0
Acrylonitrile Occupational Exposure	42300	51.5
Coke Ovens Occupational Exposure	7200	63.5
Hazardous Waste Land Disposal	2	4190.2
Municipal Solid Waste Landfill Standard	1	19107.0
Hazardous Waste: Wood Preservatives	<1	5,700,000

The risks shown relate to numbers of mortalities for the relevant exposed population. All the hazards shown are the subject of environmental legislation in the USA, so, for example, the risk that is affected by the piece of legislation is the numerical value shown here. Notice that expressing the risks as "per million" makes some of them look large. The largest risk, for arsenic/copper exposure, is 0.063 when expressed as a fraction, or 63 in 1000 or just over 6 in a 100. The manner in which risk is expressed often influences the extent to which people react to the risk.

The legislation costs money. The right hand column shows what happens when this cost is divided by the numbers of lives that the legislation is expected to save. In this way, cost and "effectiveness" (lives saved) can be compared - see text.

Source: The Council on Environmental Quality, *Environmental Quality: 21st Annual Report 1990*, Washington DC: US Government Printing Office.

Box 13.3 Disaster aversion

The table below shows some possible rules for deciding on the "value" of a disaster. Suppose we know that the "value of a statistical life" (V) is $2 million, i.e society is willing to pay up to £2 million to save a single life in road accidents, health programmes etc. Assume that the accident in question has a 1 in a million chance of happening (f = frequency of the event) and that it might involve 100, 500 or 1000 people dying (N = 100, 500, 1000). Then the "value of the accident" depends on how people view the group accident event. It has been suggested, and some regulatory agencies use this rule, that an accident involving 100 people is regarded as being the equivalent of 100x100 deaths in individual accidents (the "square rule"). Others suggest that it is equal to 300 times the number of actual deaths, and so on. Which rule is chosen matters a great deal. In the table it can be seen that one would spend only $4000 to avert a one in a million chance of 1000 people dying in a single accident if no aversion factor is present, but $4 million if the square rule is used.

f = 1/1,000,000		
N = 100	N = 500	N = 1000
fN = 0.0001	fN = 0.0005	fN = 0.001
fN^2 = 0.01	fN^2 = 0.25	fN^2 = 1.0
300fN = 0.03	300fN = 0.15	300fN = 0.3
vfN = £400	vfN = £2000	vfN = $4000
vfN^2 = £40,000	vfN^2 = £1,000,000	$vfN^2 \doteq$ $4,000,000
v300fN = £120,000	v300fN = £600,000	v300fN = $1,200,000

Box 13.4 Comparing perceptions of risk: Experts vs the public

US Environment Protection Agency Scientific Advisory Board Unranked Priorities	USA Public Opinion Poll March 1990 % Saying "Very serious"	UK Public Opinion Poll May 1989 % Saying "Very worried".
Ecological Risks		
Climate change	48	44
Ozone layer	60	56
Habitat change	42	45
Biodiversity loss	na	45
Health Risks		
Criteria pollutants*	56	34-40
Toxic air pollutants**	50	33
Radon	17	na
Indoor air pollution	22	na
Drinking water	46	41
Pesticides	52	46
Issues Regarded by the Public as Important but not by the Experts		
Oil spills	60	53
Hazardous waste sites	66	na
Industrial water pollution	63	na
Nuclear accidents	60	na
Industrial pollution accidents	58	64
Radioactive waste	58	58
Leaking underground storage tanks	54	na
Contaminated bathing water	na	59

Sources: UK Department of the Environment, [1990], "Counting on Science at EPA", *Science*, Vol.240, August 10, ; Pearce, D.W., et al, [1991], *The Development of Environmental Indicators*, Report to UK Department of the Environment, April.

Box 13.5 Agricultural production decisions: An application of payoff matrices

Agriculture is an uncertain activity in dryland areas due to the difficulty of predicting weather conditions. The hypothetical data below show an approach to uncertainty based on payoff matrices.

The management options are to graze sheep, grow wheat, or graze cattle. The net benefits associated with these options are calculated for high, moderate and low rainfall conditions. If the probabilities are known, a choice could be made on the basis of expected values. But suppose the probabilities are not known. A precautionary approach (the **maximin** approach) would be first to identify the worst-case payoffs -i.e., the payoffs with lowest net benefits. These are shown in bold in the first table. The best of these is then selected - in this case the decision is to graze sheep since this yields the highest benefits (the "max") from the worst case ("min") outcomes.

The **minimum regret** approach involves measuring the degree of "regret" associated with choosing an option. Regret is measured by the difference between the returns that could have been achieved and those that are achieved. The first step is to identify the maximum payoffs that might have been achieved in retrospect for each set of rainfall conditions. The opportunity losses are then calculated. For the highest original payoffs the losses (regrets) would be zero. Regrets for the other payoffs are calculated by subtracting the original values, for each set of rainfall conditions, from the corresponding original highest value. This produces a **regret matrix** shown in the second table. Minimising regret then involves choosing the option with the lowest value - in this case wheat production.

These **payoff approaches** do not dictate a decision rule: they simply show how particular perceptions of uncertainty can be translated into choices.

Rainfall			
Strategy	High	Medium	Low
Sheep	80	50	20
Wheat	170	30	14
Cattle	100	70	10

The Payoff Matrix

Rainfall			
Strategy	High	Medium	Low
Sheep	90	20	0
Wheat	0	40	6
Cattle	70	0	10

The Regret Matrix

To construct the regret matrix proceed as follows. Inspect the payoff matrix. The highest payoff for high rainfall is wheat at 170. If the sheep option is chosen and high rainfall occurs, the regret associated with sheep is then 170 - 80 = 90, i.e., the difference between what could have received and what is received.

PART V

IMPLEMENTATION

Chapter 14

Why Do Governments Intervene?

Rationales for intervention

All governments intervene in the workings of the economy. If the supply and demand for goods and services has certain characteristics then it could be argued that there would be no need for government intervention. Essentially, these characteristics reduce to the requirement that the preferences of all individuals affected by the provision of the good are reflected in the market place. In practice, we know that such a requirement is not met. First, the provision of many goods and services affects third parties through the phenomenon of **external effects**. Second, and a special case of external effects, the provision of a good to one person may automatically entail its provision to another person, and without the possibility of excluding the other person from that provision. This is the case with **public goods**. Third, even if individuals' preferences for or against the provision of a good are registered in the market, there are "social preferences" relating to the outcome of market provision. Most notably, there are concerns about the **distribution** or **equity impacts** of market outcomes, and about the **social morality** of markets. Thus, since markets work according to willingness to pay, and willingness to pay is influenced by ability to pay (income, wealth), the relatively poor may suffer under a market allocation. In the same way, simply honouring market solutions could produce markets in pornography, slavery and weapons. Most societies reject those outcomes on moral grounds.

It is important to distinguish **explanations** of government intervention from **justifications** for such activity. Much intervention is due to the political process in which political supporters of government are "rewarded" with gains and opponents with losses. This process shows up in the structure of financial subsidies, regionally biased policies, or special treatment for certain industries. In this chapter we are concerned with reasons for intervention which also have at least a plausible justification. The underlying rationale for intervention is basically that of moving society to a higher state of aggregate well-being than would be the case if no intervention was practised.

There is ample evidence that the free functioning of markets is more likely to accord with the underlying value judgement that individual preferences should count. The demand for commodities is assumed to reflect the preferences of individuals and the interaction of demand and supply determines what is supplied, how much is supplied, and the price at which it is supplied. But markets do not generally achieve this ideal of fulfilling preferences, and in some cases they fail altogether in the sense that markets do not exist. These **market failures** are fundamental to the rationale for government intervention. Governments intervene when the market fails in the following senses:

- the market **fails to produce the "right" commodities**, where "rightness" is to be judged by some moral principle which is superior to the moral principle underlying individual preference sovereignty. Goods that are valued more highly by reference to some other moral principle are often called **merit goods**;

- the market produces the "right" commodities but fails to produce them in the right quantities. The right quantity is that which maximises the well-being of the individuals who make up society, as defined in Chapter 3. Markets may **under-provide certain kinds of goods**. This will happen when the good contains the characteristics of a **public good**, i.e., a good which, if provided to individual A is also provided to individual B without B's consumption affecting A's consumption-also known as "non-rivalness" or "non-rival goods". Clean air might be an example. A second condition for a good to be called a public good is that it is not possible to prevent B consuming the good if A consumes it - "non-exclusion". Brief reflection will suffice to show that a private individual is unlikely to supply public goods because he or she cannot capture the benefits of shared consumption through pricing. Public goods can be thought of as sharing the characteristics of goods with **positive external effects** or **external benefits**.

Markets may also **over-provide certain other kinds of goods**. This will especially be true when the goods exhibit **negative external effects** or **external costs**. As long as the supplier of a good does not pay for the full costs of providing that good, the good will be under-priced and hence over-produced (costs of production are artificially low) and over-consumed (the consumer buys at an artificially low price).

- A further "failure" in market systems arises because consumers are often **ill-informed** about the benefits and costs of the product they consumer, and the manner in which it is produced. This form of failure is distinct from the presence of external effects. Externalities can arise even where the individual is fully informed, although there is no doubt that many externalities would be reduced in scale if individuals were fully informed of the consequence of their actions. **Information failure** exists when the addition of information changes the individual's willingness to pay (up or down). Note that information gathering itself uses up resources: hence there is an "optimal" level of information determined by the costs and benefits of acquiring the information.

- Externalities are especially likely to arise if there are **missing markets**. A missing market refers to a context in which there are changes in well-being which are not expressed through the medium of a direct market. Markets in clean air, for example, seem to be indirect rather than direct. Clean air is not bought and sold but it does affect property prices and avertive expenditures, a classic externality phenomenon. A missing market is an extreme form of an incomplete market, in which the market does not exist at all. Governments may intervene where there are missing markets in order to establish **property rights**. Good examples of such interventions include international environmental treaties such as the Montreal Protocol on Substances That Deplete the Ozone Layer, and the Framework Convention on Climate Change.

- A classic reason for intervention is to **influence the distribution of income**. Markets allocate goods and resources accordingly to willingness to pay which, in turn, is partly determined by income and wealth. Superficially, then, a legitimate cause for intervention is to correct for the income bias of the market in favour of a more "fair" or "equitable" distribution of benefits and costs. But this rationale needs to be used with caution. Projects are often a very inefficient way of redistributing income, although they can be used in this way to affect a particular region, e.g., by locating an investment in a depressed region as opposed to a growing one. Policies tend have national impacts and may therefore be better suited to distributional objectives, but even then there are usually better ways of securing the redistribution, e.g., via fiscal policy. But, especially in developing countries, options to redistribute income by fiscal means are often not available, in politically feasible terms anyway. In these contexts, the use of investments and specific policies may be the only legitimate way of influencing income distribution.

Governments may therefore intervene in order to supply merit goods and public goods, to curtail the production of goods with external costs, to provide information to enable better informed choices to be made, to create property rights which otherwise would not exist or which might be incompletely defined, and to influence the distribution of income.

Note that there is a special assumption in this justification for regulation. It is that the benefits of intervention - the gains in the supply of public goods, the reductions in the loss of well-being caused by external costs, for example - exceed the costs of intervention. The costs of intervention can be substantial. Governments have to acquire information and process it. They have to regulate the producer and the consumer, and regulations absorb resources directly (e.g., through paying government officers) and indirectly (e.g., by taking up productive time of the producer and consumer). **Thus, even where markets do fail, it is not necessarily the case that intervention will improve aggregate well-being. That depends on the balance of costs and benefits of intervention. Hence all regulation needs to be subjected to an assessment of its effects on individual and social well-being.** This is the theme of this chapter.

Types of intervention

Governments intervene in a number of ways. It is important to understand that all interventions have environmental impacts, regardless of whether the intervention is motivated by environmental concerns or not. Figure 14.1 illustrates this proposition in the context of (a) price interventions where prices may be set artificially high to raise the incomes of a specific social group (e.g., farmers), or may be set below the equilibrium price to protect a low income group; and (b) quantity interventions where quotas may be set below the equilibrium output or above it. The former case is typified by many rationing contexts and the latter by production targets in planned economic systems. While output quotas can have beneficial effects on the environment, society as a whole loses. Output quotas set above equilibrium levels are invariably environmentally harmful.

Social and unstable preferences

Two other justifications are often given for government intervention: "citizens' preferences" and unstable preferences.

Citizens' Preferences

The preferences of individuals tend to be self-oriented, i.e., what matters are the gains and losses to the individual him or herself. But individuals may register preferences acting as citizens, i.e., when thinking of what is best for society as a whole rather than for the individual. Clearly, the whole array of prices and quantities in the economy will differ if there is a regime of citizen preferences compared to one of purely individualistic preferences. But is this relevant to the argument for government intervention? If individuals actually express preferences on the basis of citizen values, then resource allocation in the economy will respond accordingly. There is no need for government to intervene. If they do not express citizens' preferences, then resource allocation will reflect individualistic preferences as long as free markets rule. Governments may then intervene if they wish to override individual preferences "for the good of society". But the arguments for legitimately overriding individual preferences have already been discussed. The existence of citizens' preferences adds little or nothing to the argument.

Unstable preferences and compensating the future

Preferences change over time. As such, a decision made in accordance with some consensus about today's preferences may not be in accord with preferences at a future date. **Preferences are said to**

be unstable. A distinction needs to be made between:

- preferences expressed by one group of individuals now and different preferences expressed by a different group - a future generation say - at another period of time;

- preferences expressed by one group of individuals whose own preferences change over time.

In the former situation there is a problem of first assigning moral standing to future generations. In the second situation individuals can either be expected to make some allowance in their decisions for **future regret** - in which case intervention is not required - or governments may anticipate the regret and intervene to modify current choices, e.g., through product taxation.

If, as most people accept, future generations have "rights", it is incumbent upon existing generations to take those rights into account when making decisions now that affect the welfare of future generations. This is very much the underlying premise of **sustainable development**.

Some would argue that there is no need for governments to intervene as " guardians of the future" because individuals now care for the future anyway: parents care for children and grandchildren; children for their children and grandchildren, and so on. There will be a series of **overlapping generations** and utility functions at any one time take the form:

$$W_t = f(C_t, W_{t+1}, W_{T+2})$$

where C is consumption, and the time subscripts prefer to the current generation (t) and the next two generations (t+1, t+2). But there are reasons to doubt if the existence of overlapping generations will produce resource allocations consistent with the philosophy of sustainable development. If not, then interventions are required by governments.

Two forms of rule emerge from a consideration of sustainable development:

a) maximise the well-being of the current generation subject to the requirement that the well-being of future generations is not less than that of the current generation - generally known as the **non-declining per capita utility** requirement.

b) maximise the well-being of the current generation subject to the requirement that any current action significantly impairing the well-being of future generations should either be (i) compensated, or (ii) avoided. These are the **intergenerational compensation** and **avoiding irreversibility** requirements.

Option (b) is consistent with future generations' well-being being less than the current generation's well-being - the only obligation on the current generation is to avoid those actions now which are likely to contribute to reduced future well-being. Otherwise, future generations can, as it were, "look after themselves". Option (a) has tended to give rise to the idea of leaving a **constant stock of capital to the next generation**, the so-called "constant capital" rule. Option (b) amounts to avoiding **irreversible actions**, or finding some mechanism for compensating the future. Of course, leaving capital stocks no less than those that exist now is itself a compensation mechanism and assumes that future generations accept as substitutes other forms of capital for those lost by current actions. If compensation has to be of a specific form, e.g a lost wetland now must be compensated by a recreated wetland in the future, then the instability of preferences presents a problem. We cannot know now what form of compensation would be acceptable to future generations since their preferences may have changed. This suggests a guiding principle to the effect that the compensation should be in a "malleable" form, i.e., something that can be converted into whatever future generations prefer.

Compensation and discounting

Important conclusions emerge from the integration of future generations into current decision-making. The first is that **actual compensation** is required. The second relates to the **discount rate**. In both cases, governments will need to intervene.

Actual compensation

Benefit-cost analysis typically works on the rule that a policy or project is satisfactory if its benefits exceed its costs, suitably expressed as present values. But there is no requirement for any external costs to be compensated. It is sufficient for there to be **hypothetical compensation** by the beneficiaries of the losers. Hypothetical compensation is consistent with the losers actually being worse off after the project or policy than before it. Aggregate well-being has improved because gains exceed losses. But the philosophy of sustainable development requires that **future losers should actually be no worse off** - in either the aggregate or specific sense.

We can present a brief model of actual compensation which also reveals an important observation about the discount rate. The model is due to Mäler [1991].

Suppose there is man-made capital, denoted K, and a non-renewable resource, denoted R. There are two periods reflecting two generations, 0 and 1. If generation 0 decides to reduce the stock of R_o in order to enjoy more consumption C_o, then it will reduce the consumption possibilities of generation 1 since the resource stock declines and is therefore not available to the next generation. In order to ensure that generation 1's consumption does not decline - the sustainability criterion - generation 0 must compensate generation 1 by increasing the stock of K so that generation 1 inherits more capital.

This compensation requirement can be written:

$$dI_0.F_{1K} = dR_0.F_{1R} \qquad [14.1]$$

The left hand side of [1] is the gain in period 1 and is equal to the change in investment in period 0 necessary to compensate period 1 multiplied by the marginal product of capital in period 1. [1] can be rewritten:

$$dI_0 = dR_0. F_{1R}./F_{1K} \qquad [14.2]$$

The right hand side is the loss in period 1 due to the reduction in the non-renewable resource and is equal to the change in the resource stock in 0 multiplied by the marginal product of that resource in period 1 (i.e., what it would have yielded in period 1).

The <u>net</u> change in consumption in period 0 is then:

$$dC_0 = dR_0.F_{0R} - dI_0 \qquad [14.3]$$

and is made up of the gain brought about by the extra extraction of the natural resource less the extra investment required to compensate period 1. Substituting [14.2] in [14.3] gives:

$$dC_0 = dR_0.[F_{0R} - F_{1R}/F_{1K}] \qquad [14.4]$$

which can be rewritten

$$dC_0 = dR_0 [F_{0R} - F_{1R}/\{1 + (F_{1K} - 1)\}] \qquad [14.5]$$

Now, $F_{1K} - 1 = r$, the marginal product of capital - 1, or the social rate of discount as given by the productivity of capital. Note that it is the marginal product of capital in period 1 that is relevant, not the productivity in period 0; and that it is the productivity of capital that gives rise to discounting in this context, not the rate of time preference.

Hence [14.5] can be written as:

$$dC_0 = dR_0.[F_{0R} - F_{1R}/(1 + r)] \qquad [14.6]$$

which is then the decision rule for generation 0. Sustainability is ensured if the change in consumption in period 0 equals the benefit from the use of the natural resource in 0 less the costs which equal the discounted value of the foregone future productivity of the resource.

Now consider the substitutability issue. If substitution possibilities between K and R are very small, then F_{1K} would be small and F_{1R} would be very big. Hence F_{1R}/F_{1K} would be large and, from [4], dC_0 would be negative. That is, development is <u>not</u> sustainable if resource use now involves resources which cannot be substituted for by K, or which have a low elasticity of substitution.

Two observations can be made. First, the basic benefit - cost model is preserved: that is, from the standpoint of the current generation the appropriate rule is to compute the present values of costs and benefits and to adopt the investment or policy change if benefits exceed costs, allowing for actual compensation. Second, the discount rate in the benefit cost formula is not the <u>current</u> marginal productivity of capital, but the <u>future</u> marginal productivity of capital.

The relevance of the future productivity of capital can be illustrated with the help of Figure 14.2. The diagram shows the welfare of the current and future generations on the two axes (W_C, and W_F respectively). PP' is an intertemporal production function showing the choices of output between now and the future. The 45° line shows all points where welfare now and in the future are equal. If we adopt the definition of sustainable development in which the well-being of future generations must not be less than the well-being of current generations, then all "sustainable well-being" points must lie in the area between the 45° line and the vertical axis. But benefit cost analysis is consistent with a move from an inefficient point such as A to an efficient point such as B, where future generations are in fact worse off than current generations. A move from A to a point such as C is both an efficient and sustainable move. However, the slope of the production frontier PP' at C is quite different to the slope at B. The slope is in fact the marginal product of capital, i.e., the discount rate. Hence the discount rate at C is lower than the discount rate at B. As with the model above, sustainability suggests that the future productivity of capital is the relevant variable for determining the discount rate, and that this rate is likely to be a low discount rate determined by current generational concerns only (as one would expect).

The implications of the rationales for intervention

What are the implications of the previous discussion for the environmental appraisal of projects, programmes and policies ?

They may be summarised as follows:
> •   government intervention is most likely to have a general justification in the contexts of:

- providing public goods which would otherwise be under-provided by the market. Environmental public goods are likely to be especially important - e.g., clean air, adequate assimilative capacity of the environment etc.

- providing information to improve the efficiency of markets, especially information about the environmental consequences of consumption and production decisions.

- correcting significant negative externalities, especially in the environmental context where there are "missing markets".

- ensuring that externalities imposed on future generations do not give rise to a failure to provide the foundations for sustainable development. This will be especially important where environmental damage is irreversible either technically or practically.

- setting discount rates below those that emerge from the workings of the market place.

- all regulatory intervention should itself be subject to an evaluation of the costs and benefits of that regulation since intervention is itself not costless, neither for government nor for the regulated parties.

Figure 14.1 **Types of government intervention**

Diagram (a) shows a simple supply and demand graph with S = supply (marginal cost) and D = demand (marginal benefit). MEC is marginal external cost and is added to S (MC) to give the full social cost of production. The price and quantity that should rule in the market are given by P*, Q* but this can only be achieved if governments intervene to correct the externality (we assume here that there are no private bargains over the externality). The net social surplus is given by the shaded area.

In diagram (b) the government has intervened to fix the price of the good at Ph, a price above the equilibrium ignoring the externality and above the equilibrium that emerges if the externality is corrected. Such price fixing is commonplace for agricultural commodities where governments often act to "protect" the incomes of farmers. The effect of the price fixing <u>compared to the corrected externality optimum</u> is:

(a) to reduce the consumers' surplus (by the shaded "arrow shape" shown);

(b) to artificially expand producers' surplus by the size of the effective subsidy Ph.P*.O.Qh;

(c) to damage the environment by imposing a non-optimal level of externality (shown by the dotted area).

Price intervention can thus have significant environmental effects.

In diagram (c) a quantity restriction is imposed rather than a price regulation. A quota at Ql has the effect of raising price to Ph. Consumers' plus producers' surplus is reduced by the heavy shaded triangle shown. The environment <u>improves</u> by the dotted area due to the output restriction (note that the areas cannot be compared directly due to transfer elements). A quota at Qh - which might exist under a planned economy system where there are production targets - would have the effect of lowering the price to Pl. Output expands and the externality worsens.

Overall, then, interventions in markets, for whatever reason, are likely to have environmental impacts.

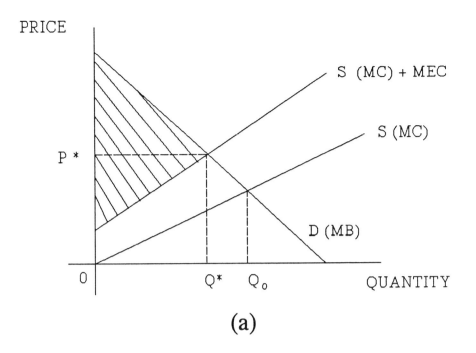

(a)

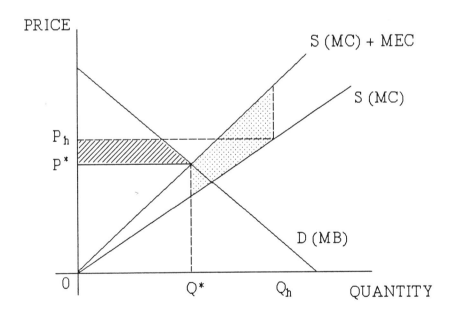

(b)

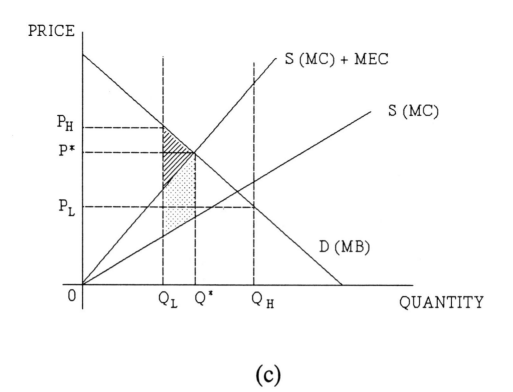

(c)

Figure 14.2 **Sustainability and the discount rate**

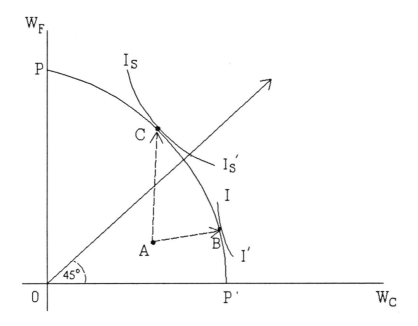

PP' is a transformation function between current well-being (Wc) and future well-being (Wf). Point A is inefficient and many policy measures and projects are concerned with moves from a point like A to a point like B, improving the well-being of current and future generations alike. But at B, future generations are still worse off than current generations, and this could be held to be inconsistent with "sustainable development". If so, only points to the north of the 45° line are consistent with sustainable development. Rather than moving from A to B, policy should aim to move from A to a point like C. At B and A the discount rate is given by the slope of the social indifference curves II' and I,I,' and the slope of the transformation function. At C the discount rate is lower than at B.

Chapter 15

Pricing

Introduction: the context of environmental resource pricing

The proper pricing of resources and economic outputs is a central weapon in the armoury of the policy analyst. Because so many environmental effects are non-marketed, one extremely important policy measure is to ensure that, as far as possible, the "true" economic value of environmental resources is accounted for when making investment and environmental policy decisions. There is therefore a fundamental connection between the issue of **economic valuation of environmental resources** and the **pricing of environmental resources**. As we shall see, all environmental resources should be priced according to their marginal economic value. The phrase "should be priced" can mean two things. First, it may mean that <u>actual</u> prices are introduced into the economy for environmental resources that were hitherto treated as free. Second, it may mean that even though actual prices are not introduced, the marginal economic value of the resource is entered into some accounting procedure such as cost-benefit analysis or national accounting (see Chapter 11). In the former case the market is then left to react to the actual price charged for the resource. In the latter case economic decisions are based on the **accounting price** or **shadow price**. In terms of the identification and measurement of the proper price the purpose does not matter much. The procedure will be the same. Both contexts may be described as **internalisation of environmental damage costs**. But the underlying rationale is important: **unless environmental resources are correctly priced - so as to be reflected in actual decisions - there will be distortions in the economy which will have the effect of biasing investment and policy decisions against environmental concerns.** A formal proof is given in Annex 11.

In case this statement appears to set the environment up as some independent goal of policy, it can be stated another way: **unless environmental resources are correctly priced, and those prices internalised in actual decisions - there will be a misallocation of resources in the economy and social well-being will not be maximised.** In this restatement, environmental resources are then not differentiated from other resources, but failing to price environmental resources correctly is seen as an instance of general misallocation and distortion in the economy.

There will generally be two contexts for the proper pricing of environmental resources: (a) when the resource is consumed directly, as with water or fuelwood; (b) when the resource is consumed indirectly, as with the receiving capacity of water and air in terms of their assimilation of wastes; and (c) when the resource is "embodied" in an economic good, as with the energy content of iron and steel or a motor vehicle. While there are various classifications, type (a) pricing involves **user charges**; type (b) involves **emissions or waste charges**; and type (c) involves **product charges**. Quite often, user, emission and waste charges are all called "user charges" because they all make an attempt to price for the use of environmental resources.

As a general rule we will find that it is best to establish prices for the environmental resources themselves. In this way, those prices will work their way through to the prices of any goods and services that embody them.

Some simple rules of environmental pricing

The basic rule for the optimal pricing of a <u>natural resource</u> is that price should be equal to the cost of extracting or harvesting the resource, plus any external costs that the extraction or harvesting causes, plus any "user cost" element.

The rule for pricing a <u>product</u> that embodies environmental resources which are unpriced or underpriced is that the product price should equal the marginal cost of production plus the value of the externality caused by the production and consumption of the good. Typically, this will result in a product price equal to the (private) cost of production plus an emissions or waste charge. In all cases, the rule will be that emissions or waste charges should equal the marginal **damage** done to the environment.

Rule 1: Pricing a resource:
$$P = MCh + MECh + MUC$$

Rule 2: Pricing products:
$$P = MCq + MECq$$

where MC is marginal cost; MEC is marginal external cost; MUC is marginal user cost; h reminds us that it is the cost of harvesting (or extraction) and q that it is the cost of production.

The term "user cost" (not be confused with a "user charge" - see below) will be dealt with shortly. One issue needs to be addressed at the outset. Which environmental costs should be embodied in the price of a product? Consider a product such as a motor vehicle. The rules above suggest that the environmental costs of production and use of the vehicle should be part of the price of the vehicle. There are at least three complications.

(a) How much externality cost should a product bear? User charges and product charges.

First, charges for the <u>use</u> of the vehicle (**user charges**) should be differentiated from the charge for the environmental cost of producing the vehicle (**product charges**). It would be inefficient to charge each vehicle the social cost of the average vehicle's use. Rather, the social costs of use should be charged separately. In the case of vehicles this could be via a road user charge or a gasoline tax. Hence it is important to differentiate charges for use from charges for production externalities. In some cases, however, it may be infeasible to charge directly for use and a product charge may have to act as a proxy for the user charge.

(b) Life cycle impacts

Second, charging for the production externality would mean incorporating the costs of, say, any air pollution arising from the manufacture of the vehicles. But what of the pollution caused by the manufacture of the steel, plastic etc. that is used to make the vehicle ? This is the issue of **life cycle impacts**. If there were no regulations or environmental taxes on pollution from upstream processes then it is arguable that a product tax should reflect all the external costs of all the processes used for the manufacture of the vehicle. But if there are regulations in place that have already raised the price of energy etc. used in manufacture, then it may be argued that the taxes will have worked their way through to the price of the vehicle. Charging for them <u>again</u> would be inefficient.

(c) Existing tax structures

A similar problem to (b) arises when taxes exist that, although they are not designed for environmental purposes, none the less act as taxes on the production or use of the product and hence regulate the amount that is produced. A conspicuous example is energy which is widely taxed in developed countries. Should it be taxed again for environmental purposes? Strictly, the answer depends on identifying the <u>amount</u> of external cost present with the non-environmental tax regime in place. If the resulting external cost level can be regarded as "optimal", then a further environmental tax would not be warranted. If, however, the prevailing tax system results in levels of externality which are non-optimal, then an environmental tax to correct that non-optimal externality level is warranted. Box 15.1 looks at this issue in the context of fuel taxation in some developed economies. Annex 12 shows why a pollution tax would be warranted in order to secure a proper allocation of resources in the economy, and derives the pricing rule in Rule 2 (for products).

Pricing non-renewable resources

Natural resources are typically divided into renewable and non-renewable resources. The term "exhaustible" is somewhat redundant since all resource are exhaustible in that they can be "mined" and over-used to extinction. This section looks briefly at the way in which a non-renewable resource should be priced. Rule 1 declares that all resources should be priced according to the sum of their extraction (harvesting) costs, any external costs and an element termed "user cost". Annex 13 explains the analytical basis of user cost. Essentially, user cost arises because, for an exhaustible resource, use of a unit of that resource today means going without it tomorrow. Keynes actually used the mining example in working out the principles of user cost and which he argued were generally applicable to all production involving durable inputs. Thus:

> "if a ton of copper is used today, it cannot be used tomorrow and the value which the copper would have for the purposes of tomorrow must clearly be reckoned as part of the marginal costs" (J.M. Keynes, [1936], *The General Theory of Employment, Interest and Money*, Macmillan, London).

The relevance of user cost in practice arises when considering how to price a new resource and in assessing whether existing prices already capture user cost. Typically, if markets are reasonably competitive the latter issue will not arise. That is, ruling prices should reflect user cost. The former case does however require such estimates to be made before deciding whether or not a resource should be exploited and, if so, what price to charge. Box 15.2 gives an illustration.

Pricing a renewable resource

The fundamental distinction between a renewable and a non-renewable resource is that the former regenerates itself whereas the latter does not. In practice, however, "renewability" is a physical <u>potential</u> rather than an actual fact. It is perfectly feasible to exhaust a renewable resource. Thus, some whale and fish stocks have been exhausted through over-fishing; forests have been lost because of over-cutting or burning; rhinoceros and elephant have disappeared from a number of African countries through poaching and land encroachment, and so on. The distinction between potential and actual renewability is important because in the case where the renewable resource is over-used relative to its rate of regeneration, it is arguable that a user cost component should be charged for the resource. Otherwise, strictly speaking, the user cost issue does not arise with respect to renewable resources[22].

The basic pricing rule for renewable resources is that already enunciated in Rule 1, but with the possibility that a user cost component may or may not be present.

For a great many renewable natural resource decisions the issue is not what price to charge but, given that there is a ruling market price which it is difficult to influence through any policy measures, at what rate should the resource be exploited? This is typically formulated in the context where "sustainability" is a constraint, i.e., it is assumed that the management policy aims to allow the resource to renew itself. The issue of how much to harvest then applies generally in cases where the rate of regeneration depends on the stock. That is, various harvest rates are possible and all are "sustainable" even though the stock will vary at each different harvest rate. This problem is not pursued further here (see any text on natural resource economics for extensive analysis of this issue).

Other decisions will, however, relate to issues such as investment in new stocks of the renewable resource - e.g., a managed fishery, a fuelwood plantation, expanded water supplies. In some of these cases, especially in poor developing countries, there may be no real markets. In such circumstances it is important to determine the **shadow price** of the resource in order to determine whether or not it should be produced and, if so, in what quantities. The shadow price is really the marginal benefit of the resource, i.e., the optimal price. In other words, the issue of optimal pricing involves the **valuation exercises** developed in Part III. In other cases, the resource may already be priced on some ad hoc basis. That is, "proper" prices do not prevail. This situation is common to both developing and developed economies. Water is a fairly conspicuous example. Many years of tradition of thinking of water as a "free good" has led to it being priced well below its true opportunity cost.

Some examples will help clarify the issues. Others are given in Part III.

A fuelwood plantation

Consider the issue of investment in a fuelwood plantation in a developing country. Fuelwood may well be bought and sold in the open market. If so, the ruling market price could be used to value the output of a fuelwood plantation. In estimating **benefits**, however, the ideal approach would be to estimate the demand for fuelwood and derive a measure of consumer surplus. Where, as is often the case in developing countries, the data do not permit this, the market price will suffice as a minimum estimate of marginal benefit. But what happens when there are no prices -i.e., when fuelwood is not traded? This is often the case outside of urban areas (where developed fuelwood markets tend to exist) and fuelwood is collected for personal use only. It is now necessary to derive a shadow price by looking at the resources used to gather fuelwood.

A procedure for doing this is as follows:

(a) using either existing surveys or specially commissioned surveys, establish the number of average hours (h_T) taken on trips to secure fuelwood. Estimate the number of trips, which may differ between the dry season and the wet season (T_D, T_W). Compute $[h_T.T_D + h_t.T_W]/2 = h^*_T$ where the division by two simply reflects the average portion of the year accounted for by the dry season and wet season.

(b) estimate the headloads per trip (S_T). This issue arises because different members of the family will be able to collect different headloads. There is a need to normalise the headloads (into, for example, "adult" headloads). In turn, to find this out it will be necessary to have a survey of who collects fuelwood. In African countries this is invariably the adult female of the household but children will also be involved

(c) estimate the weight per headload (W_s), and compute weight per trip as $W_T = S_T.W_s$.

(d) compute $C_T = h^*_T.C_h$ where C_h is the cost of an hour's labour. (This could be weighted according to the survey of who in the family collects the wood, i.e., the adult wage will overstate the average wage if children mainly collect fuelwood.)

(e) The final calculation is then:

$$Pf = C_T/W_T = C_h\{h_T[T_D + T_W]/S_T.W_s$$

where Pf is the shadow price of fuelwood.

The fuelwood pricing example relates the price of fuelwood to the opportunity cost of the time used to collect the fuelwood. If there are mixed systems where unmarketed collection occurs and fuelwood is also marketed, then a comparison can be made between the shadow price, Pf, and the market price. This is a test of the shadow price approach since, typically, one would expect the two values to be similar. If they are not, this may indicate that the value of time used in the non-market case has been mis-estimated. Mixed market, non-market systems also exist for water collection in developing countries. Where mixed market systems exist it is possible to derive implicit values of time from observations about purchasing choices for water. In turn, those values of time could be used to feed into the fuelwood pricing model: the assumption would be that individuals will not value their water collection time at any less than their fuelwood collection time (depending on who does the collecting). Alternatively, time valuation can be used directly to estimate the benefits of improved water supply. Box 15.3 gives a practical example of time valuation taken from a mixed market context in Kenya.

But water supply investments may well be of a major kind involving substantial expenditure on new reservoirs, pipelines etc. This is especially true of countries where there are **water shortages** either nationally (e.g., Malta, Cyprus, Egypt, Libya, Tunisia, Algeria, Morocco and some Middle Eastern countries especially) or locally (e.g., the South of England compared to the North of England, parts of California). Water shortages often arise because water is **underpriced**. That is, the shortage is "contrived" to the extent that past investments have not been properly priced, encouraging over-consumption relative to the true value of water.

There are two effects of this underpricing. First, the **aggregate quantity of water** consumed is too large. Second, underpricing encourages heavy water-using industries to be started where in fact they should not be. Conspicuous examples include the growing of water-intensive crops in water-scarce countries. Box 15.4 illustrates this with respect to crops in one water-scarce country, Cyprus. The procedure used is to calculate what are known as **netback values**. A netback value is calculated by calculating the total revenue (R) from the sale of a particular product and deducting all costs (Co) except the cost of the resource under investigation, in this case water (Cw)[23]. The resulting sum is then the net return:

$$Rn = R - Co$$

and is the maximum that can be paid for the water resource if profits are zero (some measure of "normal" profits would be included in Co). If X cubic metres of water are required to produce an output of Q, then X/Q is the quantity of water needed to produce one unit of output. If Pw is the efficient price of water - see below for how this is determined - then Pw.X/Q is the value of the quantity of water needed to produce one unit of output. Similarly, Rn/Q is the net return per unit of output. A rule of thumb is then that:

$$Rn/Q > Pw.X/Q$$

for any product to be justified in terms of its production in a water scarce context. Box 15.4 shows that, for Cyprus, several fruits and vegetables are not worth growing once water is properly priced.

How then is the proper price of water to be determined? Since water is (generally) a **non-tradeable resource** its economic price is determined by the marginal cost of supply. There are debates over which marginal cost concept to employ. **Short run marginal cost** (SRMC) relates to the marginal cost of expanding the quantity supplied given the existing capital stock for supplying water (dams etc.). **Long run marginal cost** (LRMC) relates to the cost of expanding the existing capacity. LRMC is the relevant concept when planning new infrastructure. Given the "lumpy" nature of investment in water supply, pricing at SRMC will tend to produce the result that prices rise as existing capacity is more and more utilised, but could fall again as new capacity is brought into being. Partly for this reason, LRMC tends to be preferred. LRMC is most often approximated by the **average incremental cost** (AIC) and this, in turn, is approximated by:

$$AIC = \Sigma_t \, (K_t + C_t)(1+r)^t \, / \, \Sigma_t \, (\triangle Q_t)(1+r)^t$$

where K is capital cost, C is operating cost, and $\triangle Q$ is the extra quantity of water that would be made available. Capital costs will include storage and transmission to the "city gate" or "farmgate", and distribution costs within the city or local area to households, farms, etc.

In water scarce countries it is important to note that the use of the AIC formula may well dictate high prices for new water supplies. The fact of scarcity tends to reflect the use already made of accessible water supplies, so that new investment can only come from major new borehole activity or, as in a growing number of countries, the introduction of desalination plant. As with all pricing and project appraisal, of course, AIC should be estimated using shadow prices rather than market prices. Estimates of AICs vary, but for arid areas desalination may cost as much as \$1.3 per cubic metre compared to "inter-basin" supply costs of \$0.5 per cubic metre.

Notice that AIC will also vary according to the <u>use</u> made of the water. While "headwork" costs (dams and reservoirs) will be common, transmission and distribution costs will vary according to the number of users and their location. The supply of water to municipalities for example will tend to cost significantly more than the cost of irrigation water.

Product pricing

Products for consumption embody natural resources, but the process of production may itself generate externalities, as indeed may the act of consuming the product. Since products "embody" resources, pricing natural resources according to Rule 1 will automatically mean that the true economic cost of the resource's extraction or harvesting will be reflected in the private costs of production of the product embodying the resource. But additional external costs from the conversion of the resource into a product would not be included. These must be added to the costs of producing the resource. The costs of consuming the resource may also exceed the price paid in the market place, for example because of disposal costs not reflected in the product price. How far the <u>product</u> should bear the cost of its disposal is arguable. Ideally, the consumer should be charged the costs of disposal. In practice, this may not always be possible and the product might then legitimately bear the disposal costs as well.

Economic instruments

Economic instruments refer to mechanisms whereby the **cost** of a natural resource, receiving environment or product is adjusted to reflect the external and user costs involved. This process of adjusting costs will therefore be environmentally beneficial. Costs may be affected in two ways: (a) through **taxes or charges**, and (b) through **tradeable quantity restrictions**, or **tradeable permits** as they are generally known. The fact that these instruments affect costs, and hence market behaviour, explains why they are often called **market-based instruments** (MBIs).

Taxes and charges are fairly obvious in their effect on costs. A tax on, say, a product or a resource appears as an additional cost of production. It will therefore affect prices or, if prices cannot be changed, profits, or both.

Quantity restrictions also affect costs. A quantity restriction which cannot be traded is not an economic instrument: it is an example of "command-and-control", the regulatory procedure whereby environmental quality standards are set and must be obeyed. Such a quantity restriction may take the form, the production of product X must not result in more than Y tonnes of emissions. In order to achieve the emissions limit of Y, it may be necessary to install pollution control equipment. Since that equipment does not contribute to profits, it is a "deadweight" cost to the polluter. Hence all quantity restrictions affect costs. To qualify as an economic instrument, however, the quantity restriction must be tradeable. In the hypothetical example this means that company A must be able to trade its limit of Y with some other company's limit. They might do this through B selling to A its "permit" to emit pollutants, so that B reduces its emissions while A expands its emissions. If the trade is "one-to-one" then the overall level of emissions will not be different than in the case where A and B have to observe their emissions quotas. The importance of this tradeability will become clearer shortly.

A subsidy also appears to qualify as an economic instrument. It affects the cost of production and could alter behaviour to the benefit of the environment if the subsidy is imposed on environmentally benign technologies - so called "clean" technologies. Subsidies are problematic, however, because they have to be paid for out of revenues raised elsewhere in the economy. The raising of that revenue may be economically inefficient if, for example, it is raised by taxing enterprise and effort. Nonetheless, many countries do use subsidies for environmentally beneficial technologies as a weapon of environmental policy[24].

One special form of tax-with-subsidy is a **deposit-refund system**. Such a system works by charging a tax on the product at the point of purchase, and then refunding the tax if the product container is returned to some agreed point for safe disposal or recycling. The most familiar examples are beverage container deposits. Deposit-refund systems are therefore further examples of economic instruments.

Why are economic instruments desirable?

The alternative to economic instruments is the command and control system of regulation (CAC). Under CAC the regulator sets a standard - which could be an emissions standard or a standard for the receiving environment. Either way, a control over emissions is implied. CAC has different degrees of flexibility. Emissions and receiving environment standards might be set and the emitter might be left to choose the technology or technique to achieve those standards. This is **flexible CAC**. Often, the emitter is not given a choice. Instead, the regulator determines which technology or technique is "best" from an environmental point of view and, provided that technology is readily accessible, that becomes the **best available technology** (or BAT). This is the technology that is then prescribed for the polluter. This is **technology based CAC** and this is perhaps the least flexible form of environmental regulation[25].

Compliance cost savings

The essence of the economic instrument approach is that it is market-based and allows flexibility of response by the polluter. Under the technology-based CAC the polluter has no option but to install the prescribed technology. Under MBIs, the polluter faces a cost, in one form or the other, and then chooses the **most efficient way of responding**. This is the first way in which MBIs promise to yield savings in the costs of complying with environmental regulation. This is **compliance cost efficiency within the firm**. As an example, it may be cheaper to engage in an energy conservation programme than to install retrofitted pollution control equipment. The energy conservation programme may not be included in the remit of "BAT" (although it should be). Of course, if the polluter behaves sensibly, a conservation programme would be introduced, emissions reduced, and perhaps the need for BAT would be avoided. In practice, CAC approaches tend to be of a "blanket" kind: i.e., the BAT is prescribed regardless of the specific circumstances of the polluter.

But there is also a second form of cost saving from MBIs. The costs of controlling pollution vary from one polluter to another. It makes sense for the pollution control to be biased towards those polluters with the lowest costs of control. If A can abate pollution at $10 per tonne of pollutant and B can abate at $20 per tonne, then requiring both polluters each to abate by one tonne - as tends to be dictated by CAC approaches - will cost $30, whereas if A cuts back by two tonnes and B does not cut back at all, the cost is $20. The overall level of pollution reduction is the same. Clearly, A would need some incentive to cut back more than B. That incentive can be provided by an **emissions tax** or a **tradeable emissions quota**. Under the tax approach, a tax of $15 per tonne would mean that A has an incentive to cut back on all emissions as long as:

$$t > MAC$$

where t is the tax and MAC is the marginal abatement cost, in this case $10 for A. But B does not have an incentive to cut back because t < MAC: he will prefer to pay the tax. By adjusting the tax to secure the desired level of cut-back in emissions (which means knowing the elasticity of emissions with respect to the tax), the emission reductions will be concentrated on the lowest abatement cost polluters. A tradeable quota works in a similar way. Suppose A and B are each given a quota such that each has to reduce emissions by one tonne. So far, this is the same as the CAC approach. But now let the quotas be tradeable. B knows that his costs of reducing the one tonne will be $20. A knows that his costs are $10. B would therefore be willing to buy A's permit for a sum less than $20 - the cost he otherwise has to pay. A will be willing to sell for more than $10: by so doing he will give up his permit and have to spend $10, but he will receive more than $10 from B. A and B both gain from the trade. As long as abatement costs vary, then, trade is likely to take place. Notice that, as with the tax, the overall costs of compliance are $20 rather than the $30 that would have occurred if both polluters had each to cut back by one tonne of emissions. **The price of the permit is effectively the same as an environmental tax.** Annex 14 takes a more detailed look at tradeable permits and illustrates them in the context of US air quality control and the management of common property fishery resources.

Dynamic incentive effects

Under the CAC procedure a polluter has no incentive to reduce pollution beyond the level ordained by the regulator, whether through an emissions limit, ambient quality level or through BAT. Under taxes and permits, however, the polluter has a **continuous incentive** to abate emissions. He will do this as long as t > MAC for a tax, and as long as p > MAC for the tradeable permit, where p is the market price of the permit.

Revenue raising

The purpose of environmental taxes is to **alter behaviour** by changing price signals in the economy. While they are not designed to raise revenue, they will tend to do this (a) during the period when the polluter is adjusting to the tax, and (b) if the tax remains in effect on the "optimal" level of pollution[26]. There are two contexts in which this revenue raising feature is of significant relevance: (a) in developed economies where the revenues may be usable to offset the "deadweight" burden of taxes on effort and enterprise, and (b) in developing countries where tax revenues may in fact be easier to raise through pollution taxes than through other taxes.

Since environmental taxes are not designed to raise revenues, they should, in principle, be **fiscally neutral,** i.e any revenues raised by government should be offset by reductions in other taxes. This "double dividend" feature is attractive since it also provides an encouragement from the polluting sectors of industry to cooperate with the tax. For this, however, they must be reasonably certain that governments will honour any promise to make the tax neutral. Available evidence suggests that, in the developed world, existing income and profits taxes give rise to as much as 20-50% deadweight welfare loss for every $1 raised. These deadweight welfare losses are avoided by reducing income taxes and replacing them with environmental taxes. Although environmental taxes will have some deadweight losses of their own, they are thought to be a small proportion of other taxes' deadweight losses. This argument has been of particular importance in discussions of **carbon taxes** since the pervasiveness of fossil fuel use in the developed world means that carbon taxes have the potential to raise very large sums in tax revenues.

In the developing world the focus on revenue raising is likely to be different, although reducing other taxes should not be forgotten as an objective. In these contexts, however, some pollution taxes may well be better at raising revenues than other forms of tax. Examples tend to include energy taxes where there is a reasonable chance of the tax being applied successfully even in countries where markets are least developed overall. As Chapter 1 noted, however, many developing countries are not at the stage in the pricing model in which prices approximate even private production costs, let alone full "social cost". In such circumstances it remains critically important to investigate movements towards the pricing of products and resources at their marginal production, harvest and extraction cost as the first stage in a longer run trend towards overall social cost pricing (Anderson [1990]).

Checklist of Economic Instruments

OECD [1991] has provided a convenient checklist of economic instruments and the circumstances under which they are likely to apply. The essentials of these checklists are repeated here with some modifications and extensions, especially allowing for developing country contexts.

Emission Charges

Definition 　　Charges on the discharge of pollutants to air, water or soil
Advantages 　　o　　save compliance costs 　　o　　dynamic incentive to reduce pollution 　　o　　raise revenues 　　o　　flexibility of response
Appropriateness: 　　o　　mainly stationary sources 　　o　　marginal abatement costs must vary 　　o　　monitoring of emissions must be feasible
Relevance to Environmental Media 　　o　　**water** high: exist in France, Germany, Netherlands 　　o　　**air** medium to high: easiest where emissions estimated by fuel consumption 　　o　　**waste**: medium: exist for hazardous waste in USA; cattle waste in Netherlands 　　o　　**noise**: high - aircraft; low - vehicle
Issues 　　o　　distributional incidence relevant in developed and developing countries 　　o　　how to allocate earmarked revenues 　　o　　complex monitoring may be required making such taxes of limited relevance to developing countries depending on state of development

Product Charges

Definition   Charges on products with negative environmental effects

Advantages
    Encourages product use reduction, product substitution and waste reduction at source
    Incentive effect
    Revenue raising
    May proxy emission charges
    Applicable to diffuse and mobile sources
    Ease of implementation
    Flexibility

Appropriateness
    Where products used in large quantities
    Products easily identifiable
    High demand elasticity
    Need to control diffuse sources
    Possible use of existing fiscal and administrative channels

Relevance to Environmental Media
    Water: high - fertiliser charges in Scandinavia; lube oils in Germany
    Air: high - sulphur content of fuels in France; leaded/unleaded gasoline differential pricing - many countries.
    Waste: high - recycling of beverage containers etc;
    Noise: medium - possible taxation of vehicles according to noisiness.

Issues
    Inapplicable where bans more appropriate (highly toxic substances)
    Trade and competitiveness implications
    Distributional incidence problems mainly in developing countries.

Definition

    Emission or resource use quotas where total of individual quotas equals environmental standard, and where the quotas are tradeable

---

Advantages

    Savings in compliance costs

    Enables economic growth without environmental quality reduction as new polluters can buy from existing polluters

    Flexibility

    "Price" of trades can be varied to reduce overall pollution: e.g., price of increased pollution by one unit could be two units of reduction elsewhere

---

Appropriateness

    Compliance costs must vary between polluters

    Harvesting costs must vary if quotas relate to a resource

    Must be significant number of traders

    Best applied to fixed sources

    Potential for technical innovation

    Environmental impact is independent of source locations

    Intermediation markets (i.e., brokers) ensure well functioning market

---

Relevance to Environmental media

    Water: low - environmental impact dependent on source location

    Air: high - see US experience (Annex 14)

    Waste: low ? Impacts vary with location of source

    Noise: low - impact dependent upon source

Issues

    Difficult to apply to more than one pollutant simultaneously - problem for integrated pollution control

    Possible "hot spots" as permits become concentrated in one area

    Economic rents arise and accrue to polluters unless permits are auctioned

    Potential high transaction costs.

    Unlikely to apply to emissions in developing countries due to need for relatively sophisticated market but could well be applied to resource quotas (e.g.,fishing) where regulatory bodies exist.

The taxation of transport fuel varies significantly by country, but in most advanced economies significant taxes are applied. Measured in per tonne of carbon content of the fuels, for example, the taxes on oil and oil products for selected countries appear as follows (there are other taxes on gas, and there are subsidies to coal):

Country	$ tonne carbon	Country	$ tonne carbon
USA	65	Japan	130
Germany	212	France	351
Italy	317	UK	297
Canada	108	Austria	267
Belgium	162	Denmark	297
Finland	189	Ireland	277
Netherlands	221	N.Zealand	235
Norway	258	Portugal	205
Spain	176	Sweden	268
Switzerland	224		

(Source for Table: Hoeller, P., and M.Wallin, [1991], *Energy Prices, Taxes and Carbon Dioxide Emissions*, Economics and Statistics Dept, Working Paper 106, OECD, Paris.).

Given these taxes, should new environmental taxes - e.g., a carbon tax - be added? Much depends on how the existing taxes are viewed. Newbery [1990, 1992] has suggested that existing transport fuel taxes and the "road tax" (the cost of licensing a vehicle) in the United Kingdom are approximately optimal if they are construed as road user charges and allowance is made for congestion. The intuitive result should be that if the existing taxes can be thought of as being at least approximately optimal taxes on congestion and use, then a new environmental tax should simply be added to the existing tax structure. Newbery [1992] demonstrates that this is so in the context of a fairly simple model of the demand for transport and the social costs that vehicle use imposes in terms of congestion and pollution. So, the presence of an existing tax structure ought not to be a material concern when devising new environmental taxes provided the existing tax structure can be thought of as providing for taxes on other externalities unrelated to the one in question.

(Newbery's argument can be found in Newbery, D., [1990], "Pricing and Congestion: Economic Principles Relevant to Pricing Roads", *Oxford Review of Economic Policy*, Vol.6 (2), 22-38; and Newbery, D., [1992], "Should Carbon Taxes Be Additional to Other Taxes ?", Department of Applied Economics, Cambridge University, January, *mimeo*.

Box 15.2 **Estimating user cost for natural gas**

Annex 13 derives the equations for estimating user cost. In a context where a new gas field is being considered for development it will be necessary to estimate the extraction cost and the user cost. The sum of these two elements (together with any environmental damage costs) makes up the optimal price of the natural gas resource.

The two equations that have to be solved are:

$$\Sigma Qt = \underline{Q}$$

and

$$Ro = [P_B - C][1 + r]^{-T}$$

where Q = extraction rate, T is the number of years to exhaustion of the resource or to the point when a backstop technology becomes competitive, P_B is the price of the backstop technology, r is the discount rate, C is extraction cost, and Ro is the initial royalty (user cost).

T is easily estimated by looking at current levels of demand or projected rates of demand for a new resource (e.g., the amount of gas needed to supply chemical feedstock, electricity generation etc.) and dividing them into the estimate of reserves Q. A study of new gas deposits in Trinidad and Tobago suggested values of T of between 55 and 69 years.

At \$9 mmbtu, or around \$54 for a barrel of oil, it was estimated that gas would be too expensive for feedstock and synthetic crude oils would become competitive, so P_B was set at \$9 mmbtu. C was estimated to be \$3.1 mmbtu for $T=69$ and \$2 mmbtu for $T=55$. So, taking $T=55$ the resulting user cost was estimated as:

$$Ro = [9 - 2]/[1.1]^{55} = \$0.037 \text{ mmbtu.}$$

User cost was therefore 3.7 cents per mmbtu. The marginal cost of extraction was independently estimated at 43.4 cents mmbtu and the transmission cost at 2.1 cents. Hence the overall optimal price of gas was put at:

$$P = 45.5 + 3.7 \text{ cents} = 49.2 \text{ cents}$$

The user cost component was thus fairly small at around 7%, reflecting the size of the reserve and hence the time to exhaustion and hence the importance of discounting. Where reserves are limited, however, user cost can easily become a significant component of the optimal price of a resource.

(The example is taken from Pearce, D.W. [1985], *Trinidad and Tobago: Energy Assessment - Natural Gas Pricing*, Report to Energy Department, World Bank, Washington DC, April.)

Box 15.3 **Valuing water supply improvements**

Villagers in Ukundu, Kenya face three options for securing drinking water supplies. They can buy from a kiosk in the village at a price Pk and with a collection time Tk. They can have a vendor deliver the water to their household at a cost Pv and a zero collection time. Or they can go to a well with zero price and collection time Tw. For kiosk users, then, the implicit value of time must lie between:

$$Pk/[Tw - Tk] \text{ and } [Pv - Pk]/Tk$$

while for vendor users it must be

$$[Pv - Pk]/Tk \text{ or } Pv/Tw$$

and for well users it must be

$$Pv/Tw \text{ or } Pk/[Tw - Tk]$$

Inspection of the different prices and times taken produced the results:

		US$ hr
kiosk users		0.12-0.64
vendor users		0.41
	or	0.51
well users		0.53

These values can be compared to the prevailing wage rate of $0.56 per hour, suggesting that ruling wage rates can be used to value resources which require time for harvesting and collection. As far as water supply investments are concerned, if those investments save time (e.g., by bringing water into a village, or by extending a single village supply to households) the saved time can be valued with ruling wage rates or with the implicit values of time derived in an exercise of this kind. The relevance for pricing is that the data can be used to estimate willingness to pay for the volume of water collected each day. For example, if 50 litres per day are collected and the time taken is 3 hours, then 50 litres would have a shadow price of, say, [$0.5 x 3]/50 = 3 cents per litre.

The value of time example is taken from Mu, X., D. Whittington, J. Briscoe, [1990], "Modelling Village Water Demand: a Discrete Choice Approach", *Water Resources Research*, Vol.26, No.4, April. 521-429.

Box 15.4 The efficient pricing of water and the choice of output mix

Cyprus is a water scarce country. Over 60% of available water is withdrawn each year, and 90% of that demand comes from agriculture. An efficient price for water is determined by calculating the long run marginal cost of water supply (see text), Pw. As the text shows, netback analysis can be used to determine the maximum willingness to pay for water. This can then be compared to the price Pw. If the maximum WTP exceeds Pw the crop in question is, in principle, economically justified. But if Pw is more than the maximum WTP the crop should not be grown.

The figures below are approximate, but reveal that several crops should not be grown once the true value of water is calculated.

Crop	maxWTP-Pw (US$/m^3)	Economically Justified?
Lemons	-0.12	no
Grapefruit	-0.37	no
Table Olives	0.08	yes
Table Grapes	-0.02	no
Apricots	0.53	yes
Artichokes	0.23	yes
Afalfa	-0.45	no
Potatoes (spring)	0.31	yes
Potatoes (autumn)	-0.45	no
Onions	0.13	yes

Source: World Bank data.

Chapter 16

Regulation

The forms of quantity regulation

In the environmental context the aim of government intervention is always to achieve some change in the natural or built environment relative to what would have occurred without the intervention. For environmental quality, this change is best measured by the **ambient quality of the receiving environment**. But interventions are also aimed at conserving a natural resource - an energy resource, soil, a forest, a groundwater supply etc. For such resources, then, the relevant measure will always involve some **indicator of quantity of the natural resource**. For some resources quantity and quality are inextricably mixed. Water is one example - abundant water of low quality is as much an environmental problem as scarce supplies of water of high quality. In practice, quantity and quality are often related. Low water quality is especially likely to arise in low flow situations.

Note that setting ambient standards or resource use restrictions embraces all forms of regulation. There are then two issues:
     (a) at what level to set ambient quality or resource use;
     (b) how to achieve that level.

Chapter 15 has already dealt with the use of **economic instruments** to achieve environmental standards. The rest of this chapter focuses on the regulatory alternatives.

Setting standards

Environmental standards tend to be of four kinds, but, as we shall see, all are related in that each implies the others. The four types of standard are:
- ambient environmental quality standards (AEQs)
- emissions (to air) standards, or effluent (to water or land) standards
- technology-based standards
- product and process standards, including total bans.

The links between these types of standard are shown in Figure 16.1. The diagram shows emissions on the vertical axis and AEQ and economic output on the two horizontal axes. AEQ and emissions are inversely related - the higher are emissions the lower is AEQ. Emissions and output are linked through technical coefficients, e.g., tonnes of SO2 per unit of energy output and quantity of energy per unit of economic output. Two coefficients are shown, e_0 and e_1, with the latter being lower than the former to illustrate the concept of lower pollution intensity of output. Any AEQ standard implies some emission standard since emissions and AEQ are linked in the manner shown. Thus, q_x corresponds to E_x. It follows that any emissions standard, such as E_x, corresponds to an AEQ standard. In the same way, a product standard - in which the "pollution content" of a product is specified - implies an emissions standard. For a given level of economic output, P_k, adoption of a product standard such as e_1 implies emissions level E_k and AEQ level q_k. Notice that a product or process standard does not, however, set an upper limit on E or AEQ. This is because process and product standards do not typically specify the <u>level of output</u>. Ambient quality and emissions standards may do this however.

Figure 16.1

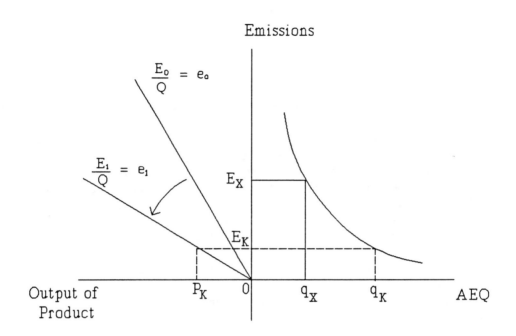

Ambient environmental quality standards

The economic approach would favour setting AEQ standards on the basis of a comparison of costs and benefits. Figure 16.2 illustrates. The benefits of improving ambient environmental quality (AEQ) are shown by the stylised total benefit function TB. The corresponding marginal benefit function, MB, is shown in the lower half of the diagram. Note that TB is assumed linear (for convenience) but has a discontinuity at Qcl. Qcl correspond to the concept of a **critical load**. Essentially, a critical load relates to the maximum level of pollution deposition that corresponds to zero damage[27]. Once pollution deposition rises above this level, critical loads are exceeded and a measure of **damage** might be:

$$D = Ql - Qcl$$

where Ql is the AEQ corresponding to a given load of pollution, and Qcl is the critical load. This function corresponds to the benefit function shown in Figure 16.2[28]. If damage is non-linear with respect to "exceedances", then an alternative function might be:

$$D = [Ql - Qcl]^a$$

where "a" is some parameter. In terms of Figure 16.2 the distance Qcl.Qmax corresponds to the receiving environment's **assimilative capacity**, so that improving the environment beyond Qcl adds nothing to benefits. This also explains the shape of the marginal benefit function in the lower half of the diagram: once Qcl is reached, MB falls to zero.

The costs of achieving any AEQ are given by TC. Figure 16.2 shows two alternatives for illustration. TC1 is drawn to illustrate the possibility that the optimum level of pollution <u>could</u> coincide with the critical load, the point of zero damage. Curve TC2 shows the case where the optimal level of pollution is greater than zero, i.e., AEQ is less than the AEQ corresponding to critical loads. The economically "optimal" standard is given by the intersection of MB and MC in each case.

Figure 16.2

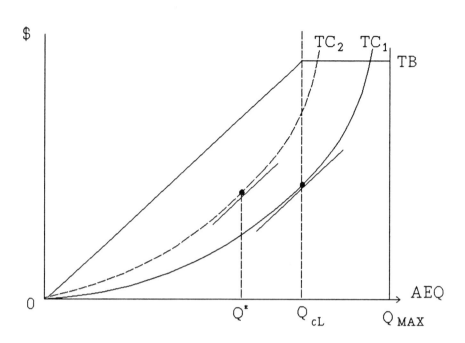

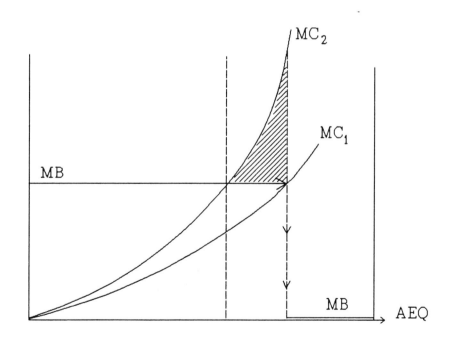

Figure 16.2 is stylised in three further senses. First, TB may often have a "stepped" appearance. This is because a given level of AEQ supports certain functions, and further functions can only be introduced if there is a discrete change in AEQ. An example might be water quality - certain levels of water quality correspond to fishing for sensitive species, slightly lower quality levels correspond to, say, drinking water and coarser fishing, lower levels still to swimming, then boating and sightseeing, and so on. As each "threshold" is reached, so the benefit function "jumps" and there are steps in the function.

The second stylisation relates to the smoothness of the cost function. In practice, it is likely that the cost function will also be "stepped" as discrete technologies are introduced for clean-up.

The real-world nature of cost and benefit functions means that rarely in practice is the "optimal" level of pollution identified by a procedure such as that implied by Figure 16.2. But if there are thresholds, it will pay to investigate their likely nature since the discontinuities <u>may</u> then correspond to optimal, or near optimal, points. To this end, identified "safe" levels of pollution concentration can be a surrogate means of identifying optima. The danger with such an approach is that the standards get set by reference only to benefits, and the costs of achieving the standards are ignored.

The third stylisation is the assumption that costs and benefits are known with certainty. In practice costs may be fairly certain, and benefits uncertain. If benefits are not known with certainty there is a case for adopting the **precautionary principle** (see Chapter 13). In terms of Figure 16.2 the precautionary principle would tend to dictate setting AEQ standards at, or near, the level of critical loads.

In line with the requirement that all regulations be assessed in terms of their costs and benefits, a policy of setting standards according to critical loads may involve society in an excess burden of cost. In terms of Figure 16.2, for example, if the relevant marginal cost curve is MC2, then setting the standard at Qcl rather than Q* involves a net social cost burden equal to the shaded area.

Emission and effluent standards

Much the same considerations as apply to ambient standards also apply to effluent and emissions standards (EESs). An EES tends to take the form of a maximum allowable concentration or quantities of pollutants that may be emitted. They are most suited to contexts where there are **point sources** (i.e., a single point of emission). They are more difficult in the **non-point source** context, i.e., where pollution emanates from many different sources. Emission standards can often be easier to implement and monitor, especially in the case where there are established emission coefficients, as tends to be the case for energy sources. Then, on the assumption that the link between AEQ and emissions has been established, it is sufficient to control emissions.

Technology-based standards

In many countries standards are based on the **best available technology** (BAT). BAT means choosing that pollution prevention or clean-up technology that "best" serves the interests of the environment. BAT is an example of command and control regulation (see below). For example, a BAT-based AEQ would be that AEQ corresponding to the use of the best environmental protection technology available. This might be flue gas desulphurisation equipment for sulphur emissions from a power plant. In terms of Figure 16.2 it is difficult to identify any particular <u>point</u> that corresponds to BAT, but most technologies corresponding to BAT come close to very high levels of pollution load removal. In the case of sulphur dioxide, for example, this might correspond to 95%-98% removal of sulphur. If so, BAT would correspond to a point a little to the left of Qcl in Figure 16.2.

Note that setting standards according to BAT means that costs are ignored altogether. Since in practice it is impossible to ignore the costs of control - industry lobbies usually ensure that - various modifications of BAT exist. These usually make reference to "practicable" means of control, having due regard to the economic cost of the technology, or BAT "not entailing excessive cost" (BATNEEC). Introducing the cost component tends to make the BAT concept closer to the cost-benefit approach to setting standards, but as the next section shows the differences are still substantial.

Product and process standards

A product standard tends to specify limits to the use of certain inputs into a product. Thus, the lead content of gasoline is regulated in many countries. Similarly, process standards specify the amount of a given input that may be used in a process. In Japan, chlor-alkali production is subject to a ban on the use of mercury cells and to mandatory replacement by diaphragm cells in order to regulate mercury emissions. One extreme form of a product or process standard is the **outright ban** which may be invoked if the external costs are thought to be especially high, as with the use of chlorofluorocarbons (CFCs) in various uses.

The costs of command and control

Command and control (CAC) measures have as their main characteristic **the absence of a choice of response** by the regulated agent. The implications of this lack of flexibility can be analyzed by looking again at technology based systems. Polluters are told to introduce the BAT, which in turn tends to be defined for them, and they are given no choice as to how to respond. This **lack of flexibility** is the hallmark of CAC measures and its shows up in the form of **higher costs of compliance** than would be the case if flexibility of response was allowed. A simple example might be that insisting on flue-gas-desulphurisation for emission control prevents adoption of other methods of control such as fuel-switching (from high sulphur to low sulphur fuels) and energy conservation. Technology-based standards tend to lock the polluter into high cost solutions to the problem at hand. This situation can be compounded if the BAT regulation is confined to new plant, with old plant being ignored (due to the acknowledged very high cost of retrofitting) or given a time schedule to catch up with new plant performance standards. One effect of this type of procedure is to delay the introduction of new plant, with existing plant being used more intensively - actually increasing pollution.

Technology-bases standards therefore tend to be inefficient in two senses: (a) high costs of compliance and (b) possibly higher levels of pollution than might otherwise have occurred. Box 16.1 provides some estimates of the difference between CAC compliance costs and the costs of the most efficient control procedure. Clearly, the differences can be substantial.

Zoning and land use control

Pollution control tends to be regulated through the use of AEQs as discussed above combined with prescriptions about best available technology. But pollution may also be regulated by **land use control** whereby certain uses of land or technology are not allowed in particular zones. Various forms of zoning exist:

- **attenuation of use**: certain uses of the land are simply prohibited. This will tend to be the case for highly polluting industries in urban districts, or land uses which make heavy demands on scarce local water supplies;

- **performance zoning**: uses are permitted subject to compliance with some performance standard, e.g., an emissions standard. Performance standards are regularly expressed in terms of ratios of open space to office or residential space

- **subdivision regulations**: the density of activity is regulated through local planning requirements such as maximum dwellings per hectare.

There are some dangers with land use zoning. First, the motives for zoning may not always be in the best interests of society. There is some evidence to show that zoning has been used in the past to exclude low income groups from the more desirable residential areas. Second, zoning affects the tax base. Areas where commercial development is allowed may generate more tax revenues, and with a lower tax base, than areas without commercial development. Depending on the jurisdictional arrangement, the result may be wide variations in the provision of public services funded from the tax revenues. Zoning may also have the effect of moving certain uses out of the zoned area on to land that is not used and which may have conservation and wilderness value.

Some of the problems with zoning can be overcome by applying economic instruments to land uses. Less desirable land uses can be taxed, for example, according to the current land use in the area. A polluting source may be charged little if it concentrates its location in an area already densely filled with similar polluting sources, and more if it wishes to locate in a relatively unpolluted area. The resulting "pollution havens" may be unattractive but they have the advantage of not distributing pollution damage across wide areas. Many zoning laws actually achieve this effect without the use of taxes. More generally, taxes on land values may, in some circumstances, assist urban environmental improvement. Low value buildings would be upgraded to attract higher rentals to meet the land value tax which is unaffected by the nature of the buildings on the land. Such a tax would work best where there is no significant supply of vacant land since there would be a major incentive to develop unspoiled land which also attracts the tax. The upgrading process may also harm low income groups, thus offending an equity principle. Alternatively, where rights to environmentally damaging activities exist - e.g., rights to deforest - the attenuation of these rights might be compensated for through payments, and the payments in turn could be tradeable. The resulting **tradeable development rights** would enable efficient solutions to be found for land uses that create conflicts of interest between those who wish the land use to be consistent with conservation and those who wish to "develop" land.

The costs and benefits of environmental regulation

Determining the costs and benefits of a proposed or actual regulation is far from simple. This section outlines the steps that need to be taken and illustrates the process with some examples.

First, there is a problem of determining the relevant **with - and without - regulation scenarios**. In order to determine the costs and benefits of the regulation it is necessary to know what would have happened without the regulation.

Second, assuming such scenarios can be constructed, it is necessary to **distinguish different groups in society** who bear costs and the different groups who reap the benefits. One reason for dividing up groups in this way is to check on the difference between **real resource costs and transfer payments**. Some of the costs accruing to one group may simply be transferred from another group. If the focus is economic efficiency, these transfer payments are not relevant to the overall cost of regulation. The second reason for dividing groups up is that distributional incidence may well be important (see above). The categorisation of groups is flexible, but is likely to involve at least national and local government, industry, consumers, and taxpayers.

Third, the efficiency effect needs to be measured in terms of the **change in the aggregate net economic surplus accruing to society**. This will be made up of changes in producer surplus and consumer surplus (see Chapter 3). Achieving this requires adoption of the best available model given the data requirements which, very often, are poor. Models vary in their complexity but generally comprise the following (Hahn and Hird [1991]):

- **partial equilibrium models**: in this approach some attempt is made to measure the changes in supply and demand as they affect the regulated sector. If the sector is significant, such partial approaches will ignore general equilibrium effects, and the latter becomes especially important if, as is often the case, environmental regulation affects the economy as a whole;

- **cost studies**: studies to determine the changes in the cost of compliance may use surveys of firms' expenditures, engineering studies, mathematical programming, and econometric estimates;

- **benefit studies**: benefit estimates make use of the techniques surveyed in Section III and try to find society's aggregate willingness to pay for the change in environmental quality that results from the regulation;

- **general equilibrium models**: where data permit, general equilibrium models (GEMs) may be constructed. GEMs simulate regulatory impacts on net surplus but usually do so on the basis of assumed perfect competition in product markets. Examples of such a procedure is given in the next section. GEMs are still controversial. Their assumption, which could be relaxed but usually is not, about the competitive state of the economy is clearly unrealistic. Their attraction is that they capture the second and nth order effects of the regulation, something that partial equilibrium models cannot do. But GEMs are also demanding of information which often does not exist, and partial approaches may often be a reasonable approximation of the net change in well-being. In the environmental sphere, GEMs typically do not control for the feedback effects of environmental benefits on productivity and health. GEMs are also difficult to validate and are not easy to understand by policy-makers (they lack "transparency");

- **macroeconomic models**: macroeconomic models do not attempt to simulate changes in each sector of the economy but focus on the overall aggregate such as investment and consumption, the balance of payments and employment. As such, macroeconomic models do not meet the requirement of estimating changes in overall net surplus arising from the regulation. Nonetheless, they are valuable in focusing on the magnitudes that are often of concern to the politician.

Example of the welfare effects of environmental regulation

Few studies exist of the impacts on aggregate well-being of environmental regulation, though a number of studies exist of the macroeconomic effects of regulation (see, for example, Jorgensen and Wilcoxen [1990]). One GEM study for the USA is that of Hazilla and Kopp [1990] which uses a computable GEM. This model estimates only the social costs of environmental regulation, and not the benefits. But estimates of benefits can be compared to the resulting cost figures. The model assumes perfect competition in all markets, and the measure of change in social cost is that derived in Part III, the compensating variation. The economy is divided into 36 producing sectors each characterised by a cost function. From these equations it is possible to derive demand equations for capital and labour, different types of energy input, and for various intermediate input. Households are modelled by assuming each household has the same preference structure. The model is then applied to the US Clean Air and Clean Water Acts both of which prescribe technology-based standards. The results are shown below and are compared with the US Environmental Protection

Agency's own estimates of the costs of compliance, which are based on engineering cost studies. Clearly, the results are very different.

Year	Social Cost (Hazilla-Kopp)	EPA's Estimate
	$b current	$b current
1975	6.8	14.1
1981	28.3	42.5
1985	70.6	56.0
1990	203.0	78.6

Notice that the Hazilla-Kopp estimates suggest that "true" compliance costs were less than EPA's own estimates in the early period but significantly higher in the later period. Part of the explanation, they suggest, is that the regulations led people to substitute leisure for consumption, reducing economic output.

Social cost studies of this kind are valuable in themselves since they can, if they are credible, indicate to government and taxpayers what regulation is costing. But they are not an adequate guide to the overall net effect of regulation because they ignore benefits. Benefit estimates for the USA Clean Air and Clean Water Acts have been produced by Freeman [1990] and Portney [1990]. Translated to 1988, Hahn and Hird [1991] suggest that the resulting benefit range is some $16 to $136 billion, with a "best guess" of $58 billion. Hahn and Hird estimate the Hazilla-Kopp compliance cost estimate at $55 to 78 billion for 1988, suggesting that costs may well have exceeded benefits for that year.

Example of the environmental effects of government intervention

Applications of economic models to environmental issues in developing countries are rare. Cruz and Repetto [1992] use a computable GEM to estimate the effects of economic policies in the Philippines on individual sectors, and then link those changes to indicators of change in natural resource endowments. Their general finding is that the Philippines experienced "illusory" economic growth in the 1970s and 1980s since growth was financed by (a) external borrowing which ended up financing low productivity investments, and (b) running down natural resource stocks. This can be seen by inspecting the data in Box 16.2. There it is seen that there is a persistent deficit between domestic savings and investment, so that the extra investment had to be financed by foreign borrowing. But hidden from the economy because of the absence of environmentally modified national accounts was the running down of environmental assets such as forests, soil and coastal fisheries. Their depreciation is recorded in Box 16.2 in terms of the value of the change in the total stock of assets. The end result could have been "sustainable" had the proceeds of this disinvestment been allocated to profitable investments in man-made capital assets. But, instead, the investment that took place had low productivity, as indicated by the incremental capital output ratio (ICOR).

The Philippines example illustrates how environmental impacts relate to economic regulation as a whole, i.e., to macroeconomic policies within a country.

262

Box 16.1 The costs of compliance with inefficient regulation

The following table shows the ratio of the costs of complying with command and control regulations relative to the costs of compliance that would have occurred had the least-cost market-based approach been employed.

Pollutant	Area	Ratio of CAC Least Cost
Particulates	St.Louis	6.0
SO2	Utah	4.2
Sulphates	Los Angeles	1.1
NO2	Baltimore	6.0
NO2	Chicago	14.4
Particulates	Baltimore	4.2
SO2	Lower Delaware	1.8
Particulates	Lower Delaware	22.0
Noise	USA	1.7
Hydrocarbons	USA	4.2
CFCs	USA	2.0

Source: Tietenberg [1990].

Box 16.2 Unsustainable economic growth in the Philippines

	1961-70	1971-75	1976-80	1981-85	1986-89
Growth rate of GDP %	4.8	6.2	6.2	-0.5	4.6
	1970	**1973**	**1978**	**1983**	**1985**
I/Y-S/Y %	-	-	5.3	8.2	0.6
Debt/Y %	-	-	34.0	70.8	82.0
Resource Deprec- iation as % GDP	5.6	5.0	3.7	3.1	3.0
	1960-69	**1970-74**	**1975-82**	**1983-88**	
ICOR*	4.1	3.5	5.5	9.5	

*Incremental capital output ratio = ratio of fixed capital formation in year t to the increase in GDP in t-1. A rising ICOR thus signifies less efficient investment.

Annex 1

Capital Budgeting

Economists and financial analysts have developed investment criteria such as the internal rate of return, net present value, pay-off period, and cost/benefit ratio for use as decision rules to help decide whether or not to proceed with a given project. Such investment criteria are also often used to rank projects. The purpose of project ranking is to see which projects should be selected given that there are limited funds. In other words, there is a budget constraint. The need to rank projects does not arise if there is no budget constraint because one can simply select all projects with a positive net benefit.

A "capital budgeting" problem arises when a government agency or firm must decide which of many investment projects to select given that available funds are limited. In other words, from among a large number of potential projects, a subset of projects must be chosen. This subset of selected projects is termed the "investment programme". Once financial and budget realities are introduced into the project selection problem, simple decision rules may be inadequate guides to optimal project selection. Mathematical programming models offer a better means for both formulating and solving capital budgeting problems. Mathematical programming models enable us to consider conceptually the nature of the capital budgeting problem, and how best to solve it, rather than search for simple decision rules that will inevitably miss some of the complexity of the problem.

In this annex we start our discussion with the application of linear programming models to capital budgeting problems because this is the simplest model formulation. We then consider integer programming formulations that can more accurately represent project interdependencies.

Divisible projects: Linear programming models

A relevant and important objective for the agency or firm would be to maximize the net present value obtained from the subset of projects selected. If it is reasonable to assume that the size or scale of the potential projects can be easily varied, then we can think of the capital budgeting problem as a series of interrelated decisions on how much money should be invested in each of the available projects. With this conceptualization of the problem, it is necessary to assume that there is an upper limit on the amount of money that can be invested in a particular project; otherwise the optimal decision will always be to invest all of the available funds in the single project with the highest returns. Let C_j equal the upper limit on the amount of money that can be invested in project j.

Assume that the costs and benefits of each project are known, and that the agency or firm has a limited amount of money to spend. A simple linear programming model for this problem is presented below. Let $j = 1 \ldots N$ be the set of potential projects, and y_j equal the amount of money (capital) invested in project j. If the decision variable y_j is equal to zero in the final model solution, this means that no funds were invested in this project. If the costs and benefits of each potential project are known, then it is a simple matter to calculate the net present value of each project. Let b_j equal the net present value of project j if C_j is invested in it. The objective function is then given by:

Maximize net present value $= \sum_{j=1}^{N} \beta_j y_j$ (A1.1)

where β_j = net present value of project j per dollar of investment (b_j / $)

This objective function is maximized subject to two general types of constraints:

(1) The amount of money invested in a project must be less than or equal to the upper limit for that project.

$$y_j \le C_j \qquad j = 1 \dots N \tag{A1.2}$$

(2) The total amount of money invested in all projects selected must be less than or equal to the budget available.

$$\sum_{j=1}^{N} y_j \le K \tag{A1.3}$$

where K = budget constraint for the investment programme.

Another way of formulating this linear programming model is to think of the decision variable as the percent of project j that is accepted. We change the notation of the decision variables from y_j to x_j to reflect this change. If the decision variable x_j is equal to zero, this means that zero percent of this project is to be undertaken. The objective function is again to maximize the net present value of the investment programme, which is now given by:

$$\text{Maximize net present value} = \sum_{j=1}^{N} b_j x_j \tag{A1.4}$$

and the constraints require that

(1) No more than 100 percent of a project can be undertaken:

$$O \le x_j \le 1 \quad j = 1 \dots N \tag{A1.5}$$

(2) The total amount of money invested in all projects selected must be less than or equal to the budget available:

$$\sum_{j=1}^{N} x_j C_j \le K \tag{A1.6}$$

These two formulations are equivalent, and, in fact, the solution to both these formulations is easy to find without actually solving the linear programming model. The objective function coefficients in equation (A10.1) can be used to create a simple ranking function. The decision rule would be to simply select first the project with the highest net present value per dollar invested until the upper limit for that project was reached, and then invest in the project with the next highest net present value per dollar invested. The analyst would proceed in this manner until the overall budget was exhausted.

However, real-life capital budgeting problems are typically not so simple - even if it can be assumed that projects are divisible. For example, the costs of each project may be incurred in different periods and the government agency or corporation may face overall cash flow constraints in each period. Let us consider how the second linear programming formulation above could be modified to capture this additional complexity.

We explicitly introduce a time dimension in the model by adding an index t, t = 1 ...T, where T is the end of the planning horizon. Let C_{jt} equal the cash outflow required by project j in year t, and K_t equal the budget constraint in year t. Our basic model is still given by equations (A10.4) - (A10.6), but now we have an additional, third set of financial constraints, one for each time period:

$$\sum_{j=1}^{N} C_{jt} x_j \leq K_t \qquad t = 1 \dots T \qquad\qquad (A1.7)$$

where C_{jt} is the funds (cash flow) required by project j in period t. This set of constraints ensures that the money required by all the selected projects in a given period does not exceed the amount available to the government agency or firm in that period.

Indivisible projects: Integer programming models

In many situations it is unrealistic to assume that the size or scale of projects can be infinitely variable. Often the size of a project is determined (or there are only a few possible sizes), and the relevant decision is whether or not to proceed with the project given the specified size. In such cases an integer programming formulation of the capital budgeting problem can better represent the physical realities of the investment choice.

In the integer programming model, the decision variables, x_j, can only take the values of zero and one, depending on whether or not project j is selected as part of the investment programme

$$x_j = \begin{cases} 1 \text{ if project j is selected (accepted)} \\ \\ 0 \text{ if project j is not selected} \end{cases} \qquad (A1.8)$$

The objective function of the model still requires that the net present value of the investment programme be maximized, and the constraints ensure that each potential project is either chosen or not (i.e., partial projects are not allowed) and the budget constraints in each period are met;

$$\text{Max net present value} = \sum_{j=1}^{N} b_j x_j \qquad\qquad (A1.9)$$

subject to
$$\sum_{j=1}^{N} C_{jt} x_j \leq K_t; \quad t = 1 \dots T \qquad\qquad (A1.10)$$

$$x_j = [0,1] \qquad ; \quad j = 1 \dots N \qquad\qquad (A1.11)$$

where all variables are defined as before.

Although computationally more difficult to solve than a linear programming model, an integer (or mixed integer) programming model offers the analyst great flexibility in characterizing the physical, economic, and financial interrelationships among projects. In the following discussion we show how integer variables can be used to represent several types of interdependencies.

Mutually exclusive projects

A set of projects are said to be "mutually exclusive" if it is only feasible to select one project in the set. For example, this might occur if two dam sites were being considered, and a dam would only be built at one of the two sites. The following constraint will ensure that the acceptance of one project precludes doing any of the other projects.

$$\sum_{k=1}^{M} x_k \leq 1 \tag{A1.12}$$

where $k = 1 \ldots M$ defines the set of mutually exclusive projects.

The set of mutually exclusive projects, M, may itself be any subset of the total number of projects to be considered for the investment programme.

This type of constraint is very flexible. For example, changing the right-hand side constant to "2" will require that *at most* two of the projects in the subset M can be accepted. If the inequality were then changed to an equality, this would *require* that two (and only two) projects in the subset M be chosen:

$$\sum_{k=1}^{M} x_k = 2 \tag{A1.13}$$

Contingent (or "prerequisite") projects

Sometimes it is not possible to undertake a project unless another project is also selected. For example, an aluminium smelter may require that an electric power plant be built (or hydroelectric power unit installed on a dam). It may not make sense to build a food-processing plant unless a road is constructed to enable farmers to get their produce to it. On the other hand, it may make sense to build the electric power plant, but not build the aluminium smelter (or to build the road but not the food-processing plant).

Suppose that the analyst decides that project B should never be selected unless Project A is also selected. The following constraint will ensure this:

$$x_B \leq x_A \tag{A1.14}$$

Consider how this simple constraint works. If project A is not selected, then x_A is equal to zero. In this case x_B must be equal to zero because it can only take the values of zero and one. If project A is selected, then x_A is equal to one. In this case Project B can be selected, but it is not required that it be selected (i.e., x_B can either take the value of one or zero).

Again, the integer programming formulation provides great flexibility. The analyst might decide that Project B should not be undertaken unless both Project A and Project C are chosen. This can be accomplished by the inclusion of the following two constraints:

$$x_B \leq x_A$$
$$x_B \leq x_C \tag{A1.15}$$

Positive or negative Interactions Among Projects

Sometimes the project interactions are not so black and white as is assumed with mutually exclusive or contingent projects. It may, for example, be feasible to build both Project A and Project B, but because the projects are near each other and relate to each other in various ways, the net present value of doing both Project A and Project B is not the same as the sum of the net present values of doing Project A and Project B separately. For instance, it may be possible to build two dams on a river at different sites upstream of a city at risk of flooding. Building both dams would provide more flood control benefits than either alone, but the total flood control benefits from both dams is less than the sum of the benefits of either dam alone. This is because if either dam is built alone, it will prevent the worst of the flood damages. The second dam built (whichever one it is) only provides an added margin of safety. In this case the two projects interact to reduce the total benefits.

To illustrate, suppose that the benefits of Project A and Project B are b_A and b_B if either project is done separately. However, if both Project A and Project B are done, then the combined benefits are only 70 percent of the total of the two projects done separately. To characterize this relationship, the first step is for the analyst to define a "new" project, x_{A+B}, with the following net present value:

$$\text{NPV}_{A+B} = 0.7(b_A + b_B) \qquad\qquad (A1.16)$$

and introduce this coefficient and the new decision variable x_{A+B} in the objective function. It is obviously impossible to build all three projects (A, B, and A + B). The second step is to add the following constraint to the integer programming model in order to prevent this from happening:

$$x_A + x_B + x_{A+B} \le 1 \qquad\qquad (A1.17)$$

This constraint precludes the acceptance of both the original projects A and B, and the new combined project. If the model solution includes the new project A+B ($x_{A+B} = 1$), then the objective function is increased by the amount: $0.7\ (b_A + b_B)$. In this case, since x_A and x_B must *both* be zero, the objective function cannot be increased by b_A or by b_B.

Two projects could be complementary in the sense that they interact positively. In this case the net present value of doing Project A and Project B is more than the sum of the benefits of each done individually. For example, the health benefits to households available from the installation and use of an improved potable water supply project are positive. Similarly the health benefit from the use of an improved sanitation system are positive. However, if households in a community improve both their water and sanitation system, the health benefits may be greater than the sum of the benefits of each done separately. Such a situation can be represented in an exactly analogous way as the case when projects interact negatively. However, in this situation the objective function coefficient associated with x_{A+B} is greater than $(b_A + b_B)$. This ensures that if both projects are selected, the contribution of the combined project to the objective function is greater than the sum of the two projects done separately.

Delaying Projects

A different kind of project interdependency involves the question of *when* a project should be initiated during the planning horizon of the investment programme. It is often possible to delay the starting date of a project; this might be desirable, for example, in order to stay within an *annual* budget constraint (i.e., as defined by equation (A10.7)). It may, however, be impossible to build a similar project more than once during the planning period. If the different starting dates for a single project are thought of as defining a set of different projects, then the issue of project delay can be handled analytically in a manner similar to that for mutually exclusive projects.

Suppose, for example, that Project A can begin in period 1, 2, or 3. For purposes of illustration, assume that the initial costs of Project A are $1, and that these costs are incurred in whatever period the project begins. Project A then yields returns of $0.50 for the next four periods. The time profile of costs and returns, and the net present value in period 1 of each profile is given over[29]:

Project	Net Present Value in Period 1	Time Profile of Costs and Benefits Period						
		1	2	3	4	5	6	7
A_1	+0.59	-1.00	0.50	0.50	0.50	0.50		
A_2	+0.53		-1.00	0.50	0.50	0.50	0.50	
A_3	+0.48			-1.00	0.50	0.50	0.50	0.50

If Project A_1 is selected, it starts in period 1, and $x_{A1} = 1$. If Project A_1 is not selected, $x_{A1} = 0$. To incorporate the possibility of project delay, the following constraint must be added to the integer programming model:

$$x_{A1} + x_{A2} + x_{A3} \leq 1 \qquad\qquad (A1.18)$$

This constraint ensures that the model will not select Project A more than once, but the model does have the flexibility to determine when it is optimal to begin Project A. Clearly the net present value of Project A is higher if the project begins as soon as possible (i.e., in period 1). However, this does not take account of other constraints on the overall investment programme. Project A is still desirable even if its starting date must be delayed until period 2 or 3 (i.e., its net present value is still positive).

Summary

These four examples illustrate how integer variables can be used to represent different kinds of interrelationships among projects that are being considered for inclusion in an investment programme. Such interrelationships are not dealt with adequately by the use of simple decision rules, such as selecting the project with the highest internal rates of return, or the project with the largest cost-benefit ratio. The solution of even moderately complex capital budgeting problems requires careful examination of the agency or firm's objectives and the financial, economic, and physical relationships among projects in the investment programme.

Alternative Functional Forms For Hedonic Price Functions

The price of the property (or the wage level for wage risk estimations) is given by R.
The pollution variable (or risk variable for wage risk estimation) is given by P.

Linear	$R = a + bP$
Quadratic	$R = a + bP + cP^2$
Log	$R = aP^b$
Semi-log	$\log R = a + bP$
Inverse Semi-log	$R = \log a + b \log P$
Exponential	$R = a + bP^c$ where $c(>0)$ is an unknown parameter
Semi-log exponential	$\log R = a + bP^c$ where $c(>0)$ is an unknown parameter
Box-Cox Transformation	$\dfrac{R^c - 1}{c} = a + bP$ where c is an unknown parameter

Valuing Marginal Damages

If (a) a producer is a profit maximiser and price taker, (b) pollution changes result in marginal changes in outputs and inputs, and (c) prices are not affected by the changes in inputs and outputs, then the appropriate measure of the value of the change in damage following the change in pollution level is the change in value of gross output.

The production function for a single output y is given by

$$y = F(X, Z)$$

where X is a vector of inputs and Z is the input of the unpriced environmental resource. Prices of inputs are given by the price vector P, and the price of output is given by s. The unpriced environmental resource influences the output directly but not the other inputs.

The profit function for the producer is given by

$$\Pi = \Phi(s, P, Z)$$

We are interested in the change in profit that results from the change in Z, i.e., in

$$\delta\Pi/\delta Z$$

By the definition of the profit function

$$\Pi = MAX\ [s.y - P.X] = MAX\ [s.\Phi(X,Z) - (P.X)]$$

which gives

$$\delta\Pi/\delta Z = s.\ \delta\Phi/\delta Z - P.\ \delta X/\delta Z = s.\ \delta\Phi/\delta Z$$

which follows from the envelope theorem.

This final expression is the gross value of the change in yield.

Annex 4

Soil Erosion In Mali

Another example of dose-response in developing countries is in valuing soil erosion from crop responses. This problem is endemic to many developing countries. Soil erodes "naturally" but lack of investment in conservation, poor extension services, inability to raise credit and insecure land tenure all contribute to poor management of soils. Using the Universal Soil Loss Equation (USLE), estimates of soil loss can be found by relating soil loss to rainfall erosivity, R; the "erodibility" of soils, K; the slope of land, SL; a "crop factor", C, which measures the ratio of soil loss under a given crop to that from bare soil, and conservation practice, P, (so that "no conservation" is measured as unity). The USLE is then:

$$\text{Soil Loss} = R.K.SL.C.P = x$$

The next step is to link soil loss to crop productivity. In a study of soil loss effects in southern Mali, researchers applied the following equation to estimate the impact.

$$\text{Yield} = C^{-bx}$$

where C is the yield on newly cleared and hence uneroded land, b is a coefficient varying with crop and slope and x is cumulative soil loss. Finally, the resulting yield reductions need to be valued. Again, a crude approach is simply to multiply the estimated crop loss by its market value if it is a cash crop. But the impact of yield changes on farm incomes will generally be more complex than this, e.g., yield reductions would reduce the requirement for weeding and harvesting. This can be allowed for by looking at the total impact on farm budgets with and without erosion.

Source: Bishop and Allen [1989]

Annex 5

Pollution And Materials Corrosion

Air pollution affects exposed surfaces and causes corrosion of metals and deterioration of building surfaces.

The pollutants most widely implicated in materials damage are the sulphur compounds, particulate matter, oxidants and nitrogen oxides. The materials damaged range from electrical contacts and components, to paints, metals - especially zinc and steel - fibres, textiles, rubber and elastomers. Most of the quantitative work on dose-response relationships has been on sulphur compounds and sulphate particulates. Nitrogen oxides may, however, be important with respect to the corrosion of electrical contacts.

The fundamental problem of valuation lies not in determining economic parameters, but in estimating the dose-response relationship. The interaction between pollutants and materials/buildings is very complex and imprecisely understood. The deposition of pollutants on building surfaces depends not only on their atmospheric concentration, but also on climatic factors (such as the strength and direction of the wind, rain intensity and humidity). The natural structure and reactivity of different materials and the degree to which they are protected also influences the degree of damage done. A further complication is that natural factors produce the same types of damage as man-made pollutants, which makes it difficult to determine how much of the damage is due to natural causes such as weathering. Additionally, there is concern over threshold levels, synergistic effects and the memory effect.

One major problem for empirical estimation of materials damage is determining the size of the inventory of materials exposed to pollution. There is some evidence that the stock-at-risk can be estimated through probability density functions for modern buildings in which surfaces of buildings and materials are estimated by taking a detailed sample of a particular tract and then extrapolating the results to a larger area.

The stages in a damage function exercise are typically:

1.   estimate a physical dose-response function of the form

$$D = f(P, W, N)$$
where D = damage e.g., in the form of corrosion.
        P = pollution concentration.
        W = is a climate variable.
        N = any other factor thought to be relevant.

2.   estimate the physical stock of exposed materials.

3.   estimate one of (per unit of material):

● costs of repair or extra maintenance
● material replacement cost
● loss of the perceived consumer value of the material
● the cost of developing pollutant resistant materials, such as fade resistant dyes.

274

Costs per unit are multiplied by the stock at risk to find the cost for the total stock.

Since materials damage from pollution shows up as a reduction in the useful life of a material causing more frequent replacement, we can calculate damages as an annual flow. First we need to work out the present value of the difference in the stream of replacement costs in a with and without pollution scenario. Call this PV_{dam}.

The annual equivalent flow of damages is then, $DAM = PV_{dam} [i(1+i)^n / (1+i)^n-1]$
where n is the useful life of the system in years and, i is the interest rate.

Materials damage from pollution then, will tend to show up in more frequent replacement, maintenance and repair of materials, and it is these extra costs which are most typically used to value damage. The issue arises as to whether this can be used as a basis for valuation? Such an approach is relevant only if the preferences of the people for the repair/restoration exceed the costs of restoration. Many empirical studies assume that this relationship does exist. If it does, then the costs of restoration are a lower bound of the "true" value. If the relationship between preferences and costs cannot be assumed then the restoration cost approach is not legitimate as an estimator of damage.

Glomsrod and Rosland [1988] use a dose-response function to estimate the direct costs of materials damage due to sulphur dioxide in Norway. They also employ a multi-sectoral macroeconomic growth model to estimate the indirect costs of S02 due to allocational effects.

The materials studied include galvanised steel, paint on steel, wood and stone, and stain on wood. Damages to other materials are not included due to lacking dose-response functions. Other air pollutants can also have corrosive effects e.g., nitrogen oxides, but Norwegian results so far have shown this effect to be small. However, N0x can increase the corrosion of the zinc cover on galvanised steel in S02-polluted air. This effect is difficult to quantify and has not been taken into account in this study.

The dose-response functions used are linear. The most researched function is that for galvanised steel based on five years of observation in southern Norway. The function describing the number of years (LG) needed to corrode 1um of the zinc cover of galvanised steel is given below:
    (1) $LG = E/K = 7.1 / (0.45 \times (SO2) + 0.7)$.

where E is the specific weight of zinc in g/cm^3 and K is the speed of corrosion given in $g/m^2/year$.

Based on data from the U.S.A. and Norway the Norwegian Institute for Air Research estimated the following dose-response function between S02-concentrations and the lifetime (LPS), measured in years, for paint and steel:
    (2) $LPS = 11.7 - 0.0042 \times (SO2)$.

Annex 6

Applications Of Dose-Response Techniques

Environmental Area/ Physical Indicator	Benefit Category	Receptor Impact	Link to Economic Benefits	Unit Damage Values Used
Air pollution/ ambient pollutant concentrations/ acid rain	Human health illness	Respiratory illness	Restricted activity days Work days lost Health care expenditures	Market Values (wage)
		Respiratory-related mortality	Risk of death	Value of Life
	Reproducible output flows	Crop damage, timber, etc	Crop loss, cropping pattern or quality	Market Prices
	Reproducible stocks	Damage to materials	Maintenance and repair	"
	Non-reproducible stocks	Damage to materials, natural resources	Maintenance and repair	Market Prices Costs of repair/replacement
Global air pollution Ozone layer	Human health	Skin Cancer	Risk of death	Value of Life
Greenhouse effect	Human health	Climatic change/drought/ floods/desertification	Risk of death Famines	Value of Life

Environmental Area/ Physical Indicator	Benefit Category	Receptor Impact	Link to Economic Benefits	Unit Damage Values Used
	Reproducible output flows	Sea level rise/ salinisation	Crop losses	Market Prices
	Reproducible stocks	Sea level rise	Defence of infrastructure buildings, etc	"
	Non-reproducible stocks	Sea level rise	Loss of land	"
Water pollution Ambient pollutant	Human health	Health risks from drinking water	Restricted activity days Work days lost Health care expenditures Mortality	Market Values (wage)
	Reproducible output flows	Crop damage, fish stock damage, Industrial production	Crop loss, cropping pattern or quality Purification	Market Prices
	Reproducible stocks	Corrosion	Maintenance and repair	Market Prices
Soil pollution (and toxic waste)	Human health	Non-lethal poisoning	Restricted activity days Work days lost Health care expenditure	Market Values (wage)
		Mortality	Death	Value of Life
	Reproducible output flows	Crop losses	Crop loss/cropping pattern/quality	Market Prices
	Non-reproducible stocks	Loss of soil fertility		
Radiation local indoor concentrations	Human health	Non-lethal risks	Restricted activity days Work days lost Health care expenditure Averting behaviour	Market Values (wage) Market Prices
		Lethal risks	Death	Value of Life

277

Environmental Area/ Physical Indicator	Benefit Category	Receptor Impact	Link to Economic Benefits	Unit Damage Values Used
Radiation Nuclear Accident	Human health	Non-lethal risks	Restricted activity days Work days lost Health care expenditure Averting behaviour	Market Values (wage) Market Prices
		Lethal risks	Death	Value of Life
	Reproducible output flows	Crop losses, Industrial production		Market Prices
	Reproducible stocks	Infrastructure		Market Prices
	Non-reproducible stocks	Water contamination		Market Prices
	Other	Evacuation, decontamination		?
Noise Local noise levels	Human health	Health risks	Restricted activity days Work days lost Health care expenditure	Market Values (wage) Market Prices
	Living environment	Learning problems	Job opportunities	?

Market Prices should be adjusted to shadow prices where necessary

Benefit Transfer: A Case Study Of The Benefits Of Reducing Wastewater Discharges At Twenty One Pulp And Paper Mills In The Eastern United States

In order to better illustrate the concept of benefit transfer, we summarize a case study of an analysis carried out by William H. Desvousges, Michael Naughton, and George Parson [1992d]. In their study Desvousges et. al. attempted to determine the economic benefits of a regulation proposed by the United States Environmental Protection Agency that would require twenty one pulp and paper mills in the eastern United States to reduce their wastewater discharges. Specifically, the water pollution control regulation would require that each plant adopt the "best conventional control technology" for water pollution abatement. The regulation would require reductions in loadings of either biological oxygen demand or total suspended solids (or both) at each of the twenty one industrial facilities. Because the twenty one plants are located on twelve different rivers with different existing ambient water quality and flow rates, and because recreational opportunities and socioeconomic characteristics of the population are different in the various locations, one would expect the benefits of reducing effluent loadings at each of the twenty one plants to be different.

As a first step, Desvousges et. al. found eight existing studies that provided estimates of the economic value of water quality improvements in the United States, and that they judged to be of sufficiently high quality for use for benefit transfer. Five of these were contingent valuation studies, two used travel cost models, and one was a participation study. However, five of the eight studies were carried out in the western part of the United States. Since the policy sites were in the eastern United States, Desvousges et. al. judged these five study sites to be too different from the twenty one policy sites to use them for benefit transfer. Of the three remaining studies, two examined the value of water quality improvements on the same eastern river, the Monongahela in Pennsylvania (Smith et. al., [1986]; Desvousges, et. al. [1983]). The remaining study examined the value of water quality improvements in the Charles River in Massachusetts (Gramlich, [1977]).

The remaining three studies were by no means ideal. Desvousges et. al. note that the contingent valuation study of the Charles River had problems with questionnaire design, sampling procedure, and econometrics. The contingent valuation study of the Monongahela (Desvousges, et. al. [1983]) did not account for the influence of substitute sites. The other study of the Monongahela (Smith, et. al., [1986]) used a variation of the travel cost model, but the sample size was quite small (69). Nevertheless, these were the best studies available and Desvousges et. al. made the judgment that despite these limitations they could be used for benefit transfer to the policy sites. They carried out benefit transfer from *each* of these three studies to the policy sites independently, thus obtaining three different sets of estimates of the value of water quality improvements at the policy sites.

Table A7.2 compares several characteristics of the study sites (i.e., Monongahela and Charles Rivers) and the policy sites. Neither the study sites nor the policy sites attract recreational users from far way; all are used primarily by local residents. However, the types of fish caught in the study and policy sites are different. Ideally Desvousges et. al. would have liked to select study sites with recreational fishing opportunities more similar to their policy sites, but such studies were simply not available.

After identifying the three study sites, Desvousges et. al. faced four principal problems in implementing the benefit transfer. The **first** was in determining the extent of the market. They found that the information available on both own and substitute price effects was not sufficient to use to define the point at which households would no longer use a river for recreational purposes (i.e., where willingness to pay declined to zero). They simply assumed that the market boundary was defined by the county boundary of those counties adjacent to that portion of the river affected by the regulation. An important advantage of using the county boundaries to define the extent of the market is that population and socioeconomic information on households is easily available in the United States for county units. Using this rule of thumb, ten of the twelve policy sites had market sizes falling in the range of 40-88 kilometres from the river. The sample for the Charles River study site was considerably smaller than this (13 kilometres), so there is some question whether the benefit information from the Charles river study can be reliably transferred to the market sizes assumed in the policy sites.

Second, the benefit estimates from the existing studies were for large, qualitative improvements in water quality (e.g., from boatable to fishable). On the other hand, the actual water quality improvements that would result from implementation of the EPA water pollution control regulation for pulp and paper mills are expected to be often quite small. However, Desvousges et. al. did not have quantitative estimates of the water quality improvements that would result in portions of the river downstream of the pulp and paper mills.

To address this problem, they first determined the current water quality at each policy site (see Table A7.1). They assumed that the water quality improvement that was valued in the Charles River contingent valuation study was equivalent to a full qualitative change in the potential recreational use of the river (i.e., from boatable to swimmable), and for the transfers using this study assumed that this same change would occur at all the policy sites. In the Monongahela contingent valuation study, benefits were estimated for two increments of water quality improvement: boatable to fishable, and fishable to swimmable. For the benefit transfers using the demand relationship from the Monongahela contingent valuation study, Desvousges et. al. assumed that the water quality improvement at two of the policy sites would be from boatable to fishable (Hudson and Oswegatchie Rivers) and from fishable to swimmable for all the other rivers.

Because the travel cost study provided a relationship between the value of water quality improvements and a continuous measure of water quality change, it was possible to use a more refined measure of the estimated water quality change at the policy sites. Desvousges et. al. assumed that the regulation of pulp and paper mills would be sufficient to improve the water quality in the relevant portion of a policy site river by either 10%, 25%, or 50% of the relevant broad increment in water quality improvement (boatable to fishable for the Hudson and Oswegatchie Rivers; fishable to swimmable for all the other rivers). Based on a judgmental assessment of dilution rates, current loadings, and the magnitude of the proposed reduction, they assumed the regulations would result in an improvement of 10% of the increment from fishable to swimmable for the Kennebec River, 25% for the Androscoggin, St. John, and Black Rivers, and 50% for the remaining rivers (it is unclear how this procedure worked for the Westfield and Ashuelot Rivers, which were judged to have swimmable water before the implementation of the regulation--see Table A7.1).

Third, Desvousges et. al. found that none of the three existing studies seriously considered the relationship between the benefits of water quality improvements and the characteristics of the recreation sites (such as ease of access), nor did they provide usable information on prices of alternative recreational opportunities (i.e., the prices of substitutes). The omission of these important determinants of value could result in potentially large errors in the benefit transfer. Without proper control for site characteristics and the prices of close substitutes, an analyst can only hope that the site characteristics at the study site(s) and the prices of alternative recreational opportunities at the study site(s) closely resemble those at the policy site(s). Desvousges et. al. speculate that the omission of information on site characteristics in the demand models from the study sites would lead to an upward bias in their benefit estimates for the policy sites because they feel that access is easier at the study sites.

Fourth, the existing studies measure different components of value. The travel cost study (Smith et.

al., [1986]) measured use value; the contingent valuation studies (Gramlich, [1977]; Desvousges, et. al. [1983]) measured both use and nonuse value. In their benefit transfer procedure Desvousges et. al. attempted to adjust the travel cost results to make them comparable to the contingent valuation results. (They multiplied the use values from the travel cost study by two different estimates of the ratio of total value to use value.)

The transfer procedure itself involved multiplying the estimated average benefits per household for each policy site by the number of affected households in the assumed market area around that site. Both the Charles River contingent valuation study and the Monongahela travel cost study estimated the relationship between the distance of a household to the recreation site and the value of a water quality improvement. Thus, for transfers using these studies Desvousges et. al. could adjust the average benefits per household to reflect the fact that the benefits to households living farther away from the recreation site were less than to households living nearby.

They made this adjustment by dividing the market area for each policy site into two zones: one "near" to and one "far" from the river. They assumed that all households in the inner zone are located 11 kilometres from the river. All households in the outer zone were assumed to be located at the average distance between the edge of the market boundary and 7 kilometres from the river. Because the market boundaries are different distances from the river for different policy sites, the distance from the representative household in the outer zone to the river is different for each policy site. No such adjustment in average household benefits was made for the Monongahela contingent valuation study because in this study the relationship between distance from the site and value of the water quality improvement was not statistically significant. Desvousges et. al. were thus forced to use a single representative household for these transfers.

The demand models in all three existing studies provided information on the relationship between benefits and household characteristics such as income and education. Desvousges et. al. adjusted the average benefits per household in the inner and outer zones in a specific policy site to reflect the household characteristics at that site. Table A7.2. summarizes the average household income and education levels for the study and policy sites.

Table A7.3 presents the per-household benefit estimates for the expected water quality improvement for the twelve policy sites derived from each of the three existing studies. Two estimates are presented for the Monongahela contingent valuation study because the study included demand relationships for two different questionnaire formats. Several aspects of these results are particularly noteworthy.

First, for both contingent valuation studies, there is little variation in the per-household benefit estimates for the majority of the policy sites. For most policy sites the per-household benefits based on the Monongahela contingent valuation study are $25 for one questionnaire format and $17 for the other format. The per-household benefits based on the Charles River contingent valuation study are usually $44-47 for the inner zone and $0-1 for the outer zone. The per-household benefit estimates based on the travel cost study exhibit considerably more variation. This is to be expected because these transfers incorporate more variation in the expected water quality improvement. Since transfers using all three studies adjust for income and education differences between the study and policy sites, such socioeconomic characteristics appear to be less important determinants of variations in per-household estimates than either the distance of the household to the river or the magnitude of the water quality change.

Second, comparing the inner zone estimates from the Charles River study with the inner zone estimates from the Monongahela travel cost study, the estimates based on the Charles River study are always much higher (2-10 times higher). **Third,** eight out of the twelve outer zone benefit estimates based on the Charles River study are zero, in contrast to the outer zone estimates based on the Monongahela travel cost model. **Fourth,** if one considers the three *average* per-household benefit estimates for each of the twelve policy sites, they are generally of the same order of magnitude.

Desvousges et. al. also calculated the total benefits of the regulatory action (summing over all the policy sites) for each of the three sets of benefit transfer estimates. The estimated aggregate benefits of the proposed regulations on the pulp and paper industry were in the range of $18-26 million per year if one used the benefit transfer based on the two contingent valuation studies, and about $11 million per year based on the travel cost study.

This case study illustrates the numerous judgments and assumptions that the analyst is required to make in order to carry out a benefit transfer analysis. Many of these assumptions appear quite ad hoc and are necessitated by the limitations of the existing studies and available data. Nevertheless, in the end Desvousges et. al. were able to derive aggregate benefit estimates that one might best describe as "crude" or "order of magnitude". It will depend on the specific decision context whether policy makers will find such "ballpark" estimates of value.

Table A7.1   Policy sites

Policy Site River	Largest City in Market Area	Current Water Quality [a]	Current Loadings,[a] mg/L		Reductions in Current Loadings,[a] %		Dilution Rate[a,c]	Affected Reach Length, miles[d]	Qualitative Assessment of Per-Family Benefits Due to Reduction[e]
			BOD[b]	TSS[b]	BOD	TSS			
Westfield	Northampton, Ma.	swimmable	13.77	4.49	45	0	9.62	20-25	moderate
Hudson	Glen Falls, NY	boatable	11.67	6.42	57	0	16.42	25-35	moderate
Schuylkill	Philadelphia, Penn.	fishable	22.09	2.15	86	0	44.74	5-10	low/moderate
Salmon	Oswego, NY	boatable	4.6	1.97	35	0	6.88	10-20	low/moderate
Oswegatchie	Canton, NY	fishable	4.11	5.35	0	12	3.97	20-30	low/moderate
St. John	Presque Isle, Maine	fishable	6.6	3.48	55	0	32.28	20-30	low/moderate
Androscoggin	Berlin, New Hampshire	fishable	3.4	2.72	12	0	48.08	20-25	low/moderate
Limestone	Syracuse, NY	fishable	10.52	21.24	75	73	5.88	5-10	low
Fox	Green Bay, Wisconsin	fishable	6.56	11.97	0	22	11.92	20-30	low
Kennebe	Augusta, Maine	fishable	18.26	30.76	51	59	225.21	10-15	low
Ashuelot	Keene, New Hampshire	swimmable	10.40	8.33	55	16	42.86	5-10	low
Black	Lowville, NY	fishable	21.21	28.71	54	46	50.81	20-25	low

1 mile equals 1.609 km.

[a] Source: EPA, Office of Water Regulations and Standards.

[b] BOD denotes biological oxygen demand; TSS, total suspended solids.

[c] Dilution rate is the ration of the river's low flow to the point source (pulp and paper plants) flow.

[d] The affected reach length is a qualitative assessment based on the current loadings and expected percentage reduction in loadings in consultation with state water quality officials.

[e] Moderate denotes noticeable water quality improvement which should affect recreational/aesthetic enjoyment. Low denotes minor water quality improvement which may affect recreational/aesthetic enjoyment.

SOURCE:

Desvousges, W.H., M.C. Naughton, and G.R. Parsons, [1992d], "Benefit Transfer: Conceptual Problems in Estimating Water Quality Benefits Using Existing Studies", *Water Resources Research*, Vol. 28, No. 3, March, [Special Section: Problems and Issues in the Validity of Benefit Transfer Methodologies.]

Table A7.2 Study and policy site attributes

	Market Size, Households	Distance From Site, Miles		Percent Urbanization	Household Income 1980 dollars	Education, % college	Access Level [a]	Recreation Types	Fish Types (cold or warm water)
		Mean	Maximum						
					Study Site Rivers				
Charles	716,245	2	8	95	23,376	39	good	boating, picnicking, hiking, biking	warm
Monongahela	616,800	15	40	81	21,542	14	good	camping, boating, Swimming, fishing picnicking	warm
					Policy Site Rivers				
Westfield	116,294	7	30	90	21,661	14	adequate	canoeing, fishing, swimming	cold
Hudson	78,825	13	40	47	19,700	16	adequate	boating	warm
Schuylkill	415,891	6	12	100	18,891	11	adequate	boating, fishing, water skiing	warm
Salmon	28,201	14	25	29	20,017	11	good	fishing, boating	cold and anadromous
Oswegatchie	26,650	28	50	41	18,643	13	adequate	boating, fishing, picnicking, hiking	cold
St. John	23,775	61	110	45	15,934	11	limited	scenic view, rare plants	cold
Androscoggin	22,975	18	55	29	17,705	10	adequate	fishing, boating	cold
Limestone	116,861	10	25	82	23,524	19	limited	fishing, picnicking	warm
Fox	77,276	12	25	77	24,182	14	limited	fishing	warm
Kennebec	32,079	11	40	56	19,120	12	adequate	boating, fishing, picnicking, hiking	cold
Ashuelot	16,127	14	30	39	20,766	18	adequate	canoeing, fishing	cold
Black	6,383	6	30	13	18,448	10	good	white water rafting and fishing	cold

1 mile equals 1.609 km.

[a] Good denotes plenty of easy access sites; adequate, a moderate level of access sites and/or some degree of difficulty in accessing the river; limited, a few access sites and/or very difficult river access (e.g., steep embankments or no public accommodations).

SOURCE:
Desvousges, W.H., M.C. Naughton, and G.R. Parsons, [1992d], "Benefit Transfer: Conceptual Problems in Estimating Water Quality Benefits Using Existing Studies", *Water Resources Research*, Vol. 28, No. 3, March, [Special Section: Problems and Issues in the Validity of Benefit Transfer Methodologies.]

Table A7.3 Transfer estimates of per-household water quality benefits (in 1984 dollars):

| | Gramlich Contingent Valuation | | | DSM Contingent Valuation | | SDF Travel Cost | | | Qualitative |
	Inner:	Outer:	Average:	High:	Low:	Inner:	Outer:	Average:	Assessment
Westfield River	47.26	19.37	31.64	25.70	17.72	24.02	17.28	20.24	moderate
Hudson River	14.57	0	15.15	40.57	27.45	29.40	16.42	20.84	moderate
Schuylkill River	44.82	12.28	33.76	25.75	17.77	9.10	2.00	7.08	low/moderate
Salmon River	48.28	0	2.90	25.73	17.75	21.14	8.43	9.19	low/moderate
Oswegatchie River	46.67	0	4.20	40.32	27.20	35.36	11.03	13.22	low/moderate
St. John River	46.58	0	6.06	25.51	17.53	21.74	2.89	5.03	low/moderate
Androscoggin River	19.54	0	15.36	26.62	17.64	16.37	2.07	9.94	low/moderate
Limestone Creek	47.38	0.89	23.21	25.63	17.65	19.60	8.79	13.99	low
Fox River	57.01	1.23	33.02	25.79	17.81	22.23	8.86	16.49	low
Kennebec River	47.68	0	25.27	25.63	17.65	4.78	2.20	3.57	low
Ashuelot River	52.29	0	5.23	25.51	17.53	10.70	5.20	5.69	low
Black River	45.54	0	32.33	25.68	17.70	10.38	5.06	8.84	low

SOURCE:

Desvouges, W.H., M.C. Naughton, and G.R. Parsons, [1992d], "Benefit Transfer: Conceptual Problems in Estimating Water Quality Benefits Using Existing Studies", *Water Resources Research*, Vol. 28, No. 3, March, [Special Section: Problems and Issues in the Validity of Benefit Transfer Methodologies.]

Annex 8

Deriving the Consumption Rate of Interest

Let an individual's well-being, U, be given by:

$$U = \frac{C^{1-u}.e^{-pt}}{1-u}$$

where u = the elasticity of the marginal utility of consumption, p = the utility discount rate, and t = time.

Then,

$$\frac{dU}{dC} = 1/(1-u).\{e^{-pt}.(1-u).C^{-u}\}$$

$$= C^{-u}.e^{-pt}$$

Define the CRI as the rate of fall over time of the marginal utility of consumption, i.e., as

$$\frac{-d(dU/dC)/dt}{dU/dC} = (-1) \times \frac{\{-p.e^{-pt}.c^{-u} + e^{-pt}.-uc^{-u-1}\}.dC/dt}{c^{-u}.e^{-pt}}$$

$$= (-1) \times \{-p - \frac{u.dC}{c.dt}\}$$

$$= p + ug$$

where $g = \frac{dC/dt}{C}$

Annex 9

Discounting and Sustainability

Mäler [1990] suggests a model to illustrate the capital substitutability issue. What follows is a further simplification to capture the essential ideas.

Suppose there is man-made capital, denoted K, and a non-renewable resource, denoted R. There are two periods reflecting two generations, 0 and 1. If generation 0 decides to reduce the stock of R_o in order to enjoy more consumption C_o, then it will reduce the consumption possibilities of generation 1 since the resource stock declines and is therefore not available to the next generation. In order to ensure that generation 1's consumption does not decline - the sustainability criterion - generation 0 must compensate generation 1 by increasing the stock of K so that generation 1 inherits more capital.

This compensation requirement can be written:

$$dI_0.F_{1K} = dR_0.F_{1R} \qquad [A9.1]$$

The left hand side of [A10.1] is the gain in period 1 and is equal to the change in investment in period 0 necessary to compensate period 1 multiplied by the marginal product of capital in period 1.

[A10.1] can be rewritten:

$$dI_0 = dR_0. F_{1R}./F_{1K} \qquad [A9.2]$$

The right hand side is the loss in period 1 due to the reduction in the non-renewable resource and is equal to the change in the resource stock in 0 multiplied by the marginal product of that resource in period 1 (i.e., what it would have yielded in period 1).

The <u>net</u> change in consumption in period 0 is then:

$$dC_0 = dR_0.F_{0R} - dI_0 \qquad [A9.3]$$

and is made up of the gain brought about by the extra extraction of the natural resource less the extra investment required to compensate period 1.

Substituting [A10.2] in [A10.3] gives:

$$dC_0 = dR_0.[F_{0R} - F_{1R}/F_{1K}] \qquad [A9.4]$$

which can be rewritten

$$dC_0 = dR_0 [F_{0R} - F_{1R}/\{1 + (F_{1K} - 1)\} \qquad [A9.5]$$

Now, $F_{1K} - 1 = r$, the marginal product of capital - 1, or the social rate of discount as given by the productivity of capital. Note that it is the marginal product of capital in period 1 that is relevant, not the productivity in period 0; and that it is the productivity of capital that gives rise to discounting in this context, not the rate of time preference.

Hence [A10.5] can be written as:

$$dC_0 = dR_0.[F_{0R} - F_{1R}/(1 + r)] \qquad\qquad [A9.6]$$

which is then the decision rule for generation 0. Sustainability is ensured if the change in consumption in period 0 equals the benefit from the use of the natural resource in 0 less the costs which equal the discounted value of the foregone future productivity of the resource.

Now consider the substitutability issue. If substitution possibilities between K and R are very small, then F_{1K} would be small and F_{1R} would be very big. Hence F_{1R}/F_{1K} would be large and, from [A10.4], dC_0 would be negative. That is, development is not sustainable if resource use now involves resources which cannot be substituted for by K, or which have a low elasticity of substitution.

Costs And Benefits Of Pollution Control In An Expected Value Framework

This annex is based on OECD [1991]. The problem is to weigh up the costs and benefits of pollution control when:

(a) the benefits of control, in terms of reduced damage, are uncertain;
(b) there is uncertainty about the effectiveness of the policy measure.

The expected value of reduced pollution damage is:

$$bD + (1-b)0 = bD \qquad (A10.1)$$

where D is the avoided or reduced damage and b is the probability that the control measure will be effective. If the control is ineffective, reduced damage = 0.

Hence any control measure will be worthwhile if

$$C < bD \qquad (A10.2)$$

(A10.2) can be rewritten:

$$\frac{D - C}{C} > \frac{1 - b}{b} \qquad (A10.3)$$

That is, the net benefit (D-C) as a proportion of cost (C)
must be greater than the ratio of the two probabilities of ineffectiveness and effectiveness respectively.

As an example, if b = 0.5 (there is a 50% chance of success), then

$$\frac{1 - b}{b} = 1$$

so D - C > C, or D > 2C,

the damage reduction must be at least twice the cost.

We can define $\quad \frac{(1 - b)C}{b} \quad$ as the cost of the risk of ineffectiveness, Cr.

Inequality (A10.3) can therefore be rewritten

$$D - C > Cr$$
or $\quad C + Cr < D \qquad (A10.4)$

Now we can introduce uncertainty about <u>damage</u> such that a is the probability that damage = D and (1-a) is the probability that damage is a fraction (g) of D.

Then the condition C < bD becomes

$$C < b[aD + (1-a)gD]$$

or $$\underset{b}{C} < D[a + (1-a)g] \qquad\qquad (A10.5)$$

But $$\underset{b}{C} = C + \underset{b}{(1-b)}C = C + Cr$$

and $$D[a + (1-a)g] = D - (1-g)(1-a)D = D - Dr$$

where (1-g)(1-a)D can be defined as the cost of the uncertainty about the damage.

Hence the cost-benefit rule becomes:

$$\boxed{C + Cr < D - Dr \qquad\qquad (A10.6)}$$

Inequality (A10.6) can be expanded to give an expression for the net benefits of pollution control as:

$$NB = D - (1-g)(1-a)D - C - (1-b)C/b$$

or $$NB = bD[a + g(1-a)] - C \qquad\qquad (A10.7)$$

Using equation (A10.7) the matrix below presents expressions for net benefits under the differing assumptions:

	b=0 (i.e., the policy is ineffective)	b=1 (i.e., the policy is effective)
a=0 (damage is gD rather than D)	NB = -C	NB = gD-C
a=1 (damage is D rather than gD)	NB = -C	NB = D - C

Why The Failure To Secure Proper Prices For Environmental Resources Reduces Aggregate Social Well-being.

Assume a simple economy in which there are two products, steel and fish, and two resources, labour and "the environment". Let the two production functions be:

$$Xs = Xs(Ls)$$

and

$$Xf = Xf(Lf,Xs)$$

where L is labour, X is output, s is steel and f is fish. Note how the environmental resource enters the picture: the output of fish is partly dependent upon the output of steel because steel production gives rise to pollution which damages the fishery through, say, water pollution.

The marginal products of labour for the two outputs are respectively:

$$dXs/dLs = MPs$$

and

$$dXf/dLf = MPf$$

But the <u>social</u> marginal products (SMPs) are:

$$SMPs = dXs/dLs - dXf/dLs$$

and

$$SMPf = dXf/dLf$$

The expression deducted from MPs is the output of fish affected by the input of labour to steel. This can be thought of as a "chain" of effects: the output of fish affected by the output of steel and the output of steel affected by the input of labour to steel.

Now, we know that, without the externality, social output is maximised where:

$$dXs/dLs = dXf/dLf$$

If this were not so, we could raise output in the economy by reallocating resources from fish to steel or steel to fish. <u>Provided the externality effect of steel on fish is ignored this equivalence of marginal products would be achieved in a competitive economy</u>.

But this equivalence of <u>private</u> marginal products is inefficient. To see this, we need to recognise that the required equivalence is between social marginal products, i.e., the marginal products after the interdependence between steel and fish outputs has been taken into account. The equivalence of SMPs gives:

$$[dXs/dLs - dXf/dLs] = dXf/dLf$$

which means that, for maximum social output, steel output should be <u>less</u> than it would be if the externality was ignored.

Note that the failure of the market here arises from the lack of any means to <u>internalise</u> the cost of steel on fish in the decisions made by steel. But note also that, for this internalisation to take place, the externality must be correctly <u>valued</u>.

Annex 12

Deriving An Externality Tax

Annex 11 established the conditions for maximum output in a simple economy comprising fish and steel. In terms of marginal products the required equivalence was:

$$[dXs/dLs - dXf/dLs] = dXf/dLf$$

or

$$MPs - CMPfs = MPf$$

where "CMPfs" means the cross marginal product of steel on fish.

This condition expressed in terms of the <u>value</u> of marginal products is then:

$$Ps. MPs - Pf/CMPfs = Pf.MPf$$

Rearranging this becomes:

$$Ps = \frac{Pf [MPf + CMPfs]}{MPs}$$

or

$$\frac{Ps}{Pf} = \frac{MPf}{MPs} + \frac{CMPfs}{MPs}$$

For either industry, the <u>marginal cost</u> of production is given by:

$$W.dXi/dLi$$

where W is the ruling wage rate. Hence, MPi = W/MCi. Substituting this in the last expression we have:

$$Ps/Pf = MCs/MCf + CMPfs/MPs$$

Now, CMPfs/MPs is equal to:

(dXf/dLs)/(dXs/dLs) which can be re-expressed as dXf/dXs (see Annex 11). Hence the required equivalence is now:

$$Ps/Pf = MCs/MCf + dXf/dXs$$

If price equals marginal cost in the fishery, we have

$$Ps/Pf = MCs/Pf + dXf/dXs$$

Multiplying through by Pf gives:

$$Ps = MCs + Pf.dXf/dXs$$

But the last expression is the marginal value of the externality or the <u>marginal external cost</u>. So, for optimality we require that steel face a tax equal to:

$$t = Pf.dXf/dXs.$$

The second expression is the monetary value of the interdependence, i.e., the value of the externality. It is simply the physical loss of output of fish due to steel production (shown here in terms of units of labour used to make steel), multiplied by the price of fish.

Annex 13

Deriving User Cost

Consider a natural resource which is finite in supply. The social benefits from the resource are Bt every year until year T when the resource is exhausted. The costs of extraction are Ct, assumed constant, i.e., $Ct = C$. Let r be the social discount rate. The quantity extracted each year is Qt and the total amount of the resource available is $\underline{Q}$. Social well-being is maximised according to the solution of:

$$\max \Sigma[Pt.Qt - C.Qt][1+r]^{-t} \text{ subject to } \Sigma Qt = \underline{Q}.$$

Form the Lagrangean:

$$\max S = \Sigma[Pt.Qt - C.Qt][1+r]^{-t} - \mu[\Sigma Qt - \underline{Q}]$$

The first order condition is:

$$dS/dQt = [Pt - C][1+r]^{-t} - \mu = 0$$

so that

$$Pt = C + \mu[1+r]^{t}$$

This result tells us that the optimal price of the exhaustible resource is made up of two components: the extraction cost, C, and the expression $\mu[1+r]^{t}$ which is the <u>user cost</u> or <u>depletion premium</u>, <u>rent</u> or <u>royalty</u>.

In turn, we can write

$$Rt = Pt - C = \mu[1+r]^{t}$$

So that

$$\frac{Rt+1 - Rt}{Rt} = r$$

that is, the royalty should rise through time at the rate of discount: this is the "Hotelling rule".

Finally, note how user cost can be estimated. If $Rt = \mu(1+r)^{t}$, then $Ro = \mu(1+r)$ and $R_T = \mu(1+r)^{T} = Ro(1+r)^{T}$, where o is the initial period, and T is the period in which the resource is exhausted or in which a "backstop technology" (B) is available for the same price. Hence in period T we can write $P_T = P_B$. It follows that:

$$Ro = \mu = R_T (1+r)^{-T} = [P_B - C][1 + r]^{-T}$$

This equation for Ro needs to be solved together with the equation $\Sigma Qt = \underline{Q}$. Box 15.2 gives an example.

Annex 14

Tradeable Emission And Resource Harvesting Permits

The basic idea underlying tradeable permits is simple. First, an acceptable level of pollution is determined. This may be expressed as some allowable concentration of, say, lead in gasoline; a production or consumption target for chemicals, e.g., CFCs; or an allowable national emission level as is likely with carbon dioxide some time in the future. Permits are then issued for the level of emissions etc. up to the allowable level. If, say, 100 units of pollution is allowable, 100 permits each with a value of 1 unit of emission might be issued. There are various ways of determining the initial issue of the permits. Because of the disruption that might ensue by alternative allocations, a popular initial allocation is one based on historical emission levels. This is known as grandfathering: rights to pollute are based on past emission levels. While this is not the only way to determine the initial allocation, the experience so far with tradeable permits shows that it is important to find an acceptable formula for this initial allocation, and that grandfathering tends to be acceptable to all parties. Clearly, grandfathering does nothing to reduce pollution or excessive resource use unless either (a) the initial allocation is for less pollution than already takes place (i.e., quotas are allocated pro rata to existing emissions but the overall level is less than the current total), or (b) the initial allocation is reduced over time. Any polluter achieving lower pollution than the number of permits he possesses receives a credit. For example, polluter A has permits to emit 10 units of pollution but actually emits 8. The credit of two is then tradeable. This works to advantage of polluter A if reducing his pollution by 2 units is cheaper than the price he can get by selling permits equal to 2 units. In technical terms, there is an incentive to sell permits if the (marginal) abatement costs are below the ruling price for permits, and to buy if abatement costs are above the price of permits.

Once the initial allocation is made, polluters are then free to trade the pollution rights. It is this tradeability that is the hallmark of the permit system since it is tradeability that accounts for the main attraction of such a system - its role in keeping down the costs of complying with regulations. Basically, a firm that finds it comparatively easy to abate pollution will find it profitable to sell its permits to a polluter who finds it expensive to abate pollution. Essentially, it will sell the permit if it receives a price higher than the costs it will have to bear of abating pollution now that it has no permit. The high cost polluter, on the other hand, will find it profitable to buy permits if the price is below what it will otherwise cost him to abate pollution. Both low and high cost polluter therefore stand to gain and this provides the incentive for them to trade. Moreover, by trading the control of pollution will tend to be concentrated among those polluters who find it cheap to pollute. Permit holding will tend to be concentrated among those who find it expensive to control pollution. Yet the overall environmental standard is safeguarded because nothing has happened to alter the overall number of permits and it is this that determines the level of pollution.

Clearly, such a description is simplistic, but it captures the essence of the tradeable permit system. One important point to note is that trade need not be between different polluters (external trading). It can be between different sources within a single firm (internal trading). The result is the same, however, because the firm will gain by concentrating abatement in its low cost sources and concentrating permits in the high cost sources.

We would expect the actual experience of permit trading to result in no decline in environmental standards and a reduction in the costs of compliance compared to what would have been incurred in a CAC system. By and large, this is the experience of the USA where a tradeable permits system exists as part of the US Clean Air Acts of the 1970s, and which have been expanded under the new Clean Air Act of 1991.

Some terminology is needed to understand the US system. Netting, introduced in 1974, is a procedure whereby a firm can create a new emissions source provided it offsets the resulting emissions by reductions elsewhere in the same plant. Netting always involves internal trading - i.e., the firm is not allowed to acquire permits from outside. Offsets were introduced in 1976 in areas where the Clean Air Act standards had not been met ("non-attainment areas"). Stringent rules applied to new sources would have meant that such areas could attract little or no new industry. However, by offsetting the new source by even greater reductions in existing sources, these areas are allowed to acquire new industry. Such offsets can be obtained by internal and external trading, i.e., from buying up permits from within the same source or from other firms. Bubbles are perhaps the most famous part of the US tradeable permits system. They were introduced in 1979. A "bubble" is an hypothetical aggregate limit for existing sources of pollution (whereas netting and offsets relate to new sources). Within the overall bubble limit firms are free to vary sources of pollution so long as the overall limit is not breached. Bubbles are allowed to extend beyond a single firm, but in practice bubbles have tended to be placed round single firms. Banking was introduced in 1979 and operates just like a bubble but through time, i.e., the firm is allowed to bank credits and use them at some stage in the future.

The table below summarises the US experience and shows the effects on cost savings and on environmental quality. The table reveals the following:

(a) nearly all trading has been internal. Only the offset system has resulted in moderate external trading. While the bubble system does permit external trading, hardly any has occurred. This appears to be due to the high costs of acquiring information about other firms' willingness to trade, and the costs of obtaining the regulator's permission to trade;

(b) the cost savings are considerable, with a minimum of $1 billion and perhaps as much as $13 billion having been saved;

(c) banking has hardly been used at all;

(d) the extensive use of netting compared to bubbles, even allowing for the predominance of internal trades, is surprising since bubbles apply to existing sources whereas netting applies only to new or modified sources.

Explaining the less than hoped-for level of trading activity in the US permits system so far is not easy. Companies such as Armco, Du Pont, USX and 3M have traded permit credits, but the take-up has otherwise been quite low. Commentators have suggested four main reasons:

(i) new sources are subject to far stricter regulations about emissions quality. This means that firms are keen to adopt any offsetting procedure when a new source starts up. Netting is the appropriate procedure in these cases and this does much to explain the dominance of netting in the US system. Moreover, existing sources have inherited abatement equipment, bought before the bubble policy was introduced in 1979, so that the costs of adjustment under a bubble policy are high;

(b) uncertainty about pollution credits. There has been considerable uncertainty about just what emission credits ensue under the banking legislation. Firms are not always sure how the regulator will determine baseline emissions and hence how emission credits will be determined. This uncertainty is heightened when other firms' credits are the subject of the trade (i.e., when external trading is involved). Firm A has to be sure that firm B really will reduce emissions to create credits that can be traded. In contrast, internal trading involves far greater certainty because the firm is dealing only with itself;

(c) it is more expensive to acquire information about external trading since firm A needs to find out what other firms have banked credits, and the price at which trade is likely to take place. Similar problems have arisen in other countries where attempts have been made to establish waste exchange information services;

(d) firms will not trade with other firms because of the prospect of permit prices rising. Permits will be hoarded as long as the expected price rise is greater than the cost of hoarding, i.e., greater than interest rate;

(e) hoarded permits can be used as a deterrent to new entrants.

Permit trading is the central feature of a more recent US Clean Air Act in the context of acid rain control. Regulators claim they have learned from the experience of the previous tradeable permit systems and that most of the problems should be avoidable in the new system.

Objections have been raised by various "interest groups": environmentalists, industry, and government.

In the USA environmentalists' objections have been focused on two main issues: whether environmental quality is sacrificed under a tradeable permits system, and whether it is morally right to "permit" pollution even for a price. The table shows that the environmental quality argument has little or no foundation. The second objection has to be countered by an educative process. All regulatory systems "permit" pollution if by pollution is meant waste. No economic process is waste free. The issue has therefore to be one of whether a tradeable permits system somehow permits more waste than a CAC system. As we have seen, there is no reason at all for this to be the case. It is significant that many environmental organizations in the USA now welcome tradeable permits.

The US experience suggests that certainty about the regulatory system is highly valued. With CAC systems the firm is, by and large, clear about the nature of the regulation and what is and what is not permitted. This is also true for CAC systems that are less rigid, such as the UK system in which there is considerable scope for flexible adjustments in light of dialogue with the Inspectorate of Pollution. As European Community Directives play an increasingly important role, however, we might expect more and more "standard setting" to replace the system of negotiation over achieving standards.

Regulators will naturally be sensitive to the concerns of both environmentalists and industry. Nonetheless they will also have their own concerns, primarily arising from the costs of considering, formulating and implementing any departure from the established CAC approach. It is worth remembering that the CAC mode of thinking is ingrained in environmental regulation in most countries, reflecting as it does the experience of over 100 years of public health, workplace and environmental legislation. Anxiety also tends to increase the less is known about the new system.

Regulators and industry are also likely to be concerned about the administrative costs of any regulatory system. Under a tradeable permits system, the administrative costs could be very high if there are a great many polluters. Where there are comparatively few the costs of administration are low, but a new problem arises in that one or two polluters may corner the market in permits and refuse to trade them. This would act like a barrier to entry for new firms and the permits could therefore contribute to non-competitive behaviour.

Tradeable permits can also be used to regulate excessive resource use, as with over-fishing. The New Zealand Individual Transferable Quotas Scheme (ITQ) was introduced in 1986. Australia also has an ITQ system for southern bluefin tuna, proposes another for the southeast trawl fishery and the USA has recently introduced one or the Atlantic surf clam industry. In the New Zealand system initial quotas were grandfathered (fishermen were allowed to dispute historical catch records). Government then bought back some quotas at ruling market prices, thus reducing the total allowable catch (TAC). After that, a fixed price of 80% of the first stage price was offered to remaining fishermen. Finally, any remaining reductions needed to get to TAC were pro-rated across the remaining fishermen. Fishermen can resell quotas to other New Zealand fishermen. New entrants face minimum quota allocations. Quotas and actual catches are matched at the end of each month. Fishermen also pay a royalty to the government for the quotas, and the royalty is doubled if foreign vessels are leased for the catch. Since catch was already monitored, the ITQ system has imposed few additional administrative burdens.

The ITQ system has worked well, despite having to face substantial changes in some TACs as better information came to light. Large outlays of government money to buy back quotas have been avoided by making some quotas a proportion of the TAC. Trade in quotas has been facilitated by a Quota Trading Exchange which has brokers who act as intermediaries. But in fact most trades have taken place privately, with all trades being reported to the quota managers. Some oddities have emerged. Observed prices for quotas sometimes seem well above their value in terms of permitted catch, and there has been a wide variation in the price of quotas for the same catch. Analysis suggests that these events may be expected during the transition from an "open access" fishery to a managed regime, but that lack of information and some inherent stability in quota markets is also present. Some "deterrent pricing" may also be occurring, whereby larger firms bid up the price of quotas to deter entry by new fishermen (a standard potential problem with tradeable permits). The other main problem has been disputes about the government's changes in the royalties charged - and this has been resolved by agreeing fixed charges for 5 year periods.

The New Zealand experience suggests:

(a) that grandfathering is a politically acceptable allocation system, followed by buy-back or proportional reductions. This would be highly appropriate for any European resource use control system;

(b) that the "royalty" charges need to be specified at the outset and maintained so as to induce certainty in expectations about the system;

(c) that control is comparatively easy when an in-place monitoring system - the catch records - exist. In the pollution context there is an obvious need to monitor the pollutant itself, so that one would expect such a system to work least well when monitoring is subject to significant error.

Tradeable resource and pollution permits offer an innovative and challenging way of tackling many environmental problems. Because they leave the polluter with the flexibility as to how to adjust to the environmental standard, they make compliance with regulations less expensive than would be the case with CAC. They do not sacrifice environmental quality because the overall level of quality is determined by the overall number of permits, and that is set by the regulatory authority. They appear to be more acceptable to resource users and polluters, at least once they have been in operation for a while and bureaucratic control is minimised. Their potential is not limited to traditional pollutants. As we have seen, they are being experimented with fairly successfully in the control of resource over-use. They have significant potential for controlling carbon dioxide emissions as well. Indeed, it is quite widely suggested that there could be <u>internationally traded</u> carbon dioxide permits. The attraction would be that countries which find it costly to reduce CO_2 emissions would buy permits while those finding it easy to cut back emissions could sell permits. There may also be some attraction to "overissuing" permits to poor countries who could then sell them to richer countries.

USA EXPERIENCE WITH TRADEABLE PERMITS

	Bubbles Federal	Bubbles State	Offsets	Netting	Banking
Number of trades:	42	89	2000	5000-12000	<120
Cost savings $US million	300	135	large	525-12300	small
Air quality impact	zero	zero	zero	probably insig.	probably insig.
Nature of trade: internal	40	89	1800	5000-12000	<100
external	2	0	200	0	< 20

Source:

Hahn, R., and G. Hester [1989], "Where Did All the Markets Go? An Analysis of EPA's Emissions Trading Program", *Yale Journal of Regulation*, Vol.6, No.1, Winter, 109-153. See also Hahn, R., [1987], "The Market for Bads: EPA's Experience with Emissions Trading", *Regulation*, Nos 3/4.

Notes

1. It is easy to understand why this monetary measure of the change in well-being could be infinite. Suppose a child is suffering from a life-threatening disease and needs an organ transplant. The government wishes to know the gain in well-being to the parents of the child of a policy that would ensure the availability of donor organs to all who need them. If the parents are asked how much they would be willing to pay in order to have this policy adopted and thus have an organ provided to their child (i.e., their compensating variation), their answer would be limited by their total wealth. On the other hand, if the parents were asked how much they would accept as compensation in order to forgo the implementation of such a policy (i.e., their equivalent variation), it is perfectly clear that their answer could be infinite. This is because it is reasonable to presume that there is no way that money could compensate them for the death of their child.

2. In other words, the implementation of A_0 results in the state of the world S_0; A_1 results in S_1; and A_2 results in S_2.

3. By defining the status quo as the baseline against which all other policy alternatives will be judged (or measured), we are in effect "netting out" one of the policy alternatives, thus reducing the number of alternatives by one. It is customary to net out the alternative of "doing nothing," but this is not necessary: any policy alternative could be used as the baseline.

4. Because such concrete criteria are often easier for the general public to understand than abstract measures of the "public good," they are often of more interest in public debates and may facilitate wider consensus on the desirable policy option. However, such concrete criteria will typically overlap with more general ethical values (or criteria) so that they are measuring the same change in human well-being.

5. This does not mean, however, that society grants *no* standing to criminals. Even if they have no right to have the benefits from stolen property included in a policy analysis, criminals may still be entitled to be free from "cruel and unusual punishment."

6. To see this, substitute $1/(1+r)^t$ for w_t in equation (4-17)

$$\frac{w_t - w_{t+1}}{w_{t+1}} = \frac{1/(1+r)^t - 1/(1+r)^{t+1}}{1/(1+r)^{t+1}}$$

$$K = (1+r) - 1$$
$$K = r$$

301

7.   Shadow prices are sometimes called "accounting prices" and shadow priced inputs and outputs are often called "economic values".

8.   The border price approach is also known as the foreign exchange, world price or "Little-Mirrlees" approach; the domestic price approach is also known as the willingness to pay approach, consumption numeraire approach, the UNIDO approach or the "Dasgupta-Sen-Marglin" approach.

9.   More precisely, the ACF is given by:

$$ACF = \frac{M + X}{(M + Tm - Sm) + (X - Tx + Sx)}$$

where M is the total value of imports, X the total value of exports, Tm and Tx are total trade taxes on imports and exports respectively, and Sm and Sx are total trade subsidies on imports and exports.

10.   There is an important difference between the contingent valuation method and the contingent behaviour method that should be noted. The CVM can be used to measure existence values, i.e., an individual's response to a willingness-to-pay question may include the value he assigns to the preservation of an environmental asset even though he never intends to use it. If the CBM asks about changes in an individual's use of a resource under a hypothetical set of circumstances, information on existence value will not be obtained. On the other hand, a CBM question that asks how a respondent would vote in a hypothetical referendum can measure existence values.

11.   Similarly individuals who offer protest bids (often indicated by a zero willingness to pay) are likely to have socioeconomic characteristics different from the general population.

12.   The spikes in the frequency distribution in Figure 7.1 at 500 and 1000 cedis per month occur at the two values offered in the abbreviated bidding game, and show the "anchoring" of responses around these offered amounts.

13.   Source: Choe, K., W.R. Parke, and D. Whittington "A Monte Carlo Comparison of OLS Estimation Errors and Design Efficiencies in a Two-Stage Stratified Random Sampling Procedure for a Contingent Valuation Study.", June 1993. Department of City and Regional Planning, University of North Carolina, Chapel Hill, North Carolina. 32 pages.

14.   Source: Whittington, D., D.T.Lauria and X. Mu, [1991]

15.   In practise the bias is thought to be small with crude estimates found using the simple multiplication approach being around 20% higher than sophisticated behavioural and price modelling estimates (see Adams, Crocker and Thanavibulchai[1982]).

16.   For example, Desvousges et. al. [1992] note that few articles reporting multisite travel cost models present enough information on their estimation procedures to permit their use for benefit transfer applications.

17.   The difference between the two being that GNP includes earnings from abroad. The difference between GDP and GNP is known as net income from abroad.

18. Indeed, the expected value criterion implies <u>risk neutrality</u>. Compare the certainty of getting £50 with the gamble of a 0.5 chance of £100 and a 0.5 chance of getting nothing. The expected value of the gamble is also £50. If you are indifferent between the certain £50 and the gamble, then you are risk neutral. If you prefer the certain £50 you are risk averse. If you prefer the gamble you are a "risk lover".

19. The example is extremely simplistic since expected utility involves translating each return into a utility value based on what is called a "utility function".

20. Article 130R of the Single European Act, for example, refers to "prudent and rational utilisation" and to the "principles of preventive action".

21. The concept of a "precautionary measure" is mentioned in the Preamble to the Montreal Protocol on substances that deplete the ozone layer (1987), although it is also said that measures "should be based on relevant scientific knowledge, taking into account technical and economic consideration".

22. Although there are what is known as "marginal stock effects" -i.e. the rate of use today affects the stock in the future and hence the regeneration rate in the future.

23. An alternative widely used approach is to estimate the value of the marginal product of water by using data on the responsiveness of crop output to water inputs. Experimental research station data will often provide this. See Gibbons, D., [1986], *The Economic Value of Water*, Resources for the Future, Washington DC.

24. OECD guidelines make it clear that subsidies are not generally regarded as being consistent with the "Polluter Pays Principle", but the guidelines indicate that there are cases in which subsidies would be regarded as being acceptable. See OECD, [1991], *Environmental Policy: How to Apply Economic Instruments*, OECD, Paris.

25. A degree of flexibility is usually introduced by qualifying BAT according to cost considerations. Thus **best practicable means** (BPM) tends to emphasise the practicability of the technology from a cost point of view, whilst **best available technology (and technique) not entailing excessive cost** (BATNEEC) makes overt reference to the cost of introducing the clean technology. It is not, however, entirely clear what BATNEEC means. See Pearce, D.W. and I. Brisson, [1993].

26. An environmental tax tends to be of the form $t per unit of product output, or $t per unit input, or $t per unit emissions or wastes. Not all emissions, waste,etc., are non-optimal. Those emissions which are more costly to remove than the benefit of removing them can be said to be "optimal" emissions. The tax may therefore be present even for these emissions, in which case the polluter carries on paying taxes even though the optimal level of pollution has been reached. The same observation holds if, instead of the optimal level of pollution, we substitute regulatory acceptable levels of pollution.

27. For convenience, we assume economic and physical damage coincide.

28. Note that benefits are formally identical to avoided environmental damage.

29. Assumes a discount rate of 10 percent.

Bibliography and References

Aakerman, J. [1988], Economic Valuation of Risk Reduction: The Case of In-Door Radiation, Mimeo, Stockholm School of Economics, Stockholm, Sweden.

Aakkula, J. [1991], "Maisemamaatalouden Mahdollisuudet Suomessa (The Potentiality of Scenic Agriculture in Finland - The Value of Agricultural Landscape Estimated by Means of WTP and WTA)", (in Finnish), Paper Presented at Workshop on Resource and Environmental Economics, Oulu, Finland.

Aarkskog, E.M. [1988], "Willingness-To-Pay For Cleaning Up The Inner Oslo Fjord", M.Sc Thesis, Department of Economics, University of Oslo.

Abala, D.O. [1987], "A Theoretical and Empirical Investigation of the Willingness to Pay for Recreational Services: A Case Study of Nairobi National Park", *Eastern Africa Economic Review*, Vol. 3, No. 2, 111-119.

Abelson, P.N. [1979], "Property Prices and the Value of Urban Amenities", *Journal of Environmental Economics and Management*, Vol. 6, 11-28.

Acton, J.P. [1973], *Evaluating Public Progress to Save Lives: The Case of Heart Attacks*, Rand Research Report R-73-02, Rand Corporation, Santa Monica, CA.

Adams, R.M. and Crocker, T.D. [1989], "Economically Relevant Response Estimation and the Value of Information: Acid Deposition", in *Economic Perspective on Acid Deposition Control*, Crocker (ed.), Butterworth Publishers, Boston.

Adams, R.M. et al. [1985], "An Assessment of the Economic Effects of Ozone on US Agriculture", *Journal of the Air Pollution Control Association*, Vol. 35.

Adams, R.M. et. al. [1989], "User Fees and Equity Issues in Public Hunting Expenditures: The Case of Ring-Necked Pheasant in Oregon", *Land Economics* Vol. 65, No. 4, 376-385.

Adams, R.M., T.D. Crocker and N. Thanavibulchai [1982], "An Economic Assessment of Air Pollution to Selected Annual Crops in Southern California", *Journal of Environmental Economics and Management*, Vol.9, 42-58.

Aedo, C. [1992], "Estudio de Determinacion de Indicadores de Rentabilidad de Seleccion de Parametros de Alcantarillado de Aguas Servidas", *Analisis Econometrico y Evaluacion Economicica*, Santiago, Chile.

Ahearn, M.C. [1984], "An Analysis of Contingent Valuation Applied to Air Quality and Public Safety from Crime", Dissertation, *DAI*, 45, 578, Oregon State University.

Altaf, M.A. [1992], How Far Will Self-Provisioning Go: Household Response to Lack of Public Investment in Water and Sanitation Services in the Punjab, Pakistan, Mimeo, Department of Environmental Sciences and Engineering, University of North Carolina, Chapel Hill.

Amundsen, B.T. [1987], "Recreational Value of the Fish Populations in the Recreational Area Oslomarka", M.Sc Thesis, Agricultural University of Norway.

Anderson, D. [1987], *The Economics of Afforestation: A Case Study in Africa*, World Bank Occasional Paper, Johns Hopkins University Press, Baltimore, MD.

Anderson, R.J. and T.D. Crocker [1971], "Air Pollution and Residential Property Values", *Urban Studies*, Vol. 8, 171-180.

Anderson, E. and D. Devereaux [1986], "Testing For Two Kinds of Bias in a Contingent Valuation Survey of Anglers Using An Artificial Reef", Paper Presented at the Annual Meeting of the Eastern Economic Association, Philadelphia, PA.

Arnould, R.J. and L.M. Nichols, [1983], "Wage-Risk Premiums and Worker's Compensation: A Refinement of Estimates of Compensating Wage Differentials", *Journal of Political Economy*, Vol. 91, 332-340.

Arntzen, J. [1990], "A Framework for Economic Evaluation of Collective Fencing in Botswana", in Dixon et al (ed.), *Dryland Management: Economic Case Studies*, Earthscan Publications, London.

Arrow, K., R. Solow, H. Schuman, R. Ragner, and P. Portney [1993], "Report to the NOAA Panel on Contingent Valuation." *U.S. Federal Register*, January 15, 1993, Vol.58, No.10, 4602-4614.

Asabere, P.K. [1981], "The Determinants of Land Values in an African City: The Case of Accra, Ghana", *Land Economics*, Vol.57 No.3, 385-397.

Asian Development Bank [1986], "Economic Analysis of the Environmental Impacts of Development Projects", Staff Paper No. 31, Manila.

Atkinson, S.E., T.D. Crocker, and J.F. Shogen [1992] "Bayesian Exchangeability, Benefit Transfer, and Research Efficiency", *Water Resources Research*, Vol.28, No.3, March, [Special Section: Problems and Issues in the Validity of Benefit Transfer Methodologies.]

Balson, W.E. et al. [1990a], A Review and Critique of the Applicability of Visibility Valuation Studies to a Navajo Generating Station BART Decision, Draft Report to the Salt River Project, Los Altos, CA: Decision Focus.

Balson, W.E., R.T. Carson and M.B. Conaway [1990b], *Development and Design of a Contingent Valuation Survey for Measuring the Public's Value for Visibility Improvements at the Grand Canyon National Park*, Report to the Salt River Project, Los Altos, CA: Decision Focus.

Barbier, E.B. [1989], Economic Evaluation of Tropical Wetland Resources: Applications in Central America, Unpublished Report for the Centro Agronomico Tropical de Investigacion Ensenanza and the IUCN, May.

Barde, J-P. and D.W. Pearce [1991], *Valuing the Environment - Six Case Studies*, Earthscan, London.

Barry, B. [1977], "Justice Between Generations", in P.Hacker and J.Raz (eds.), *Law, Morality and Society*, 268-84, Clarendon Press, London.

Bartelmus, P. [1989], "Environmental Accounting and the System of National Accounts", In Ahmad, Y.J. et al. *Environmental Accounting for Sustainable Development*, World Bank, Washington, D.C.

Bartik, T.J. [1988a], "Measuring the Benefits of Amenity Improvements in Hedonic Price Models", *Land Economics*, Vol. 64, 172-183.

Bartik, T.J. [1988b], "Evaluating the Benefits of Non-Marginal Reduction in Pollution Information on Defensive Expenditures", *Journal of Environmental Economics and Management*, Vol. 15, 111-127.

Bateman, I.J. et al. [1990], "Economic Appraisal of the Consequences of Climate-Induced Sea Level Rise: A Case Study of East Anglia", Paper Presented at the Annual Conference of River and Coastal Engineers, Loughborough.

Bateman, I.J., C.H. Green, S.M. Tunstall and R.K. Turner [1991], The Contingent Valuation Method: The Environmental Effects of New Roads, Report to the Transport and Road Research Laboratory, Flood Hazard Research Centre, Enfield, Great Britain.

Bateman, I.J. et al. [1992], Recreation and Environmental Preservation Value of the Norfolk Broads: A Contingent Valuation Study, Mimeo, Environmental Appraisal Group, University of East Anglia, Norwich, Great Britain.

Beckerman, W. [1976], *An Introduction to National Income Analysis*, 2nd ed., Wiedenfeld and Nicolson, London.

Bennett, J.W. [1984], "Using Direct Questioning to Value the Existence Benefits of Preserved Natural Areas", *Australian Journal of Agricultural Economics*, Vol. 28, No. 2, 136-152.

Bentkover, J.D., V. Covello and J. Mumpower [1986], *Benefits Assessment: The State of the Art*, D. Reidel Publishing Company, Dordrecht, Netherlands.

Bergstrom, J.C., B.L. Dillman and J.R. Stoll [1985], "Public Environmental Amenity Benefits of Private Land: The Case of Prime Agricultural Land", *Southern Journal of Agricultural Economics*, Vol. 17, No. 1, 139-149.

Berger, M.C., G.C. Blomquist, D. Kenkel and G.S. Tolley [1987], "Valuing Changes in Health Risks: A Comparison of Alternative Measures", *Southern Economic Journal* Vol. 53, 967-984.

Bergstrom, J.C., H. K. Cordell and D. Klinko [1989], "Recreational Benefits of Reservoir Water-Level Management", Paper Presented at the Annual USDA W-133 Meeting, San Diego, CA.

Bergstrom, J.C., J.R. Stoll, J.P. Titre and V.L. Wright [1990], "Economic Value of Wetlands-Based Recreation", *Ecological Economics*, Vol. 2, No. 2, 129-147.

Bernstein, J. [1991], Alternative Approaches to Pollution Control and Waste Management, Urban Management Program, Discussion Paper No.3, World Bank, Washington DC.

Binkley, C.S. and W.M. Hanemann, *The Recreation Benefits of Water Quality Improvement: Analysis of Day Trips in an Urban Setting*, Report to the U.S. Environmental Protection Agency, Washington, DC.

Birkan, S., J.P. Hoehn and E.O. van Ravensway [1992], "The Economics of Consumer Response to Health Risk Information on Food", Staff Paper No. 92-20, Department of Agricultural Economics, Michigan State University.

Bishop, J. and J. Allen [1989], *The On-Site Costs of Soil Erosion in Mali*, Working Paper 21, World Bank, Environment Department, Washington, D.C.

Bishop, R.C. and K.J. Boyle [1985], *The Economic Value of Illinois Beach State Nature Preserve*, Final Report to Illinois Department of Conservation, Heberlein Baumgartner Research Services, Madison, WI.

Bishop, R.C. and K. Boyle [1986], "The Economic Value of Endangered Species of Wildlife", in *Transactions of the 51st North American Wildlife and Natural Resources Conference*.

Bishop, R.C. and K.J. Boyle [1987], "Valuing Wildlife in Benefit-Cost Analysis: A Case Study Involving Endangered Species", *Water Resources Research*, Vol. 23, No. 5, 943-950.

Bishop, R.C., K.J. Boyle and M.P. Welsh [1987], "Toward Total Economic Valuation of Great Lakes Fishery Resources", *Transactions of the American Fisheries Society*, Vol. 116, 352-373.

Blank, F. et. al. [1978], Valuation of Aesthetic Preferences: A Case Study of the Economic Value of Visibility, Research Report to EPRI, Resource and Environmental Economics Laboratory, University of Wyoming, Laramie.

Blomquist, G. [1979], "Value of Life Savings: Implications of Consumption Activity", *Journal of Political Economy*, Vol. 87,540-558.

Blomquist, G. and L. Worley [1981], "Hedonic Prices, Demands for Urban Housing Amenities, and Benefit Estimates", *Journal of Urban Economics*, Vol. 9, 212-221.

Boadu, F. [1992], "Contingent Valuation for Household Water in Rural Ghana", *Journal of Agricultural Economics*, Vol. 43.

Bockstael, N.E and McConnel, K.E [1983], "Welfare Measurement in the Household Production Framework", *American Economic Review*, Vol. 73, 806-814.

Bockstael, N.E., K.E. McConnell and I.E. Strand [1989], "Measuring the Benefits of Improvement in Water Quality: The Chesapeake Bay", *Marine Resource Economics*, Vol. 6, 1-18.

Bockstael, N.E., W.M. Hanemann and C.L. Kling [1987a], "Modeling Recreational Demand in a Multiple Site Framework", *Water Resources Research*, Vol.23, 951-960.

Bockstael, N.E., W.M. Hanemann and C.L. Kling [1987b], "Estimating the Value of Water Quality Improvements in a Recreational Demand Framework", *Water Resources Research*, Vol. 23, 951-960.

Bockstael, N.E., W.M. Hanemann and I.E. Strand, Jr. [1987], *Measuring the Benefits of Water Quality Improvements Using Recreation Demand Models*, Report (Vol. 2) to the U.S. Environmental Protection Agency, Department of Agriculture and Resource Economics, University of Maryland.

Bohm, R.A., T. Essenburg and W.F. Fox [1993], "Willingness to Pay for Potable Water Services in the Philippines", *Water Resources Research*, Forthcoming.

Bojo, J. [1985], "Kostnadsnyttoanalys av Fjallnara Skogar. Fallet Valadalen (A Cost-Benefit Analysis of Mountainous Forests. The Case of the Vala Valley)", Stockholm School of Economics, Stockholm, Sweden.

Bojo, J. [1987], CBA of the Farm Improvements With Soil Conservation Project, Mohale's Hoek, Lesotho, Internal Paper for SADCC Co-ordination Unit, Lesotho.

Bojö, J., K-G. Mäler and L. Unemo [1990], *Environment and Development: An Economic Approach*, Kluwer Academic Publishers, Dordrecht, Netherlands, and Boston, Mass.

Bonnieux, F., J.P. Boude, C. Guerrier and A. Richard [1991], "La Peche sportive du Saumon et de la Truite de mer en Basse-Normandi: Analyse Economique (Angling for Salmon and Sea Trout in Normandie: An Economic Analysis)", Working Paper CSP (in French), INRA-ENSA - Rennes, France.

Boyle, K.J. and J.C. Bergstrom [1992] "Benefit Transfer Studies: Myths, Pragmatism, and Idealism", *Water Resources Research*, Vol.28, No.3, March, [Special Section: Problems and Issues in the Validity of Benefit Transfer Methodologies.]

Boyle, K.J. and R.C. Bishop [1979], "Toward the Total Valuation of the Great Lakes Fishery Resources", *Water Resources Research*, Vol. 5, 943-990.

Boyle, K.J. and R.C. Bishop [1987], "Valuing Wildlife in Benefit Cost Analysis: A Case Study Involving Endangered Species", *Water Resources Research*, Vol.23, 943-950.

Boyle, K.J., S.D. Reiling and M.L. Phillips [1990], "Species Substitution and Questions Sequencing in Contingent Valuation Surveys Evaluating the Hunting of Several Types of Wildlife", *Leisure Science*, Vol. 12, 103-118.

Braden, J., C. Kolstad, R. Woock and J. Machado [1992], "The Demand for Synthetic Fuels: Contingent Valuation of Quality-Differentiated Factors of Production", Paper Presented at the Annual Meeting of the European Association of Environmental and Resource Economists, Cracow, Poland.

Braden, J.B. and C.D. Kolstad [1991], *Measuring the Demand for Environmental Quality*, North-Holland, Amsterdam.

Briones, N. [1986], "Estimating Erosion Costs: A Philippines Case Study in the Lower Agno River Watershed", in Easter, W. et al. (ed.), *Watershed Resources Management: An Integrated Framework with Studies from Asia and the Pacific*, Institute of South East Asian Studies, Singapore.

Briscoe, J. et. al. [1990], "Toward Equitable and Sustainable Rural Water Supplies: A Contingent Valuation Study in Brazil", *World Bank Economic Review*, Vol. 4, No. 2, 115-134.

Bristow, A.L., P.G. Hopkinson, C.A. Nash and M. Wardman [1990], Evaluation of the Use and Non-Use Benefits of Public Transport, Mimeo, Institute for Transport Studies, University of Leeds.

Bromley, D.W. [1989a], *Economic Interests and Institutions: The Conceptual Foundations of Public Policy*, Blackwell, Oxford.

Bromley, D.W. [1989b], "Entitlements, Missing Markets, and Environmental Policy", *Journal of Environmental Economics and Management*, Vol. 17, 181-194.

Brooks, K.N. et al. [1982], "Economic Evaluation of Watershed Projects - An Overview Methodology and Application", *Water Resources Bulletin,* April.

Brooks, R. [1991], *Warm Water Fishing in Montana: A Contingent Valuation Assessment of Angler Attitudes and Economic Benefits for Selected Waters Statewide*, Report Prepared for State of Montana Department of Fish, Wildlife, and Parks, Helena, MT.

Brookshire, D. and H.R. Neill [1992], "Benefit Transfers: Conceptual Issues and Empirical Issues", *Water Resources Research*, Vol.28, No.3, March, [Special Section: Problems and Issues in the Validity of Benefit Transfer Methodologies.]

Brookshire, D.S., A.S. Randall and J.R. Stoll [1980], "Valuing Increments and Decrements in Natural Resource Service Flows", *American Journal of Agricultural Economics*, Vol. LXII, 477-488.

Brookshire, D.S. and T.D. Crocker [1979], *The Use of Survey Instruments in Determining the Economic Valuation of Environmental Goods*, Report, Rocky Mountain Forest and Range Experimental Station, Fort Collins, CO.

Brookshire, D.S., L.S. Eubanks and A.Randall [1983], "Estimating Option Prices and Existence Values for Wildlife Resources", *Land Economics*, Vol. 59, 1-15.

Brookshire, D.S., L.S. Eubanks and A. Randall [1978], "Valuing Wildlife Resources: An Experiment", in *43rd Transactions of the North American Wildlife Conference*, Wildlife Management Institute, Washington, DC.

Brookshire, D.S., M.A. Thayer, W.D Schulze and R.C. d'Arge [1982], "Valuing Public Goods: A Comparison of Survey and Hedonic Approaches", *American Economic Review*, Vol.72, 165-178.

Brookshire, D.S., R.C. d'Arge, W.D. Schulze and M.A. Thayer [1979a], "Experiments in Valuing Non-marketed Goods: A Case Study of Alternative Benefit Measures of Air Pollution Control in the South Coast Air Basin of Southern California", *Methods Development for Assessing Tradeoffs in Environmental Management*, Vol. 2, National Technical Information Service, Washington, DC.

Brookshire, D.S., R.C. d'Arge, W.D. Schulze and M.A. Thayer [1979b], *Methods Development for Assessing Trade-Offs in Environmental Management*, EPA report 600-6-79-0016, U.S. Environmental Protection Agency, Washington, DC.

Brown, C. [1980], "Equalizing Differences in the Labor Market", *Quarterly Journal of Economics*, Vol. 94, 113-134.

Bruce, D.S. [1986], A Review of the Environmental Implications of Nitrogen Oxides.

Butler, R.J. [1983], "Wage and Injury Rate Responses to Shifting Levels of Workers' Compensation", in J.D. Worrall (ed.), *Safety and the Work Force*, Cornell University:ILR Press, Ithaca.

Button, K. and Pearce, D.W. [1989], "Infrastructure Restoration as a Tool for Stimulating Urban Renewal: The Glasgow Canal", *Urban Studies*, 26.

Camerer, C. and H. Kunreuther [1989], "Decision Processes for Low Probability Events: Policy Implications", *Journal of Policy Analysis and Management*, Vol.8, No.4, 565-592.

Cameron, T.A. and M. James. [1987], "Efficient Estimation Methods for 'Closed-ended' Contingent Valuation Surveys", *Review of Economics and Statistics*, Vol.69, 269-275.

Cameron, T.A. [1988], "A New Paradigm for Valuing Non-market Goods Using Referendum Data", *Journal of Environmental Economics and Management*, Vol.15, 355-379.

Carlsen, A.J. [1987], "Economic Valuation of Hydroelectric Power Production and Salmon Fishing", in *Proceedings of the UNESCO Symposium on Decision Making in Water Resources Planning*, Oslo, Norway.

Carson, R.T. [1989], "Value of Diamonds and Water: Water Supply Reliability in Southern California", Paper Presented at the Association for Public Policy Analysis and Management, Washington, DC.

Carson, R.T. [1991a], The Australian Resource Assessment Commission's Kakadu Conservation Zone Contingent Valuation Study: Remarks on the Brunton, Stone, and Tasman Institute Critiques, Comments Submitted to the Australian Resource Assessment Commission, Canberra; University of California, San Diego.

Carson, R.T. [1991b], *Comments on the ABARE Submission*, Report, Australian Resources Assessment Commission.

Carson, R.T. [1991c], "Constructed Markets", in J.B. Braden and C.D. Kolstad (eds.), *Measuring the Demand for Environmental Quality*, 121-162, Elsevier Scientific Publishers, Amsterdam, The Netherlands.

Carson, R.T. [1992], "Kakadu Conservation Zone", in *Natural Resource Damages: Law and Economics*, Wiley Law Publications, New York.

Carson, R.T. and K.M. Martin [1991], "Measuring the Benefits of Freshwater Quality Changes: Techniques and Empirical Findings", in A. Dinar and D. Zilberman, (eds.), *The Economics and Management of Water and Drainage in Agriculture*, Kluwer Academic Press, Boston.

Carson, R.T. and R.C. Mitchell [1987], *Economic Value of Reliable Water Supplies for Residential Water Users in the State Water Project Service Area*, Report Prepared for the Metropolitan Water District of Southern California, Resources for the Future, Washington, DC.

Carson, R.T. and R.C. Mitchell [1991a], "The Value of Diamonds and Water", Paper Presented at the Meeting of the European Association of Environmental and Resource Economists, Stockholm.

Carson, R.T. and R.C. Mitchell [1991b], *The Value of Clean Water: The Public's Willingness to Pay for Boatable, Fishable, and Swimmable Quality Water*, Report to U.S. Environmental Protection Agency Economic Analysis and Research Branch, University of California, San Diego.

Carson, R.T. and P.A. Ruud [1991c], *Grand Canyon Visibility Benefits Calculations* , Report to W.E. Balson, Decision Focus, Los Altos, CA.

Carson, R.T. and D. Steinberg [1990a], "Experimental Design for Discrete Choice Voter Preference

Surveys", in *1989 Proceeding of the Survey Methodology Section of the American Statistical Association*, American Statistical Organization, Washington, DC.

Carson, R.T. et. al. [1991d], Valuation of Nonmarket Aspects of Municipal Water Systems, Technical Report for Project UCAL-W-722, Submitted to the University of California Water Resources Center, University of California, San Diego.

Carson, R.T. et. al. [1991e], Comments on the Benefit Analysis in the U.S. Environmental Protection Agency's Proposed Navajo Generating Station BART Action, Submitted to U.S. Environmental Protection Agency, Decision Focus, Los Gatos, CA.

Carson, R.T., W.M. Hanemann and R.J. Kropp [1991f], Comments on the United States Department of the Interior's Notice of Proposed Rulemaking 43 CFR Part II Natural Resource Damage Assessment, Department of Economics, University of California, San Diego.

Carson, R.T., W.M. Hanemann and D. Steinberg [1990b], "A Discrete Choice Contingent Valuation Estimate of the Value of Kenai King Salmon", *Journal of Behavioral Economics*, Vol. 19, No. 1, 53-68.

Carson, R.T., R.C. Mitchell and P.A. Ruud [1990c], "Valuing Air Quality Improvements: Simulating a Hedonic Pricing Equation in the Context of a Contingent Valuation Scenario", in C.V. Mathai, (ed.), *Visibility and Fine Particles*, Air and Waste Management Association, Pittsburgh.

Carson, R., R.C. Mitchell, W.M. Hanemann, R.J. Kopp, St. Presser, and P.A. Ruud [1992], *A Contingent Valuation Study of Lost Passive Use Values Resulting From the Exxon-Valdez Oil Spill*, A Report to the Attorney General of the State of Alaska.

Caudill, J.D. and J.P. Hoehn [1992], "The Economic Valuation of Groundwater Pollution Policies: The Role of Subjective Risk Perceptions", Staff Paper No. 92-11, Department of Agricultural Economics, Michigan State University.

Cesario, F.J. [1976], "Value of Time in Recreation Benefit Studies", *Land Economics*, Vol.52, 32-41.

Chestnut, L.G. and R.D. Rowe [1990], Review and Response to: Development and design of a Contingent Value Survey for Measuring the Public's Value for Visibility Improvements at the Grand Canyon National Park, Draft Report Prepared by RCG/Hagler, Bailly, Inc. for Economic Analysis Branch, Office of Air Quality Planning and Standards, U.S. EPA, Boulder, CO.

Chestnut, L.G. and R.D. Rowe [1990a], *Preservation Values for Visibility Protection at the National Parks*, Report Prepared by RCG/Hagler, Bailly, Inc. for the Office of Air Quality Planning and Standards, U.S. EPA, and the National Park Service, Boulder, CO.

Chestnut, L.G. and R.D. Rowe [1990b], "New National Park Visibility Value Estimates", in C.V. Mathai, (ed.), *Visibility and Fine Particulates*, Air and Waste Management Association, Pittsburgh, PA.

Chestnut, L.G. and R.D. Rowe [1991], Economic Changes in Visibility: A State of the Science Assessment for NAPAP, SOS 27 for the National Acidic Precipitation Assessment Program.

Chestnut, L.G. et. al. [1988], *Heart Disease Patients' Averting Behavior; Costs of Illness and Willingness to Pay to Avoid Angina Episodes*, Final Report (EPA-230-10-88-042), Cooperative

Agreement No. CR-812826, Office of Policy Analysis, U.S. Environmental Protection Agency.

Chestnut, L.G., L.R. Keller, W. Lambert and R.D. Rowe [1992], "Measuring Heart Patients' Willingness to Pay for Changes in Angina Symptoms: Some Methodological Implications", Graduate School of Management, University of California, Irvine, CA.

Choe, K., W.R. Parke and D.W. Whittington [1993], A Monte Carlo Comparison of OLS Estimation Errors and Design Efficiencies in a Two-Stage Stratisfied Random Sampling Procedure for a Contingent Valuation Study, Department of City and Regional Planning, University of North Carolina, Chapel Hill, North Carolina.

Cichetti, C., A. Fisher, and V.K. Smith [1971], "An Econometric Evaluation of a Generalized Consumer Surplus Measure: The Mineral King Controversy", *Econometrica*, Vol.39, 813-827.

Clawson, M. and J.L. Knetsch [1966], *Economics of Outdoor Recreation*, Johns Hopkins University Press, Baltimore, MD.

Clawson, M. [1959], *Methods of Measuring the Demand for and Value of Outdoor Recreation*, Resources for the Future reprint No. 10, Washington, DC.

Cline, W. [1992], *The Economics of Climate Change*, Institute for International Economics, Washington DC.

Coase, R.H. [1960], "The Problem of Social Cost", *Journal of Law and Economics*, October, Vol. 3, 1-44.

Cobb, S.A. [1977], "Site Rent, Air Quality, and the Demand for Amenities", *Journal of Environmental Economics and Management*, Vol. 4, 214-218.

Cocheba, D.J. and W.A. Langford [1978], "Wildlife Valuation: The Collective Good Aspect of Hunting", *Land Economics*, Vol. 54, No. 4, 490-504.

Cohon, J.L. [1978], *Multiobjective Programming and Planning*, Academic Press.

CONSPLAN [1992], "A Contingent Valuation of the Benefits of Drainage and Sanitation in Fortaleza, Brazil."

Courant, P.N. and R.C. Porter [1981], "Averting Expenditures and the Cost of Pollution", *Journal of Environmental Economics and Management*, Vol.8, 321-329.

Coursey, D.L., J.L. Hovis and W.D. Schulze [1987], "The Disparity Between Willingness to Accept and Willingness to Pay Measures of Value", *The Quarterly Journal of Economics*, August, 679-690.

Cousineau, J.M., R. Lacroix and A.M. Girard, [1988], "Occupational Hazard and Wage Compensating Differentials", Centre de Recherche et Développement Economique, University de Montréal.

Crocker, T.D. [1985], "On the Value of the Condition of a Forest Stock", *Land Economics*, Vol. 61, No. 3, 244-254.

Cropper, M.L. and Freeman, A.M. III [1991], "Environmental Health Effects", in Braden, C. et al.

(ed.), op cit.

Cropper, M.L., L.B. Deck and K.E. McConnell [1988], "On the Choice of Functional Form for Hedonic Price Functions", *Review of Economics and Statistics*, Vol.70, 668-675.

Cropper, M.L. [1981], "Measuring the Benefits from Reduced Morbidity", *American Economic Review*, Vol.71, 235-240.

Cruz, W and R. Repetto [1992], *The Environmental Effects of Stabilization and Structural Adjustment Programs: the Philippines Case*, Washington DC: World Resources Institute.

Cummings, R.G., D.S. Brookshire, and W.D. Schulze. [1986], *Valuing Environmental Goods: An Assessment of the Contingent Valuation Method*, Rowman & Allanheld, Totowa, NJ.

Cummings, R.G., L.A. Cox, Jr. and A.M. Freeman III [1986], "General Methods for Benefits Assessment", In J.D. Bentkover et al.(eds.), *Benefits Assessment : The State of the Art*, D Reidel Publishing Co, Dordrecht, Netherlands.

Curry, S. and J. Weiss [1993], *Project Analysis in Developing Countries*, Macmillan, London.

d'Arge, R.C. and J.F. Shogren [1985], *Water Quality Benefits: An Analysis of the Lakes at Okoboji, Iowa*, Final Report (#CR 808893-02-2), U.S. Environmental Protection Agency, Office of Planning Management, Washington, DC.

Dahle, L., B. Solberg and D.P. Sydal [1987], Attitudes Toward and Willingness to Pay for Brown Bear, Wolverine and Wolf in Norway, Report No. 5/1987 (in Norwegian), Department of Forest Economics, Agricultural University of Norway.

Dalgard, M. [1989], Drammentsvassdraget - en Undersokelse av Betalingsvillighet (Willingness to Pay for Regulatory Actions Towards Water Pollution in the Drammen Fjord), Report No. 881108-2, in Norwegian; Centre for Industrial Research, University of Oslo, Norway.

Dardis, R. [1980], "The Value of a Life: New Evidence from the Market Place", American Economic Review, Vol. 70, 1077-1082.

Dasgupta, P., S.Marglin and A.Sen - see UNIDO [1972],

David, E.L. [1968], "Lake Shore Property Values: A Guide to Public Investment in Recreation", *Water Resources Research*, Vol. 4, No. 4, 697-707.

Davis, R.K. [1963], "Recreational Planning as an Economics Problem", *Natural Resource Journal*, 238-249.

Davis, R.K. [1964], "The Value of Big-Game Hunting in a Private Forest", in *Transactions of the Twenty-Ninth North American Wildlife Conference*, Wildlife Management Institute, Washington, DC.

Desvousges, W.H., V.K. Smith and M.P. McGivney [1983], *A Comparison of Alternative Approaches for Estimating Recreation and Related Benefits of Water Quality Improvements*, EPA Report 230-05-83-001, U.S. Environmental Protection Agency, Office of Policy Analysis, Washington, DC.

Desvousges, W.H. et. al. [1992a], Measuring Nonuse Damages Using Contingent Valuation: An Experimental Evaluation of Accuracy, Research Triangle Institute, Research Triangle Park, NC.

Desvousges, W.H. et. al. [1992b], "Measuring Natural Resource Damages with Contingent Valuation: Tests of Validity and Reliability", Paper Presented at the Cambridge Economics, Inc. Symposium, Contingent Valuation: A Critical Assessment, Washington, DC.

Desvousges, W.H. et. al. [1992c], "Measuring Natural Resource Damages with Contingent Valuation", Paper Presented at Association of Environmental and Resource Economists meeting, Baltimore, MD.

Desvousges, W.H., M.C. Naughton, and G.R. Parsons [1992d], "Benefit Transfer: Conceptual Problems in Estimating Water Quality Benefits Using Existing Studies", *Water Resources Research*, Vol.28, No.3, March, [Special Section: Problems and Issues in the Validity of Benefit Transfer Methodologies.]

Deyak, T.A. and V.K. Smith [1974], "Residential Property Values and Air Pollution: Some New Evidence", *Quarterly Review of Economics and Business*, Vol. 14, 93-100.

Diamond, D.B., Jr. and G. Tolley, eds. [1982], *The Economics of Urban Amenities*, Academic Press, New York.

Diamond, D.B., Jr. [1980a], "Income and Residential Location: Muth Revisited", *Urban Studies*, 1-12.

Diamond, D.B., Jr. [1980b], "The Relationship Between Amenities and Urban Land Prices", *Land Economics*, 21-32.

Dickens, W.T. [1984], "Differences Between Risk Premiums in Union and Nonunion Wages and the Case for Occupational Safety Regulation", *American Economic Review*, Vol.74, 320-323.

Dickie, M. and S. Gerking [1989a], "Valuing Nonmarket Goods: A Household Production Approach", Paper presented at the Association of Environmental and Resource Economists conference on Estimating and Valuing Morbidity in a Public Context, June 8-9, 1989, Research Triangle Park, NC.

Dickie, M. and S. Gerking [1989b], "Benefits of Reduced Morbidity from Air Pollution: A Survey Valuation Methods and Policy Making", in H. Folmer and E. van Ierland, (eds.), *Valuation Methods and Policy Making in Environmental Economics*, North-Holland, Amsterdam.

Dickie, M. and S. Gerking [1991a], "Health Benefits of PMP Control: The Case of Stratospheric Ozone Depletion and Skin Damage Risks", In J.B. Opschoor, and D.W. Pearce. (eds), *Persistent Pollutants: Economics and Policy*, Kluwer Academic Publications, Dordrecht, Netherlands.

Dickie, M. and S. Gerking [1991b], "Willingness to Pay for Ozone Control: Inferences from the Demand for Medical Care", *Journal of Environmental Economics and Management*, Vol. 21, 1-16.

Dillingham, A. [1979], "The Industry Risk Structure of Occupations and Wages", Unpublished PhD Dissertation, Cornell University, Ithaca, N.Y.

Dillingham, A. [1985], "The Influence of Risk Variable Definition on Value of Life Estimates",

Economic Inquiry, Vol. 24, 277-294.

Dillman, D.A. [1978], *Mail and Telephone Surveys: The Total Design Method*, John Wiley and Sons, New York.

Dixon, J. [1991], "Valuation of Protected Areas in Developing Countries", in Valuing Environmental Benefits in Developing Economies", Proceedings of a Seminar Series Held February-May 1990, at Michigan State University, Special Report 29.

Dixon, J. and M. Hufschmidt, eds. [1986], *Economic Valuation Techniques for the Environment: A Case Study Workbook*, Johns Hopkins University Press, Baltimore, Md.

Dixon, J., et al. [1988], *Economic Analysis of the Environmental Impacts of Development Projects*, Earthscan Publications in Association with the Asian Development Bank, London.

Doane, M., G.H. McClelland, W.D. Schulze and C.K. Woo [1989], The Value of Electrical Power Outages: A Contingent Valuation Study, Report Submitted to Niagra Mohawk Electric Power Company.

Doane, M.J., G.H. McClelland, W.D. Schulze and C.K. Woo [1990], Residential Outage Cost Survey, Report Submitted to Niagra Mohawk Electric Power Corporation.

Doane, M.J., R.S. Hartman and C.K. Woo [1988], "Household's Perceived Value of Service Reliability: An Analysis of Contingent Valuation Data", *Energy Journal*, Vol. 9, 135-150.

Donnelly, D.M. and L.J. Nelson [1986], "Net Economic Value of Deer Hunting in Idaho", *U.S. Forest Service Resource Bulletin RM-13*, Rocky Mountain Forest and Range Experiment Station, U.S. Forest Service, Fort Collins, CO.

Donnelly, D.M., J.B. Loomis, C.F. Sorg and L.J. Nelson [1985], "Net Economic Value of Recreational Steelhead Fishing in Idaho", *U.S. Forest Service Bulletin RM-9*, Rocky Mountain Forest and Range Experiment Station, Fort Collins, CO.

Dorsey, S. and N. Walzer (1983), "Workers' Compensation, Job Hazards and Wages", *Industrial and Labor Relations Review*, Vol. 36, 643-654.

Dragun, A.K. [1991], An Economic Study of Commercial and Recreational Fishing Conflicts in Port Philip Bay and Western Port, Victoria, Australia, Report Prepared for the Victorian Department of Conservation and Environment, Department of Legal Studies, La Trobe University.

Drake, L. [1993], "The Non-Market Value of the Swedish Agricultural Landscape", *European Review of Agricultural Economics*, forthcoming.

Duffield, J.W. [1988], *The Net Economic Value of Elk Hunting in Montana*, Report to Montana Department of Fish, Wildlife, and Parks, Helena, MT.

Duffield, J.W. [1991a], "Elk Economics: Implications for Management of Elk Security", in A.G. Christensen, (ed.), *Proceedings of Elk Vulnerability - A Symposium*, The Wildlife Society, Bozeman, MT.

Duffield, J.W. [1991b], "Existence and Nonconsumptive Values for Wildlife: Application to Wolf

Recovery in Yellowstone National Park", Paper Presented at the Annual USDA W-133 meeting, Monterey, CA.

Duffield, J.W. [1991c], "Total Valuation of Wildlife and Fishery Resources: Applications in the Northern Rockies", Paper Presented at the National Conference on the Economic Value of Wilderness, U.S. Forest Service and Society of American Foresters, Jackson Hole, WY.

Duffield, J.W. and S. Allen [1988], *Contingent Valuation of Montana Trout Fishing by River and Angler Subgroup*, Angler Preference Study Final Economic Report Prepared for Montana Department of Fish, Wildlife, and Parks, Helena, MT.

Duffield, J.W. and C. Neher [1991], *Montana Waterfowl Hunting: A Contingent Valuation Assessment of Economic Benefits and Hunter Attitudes*, Report to Montana Department of Fish, Wildlife, and Parks, Helena, MT.

Dwyer, J.F. and M.D. Bowes [1978], "Concepts of Value for Marine Recreational Fishing", *American Journal of Agricultural Economics*", Vol. LX, 1008-1012.

ECO Northwest, et al. [1983], Economic Analysis of the Environmental Effects of the Coal-Fired Electric Generator at Broadman, Oregon, for Bonneville Power Administration.

ECO Northwest et al. [1984], *Economic Analysis of the Environmental Effects of a Combustion-Turbine Generating Station at the Fredrickson Industrial Park, Pierce County, Washington*, Final Report, Bonneville Power Administration.

ECOTEC [1990], Identification and Assessment of Materials Damage to Buildings and Monuments by Air Pollution, ECOTEC Research and Consulting Ltd., Birmingham.

Edwards, S.F. [1988], "Option Prices for Groundwater Protection", *Journal of Environmental Economics and Management*, Vol. 15.

Enis, R. and Shechter, M. [1972], Quarries and Landscape, Centre for Urban and Regional Studies, Israel Institute of Technology, Haifa.

Eom, Y.S. [1992], "Consumers' Stated Preferences for Food Safety: The Case of Pesticide Residues on Fresh Produce", Paper Presented at the Annual Meeting of the Association of Environmental and Resource Economists.

Everett, R.D. [1979], "The Monetary Value of the Recreational Benefits of Wildlife", *Journal of Environmental Management*, vol. 9.

Ewers, H.J. et al. [1986], "On the Monetization of Forest Damages in the Federal Republic of Germany", in *Kosten der Umweitverschmutzung*, Umweltbundesamt, Berichte 7/86.

Feenstra, J.F. [1984], Cultural Property and Air Pollution, Ministry of Housing, Physical Planning and Environment, Leidschendam.

Fenger, J. et al [n.d.], Forsuringsprojektet: Materialeskader (Acidification Project: Material Damage, Miljominiesteriet, Copenhagen.

Fink, F.W. et al. [1971], Technical Economic Evaluation of Air Pollution Corrosion Costs on Metals in the US, Batelle Memorial Institute.

Finney, C.E and Western, S. [1986], "An Economic Analysis of Environmental Protection and Management: An Example From the Philippines", *The Environmentalist*, 6(1).

Fisher, A., L.G. Chestnut and D.M. Violette [1989], "The Value of Reducing Risks to Death: A Note on New Evidence", *Journal of Policy Analysis and Management*, Vol.8, No.1, 88-100.

Flemming, W.M. [1983], "Phewa Tal Catchment Management Program: Benefits and Costs of Forestry and Soil Conservation in Nepal", in Hamilton (ed.), *Forest and Watershed Development and Conservation in Asia and Pacific*, Westview Press, Boulder, CO.

Follain, J.R. and E. Jimenez [1985], "Estimating the Demand for Housing Characteristics: A Survey and Critique", *Regional Science and Urban Economics*, Vol. 15, 77-107.

Forster, B.A. [1989], "Valuing Outdoor Recreational Activity: A Methodological Survey", *Journal of Leisure Research*, Vol. 21, No. 2, 188-201.

Freeman, A.M., III [1971], "Air Pollution and Property Values: A Methodological Comment", *Review of Economics and Statistics*, Vol. 53, 415-416.

Freeman, A.M., III [1974a], "Air Pollution and Property Values: A Further Comment", *Review of Economics and Statistics*, Vol. 56, 554-556.

Freeman, A.M., III [1974b], "On Estimating Air Pollution Control Benefits from Land Value Studies", *Journal of Environmental Economics and Management*, Vol. 1, 277-288.

Freeman, A.M. III [1979], *The Benefits of Environmental Improvement: Theory and Practice*, Johns Hopkins University Press, Baltimore.

Freeman, A.M. III [1982], *Air and Water Pollution Control: A Benefit-Cost Assessment*, Wiley, New York.

Freeman, A.M. III [1985], "Methods for Assessing the Benefits of Environmental Programs", In A.V. Kneese and J.L. Sweeney (eds.), *Handbook of Natural Resource and Energy Economics*, Vol. 1, pp. 223-270, North-Holland Publishing Company, Amsterdam.

Freimund, W.A. [1990], "The Effects of Gypsy Moth Caused Tree Mortality or Aesthetic Preference and Behavior Intentions", Thesis, West Virginia University.

Garen, J. [1988], "Compensating Wage Differentials and the Endogeneity of Job Riskiness", *The Review of Economics and Statistics*, Vol. 70, 9-16.

Gegax, D., S. Gerking and W. Schulze [1985], "Perceived Risk and the Marginal Value of Safety", Working paper, U.S. Environmental Protection Agency, Washington, DC.

Georgiou, S. [1992], "Valuing Statistical Life and Limb: A Compensating Wage Differentials Evaluation for Industrial Accidents in the UK", Centre for Social and Economic Research on the Global Environment, Working Paper GEC 92-13.

Gerking, S. and L.R. Stanley [1986], "An Economic Analysis of Air Pollution and Health: the Case of St. Louis", *Review of Economics and Statistics,* Vol.68, 115- 121.

Gilbert, A.A., R. Glass and T. More [1991], "Valuation of Eastern Wilderness: Extramarket Measures of Public Support", in *National Conference on the Economics of Wilderness,* U.S. Department of Agriculture, Forest Service, Jackson Hole, WY.

Gillette [1975], "Sulphur Dioxide and Materials Damage", *Air Pollution Control Association Journal.*

Gittinger, H.P. [1982], *Economic Analysis of Agricultural Products,* 2nd edition, Johns Hopkins University Press, Baltimore.

Glomsrod, S. and A. Rosland [1988], Air Pollution and Materials Damages: Social Costs, Report 88/31, Central Bureau of Statistics of Norway.

Goodin, R. [1986], *Protecting the Vulnerable,* University of Chicago Press, Chicago.

Gordon, I.M. and J.L. Knetsch [1979], "Consumer's Surplus Measures and the Evaluation of Resources", *Land Economics,* February, Vol. 55, No. 1, 1-10.

Gramlich, F.W. [1977] "The Demand for Clean Water: The Case of the Charles River", *National Tax Journal,* 30, 183-194.

Grandstaff, Dixon, and Eutriak, [1986], "Case Study: Lumpinee Public Park, Bangkok", in Dixon and Hufschmidt (ed.), *Economic Valuation Techniques for the Environment: A Case Study Workbook,* Johns Hopkins University Press, Baltimore, MD and London.

Grandstaff, S. and J.A. Dixon [1986], "Evaluation of Lumpinee Park in Bangkok, Thailand", in J.A. Dixon and M.M. Hufschmidt, (eds.), *Economic Valuation Techniques for the Environment: A Case Study Workbook,* Johns Hopkins University Press, Baltimore, MD.

Grayson, A.J. et al [1975], "Some Aspects of Recreational Planning in the Forestry Commission", in Searle G.A.C. (ed.), *Recreational Economics and Analysis,* Longman, London.

Green, C.H. et al [1988], "Evaluating the Benefits of River Water Improvements", Middlesex Polytechnic Flood Hazard Research Centre.

Green, C.H. et al [1989], Water Quality: The Public Dimension, in Wheeler, D. et al. (ed.), *Watershed 89: The Future for Water Quality in Europe,* Oxford, Pergamon.

Green, C.H. and Tunstall, S.M. [1990a], "The Benefits of Coast Protection. Results from Testing the Contingent Valuation Method for Valuing Beach Recreation", Flood Hazard Research Centre, Publication No. 168, Middlesex Polytechnic.

Green, C.H. and Tunstall, S.M. [1990b], The Benefits of River Water Improvement, Report from the Flood Hazard Research Centre, Middlesex Polytechnic.

Green, C.H. and Tunstall, S.M. [1991], "The Amenity and Environmental Value of River Corridors", Flood Hazard Research Centre, Publication No. 171, Middlesex Polytechnic.

Green, C.H. and S.M. Tunstall [1991], "The Evaluation of River Water Quality Improvements by the Contingent Valuation Method", *Applied Economics,* Vol. 23, No. 7, 1135-1146.

Grieson, R.E. and J.R. White [1989], "The Existence and Capitalization of Neighborhood Externalities: A Reassessment", *Journal of Urban Economics*, Vol. 25, 68-76.

Griliches, Z., ed. [1971], *Price Indexes and Quality Change*, Harvard University Press, Cambridge, MA.

Hahn, R. and G. Hester. [1989], "Marketable Permits: Lessons for Theory and Practice", *Ecology Law Quarterly*, Vol. 16, No.2, 361-406.

Hahn, R. and J. Hird [1991], "The Costs and Benefits of Regulation: Review and Synthesis", *Yale Journal of Regulation*, Vol. 8, No.1, Winter.

Halstead, J.M., B.E. Lindsay and C.M. Brown [1991], "Use of the Tobit Model in Contingent Valuation: Experimental Evidence from Pemigewasset Wilderness Area", *Journal of Environmental Management*, Vol. 33, No. 1, 79-89.

Halvorsen, R. and H.O. Pollakowski [1981], "Choice of Functional Form for Hedonic Price Equations", *Journal of Urban Economics*, Vol.10, 37-49.

Hammack, J. and G.M. Brown, [1974], *Waterfowl and Wetlands: Toward Bioeconomic Analysis*, The Johns Hopkins University Press for Resources for the Future, Baltimore.

Hammitt, J.K. [1986], *Estimating Consumer Willingness to Pay to Reduce Food-Borne Risk*, Report R-3447-EPA, RAND Corporation, Santa Monica, CA.

Hanemann, W.M. [1984], "Welfare Evaluations in Contingent Valuation Experiments with Discrete Responses", *American Journal of Agricultural Economics*, Vol.66, 322-341.

Hanemann, W.M. [1992], "Willingness-to-Pay versus Willingness-to-Accept: How Much Can They Differ?", *American Economic Review*,

Hanley, N.D. [1986], "An Economic Analysis of Agricultural Externalities with Special Reference to Straw-Burning", Dissertation, Department of Agricultural Economics, University of Newcastle-on-Tyne, Great Britain.

Hanley, N.D. [1988], "Using Contingent Valuation to Value Environmental Improvements", *Applied Economics*, 20.

Hanley, N.D. [1989a], "Valuing Non-Market Goods Using Contingent Valuation", *Journal of Economic Surveys* Vol. 3, 235-252.

Hanley, N.D. [1989b], "Contingent Valuation as a Method for Valuing Changes in Environmental Service Flows", paper presented at the University of Uppsala, Uppsala, Sweden.

Hanley, N.D. [1989c], "Problems in Valuing Environmental Improvement Resulting from Agricultural Policy Changes", in A. Dubgaard and A. Nielson, eds., *Economic Aspects of Environmental Regulation in Agriculture*, Kiel, Germany: Wissenschaftsverlag Vauk Kiel.

Hanley, N.D. [1989d], "Valuing Rural Recreation Benefits: An Empirical Comparison of Two Approaches", *Journal of Agricultural Economics* Vol. 40, 361-374.

Hanley, N.D. and M.S. Common [1987a], Estimating Recreation, Wildlife and Landscape Benefits Attached to Queen Elizabeth Forest Park, Final Report to Forestry Commission, Edinburgh, Great Britain.

Hanley, N.D. and M.S. Common [1987b], "Evaluating the Recreation, Wildlife and Landscape Benefits of Forestry: Preliminary Results from a Scottish Study", Papers in Economics Finance and Investment, No. 141, University of Stirling, Great Britain.

Hanley, N.D. and S. Craig [1991], "The Economic Value of Wilderness Areas: An Application to the Krutilla-Fisher Model to Scotland's Flow Country", in F. Dietz, R. van der Ploeg and J. van der Straaten, (eds.), *Environmental Policy and the Economy*, North Holland, Amsterdam.

Harberger, A. [1976], *Project Evaluation: Collected Papers*, University of Chicago Press, Chicago.

Harford, J.D. [1984], "Averting Behaviour and The Benefits of Reduced Soiling", *Journal of Environmental Economics and Management*, Vol. 11, 292-302.

Harley, D. and N.D. Hanley [1989], "Economic Benefits for Nature Reserves: Methods and Results", Discussion Paper, Department of Economics, University of Stirling, Stirling, Great Britain.

Harris, B.S. [1984], "Contingent Valuation of Water Pollution Control", *Journal of Environmental Management*, Vol. 19, 199-208.

Harrison, D., Jr. and D.L. Rubinfield [1978], "Hedonic Housing Prices and the Demand for Clean Air", *Journal of Environmental Economics and Management*, Vol. 5, 81-102.

Hartwick, J.M. [1990], "National Accounting and Economic Depreciation", *Journal of Public Economics*, Vol.43, 291-304.

Hay, M.J. [1988a], *Net Economic Recreation Value for Deer, Elk and Waterfowl Hunting and Bass Fishing*, Report 85-1, U.S. Department of the Interior, Fish and Wildlife Service, Washington, DC.

Hay, M.J. [1988b], *Net Economic Value of Nonconsumptive Wildlife-Related Recreation*, Report 85-2, U.S. Department of the Interior, Fish and Wildlife Service, Washington, DC.

Hayes, K.M. [1987], An Analysis of the Benefits of Improving Water Quality in Narragansett Bay: An Application of the Contingent Valuation Method, Mimeo.

Hazilla, M. and R. Kopp [1990], "Social Cost of Environmental Quality Regulations: A General Equilibrium Analysis", *Journal of Political Economy*, Vol.98, No.4.

Heiberg, A. and K.G. Hem [1987], "Use of Formal Methods in Evaluating Countermeasures to Coastal Water Pollution. A Case Study of the Kristiansand Fjord, Southern Norway", in H.M. Siep and A. Heiberg, (eds.), *Risk Management of Chemicals in the Environment*, Plenum Press, London.

Heiberg, A. and Hem, K-G. [1988], Regulatory Impact Analysis for Inner Oslo Fjord: A Comparison of Three Different Methods, Centre for Industrial Research, Report 88 0105-1, September 1988.

Heinz, I. [1986], "Zur Okonomischen Bewertung von Materialschaden durch Luftverchmutzung" (On the Economic Valuation of Materials Damages by Air Pollution), in, *Kosten der Umweltverchmutzung*, Umweltbundesamt, Berichte, 7/86.

Hervik, A. et. al. [1987], "Implicit Costs and Willingness-to-Pay for Development of Water Resources", in Carlsen (ed), *Proceedings. UNESCO Symposium on Decision Making in Water Resources Planning*, Oslo, 1986.

Herzog, H.W., Jr and A.M. Schlottmann [1987], "Valuing Risk in the Workplace: Market Price, Willingness to Pay, and the Optimal Provision of Safety", University of Tennessee Working Paper.

Hicks, J.R. [1939], *Value and Capital*, Clarendon Press, Oxford.

Hill, J.W. [1988], "Valuing Reductions in the Risk of Breast Cancer Mortality: A Comparison of Revealed Preference and Contingent Valuation Methods", Dissertation, *DAI* Vol. 50, 2992, University of Wisconsin - Madison.

Hjalte, K. et al. [1982], Economic Consequences of Water Quality Changes in Lakes, March 1982 Report, TEM University of Lund.

Hoehn, J.P. [1987], "Contingent Valuation in Fisheries Management: The Design of Satisfactory Contingent Valuation Formats", *Transactions of the American Fisheries Society*, Vol. 116, 412-419.

Hoehn, J.P. and G. Fishelson [1987], "Measuring the Economic Impact of Visibility", Staff Paper No. 87-21, Department of Agricultural Economics, Michigan State University.

Hoehn, J.P. and D. Walker [1988], "Measuring the Economic Damages of Groundwater Contamination: The Case of Nitrates", Staff Paper No. 88-84, Department of Agricultural Economics, Michigan State University.

Hoen, H.F. and G. Winther [1991], Attitudes to, and Willingness to Pay for, Multiple-Use Forestry and Preservation of Coniferous Forests in Norway, Report to the Department of Forestry, Agricultural University of Norway.

Hoffmann, J.V. [1984], "Air Traffic Noise and the Value of Housing Properties - 1984", Working Paper, Institute of Transport Economics.

Horst, R.L et al. [1986], *A Damage Function Assessment of Building Materials: The Impact of Acid Deposition*, Mathtech Inc., Princeton, New Jersey, Report Prepared for EPA, Washington DC.

Horst, R.L. et al. [1990], *Economic Assessment of Materials Damage in the South Coast Air Basin: A Case of Acid Deposition Effects On Painted Wood Surfaces Using Individual Maintenance Behavior Data*, Mathtech Inc., Princeton, New Jersey.

Howe, C.W. and M.G. Smith [1991], "Optimizing the Reliability of Urban Water Supplies", Paper Presented at the Annual Meeting of the European Association of Environmental Resource Economists, Stockholm School of Economics.

Howwit, R.E., Gossard, T.W. and Adams, R.M. [1984], "Effects of Alternative Ozone Levels and Response Data on Economic Assessments: the Case for California Crops", *Journal of Air Pollution Control Association*, Vol. 34.

Hufschmidt, M., D. James.,A. Meister.,B. Bower and J. Dixon [1983], *Environment, Natural Systems and Development: an Economic Valuation Guide*, Johns Hopkins University Press, Baltimore.

Huppert, D.D. [1989], "Measuring the Value of Fish to Anglers: Application to Central California Anadromous Species", *Marine Resource Economics*, Vol. 6, 89-107.

Hylland, A. and Strand, J. [1983], "Valuation of Reduced Air Pollution in the Greenland Area", Department of Economics, University of Oslo, Memo. No. 12-83, pp 135.

International Institute for Applied Systems Analysis (IIASA) Forest Study [1991], "European Forest Decline: the Effects of Air Pollutants and Suggested Remedial Policies".

Ippolito, P.M. and R.A. Ippolito [1984], "Measuring the Value of Life Saving from Consumer Reactions to New Information", *Journal of Public Economics*, Vol. 25, 53-81.

Isecke, B. et al. [1990], in English, Economic Losses Resulting from Material Damage Caused by Environmental Pollution in the FDR, Umweltbundesamt.

Jansen, H.M.A. and Olsthootn, A.A. [1982], "Economische Waardering van de Nationale Schade door Luchtverontreiniging", in *Mozaiek van de Milieuproblematiek*, IVM-VU, Amsterdam.

Jansen, H.M.A. et al [1974], "Een Raming van de Schade Door Luchtverontreiniging in Nederland in 1970", Institut Voor Milieuvraagstukken, Amsterdam.

Johannesson, M., and B. Jonsson [1991a], "Willingness to Pay for Antihypertensive Therapy - Results of a Swedish Pilot Study", *Journal of Health Economics*, Vol. 10, 461-474.

Johannesson, M., and B. Jonsson [1991b], "Economic Evaluation in Health Care: Is There a Role for Cost-Benefit Analysis?" *Health Policy*, Vol. 17, 1-23.

Johannesson, M., P-O. Johansson and B. Jonsson [1992], "Economic Evaluation of Drug Therapy: A Review of the Contingent Valuation Method", *PharmacoEconomics*, Vol. 1, No. 5, 325-337.

Johansson, P-O. [1987], *The Economic Theory and Measurement of Environmental Benefits*, Cambridge University Press, Cambridge.

Johansson, P-O. and B. Kristrom [1988a], "Measuring Values for Improved Air Quality from Discrete Response Data: Two Experiments", *Journal of Agricultural Economics*, Vol. 39, 439-445.

Johansson, P-O. and B. Kristrom [1988b], "Asymmetric and Symmetric Discrete Response Models in Contingent Valuation Experiments", Discussion Paper, University of Umea, Sweden.

Jones-Lee, M.W. [1976], *The Value of Life: An Economic Analysis*, Chicago: University of Chicago Press.

Jones-Lee, M.W. [1989], *The Economics of Safety and Physical Risk*, Blackwell, Oxford.

Just, R., D. Hueth and A. Schmitz [1982], *Applied Welfare Economics and Public Policy*, Prentice-Hall, Englewood Cliffs N.J.

Kahneman, D. [1986], "Comments by Professor Daniel Kahneman", In R.G. Cummings, D.S. Brookshire and W.D. Schulze (eds), *Valuing Environmental Goods: An Assessment of the Contingent Valuation Method*, Rowman and Allanheld, Totowa, N.J. .

Kahneman, D. and A. Tversky [1979], "Prospect Theory: An Analysis of Decision under Risk", *Econometrica*, Vol. XLVII, 263-291.

Kahneman, D., J.L. Knetsch, and R.H. Thaler [1990], "Experimental Tests of the Endowment Effect and the Coase Theorem" *Journal of Political Economy*, Vol. 98, No. 6, 1325-1348.

Kanerva, V. and Matikainen [1972], The Economic Losses Caused by Water Pollution in Lake Saimaa, Rakennustalouden Laboratorio 7, Otaniemi Marraskuu, Report from the Technical Research Centre in Finland.

Kaoru, Y. [1991], Differentiating Use and Nonuse Values for Coastal Pond Water Quality Improvement, Mimeo, Marine Policy Center, Woods Hole Oceanographic Institution, Woods Hole, MA.

Katz, K. and T. Sterner [1990], "The Value of Clean Air: Consumers' Willingness to Pay for a Reduction in Gasoline Vapors at Filling Stations", *Energy Studies Review*, Vol. 2, No. 1, 39-47.

Kim and Dixon [1987], in Dixon et al. (ed.), *Economic Valuation Techniques for the Environment: A Case Study Workbook*, Johns Hopkins University Press, Baltimore, MD and London.

King, D. A., D.J. Bugorsky and W.W. Shaw, eds. [1987], "Contingent Valuation: An Application to Wildlife", Proceedings of the 18th International Union of Forestry Research Organizations World Congress Economic Value Analysis of Multiple-Use Forestry, International Union of Forestry Research Organizations.

King, D.A. and D.J. Flynn [1989], "Total and Existence Values of a Herd of Desert Bighorn Sheep", Paper Presented at the Annual USDA W-133 meeting, San Diego, CA.

Kneese, A.V. [1984], *Measuring the Benefits of Clean Air and Water*, Resources for the Future Inc., Washington DC.

Knetsch, J.L. [1987], "The Persistence of Evaluation Disparities", *The Quarterly Journal of Economics*, August.

Knetsch, J.L. [1990], "Environmental Policy Implications of Disparities between Willingness to Pay and Compensation Demanded Measures of Values", *Journal of Environmental Economics and Management*, vol.18, No.3, 227-237.

Knetsch, J.L. and R.K. Davis [1977], "Comparisons of Methods for Recreation Evaluation", In R. Dorfman and N.S. Dorfman (eds.), *Economics of the Environment - Selected Readings*, 2nd ed., Norton and Co, New York.

Knetsch, J.L. and J.A. Sinden [1984], "Willingness to Pay and Compensation Demanded: Experimental Evidence of an Unexpected Disparity", *The Quarterly Journal of Economics*, August, Vol. XCIX, No. 3, 507-521.

Kniesner, T.J. and J.D. Leeth [1991], "Compensating Wage Differentials for Fatal Injury Risk in Australia, Japan, and the United States", *Journal of Risk and Uncertainty*, Vol. 4, No. 1, 75-90.

Kuik, O., H. Jansen and J. Opschoor [1991], "The Netherlands", Chapter 4 of Barde, J-P. and D.W. Pearce (eds.), *Valuing the Environment: Six Case Studies*, Earthscan, London.

Kula, E. [1984], "Derivation of Social Time Preference Rates for the United States and Canada", *Quarterly Journal of Economics*, Vol. 99, No.4, 873-882.

Kula, E. [1985], "An Empirical Investigation of the Social Time Preference Rate for the United Kingdom", *Environment and Planning*, Vol. 17, 99-112.

Kula, E. [1986], An Analysis of the Social Interest Rate in Trinidad and Tobago, University of Ulster, Mimeo.

Kyber, M. [1981], "Harmful Effects of Water Pollution on Recreation and Their Estimation at an Inspection", Research Notes 23/1981, Technical Research Centre of Finland.

Lant, C.L. and J.B. Mullens [1991], "Lake and River Quality for Recreation Management and Contingent Valuation", *Water Resources Bulletin*, Vol. 27, No. 3, 453-460.

Lant, C.L. [1988], "Greenbelts: An Economic Analysis of Riparian Corridors in the Agricultural Midwest", Dissertation, *DAI* 50, 1050, University of Iowa.

Lantinng, R.W. and Morree, J.C. [1984], "Aantasting van Materiallen door Luchtverontreiniging (Effects of Air Pollution on Materials)", TNO-G-1157, Delft, Netherlands, Instituut voor Milieuhygiene en Gezondheidstechniek.

Larsen, O.I. [1985], Road Traffic and the Value of Housing Properties, Project Report, (1985), Institute of Transport Economics.

Lauria, D.T., D. Whittington and K. Choe [1993], *Households' Willingness to Pay for Improved Sanitation Services in Calamba, Philippines*, A Report to the World Bank, CVM Inc., Chapel Hill, NC, May 1993.

Lave, L.B. and E.P. Seskin [1971], "Air Pollution and Human Health", *Science*, No.169, 723-731.

Lazo, J. and W. Schulze [1992], "Do Existence Values Exist for Groundwater?", Paper Presented at the Association of Environmental and Resource Economists Meeting, Baltimore, MD.

Leigh, J.P. [1987], "Gender, Firm Size, Industry and Estimates of the Value of Life", *Journal of Health Economics*, Vol. 6, 255-273.

Leigh, J.P. [1991], "No Evidence of Compensating Wages for Occupational Fatalities", *Industrial Relations*, Vol. 30, No. 3,382-395.

Leigh, J.P. and R.N. Folsom [1984], "Estimates of the Value of Accident Avoidence at the Job Depend on Concavity of the Equalizing Differences Curve", *The Quarterly Review of Economics and Business*, Vol. 24, 255-273.

Levy, D.S. et. al. [1991], "Comments on Contingent Valuation of Altered Visibility in the Grand Canyon Due to Emissions from the Navajo Generating Station", Draft Paper, Rand Corporation, Santa Monica, CA.

Li, M. and H.J. Brown [1980], "Micro-Neighborhood Externalities and Hedonic Housing Prices", *Land Economics*, 125-141.

Linder, J.W. van der and Oosterhuis, F.H. [1988], *The Social Evaluation of the Vitality of Forests and Heath*, Report VROM 80115/3 - 88 4850/101 from the Ministry of Public Housing, Physical Planning and Environmental Management.

Lipfert, F. [1987], "Effects of Acidic Deposition on the Atmospheric Deterioration of Materials", *Materials Performance,* July 1987.

Little, I. and J. Mirrlees [1969], *Manual of Industrial Project Analysis in Developing Countries*, Vols. 1 and 2, OECD, Paris.

Little, I. and J. Mirrlees [1974], *Project Appraisal and Planning for Developing Countries*, Heinemann, London.

Little, I. and J. Mirrlees [1990], "Project Appraisal and Planning Twenty Years On", *Proceedings of the World Bank Annual Conference on Development Economics 1990*, World Bank, Washington DC.

Liu, J-T. [1989], "Postponing Development of Nuclear Generating Capacity in Taiwan: A Contingent Valuation Analysis", Research Report, Academia Sinica, The Institute of Economics, Taipei, Taiwan.

Loehman, E.T. and D. Boldt [1988], Specification of Willingness to Pay Benefit Functions for Air Quality: A Comparison of Theory and Empirical Measurement, Mimeo, Purdue University, Indiana.

Loehman, E.T. [1984], "Willingness to Pay for Air Quality: A Comparison of Two Methods", Staff Paper 84-18, Department of Agricultural Economics, Purdue University, Indiana.

Loomis, J.B. [1987a], "The Economic Value of Instream Flow: Methodology and Benefit Estimates for Optimum Flows", *Journal of Environmental Management*, Vol. 24, 169-179.

Loomis, J.B. [1987b], "An Economic Evaluation of Public Trust Resources of Mono Lake", Institute of Ecology Report #30, College of Agricultural and Environmental Sciences, University of California, Davis, CA.

Loomis, J.B. [1987c], "Balancing Public Trust Resources of Mono Lake and Los Angeles Water Rights: An Economic Approach", *Water Resources Research*, Vol. 23, No. 8, 1449-1456.

Loomis, J.B. [1987d], "Expanding Contingent Value Sample Estimates to Aggregate Benefit Estimates: Current Practices and Proposed Solutions", *Land Economics*, Vol. 63, No. 4, 396-402.

Loomis, J.B. [1992], "The Evolution of a More Rigorous Approach to Benefit Transfer: Benefit Transfer Function", *Water Resources Research*, Vol.28, No.3, March, [Special Section: Problems and Issues in the Validity of Benefit Transfer Methodologies.]

Loomis, J.B. and J. Cooper [1988], *The Net Economic Value of Antelope Hunting in Montana*, Report Prepared for Montana Department of Fish, Wildlife, and Parks, Helena, MT.

Loomis, J.B., J. Cooper and S. Allen [1988], *The Montana Elk Hunting Experience: A Contingent Valuation Assessment of Economic Benefits to Hunters*, Report Prepared for Montana Department of Fish, Wildlife, and Parks, Helena, MT.

Loomis, J.B., M. Creed and J.C. Cooper [1989], "Economic Benefits of Deer in California: Hunting and Viewing Values", Institute of Ecology Report #3, University of California, Davis.

Loomis, J.B., M.B. Lockwood and T. DeLacy [1993], "Some Empirical Evidence on Embedding Effects in Contingent Valuation of Forest Protection", *Journal of Environmental Economics and Management*, Forthcoming.

Loomis, J.B., C.F. Sorg and D.M. Donnelly [1986], "Evaluating Regional Demand Models for Estimating Recreation Use and Economic Benefits: A Case Study", *Water Resources Research*, Vol. 22, 431-438.

Low S.A. and L.R. McPheters [1983], "Wage Differentials and Risk of Death: An Empirical Analysis", *Economic Inquiry*, Vol. XXI, 271-280.

Loyland, K., S. Navrud and J. Strand [1991], Betalingsvillighet for Okologiske Matvarer i Norge: En Betinget Verdsettingsstudie (Willingness to Pay for Ecologically Produced Food in Norway: A Contingent Valuation Survey), Mimeo, Norwegian Center for Research in Economics and Business Administration, Oslo, Norway.

Luken, R. [1987], Economic Analysis: Canal Cities Water and Wastewater Phase II, Unpublished Report of Waste Water Treatment in Ismailia, for USAID, Cairo.

Luken, R.A., F.R. Johnson, and V. Kibler. [1992], "Benefits and Costs of Pulp and Paper Effluent Controls Under the Clean Water Act", *Water Resources Research*, Vol.28, No.3, March, [Special Section: Problems and Issues in the Validity of Benefit Transfer Methodologies.]

Luken, R.A., F.R. Johnson and V. Kibler [1992], "Benefits and Costs of Pulp and Paper Effluent Controls Under the Clean Water Act", *Water Resources Research* Vol. 28, No. 3.

MacRae, D. and D. Whittington [1988], "Assessing Preferences in Cost - Benefit Analysis: Reflections on Rural Water Supply in Haiti", *Journal of Policy Analysis and Management*, Vol.7, No. 2, 246-263.

Magnussen, K. [1991], "Valuation of Reduced Water Pollution Using the Contingent Valuation Method - Methodology and Empirical Results", Norwegian Agricultural Economics Research Institute, Paper Presented at the Second Annual Meeting of EAERE, Stockholm, 1991.

Magnussen, K. [1992a], "Valuation of Reduced Water Pollution Using the Contingent Valuation Method - Testing for Mental Accounts and Amenity Misspecification", in S. Navrud, ed., *Pricing the European Environment*, Oxford University Press, Oslo, Norway.

Magnussen, K. [1992b], "Valuation of Reduced Water Pollution Using the Contingent Valuation Method - Methodology and Empirical Results", Paper Presented at Conference on Water Quantity/Quality Disputes and Their Resolution, Washington, DC.

Magreth, W. and Arrens, P. [1989], *The Costs of Soil Erosion in Java: a Natural Resource Accounting Approach*, Environment Department Working Paper No. 18, World Bank.

Mäler, K-G. [1985], "Welfare Economics and the Environment", In A.V. Kneese and J.L. Sweeney (eds.), *Handbook of Natural Resources and Energy Economics*, Vol. 1, North Holland Publishing Company, Amsterdam.

Mäler, K-G. [1991a], "Production Function Approach in Developing Countries, in Valuing Environmental Benefits in Developing Economies", Proceedings of a Seminar Series Held February-May 1990, at Michigan State University, Special Report 29.

Mäler, K-G. [1991b], Measuring Environmental Damage - The Production Function Approach, Beijer Institute Stockholm, Mimeo.

Malpezzi, S. and S.K. Mayo (with D.J. Gross) [1985], "Housing Demand in Developing Countries", World Bank Staff Working Paper No. 733.

Mantymaa, E. [1991], "Some New Ideas and Preliminary Results for Using the CVM in Measuring the Environmental Benefits of a Lake", University of Oulu, Research Institute of Northern Finland, Paper Presented at Autumn Workshop in Environmental Economics, 1991.

Marin, A. and G. Psacharopoulos [1982], "The Reward for Risk in the Labor Market: Evidence From the United Kingdom and a Reconciliation With Other Studies", *Journal of Political Economy*, Vol.90, 827-853.

Markandya, A. and D.W. Pearce [1988], *Environmental Considerations and the Choice of the Discount Rate in Developing Countries*, Working Paper No.9, Environment Department, World Bank, Washington DC.

Markandya, A. and J. Richardson [1992], *The Earthscan Reader in Environmental Economics*, Earthscan, London.

Mathews, S.B. and G.S. Brown [1970], Economic Evaluation of the 1967 Sport Salmon Fisheries of Washington, Technical Report No. 2, Washington Department of Fisheries, Olympia.

McClelland, G.H. et. al. [1992], "Methods for Measuring Non-Use Values: A Contingent Valuation Study of Groundwater Cleanup", U.S. Environmental Protection Agency Cooperative Agreement #CR-815183, Center for Economic Analysis, University of Colorado, Boulder, CO.

McClelland, G.H. et. al. [1991], *Valuing Eastern Visibility: A Field Test of the Contingent Valuation Method-Innovative Approaches for Valuing Perceived Environmental Quality*, U.S. Environmental Protection Agency Cooperative Agreement #CR-815183-01-3, U.S. Environmental Protection Agency, Washington, DC.

McConnell, K.E. [1990], "Models for Referendum Data: The Structure of Discrete Choice Models for Contingent Valuation", *Journal of Environmental Economics and Management*, Vol.18, No.1, 19-34.

McConnell, K.E. [1992], "Model Building and Judgment: Implications for Benefit Transfers with Travel Cost Models", *Water Resources Research*, Vol.28, No.3, March, [Special Section: Problems and Issues in the Validity of Benefit Transfer Methodologies.]

McConnell, K.E. and I.E. Strand [1981], "Measuring the Cost of Time in Recreation Demand Analysis", *American Journal of Agricultural Economics*, Vol.63, 153-156.

McConnell, K.E. and J.H. Ducci [1989], "Valuing Environmental Quality in Developing Countries: Two Case Studies", Paper Presented at annual Association of Environmental and Resource Economics meeting, Atlanta, GA.

McKillop, W. [1992], "Use of Contingent Valuation in Northern Spotted Owl Studies - A Critique", *Journal of Forestry*, Vol. 90, No. 8, 36-37.

McMillan, M.L., B.G. Reid and D. W. Dilen [1980], "An Extension of the Hedonic Approach for Estimating the Value of Quiet", *Land Economics*, 315-328.

Melinek, S.J. [1974], "A Method for Evaluating Human Life for Economic Purposes", *Accident Analysis and Prevention*, Vol. 6, 103-114.

Mendelsohn, R. [1987], "Modeling the Demand for Outdoor Recreation", *Water Resources Research*, Vol.23, 961-967.

Meta Systems, Inc., HBRS and Analysis Group [1986], *Residential Outage Cost Estimation*, Final Report prepared for Pacific Gas and Electric.

Meyer, P.A. [1978], *Updated Estimates for Recreation and Preservation Values Associated with the Salmon and Steelhead of the Fraser River*, Report, Environment Canada, Vancouver, British Columbia.

Meyer, P.A. [1979], "A Publicly Vested Values for Fish and Wildlife: Criteria in Economic Theory and Interface with the Law", *Land Economics*, Vol. 55, No. 2, 223-235.

Meyer, P.A. [1980], *Recreational/Aesthetic Values Associated with Selected Groupings of Fish and Wildlife in California's Central Valley*, Report to the U.S. Fish and Wildlife Service, Sacramento, CA.

Meyer, P.A. [1987], The Value of King Salmon, Harbor Seals and Wetlands of San Francisco Bay, The Bay Institute of San Francisco, San Francisco, CA.

Michaels, R.G. and V.K. Smith [1990], "Market Segmentation and Valuing Amenities with Hedonic Models: The Case of Hazardous Waste Sites", *Journal of Urban Economics*, Vol. 28, 223-242.

Michalson, E.L. and R.L. Smathers, Jr. [1985], "Comparative Estimates of Outdoor Recreation Benefits in the Sawtooth National Recreation Area, Idaho", Agricultural Economics Research Paper Series 249, University of Idaho.

Miller, R. [1980], "The Demand for the Colorado Deer Hunting Experience", Dissertation, Colorado State University.

Milon, J.W. [1986], "Economic Evaluation of Artificial Habitat for Fisheries: Progress and Challenges", Discussion paper, Food and Resource Economics Department, University of Florida-Gainesville.

Mishan, E.J. [1982], *Cost - Benefit Analysis*, 3rd Edition, George Allen & Unwin, London.

Mitchell, R.C. [1982], *On the Use of the Contingent Valuation Approach to Value Public Services in Developing Nations (Kenya)*, Report Prepared for the World Bank, Clark University, Worcester, MA.

Mitchell, R.C. and R.T. Carson [1981], *An Experiment in Determining Willingness to Pay for National Water Quality Improvements*, Report to the U.S. Environmental Protection Agency.

Mitchell, R.C. and R.T. Carson [1986a], *The Use of Contingent Valuation Data for Benefit-Cost Analysis in Water Pollution Control*, Report to the U.S. Environmental Protection Agency, Washington, DC.

Mitchell, R.C. and R.T. Carson [1986b], *Valuing Drinking Water Risk Reductions Using the Contingent Valuation Method: A Methodological Study of Risks From THM and Giardia*, Report Submitted to the U.S. Environmental Protection Agency, Cooperative Agreement CR810466-01-6, Resources for the Future, Washington, DC.

Mitchell, R.C. and R.T. Carson [1987], "Valuing Reductions in Environmental Risk: The Case of Trihalomethanes", Paper Presented at Association for Public Policy Analysis and Management, Washington, DC.

Mitchell, R.C. and R.T. Carson [1988a], "Evaluating the Validity of Contingent Valuation Studies", in Peterson, G., B.L. Driver, and R. Gregory, (eds.), *Economic and Psychological Knowledge in Valuations of Public Amenity Resources*, Venture Publishing, State College, PA.

Mitchell, R.C. and R.T. Carson [1988b], "The Role of Social and Behavioral Sciences in Water Resources Planning and Management", in *Proceedings of an Engineering Foundation Conference in conjunction with the Universities Council on Water Resources*, American Society of Civil Engineers, New York.

Mitchell, R.C. and R.T. Carson [1988c], "How Far Out on the Learning Curve Are We with Contingent Valuation?", in A.D. Baumann and Y.H. Haimes, (eds.), *Proceedings of the Conference on the Role of Social/Behavior Science in Water Resource Management*, American Society of Civil Engineers/Engineering Foundation/Universities' Council on Water Resources, New York.

Mitchell, R.C. and R.T. Carson [1988d], Towards a Methodology for Using Contingent Valuation to Value Air Visibility Benefits, Draft Report to the Electric Power Institute, Resources for the Future, washington, DC.

Mitchell, R.B. and R.T. Carson. [1989], *Using Surveys to Value Public Goods: The Contingent Valuation Method*, Resources for the Future, Washington D.C.

Mitchell, R.C., R.T. Carson and P.A. Ruud [1989], *Cincinnati Visibility Valuation Study: Pilot Study Findings*, Report Submitted to the Electric Power Research Institute, Resources for the Future, Washington, DC.

Moore, M.J. and Viscusi, W.K. [1988a], "Doubling the Estimated Value of Life: Results Using New Occupational Fatality Data", *Journal of Policy Analysis and Management*, Vol. 7, No. 3, 476-490.

Moore, M.J. and Viscusi, W.K. [1988b], "The Quantity Adjusted Value of Life", *Economic Inquiry*, Vol. 26, No. 2, 369-388.

Moore, M.J. and Viscusi, W.K. [1990a], "Discounting Environmental Health Risks: New Evidence and Policy Implications", *Journal of Environmental Economics and Management*, Vol. 18, No. 2, pt. 2: S51-S62.

Moore, M.J. and Viscusi, W.K. [1990b], "Models for Estimating Discount Rates for Long Term Health Risks Using Labour Market Data", *Journal of Risk and Uncertainty*, Vol. 3, No. 4, 381-402.

Mueller and Stickney [1970], *Final Report on the Survey and Assessment of the Effects of Air Pollution on the Elastomers*, National Air Pollution Control Association, Columbus, Ohio.

Muller, A. and T.J. Reutzel [1984], "Willingness to Pay for Reduction in Fatality Risk: An Exploratory Survey", *American Journal of Public Health*, Vol. 74, 808-812.

Munasinghe, M. [1992], *Environmental Economics and Valuation in Development Decisionmaking*, Environment Working Paper No. 51, World Bank.

Murdoch, J.C. and M.A. Thayer [1988], "Hedonic Price Estimation of Variable Urban Air Quality", *Journal of Environmental Economics and Management*, Vol. 15, 143-146.

Musser, W.N., L.M. Musser, A.S. Laughland and J.S. Shortle [1992], "Contingent Valuation Estimates for Local Public Water Decisions", Staff Paper No. 216, Agricultural Economics and Rural Sociology Department, College of Agriculture, Pennsylvania State University.

Nachtman, S.C. [1983], "Valuation of the Maroon Valley Mass Transit System for Recreational Visitors", Thesis, Colorado State University.

NAPAP [1991], *The Causes and Effects of Acid Rain Precipitation*, NAPAP, Washington DC.

Naughton, M.C. and W.H. Desvousges [1986], "*Water Quality Benefits of Additional Pollution Control in the Pulp and Paper Industry*", Final Report to the U.S. Environmental Protection Agency, Contract 68-01-7033, Research Triangle Institute, Research Triangle Park, NC.

Navrud, S [1984], "Economic Valuation of Recreational Fishing in the River Hallingdalselv", M.Sc Thesis, Published in Norwegian Water Resources and Electricity Board's Report Series, *Biotopjusteringsprosjektet - Terskelprosjektet*, pp 121.

Navrud, S. [1988a], *Recreational Value of Atlantic Salmon and Sea Trout Angling in the River Vikedalselv in 1987 - Before Regular Liming*, Report for the Directorate for Nature Management.

Navrud, S. [1988b], *Distributional Effects of Environmental Regulations in the Ferro-Alloy Industries*, Case: Bjclvefossen A/S, Report T-712, Ministry of Finance.

Navrud, S. [1989], "Estimating Social Benefits of Environmental Improvements from Reduced Acid Depositions: A Contingent Valuation Survey", in H. Folmer and E. van Ireland, (eds.), *Valuation Methods and Policy Making in Environmental Economics*, Studies in Environmental Science, North-Holland, Amsterdam.

Navrud, S. [1991a], "Norway", Ch.5 of Barde, J-P. and D.W. Pearce, *Valuing the Environment: Six Case Studies*, Earthscan, 1991.

Navrud, S. [1991b], *Nytte-Kostnadsanalyse Av Kalding Av Innlandsfiskevann. En Studie Av Lauvann Og Seks Vann I Gjerstadskogene (Cost-Benefit Analysis of Liming Lakes. A Study of Lake Lauvann and Six Lakes in the Gjerstad Forests)*, Report to the Directorate for Nature Management, Trondheim, Norway.

Navrud, S. [1991c], *Nytte-Kostnadsanalyse Av Kalding I Audna. En Utvidet Analyse (Cost Benefit of Liming River Audna - An Extended Analysis*, Report (in Norwegian) to the Directorate for Nature Management, Trondheim, Norway.

331

Navrud, S. [1991d], "Willingness to Pay for Preservation of Species: An Experiment with Actual Payments", Paper Presented at the Second Annual Meeting of European Association of Environmental Resource Economists, Stockholm, Sweden.

Navrud, S. [1992], *Pricing the European Environment*, Scandinavian University Press, Oslo.

Navrud, S. and Strand, J. [1990], Valuation of Our Cultural Heritage - A Case Study of Historical Buildings and Monuments in Norway (Project Description), Centre for Research in Economics and Business Administration, University of Oslo.

Navrud, S., K. Siemensen, B. Solberg and M.H.A. Wind [1990], "Valuing Environmental Effects of Different Management Practices in Mountainous Forests in Norway: A Survey of Recreationists' Preferences and Willingness to Pay", Paper Presented at the XIX World Congress of International Union of Forestry Research Organizations, Montreal.

Needleman, L. [1979], "The Valuation of Changes in the Risk of Death by Those at Risk", University of Waterloo, Working Paper 103.

Nelson, J.P. [1978], "Residential Choice, Hedonic Prices, and the Demand for Urban Air Quality", *Journal of Urban Economics*, Vol. 5, 357-369.

Nelson, J.P. [1979], "Airport Noise, Location Rent, and the Market for Residential Amenities", *Journal of Environmental Economics and Management*, Vol. 6, 320-331.

Nelson, J. [1980], "Airports and Property Values: A Survey of Recent Evidence", *Journal of Transport Economics and Policy*, XIV, 37-52;

Nelson, J.P. [1981], "Estimating Demand Functions for Product Characteristics: A Comment", mimeo.

Nelson, J. [1982], "Highway Noise and Property Values: A Survey of Recent Evidence", *Journal of Transport Economics and Policy*, XVI, 117-130.

Newcombe, K.J. [1989], "An Economic Justification for Rural Afforestation: the Case of Ethiopia", in Schramm et al (ed.), *Environmental Management and Economic Development*, Johns Hobkins University Press, Baltimore, MD.

Nielsen, C. [1992], "Der Wert Stadtnaher Walder als Erholungsraum: Eine Okonomische Analyse am Beispiel von Lugano (The Value of Nearby Forests as Recreation Area: An Economic Analysis Taking as an Example Lugano)", Dissertation, University of Zurich, Switzerland.

NNM [1988], Forest Damage Scenarios: How Pollution Might Affect Norwegian Forests in a 25 year Perspective, Norwegian Ministry of Environment (NME), Oslo.

Nordhaus, W [1990], To Slow or Not to Slow: the Economics of the Greenhouse Effect, Mimeo.

North, J.H. and C.C. Griffin [1993], "Water Source as a Housing Characteristic: Hedonic Property Valuation and Willingness to Pay for Water", *Water Resources Research*, Forthcoming.

O'Byrne, P.H. et al [1985], "Housing Values, Census Estimates, Disequilibrium and the Environmental Cost of Airport Noise: a Case Study of Atlanta", *Journal of Environmental Economics and Management,* Vol. 12(2).

O'Neil, W.B. [1985], Estimating the Recreational Value of Maine Rivers: An Experiment with the Contingent Value Technique, Mimeo, Colby College, Waterville, ME.

ODA [1990], Bogota Sewage Treatment Project, An Unpublished Report for Sewage Treatment Facilities in Rio Bogota, Columbia.

Oliveira, H. [1992], A Contingent Valuation of the Benefits of Cleaning the Guanabarra Bay and the Beaches of Rio de Janeiro, Brazil, Mimeo.

Olsen, D., J. Richards and D.R. Scott [1991], "Existence and Sport Values for Doubling the Size of Columbia River Basin Salmon and Steelhead Runs", *Rivers,* Vol. 2, No. 1, 44-56.

Olson, C.A. [1981], "An Analysis of Wage Differentials Received by Workers on Dangerous Jobs", *Journal of Human Resources,* Vol.16, 167-185.

Oosterhuis, F.H. and Van der Pligt [1985], Kosten en Baten Van de Wet Geluidshinder, (Costs and Benefits of the Noise Nuisance Law), Commissie Evaluatie Wet Geluidshinder, CW-AS-06.

Organisation for Economic Cooperation and Development, *Dealing with Uncertainty,* OECD, Paris.

Oster, S. [1977], "Survey Results on the Benefits of Water Pollution Abatement in the Merrimack River Basin", *Water Resources Research,* Vol. 13, 882-884.

Ostro, B. [1983], "Air Pollution and Morbidity Revisited: A Specification Test", *Journal of Environmental Economics and Management,* Vol.14 no.1.

Ovaskainen, V., H. Savolainen and T. Sievanen [1991], "The Benefits of Managing Forests for Grouse Habitats: A Contingent Valuation Experiment", Paper Presented at Biennial Meeting of the Scandinavian Society of Forest Economics, Gausdal, Norway.

Page, T. [1977], *Conservation and Economic Efficiency,* Baltimore: Johns Hopkins University Press.

Palmquist, R.B. [1983], "Estimating the Demand for Air Quality from Property Values Studies: Further Results", Working Paper, North Carolina State University, Raleigh, NC.

Palmquist, R.B. and L.E. Danielson [1989], "A Hedonic Study of the Effects of Erosion Control and Drainage on Farmland Values", *American Journal of Agricultural Economics,* Vol. 71, 55-62.

Parfit, D. [1983], "Energy Policy and the Further Future: the Social Discount Rate", in D.Maclean and P.Brown (eds), *Energy and the Future,* Totowa: Rowman and Littlefield, 31-7.

Pearce, D.W. [1985], *Trinidad and Tobago: Energy Assessment - Natural Gas Pricing,* Report to Energy Department, World Bank, Washington DC, April.

Pearce, D.W. [1986], *Cost-Benefit Analysis,* Macmillan, London.

Pearce, D.W. [1993], *Economic Values and the Natural World,* Earthscan, London.

Pearce, D.W. and I. Brisson [1993], *BATNEEC: The Economics of Technology Based Environmental*

Standards, Oxford Review of Economic Policy, Forthcoming.

Pearce, D.W. and A. Markandya [1989], *The Benefits of Environmental Policy: Monetary Valuation*, OECD, Paris.

Pearce, D.W. and C. Nash [1981], *The Social Appraisal of Projects*, Macmillan, London.

Pearce, D.W. and R.K. Turner [1989], *Economics of Natural Resources and the Environment*, Harvester-Wheatsheaf, London.

Pearce, D.W. and R.K. Turner [1992a], *Benefit Estimates and Environmental Decision Making*, OECD, Paris.

Pearce, D.W and R.K. Turner [1992b], "United Kingdom", in S.Navrud (ed), *Pricing the European Environment*, Scandinavian University Press, Oslo.

Pearce, D.W. and J.J. Warford [1993], *World Without End: Economics Environment and Sustainable Development*, Oxford University Press, New York.

Pearce, D.W. et al, [1991], The Development of Environmental Indicators, Report to UK Department of the Environment, April.

Pearce, D.W., C. Bann and S. Georgiou [1992], *The Social Cost of Fuel Cycles*, HMSO, London.

Pearce, D.W., A. Markandya, and E. Barbier [1989], *Blueprint for a Green Economy*, Earthscan Publications, London.

Peckham, B. [1970], Air Pollution and Residential Property Values in Philadelphia, Mimeo.

Phantumvanit, D. [1982], "A Case of Water Quality Management in Thailand" in Ahmed, Y. (ed.), (1989) *Environmental Accounting for Sustainable Development*, World Bank, Washington, DC.

Pigou, A. [1931], *The Economics of Welfare*, Macmillan, London.

Poe, G.L. and R.C. Bishop [1992], "Measuring the Benefits of Groundwater Protection from Agricultural Contamination: Results from a Two-Stage Contingent Valuation Study", Staff Paper No. 341, Department of Agricultural Economics, University of Wisconsin, Madison.

Polinsky, A.M. and S. Shavell [1975]",The Air Pollution and Property Value Debate", *Review of Economics and Statistics*, Vol. 57, No. 1, 100-104.

Polinsky, A.M. and S. Shavell [1976], "Amenities and Property Values in a Model of an Urban Area", *Journal of Public Economics*, Vol. 5, 119-129.

Portney, P. [1990], "Air Pollution", in P.Portney (ed.), *Public Policies for Environmental Protection*, Resources for the Future, Washington D.C.

Powell, J.R. [1991], "The Value of Groundwater Protection: Measurement of Willingness to Pay Information, and Its Utilization by Local Government Decisionmakers", Dissertation, *DAI* Vol. 52, 622, Cornell University.

Purvis, A.K., J.P. Hoehn and F.J. Pierce [1989], "Farmers Response to a Filter Strip Program: Results from a Contingent Valuation Survey", *Journal of Soil and Water Conservation*, Vol. 44, No. 5, 501-504.

Rae, D.A. [1982], *Benefits and Costs of Improving Visibility: Case Studies of the Applications of the Contingent Valuation Ranking Methodology at Mesa Verde and Great Smoky Mountain National Parks*, Report by Charles River Associates to Electric Power Research Institute, Electric Power Research Institute, Boston, MA.

Rae, D.A. [1983], "The Value to Visitors of Improving Visibility at Mesa Verde and Great Smoky Mountain National Parks", in R.D. Rowe and L.G. Chestnut, (eds.), *Managing Air Quality and Scenic Resources at National Parks and Wilderness Areas*, Westview Press, Boulder, CO.

Rae, D.A. [1984], *Benefits of Visual Air Quality in Cincinnati: Results of a Contingent Ranking Survey*, Report by Charles River Associates to Electric Power Research Institute, Electric Power Research Institute, Boston, MA.

Rahmatian, M. [1987], "Valuing Public Goods Using the Linear Expenditure System Approach", *Journal of Environmental Management*, Vol. 24, 225-236.

Rahmatian, M. [1987], "Component Value Analysis: Air Quality in the Grand Canyon National Park", *Journal of Environmental Management*, Vol. 24, 217-223.

Randall, A. [1979], "The Economic Value of Atmospheric Visibility", in *Proceedings of the Workshop on Visibility Values*, U.S. Forestry Service Technical Report WO-18.

Randall, A., B. Ives, and C. Eastman [1974], "Bidding Games for Valuation of Aesthetic Environmental Improvements", *Journal of Environmental Economics and Management*, Vol.1, 132-149.

Randall, A., G.C. Blomquist, J.P. Hoehn, and J.R. Stoll [1985], *National Aggregate Benefits of Air and Water Pollution Control*, Cooperative Agreement CR811056-01-0, Interim report to the U.S. Environmental Protection Agency, University of Kentucky, Lexington.

Rawls, J. [1971], *A Theory of Justice*, Oxford University Press, Oxford.

Ray, A. [1984], *Cost Benefit Analysis: Issues and Methodologies*, Johns Hopkins University Press, Baltimore.

RCG/Hagler, Bailly, Inc. [1986], Value-Based Planning for Electric Utilities, Prepared for California Energy Commission, Boulder, CO.

RCG/Hagler, Bailly, Inc. [1988], Optimal Selection of Reliability Standards in Practice and Theory, Prepared for Electric Power Research Institute, Boulder, CO.

RCG/Hagler, Bailly, Inc. [1989a], *Customer Value of Service Reliability: Volume 2: Residential Customers*, Prepared for Southern California Edison Company, Rosemead, CA; Boulder, CO.

RCG/Hagler, Bailly, Inc. [1989b], *Customer Value of Service Reliability: Volume 1: Summary*, Prepared for Southern California Edison Company, Rosemead, CA; Boulder, CO.

RCG/Hagler, Bailly, Inc. [1989c], *Customer Value of Service Reliability: Volume 3: Commercial and Industrial Customers*, Final Report (reference number 1989-6012), Prepared for Southern California Edison Company, Rosemead, CA; Boulder, CO.

RCG/Hagler, Bailly, Inc. [1989d], *Customer Value of Service Reliability: Volume 4: Methodology*, Final Report, Prepared for Southern California Edison Company, Rosemead, CA.

RCG/Hagler, Bailly, Inc. [1990a], *Cost-Benefit Analysis of Power System Reliability: Determination of Interruption Costs Volume 3: Measurement of Interruption Costs for a Major Southeast Utility*, Final Report (Research Project 2878-1, Report Number EL-6791), Prepared for the Bonneville Power Administration and Electric Power Research Institute, Palo Alto, CA.

RCG/Hagler, Bailly, Inc. [1990b], *Cost-Benefit Analysis of Power System Reliability: Determination of Interruption Costs Volume 2: Measurement of Interruption Costs for the Bonneville Power Administration*, Final Report (Research Project 2878-1, Report Number EL-6791), Prepared for the Bonneville Power Administration and Electric Power Research Institute, Palo Alto, CA.

RCG/Hagler, Bailly, Inc. [1991a], *Economic Penalties Including Customer Costs for Loss of Service Continuity*, CEA No. SD-2730, Boulder, CO.

RCG/Hagler, Bailly, Inc. [1991b], *Survey of Customer Outage Costs*, (2 Volumes), Prepared for Southern Company Services, Inc., Boulder, CO.

Repetto, R. et al. [1989], *Wasting Assets: Natural Resources in the National Income Accounts*, World Resources Institute Studies, Washington, DC.

Ribaudo, M.O. [1983], "The Contingent Ranking Method for Measuring the Benefits of Water Quality Improvements: Development and Application", Dissertation, *DAI* Vol. 44, 2530, The Pennsylvania State University.

Ridker, R.G. and J.A. Henning [1967], "The Determinants of Residential Property Values with Special Reference to Air Pollution", *Review of Economics and Statistics*, Vol. 49, 246-257.

Riera, P. [1991], "Barcelona's New Ring Road for the 1992 Olympic Games: An Evaluation Using Contingency Valuation Analysis", Paper Presented at the Summer Annual Meeting of the Planning and Transport Research and Computation International Association, University of Sussex, Great Britain.

Robinson, P.R. [1988], Willingness to Pay for Rural Water: The Zimbabwe Case Study, Mimeo, Zimconsult, Harare, Zimbabwe.

Rowe, R.D. and L.G. Chestnut [1986], "Valuing Changes in Morbidity WTP versus COI Measures", Paper Presented at the American Economic Annual Meetings, Dallas, TX.

Rowe, R.D., R. Dutton and L.Chestnut [1985], *The Value of Ground Water Protection: Miami Case Study Design and Pretest*, Energy and Resource Consultants, Inc. Report to the U.S. Environmental Protection Agency, Washington, DC.

Rowe, R.D., R.C. d'Arge and D. S. Brookshire [1980], "An Experiment on the Economic Value of Visibility", *Journal of Environmental Economics and Management*, Vol. 7, 1-19.

Rubin, J., G. Helfand and J.B. Loomis [1991], "A Benefit-Cost Analysis of the Northern Spotted Owl: Results from a Contingent Valuation Survey", *Journal of Forestry*, Vol. 89, No. 12, 25-30.

Ruitenbeek, H. J. [1989], Social Cost-Benefit Analysis, Appendix 13, The Korup Project: Plan for Developing the Korup National Park and its Support Zone.

Ruud, P.A. [1986], "Contingent Ranking Surveys: Their Application and Design in Estimating the Value of Visibility", in P.S. Bhardwaja, (ed.), *Visibility Protection: Research and Policy Aspects*, Air Pollution Control Association, Pittsburgh, PA.

Salmon, R.L. [1970], Systems Analysis of the Effects of Air Pollution on Materials, Midwest Research Institute, Prepared for Economic Effects Research Division, National Air Pollution Control Administration, Kansas City, Missouri.

Samples, K.C. and J.R. Hollyer [1990], "Contingent Valuation of Wildlife Resources in the Presence of Substitutes and Complements", in R.L. Johnson and G.V. Johnson, (eds.), *Economic Valuation of Natural Resources: Issues, Theory and Applications*, Westview, Boulder, CO.

Sanghvi, A.P., R.D. Rowe and T. Lawrence [1989], Customer Value of Service Reliability: Residential, RCG/Hagler, Bailly, Inc., Prepared for Southern California Edison Company, Boulder, CO.

Sanghvi, A.P. [1990], *Cost-Benefit Analysis of Power System Reliability: Determination of Interruption Costs Volume 1: Measurement Methods and Potential Applications in Reliability Cost-Benefit Analysis*, Final Report (Research Project 2878-1, Report Number EL-6791), Prepared by RCG/Hagler, Bailly, Inc., for the Electric Power Research Institute, Palo Alto, CA; Washington, DC.

Scancke, E [1984], "Economic Valuation of the Recreational Fishing in the River Tinnelv", M.Sc Thesis, Department of Economics, University of Oslo.

Schechter, M. et al. [1988], "The Benefits of Morbidity Reduction from Air Pollution", Natural Resources and Environmental Research Centre, University of Haifa.

Schultz, S.D. and B.E. Lindsay [1990], "The Willingness to Pay for Groundwater Protection", *Water Resources Research*, 1869-1875.

Schulz, W. [1985], "Bessere Luft, Was ist sie uns wert? Eine Gesellschaftliche Bedarfs-Analyse auf der basis individuller zahlungs-bereitschftend", translated into English as, "Better Air - How Do We Value It? A Social Demand Analysis Based on Willingness To Pay"), OECD Workshop, October 1986, Technical University of Berlin, Germany.

Schulze, W.D. [1992], "Groundwater Contamination: What is Your Opinion?", Center for Economic Analysis, University of Colorado, Boulder, CO.

Schulze, W.D., D. S. Brookshire, E.G. Walter and K. Kelley [1981a], "The Benefits of Preserving Visibility in the National Parklands of the Southwest", Report to the U.S. Environmental Protection Agency, in *Methods Development for Air Pollution Control Benefits Assessment*, Resource & Environmental Economics Lab, University of Wyoming, Laramie.

Schulze, W.D., D.S. Brookshire and M.A. Thayer [1981b], "National Parks and Beauty: A Test of Existence Values", Paper Presented at the American Economic Association Annual Meeting,

Washington, DC.

Schulze, W.D. et. al. [1983a], "The Economic Benefits of Preserving Visibility in the National Parklands of the Southwest", *Natural Resources Journal*, Vol. 23, 149-173.

Schulze, W.D., R.C. d'Arge and D.S. Brookshire [1981c], "Valuing Environmental Commodities: Some Recent Experiments", *Land Economics* Vol. 57, No. 2, 151-172.

Schulze, W.D., R.G. Cummings and D.S. Brookshire [1983], *Methods Development in Measuring Benefits of Environmental Improvements: Experimental Approaches for Valuing Environmental Commodities*, Report to the U.S. Environmental Protection Agency, Office of Policy Analysis, U.S. Environmental Protection Agency, Washington, DC.

Schulze, W.D., T. Crocker, Shaul B-D. and A. Kneese [1979], *Methods Development for Assessing Air Pollution Control Benefits*, 5 Vols., Report to the U.S. Environmental Protection Agency, Resource & Environmental Economic Lab, University of Wyoming, Laramie.

Schuman, H. and S. Presser. [1981], *Questions and Answers in Attitude Surveys: Experiments on Question Form, Wording, and Context*, Academic Press, New York.

Scott, M. [1977], "The Test Rate of Discount and Changes in Base Level Income in the United Kingdom", *Economic Journal*, Vol.87, No.346.

Sen, A. [1967], "Isolation, Assurance and the Social Rate of Discount", *Quarterly Journal of Economics*, Vol.LXXXI, 112-24.

Sen, A. [1982], "Approaches to the Choice of Discount Rates for Social Cost-Benefit Analysis", in R. Lind (ed.), *Discounting for Time and Risk in Energy Policy*, Johns Hopkins University Press, Baltimore.

Shechter, M. [1989], "Valuation of Morbidity Reduction Due to Air Pollution Abatement: Direct and Indirect Measurements", Paper Presented at the Association of Environmental and Resource Economists Conference on Estimating and Valuing Morbidity in a Policy Context, Research Triangle Park, NC.

Shechter, M and Zeidner, M. [1990], "Anxiety: Towards a Decision Theoretic Perspective", *The British Journal of Mathematical and Statistical Psychology*, Vol. 43, 15-28.

Shechter, M., R. Enis and M. Baron [1974], "Mt. Carmel National Park: The Demand for Outdoor Recreation", Center for Urban and Regional Studies, Technion (Israel Institute of Technology), Haifa, Israel.

Signorello, G. [1992], Stima Del Valore di Esistenza dei Cetacei Nel Mediterraneo, Mimeo, Istituto di Estimo Rurale e Contabilita, Universita Degli Studi di Catania.

Silvander, U. [1991], "Betalningsvillighetstudier for Sportfiske och Grundvatten i Sverige (The Willingness to Pay for Fishing and Groundwater in Sweden)", dissertation (in Swedish), Swedish University of Agricultural Studies.

Silvander, U. [1991], "The Willingness-To-Pay for Angling and Ground Water in Sweden", Dissertation No 2, Swedish University of Agricultural Sciences, Department of Economics.

Singh, B., R. Ramasubban., R. Bhatia., J. Briscoe., C. Griffen and C. Kim [1993], "Rural Water Supply in Kerala, India: How to Emerge from a Low-Level Equilibrium Trap", *Water Resources Research*, forthcoming.

Small, K.A. [1975], "Air Pollution and Property Values: Further Comment", *Review of Economics and Statistics*, Vol. 57, 105-107.

Smith, N.E. [1980], "A Comparison of the Travel Cost and Contingent Valuation Methods of Recreation Valuation at Cullby Lake County Park", Thesis, Oregon State University.

Smith, R.S. [1973], "Compensating Wage Differentials and Hazardous Work", Technical Paper No. 5, Office of Policy Evaluation and Research, Department of Labor.

Smith, R.S. [1976], "The Occupational Safety and Health Act", American Enterprise Institute for Public Policy Research, Washington, DC.

Smith, V.K. [1983], "The Role of Site and Job Characteristics in Hedonic Wage Models", *Journal of Urban Economics*, Vol. 13, 296-321.

Smith, V.K. [1983], *Environmental Policy Under Reagan's Executive Order: The Role of Benefit-Cost Analysis*, University of North Carolina Press, N.C.

Smith, V.K. [1992], "On Separating Defensible Benefit Transfers from Smoke and Mirrors", *Water Resources Research*, Vol.28, No.3, March, [Special Section: Problems and Issues in the Validity of Benefit Transfer Methodologies.]

Smith, V.K. and T.A. Deyack [1975], "Measuring the Impact of Air Pollution on Property Values", *Journal of Regional Science*, Vol. 15, 277-288.

Smith, V.K. and W.H. Desvousges [1985], "The Generalized Travel Cost Model and Water Quality Benefits: A Reconsideration", *Southern Economic Journal*, Vol.52, 371-381.

Smith, V.K. and W.H. Desvousges [1986], *Measuring Water Quality Benefits*, Kluwer-Nijhoff Publishing, Boston.

Smith, V.K. and W.H. Desvousges. [1987], "An Empirical Analysis of the Economic Value of Risk Changes", *Journal of Political Economy*, Vol.95.

Smith, V.K. and Gilbert, C. [1984], "The Implicit Risks To Life: A Comparative Analysis", *Economics Letters*, Vol. 16, 393-399

Smith, V.K and Y. Kaoru [1990], "Signals or Noise? Explaining the Variation in Recreation Benefit Estimates", *American Journal of Agricultural Economics*, Vol.72, 419-433.

Smith, V.K. and Y.S. Eom [1992], "Linking Revealed and Stated Preferences Data in Describing Consumer Responses to Risk: Pesticide Residues on Food", Presented at the Annual Meeting of the Association of Environmental and Resource Economists.

Smith, V.K., W.H. Desvousges and A. Fisher [1983], *Economic Letters*, Vol. 13, No. 1, 81-86.

Smith, V.K., W.H. Desvousges, and A. Fisher [1986], "A Comparison of Direct and Indirect

Methods for Estimating Environmental Benefits", *American Journal of Agricultural Economics,* Vol.68, 280-289.

Smith, V.K., R.B. Palmquist and P. Jackus [1989], "A Non-Parametric Hedonic Travel Cost Model for Valuing Estuarine Quality", Working Paper, North Carolina State University, Raleigh, NC.

Sodal, D.P. [1989], "The Recreational Value of Moose Hunting in Norway: Towards Modelling Optimal Population Density", *Scandinavian Forest Economics*, Vol. 30, 62-78.

Sodal, D.P. [1989], "Economic Valuation of Moose Hunting", Dissertation, *DAI* Vol. 51, 507, Norges Landbrukshogskole.

Sorg, C.F. and J.B. Loomis [1984], *Empirical Estimates of Amenity Forest Values: A Comparative Review*, General Technical Report RM-107, Rocky Mountain Forest and Range Experiment Station, U.S. Forest Service, Fort Collins, CO.

Sorg, C.F. and L.J. Nelson [1986], Net Economic Value of Elk Hunting in Idaho, U.S. Forest Service Resource Bulletin RM-12, Rocky Mountain Forest and Range Experiment Station, U.S. Forest Service, Fort Collins, CO.

Southgate, D. and Macke, R. [1989], "The Downstream Benefits of Soil Conservation in the Third World Hydroelectric Watersheds", *Land Economics*, 65(1), February.

Spore, R. [1972], "Property Value Differentials as a Measure of the Economic Costs of Air Pollution", Pennsylvania State University, Center for Air Environment Studies, University Park, PA.

Squire, L and H. van der Tak [1975], *Economic Analysis of Projects*, Johns Hopkins University Press, Baltimore.

Starkie, D.M.N. and Johnson, D.M. [1973], The Valuation of Disamenity: An Analysis of Sound Attenuation, Mimeo, Department of Geography, University of Reading, 1973.

Starsa Inversion y Desarrollo S.A. [1992], "Proyecto de Saneamiento y control do Inundaciones de la Cuenca del Rio Reconquista", Buenos Aires, Argentina.

Stavins, R. (ed.) [1988], *Project 88: Harnessing Market Forces to Protect Our Environment*, a Public Policy Study Sponsored by Senators Wirth and Heinz, Washington DC, December; and its Sequel, R.Stavins (ed) [1991], *Project 88: Round II*, Washington DC, May.

Steele, W. [1972], "The Effect of Air Pollution on the Value of Single Family Owner-Occupied Residential Property in Charleston, South Carolina", Thesis, Clemson University.

Stern, N. [1977], "The Marginal Valuation of Income", in M.Artis and R.Nobay, *Studies in Modern Income Analysis*, Blackwell, Oxford.

Stevens, T.H. [1991], "CVM Wildlife Existence Value Estimates: Altruism, Ambivalence, and Ambiguity", Paper Presented at the Annual USDA W-133 Meeting, Monterey, CA.

Stocking, M. [1986], "The Cost of Soil Erosion in Zimbabwe in Terms of the Loss of the Three Major Nutrients", Working Paper No. 3, Soil Conservation Programme, Land and Water Development Division, FAO.

Stoll, J. and Johnson, L. [1984], "Concepts of Value, Non-Market Valuation, and the Case of the Whooping Crane", *Transactions of the North American Wildlife and Natural Resources Conference*, 49.

Stoll, J.R. [1980], "The Valuation of Hunting Related Amenities: A Conceptual and Empirical Approach", Dissertation, *DAI* Vol. 41, 4783, University of Kentucky.

Strand, J. [1981a], "Valuing Benefits of Recreational Fishing in Norway: the Gaula case", in Carlsen, A. J. (ed.), [1987], *Proceedings. UNESCO Symposium on Decision Making in Water Resources Planning*, Oslo, pp 245-78.

Strand, J. [1981b], Verdsetting av Ferskvannsfisk som Kollektivt Gode i Norge. Resultater fra en Intervjuundersokelse (Valuation of Freshwater Fish Populations as a Public Good in Norway. Results from a Survey), Mimeo in Norwegian, English Summary.

Strand, J [1985a], Valuing Reduced Air Pollution from Automobiles in Norway, Department of Economics, University of Oslo, Memo. No. 1-85. (For a shorter English version see: "The Value of Catalytic Converter Requirement for Norwegian automobiles: A Contingent Valuation Study". Mimeo, Department of Economics, University of Oslo).

Strand, J. [1985b], The Value of a Catalytic Converter Requirement for Norwegian Automobiles: A Contingent Valuation Study, Mimeo (in English), Department of Economics, University of Oslo.

Strotz, R. [1956], "Myopia and Inconsistency in Dynamic Utility Maximisation", *Review of Economic Studies*, Vol.23, No.3, 165-180.

Sutherland, R.J. and Walsh, R.G. [1985], "Effects of Distance on the Preservational Value of Water Quality", *Land Economics*, 61.

Swanson, T. [1991], "Conserving Biological Diversity", in Pearce D.W. (ed.), *Blueprint 2: Greening the World Economy*, Earthscan, London.

Sydal, D.P. [1989], "The Recreational Value of Moose Hunting in Norway: Towards Modelling Optimal Population Density", in Mattson and Sydal (ed.), Multiple Use of Forests - Economics and Policy, *Scandinavian Forest Economics*, No. 30.

Syme, G.J., E. Roberts and P.B. McLeod [1990], "Combining Willingness to Pay and Social Indicator Methodology in Valuing Public Services: An Example from Agricultural Protection", *Journal of Economic Psychology*, Vol. 11, 365-381.

Thaler, R. and S. Rosen [1976], "The Value of Life Savings", In N. Terleckyj (ed.), *Household Production and Consumption*, Columbia University Press, New York.

Thayer, M.A. [1981], "Contingent Valuation Techniques for Assessing Environmental Impacts: Further Evidence", *Journal of Environmental Economics and Management*, Vol.8, 27-44.

Thomas, J.F. and G.J. Syme [1988], "Estimating Residential Price Elasticity of Demand for Water: A Contingent Valuation Approach", *Water Resources Research*, Vol. 24, No. 11, 1847-1857.

Thompson, M.S. [1986], "Willingness to Pay and Accept Risks to Cure Chronic Disease", *American Journal of Public Health*, Vol. 76, No. 4, 392-396.

Tietenberg, T. [1988], *Environmental and Natural Resource Economics*, 2nd edition, Glenview Scott Foresman & Co, Illinois.

Tietenberg, T. [1990], "Economic Instruments for Environmental Regulation", in D.Helm (ed.), *Economic Policy Towards the Environment*, Blackwell, Oxford.

Tobias, D. and R. Mendelsohn [1991], "Valuing Ecotourism in a Tropical Rain-Forest Reserve", *Ambio*, Vol.20, No.2, April.

Tolley, G.S. et. al. [1985], *Results from 1984 Contingent Valuation Study of Visibility and Comparison with 1982 Results: Photos, Vehicle, Seasonality and Distribution*, Report to U.S. Environmental Protection Agency, University of Chicago.

Turner, R.K. and Brooke, J. [1988], A Cost-Benefit Analysis of the Aldeburgh Sea Defence Scheme, Environmental Appraisal Group, University of East Anglia.

Tversky, A. and D. Kahneman [1981], "The Framing of Decisions and the Psychology of Choice", *Science*, January 30, Vol.211, 453-458.

U.S. Water Resources Council [1983], *Economic and Environmental Principles and Guidelines for Water and Related Land Resource Implementation Studies*, U.S. Government Printing Office, Washington, DC.

Ulleberg, M. [1988], "The Recreational Value of Fishing for Atlantic Salmon and Sea Trout in the River Stordalselv in 1987", M.Sc Thesis, Department of Forest Economics, Agricultural University of Norway.

United Nations Development Programme [1992], *Human Development Report*, Oxford University Press, Oxford.

United Nations Industrial Development Oganisation [1972], *Guidelines for Project Evaluation*, United Nations, New York.

United States Water Resources Research Council [1983], *Economic and Environmental Principles and Guidelines for Water and Related Land Resources Implementation Studies*, United States Government Printing Office, Washington D.C.

Unnevehr, L.J. [1986], "Consumer Demand for Rice Grain Quality and Returns to Research for Quality Improvement in Southeast Asia", *American Journal of Agricultural Economics*, Vol.68, No.3, 634-641.

van Ravensway, E.O. and J.P. Hoehn [1991a], "Contingent Valuation and Food Safety: The Case of Pesticide Residues in Food", Staff Paper No. 91-13, Department of Agricultural Economics, Michigan State University.

van Ravensway, E.O. and J.P. Hoehn [1991b], "Consumer Willingness to Pay for Reducing Pesticide Residues in Fresh Produce", Staff Paper No. 91-18, Department of Agricultural Economics, Michigan State University.

Van Tongeren, J. [1991], *Integrated Environmental and Economic Accounting: A Case Study for Mexico*, Environment Working Paper No.50, World Bank, Washington D.C.

Varian, H.R. [1984], *Microeconomic Analysis*, 2nd ed, W.W. Norton and Co, New York.

Vaughn, W.J. and C.S. Russell [1982]", Valuing a Fishing Day: An Application of a Systematic Varying Parameter Model", *Land Economics*, Vol. 58, 450-630.

Veljanovski, C. [1978], The Economics of Job Safety Regulation: Theory and Evidence Part I in the Market and Common Law, Mimeo, Centre for Socio-Legal Studies, Oxford.

Viscusi, W.K. [1978], "Health Effects and Earnings Premiums for Job Hazards", *Review of Economics and Statistics*, Vol. 60, 408-416.

Viscusi, W.K. [1979], *Employment Hazards: An Investigation of Market Performance*, Cambridge, MA: Harvard University Press.

Viscusi, W.K. [1980], "Union, Labour Market Structure and the Welfare Implications of the Quality of Work", *Journal of Labor Research*, Vol. 1(1), 175-192.

Viscusi, W.K. [1981], "Occupational Safety and Health Regulation: Its Impact and Policy Alternatives", *Research in Public Analysis and Management*, Vol. 2, 281-299.

Viscusi, W.K. [1986], "Valuation of Risks to Life and Health: Guidelines for Policy Analysis", In J. Bentkover and others, eds., *Benefits Assessment: The State of the Art*, D. Reidel Publishing Company, Dordrecht, Netherlands.

Viscusi, W.K. [1992], *Fatal Tradeoffs: Public and Private Responsibilities for Risk*, Oxford University Press, New York.

Viscusi, W.K. and Moore, M.J. [1987], "Worker's Compensation: Wage Effects, Benefit Inadequacies, and the Value of Health Losses", *The Review of Economics and Statistics*, Vol. 69, 249-261.

Viscusi, W.K. and Moore, M.J. (1989), "Rates of Time Preference and Valuations for the Duration of Life", *Journal of Public Economics*, Vol. 38, 297-317.

Viscusi, W.K., W.A. Magat and J. Huber [1989], *Pricing Environmental Health Risks: Survey Assessments of Risk-Risk and Risk-Dollars Trade-Off*, Research report to U.S. Environmental Protection Agency, Washington, DC.

Walker, D.R. and J.P. Hoehn [1989], "A Framework for Estimating the Economic Damages of Groundwater Contamination: An Application to Nitrates", Staff Paper No. 89-06, Department of Agricultural Economics, Michigan State University.

Walsh, R.G. and Lynde O. Gilliam [1982], "Benefits of Wilderness Expansion with Excess Demand for Indian Peaks", *Western Journal of Agricultural Economics*, Vol. 7, 1-12.

Walsh, R.G., D.M. Johnson and J.R. McKean [1988], "Review of Outdoor Recreation Research Economic Demand Studies with Nonmarket Benefits Estimates: 1968-1988", Technical report No. 54, Colorado Water Resources Research Institute, Colorado State University, Fort Collins, CO.

Walsh, R.G., D.M. Johnson and J.R. McKean [1990], "Non-Market Values from Two Decades of Research on Recreational Demand", in A.N. Link and V.K. Smith, (eds.), *Advances in Applied*

Microeconomics, Vol. 5, JAI Press, Greenwich.

Walsh, R.G., D.M. Johnson, and J.R. McKean [1992], "Benefit Transfer of Outdoor Recreation Demand Studies, 1968-1988", *Water Resources Research*, Vol.28, No.3, March, [Special Section: Problems and Issues in the Validity of Benefit Transfer Methodologies.

Walsh, R.G., Loomis, J.B. and Gillman, R.A. [1984], "Valuing Option, Existence and Bequest Demands for Wilderness", *Land Economics*, 60.

Walsh, R.G., R. Derek Bjonback, R.A. Aiken and Donald H. Rosenthal [1990], "Estimating the Public Benefits of Protecting Forest Quality", *Journal of Environmental Management*, Vol. 30, No. 2, 1975-1989.

Walsh, R.G. [1991], "Empirical Evidence on Benefits of Protecting Old Growth Forests and the Spotted Owl", Appendix B, in *Economic Analysis of Designation of Critical Habitat for the Northern Spotted Owl*, U.S. Department of the Interior, Fish and Wildlife Service, Washington, DC.

Walter, J and Ayres, R. [1990], Global Warming: Damages and Costs, Paper Presented to the IPPC, January.

Walters, A.A. [1975], "Noise and Prices", Clarendon Press, Oxford.

Ward, W., B. Deren and E.D'Silva [1991], *The Economic Analysis of Projects: A Practitioner's Guide*, Economic Development Institute, World Bank, Washington DC.

Water Research Centre and Flood Hazard Research Centre [1989], Investment Appraisal for Sewage Schemes: The Assessment of Social Costs, Water Research Centre (WRC) and the Flood Hazard Research Centre (FHRC), Project Report, WRC, Swindon.

Whitehead, J.C. [1990], "Measuring Willingness to Pay for Wetlands Preservation with the Contingent Valuation Method", *Wetlands*, Vol. 10, No. 2, 187-201.

Whittington, D. and D. MacRae. [1986], "The Issue of Standing in Cost-Benefit Analysis", *Journal of Policy Analysis and Management*, Vol.5, No.4, 665-682.

Whittington, D. and D. MacRae [1990], "Judgments About Who Has Standing in Cost - Benefit Analysis? A Comment", *Journal of Policy Analysis and Management*, Vol.9, No.4. 536-547.

Whittington, D. et. al. [1991a], Willingness to Pay for Improved Sanitation in Kumasi, Ghana: A Contingent Valuation Study, Report to the Infrastructure and Urban Development Department, World Bank, Washington, DC.

Whittington, D. and V. Swarna.[1993a], The Economic Benefits of Potable Water Supply Projects to Households in Developing Countries, Asian Development Bank, Manila, Philippines, Forthcoming.

Whittington, D., J. Briscoe, and X. Mu [1987], *Willingness to Pay for Water in Rural Areas: Methodological Approaches and An Application in Haiti*, WASH Technical Report No. 213, U.S. Agency for International Development, Washington, DC.

Whittington, D., D.T. Lauria and K. Choe [1993b], Willingness to Pay for Improved Sanitation Services in Devao City, Philippines, Report to the World Bank, CVM Inc., Chapel Hill, NC.

Whittington, D., D. Lauria, and X. Mu. [1991b], "A Study of Water Vending and Willingness to Pay for Water in Onitsha, Nigeria", *World Development*, Vol.19, No.2/3, 179-198.

Whittington, D., D. Amaral, G. Cassidy and E. McClelland [1993c], Economic Value of Improving the Environmental Quality of Galveston Bay, Texas, Report to the Galveston Bay National Estuary Program, Webster, TX, September 1993.

Whittington, D., J. Briscoe, X. Mu and W. Baron [1990], "Estimating the Willingness to Pay for Water Services in Developing Countries: A Case Study of the Use of Contingent Valuation Surveys in Southern Haiti", *Economic Development and Cultural Change*, Vol. 38, No. 2, 293-311.

Whittington, D., M. Mujwahuzi, G. McMahon and K. Choe [1988], *Willingness to Pay for Water in Newala District, Tanzania: Strategies for Cost Recovery*, Water and Sanitation for Health Project Field Report No. 246, U.S. Agency for International Development, Washington, DC.

Whittington, D., D.L. Lauria, A.M. Wright, K. Choe, J.A. Hughes, and V. Swarna [1992a], *Household Demand for Improved Sanitation Services: A Case Study of Kumasi, Ghana*, UNDP-World Bank Water and Sanitation Program, Report No.3. Washington D.C.

Whittington, D., D.T. Lauria, A.M. Wright, K. Choe, J. A. Hughes and V. Swarna [1993d], "Household Demand for Improved Sanitation Services in Kumasi, Ghana: A Contingent Valuation Study", *Water Resources Research*, Vol. 29, No. 6, 1539-1560.

Whittington, D., D.T. Lauria, A.M. Wright, K. Choe, J.A. Hughes and V. Swarna [1993e], "Household Sanitation in Kumasi, Ghana: A Description of Current Practices, Attitudes, and Perceptions", *World Development*, Vol. 21, No. 5, 733-748.

Whittington, D., V.K. Smith, A. Okorafor, A. Okore, J.L. Lui, and A. McPhail [1992b], "Giving Respondents Time to Think in Contingent Valuation Studies: A Developing Country Application", *Journal of Environmental Economics and Management*, Vol.22, 205-225.

Wieand, K.F. [1973], "Air Pollution and Property Values: A Study of the St. Louis Area", *Journal of Regional Science*, Vol. 13, No. 2, 91-95.

Wiggins, S.L. and Palmer, O.G. [1980], "Acelhaute River Catchment Management Project, El Salvadore. Cost Benefit Analysis of Soil Conservation", ODA Land Resource Development Centre, UK.

Willig, R.D. [1976], "Consumer's Surplus Without Apology", *American Economic Review*, Vol.LXVI, 589-597.

Willis, K.G. and G.D. Garrod [1991], "Landscape Values: A Contingent Valuation Approach and Case Study of the Yorkshire Dales National Park", Countryside Change Working Paper No. 21, University of Newcastle, Newcastle, Great Britain.

Willis, K.G. and Benson, J. [1988], "Valuation of Wildlife: A Case Study on the Upper Tesdale Site of Special Scientific Interest and Comparison of Methods in Environmental Economics", in Turner, R.K. (ed.), *Sustainable Environmental Management: Principles and Practice,* Belhaven Press, London.

Willis, K.G. [1990], "Valuing Non-Market Wildlife Commodities: An Evaluation and Comparison of Benefits and Costs", *Applied Economics*, Vol. 22, 13-30.

Wilson, R., Colone, Spengler and Wilson [1980], *Health Effects of Fossil Fuel Burning: Assessment and Mitigation*, Balinger, Cambridge, USA.

Wind, M.H.A. [1991], "Contingent Valuation of Forest Management", Paper Presented at Annual Meeting of European Association of Environmental Resource Economists, Stockholm School of Economics.

Winpenny, J.T. [1991], *Values for the Environment: A Guide to Economic Appraisal*, HMSO, London.

Woo, C-K. and R.L. Pupp [1992], "Costs of Service Disruptions to Electricity Consumers", *Energy*, Vol. 17, 109-126.

World Commission on Environment and Development [1987], *Our Common Future*, Oxford University Press, Oxford.

Yankelovich, D.[1991], *Coming to Public Judgment: Making Democracy Work in a Complex World*, Syracuse University Press.

Young, J.S. et. al. [1987], "Net Economic Value of Upland Game Hunting in Idaho", Resource Bulletin RM-15, Rocky Mountain Forest and Range Experiment Station, U.S. Forest Service, Fort Collins, CO.

Zeidner, M. and Shechter, M. [1988], "Psychological Responses Towards Air Pollution: Some Personality and Demographic Correlates", *Journal of Environmental Psychology*, 8, 191-208.

Zeleny, M. [1982], *Multiple Criteria Decisionmaking*, McGraw - Hill.

MAIN SALES OUTLETS OF OECD PUBLICATIONS
PRINCIPAUX POINTS DE VENTE DES PUBLICATIONS DE L'OCDE

ARGENTINA – ARGENTINE
Carlos Hirsch S.R.L.
Galería Güemes, Florida 165, 4° Piso
1333 Buenos Aires   Tel. (1) 331.1787 y 331.2391
Telefax: (1) 331.1787

AUSTRALIA – AUSTRALIE
D.A. Information Services
648 Whitehorse Road, P.O.B 163
Mitcham, Victoria 3132   Tel. (03) 873.4411
Telefax: (03) 873.5679

AUSTRIA – AUTRICHE
Gerold & Co.
Graben 31
Wien I   Tel. (0222) 533.50.14

BELGIUM – BELGIQUE
Jean De Lannoy
Avenue du Roi 202
B-1060 Bruxelles   Tel. (02) 538.51.69/538.08.41
Telefax: (02) 538.08.41

CANADA
Renouf Publishing Company Ltd.
1294 Algoma Road
Ottawa, ON K1B 3W8   Tel. (613) 741.4333
Telefax: (613) 741.5439
Stores:
61 Sparks Street
Ottawa, ON K1P 5R1   Tel. (613) 238.8985
211 Yonge Street
Toronto, ON M5B 1M4   Tel. (416) 363.3171
Telefax: (416)363.59.63
Les Éditions La Liberté Inc.
3020 Chemin Sainte-Foy
Sainte-Foy, PQ G1X 3V6   Tel. (418) 658.3763
Telefax: (418) 658.3763

Federal Publications Inc.
165 University Avenue, Suite 701
Toronto, ON M5H 3B8   Tel. (416) 860.1611
Telefax: (416) 860.1608
Les Publications Fédérales
1185 Université
Montréal, QC H3B 3A7   Tel. (514) 954.1633
Telefax : (514) 954.1635

CHINA – CHINE
China National Publications Import
Export Corporation (CNPIEC)
16 Gongti E. Road, Chaoyang District
P.O. Box 88 or 50
Beijing 100704 PR   Tel. (01) 506.6688
Telefax: (01) 506.3101

DENMARK – DANEMARK
Munksgaard Book and Subscription Service
35, Nørre Søgade, P.O. Box 2148
DK-1016 København K   Tel. (33) 12.85.70
Telefax: (33) 12.93.87

FINLAND – FINLANDE
Akateeminen Kirjakauppa
Keskuskatu 1, P.O. Box 128
00100 Helsinki
Subscription Services/Agence d'abonnements :
P.O. Box 23
00371 Helsinki   Tel. (358 0) 12141
Telefax: (358 0) 121.4450

FRANCE
OECD/OCDE
Mail Orders/Commandes par correspondance:
2, rue André-Pascal
75775 Paris Cedex 16   Tel. (33-1) 45.24.82.00
Telefax: (33-1) 49.10.42.76
Telex: 640048 OCDE

OECD Bookshop/Librairie de l'OCDE :
33, rue Octave-Feuillet
75016 Paris   Tel. (33-1) 45.24.81.67
(33-1) 45.24.81.81
Documentation Française
29, quai Voltaire
75007 Paris   Tel. 40.15.70.00
Gibert Jeune (Droit-Économie)
6, place Saint-Michel
75006 Paris   Tel. 43.25.91.19
Librairie du Commerce International
10, avenue d'Iéna
75016 Paris   Tel. 40.73.34.60
Librairie Dunod
Université Paris-Dauphine
Place du Maréchal de Lattre de Tassigny
75016 Paris   Tel. (1) 44.05.40.13
Librairie Lavoisier
11, rue Lavoisier
75008 Paris   Tel. 42.65.39.95
Librairie L.G.D.J. - Montchrestien
20, rue Soufflot
75005 Paris   Tel. 46.33.89.85
Librairie des Sciences Politiques
30, rue Saint-Guillaume
75007 Paris   Tel. 45.48.36.02
P.U.F.
49, boulevard Saint-Michel
75005 Paris   Tel. 43.25.83.40
Librairie de l'Université
12a, rue Nazareth
13100 Aix-en-Provence   Tel. (16) 42.26.18.08
Documentation Française
165, rue Garibaldi
69003 Lyon   Tel. (16) 78.63.32.23
Librairie Decitre
29, place Bellecour
69002 Lyon   Tel. (16) 72.40.54.54

GERMANY – ALLEMAGNE
OECD Publications and Information Centre
August-Bebel-Allee 6
D-53175 Bonn 2   Tel. (0228) 959.120
Telefax: (0228) 959.12.17

GREECE – GRÈCE
Librairie Kauffmann
Mavrokordatou 9
106 78 Athens   Tel. (01) 32.55.321
Telefax: (01) 36.33.967

HONG-KONG
Swindon Book Co. Ltd.
13–15 Lock Road
Kowloon, Hong Kong   Tel. 366.80.31
Telefax: 739.49.75

HUNGARY – HONGRIE
Euro Info Service
POB 1271
1464 Budapest   Tel. (1) 111.62.16
Telefax : (1) 111.60.61

ICELAND – ISLANDE
Mál Mog Menning
Laugavegi 18, Pósthólf 392
121 Reykjavik   Tel. 162.35.23

INDIA – INDE
Oxford Book and Stationery Co.
Scindia House
New Delhi 110001   Tel.(11) 331.5896/5308
Telefax: (11) 332.5993
17 Park Street
Calcutta 700016   Tel. 240832

INDONESIA – INDONÉSIE
Pdii-Lipi
P.O. Box 269/JKSMG/88
Jakarta 12790   Tel. 583467
Telex: 62 875

IRELAND – IRLANDE
TDC Publishers – Library Suppliers
12 North Frederick Street
Dublin 1   Tel. (01) 874.48.35
Telefax: (01) 874.84.16

ISRAEL
Electronic Publications only
Publications électroniques seulement
Praedicta
5 Shatna Street
P.O. Box 34030
Jerusalem 91340   Tel. (2) 52.84.90/1/2
Telefax: (2) 52.84.93

ITALY – ITALIE
Libreria Commissionaria Sansoni
Via Duca di Calabria 1/1
50125 Firenze   Tel. (055) 64.54.15
Telefax: (055) 64.12.57
Via Bartolini 29
20155 Milano   Tel. (02) 36.50.83
Editrice e Libreria Herder
Piazza Montecitorio 120
00186 Roma   Tel. 679.46.28
Telefax: 678.47.51
Libreria Hoepli
Via Hoepli 5
20121 Milano   Tel. (02) 86.54.46
Telefax: (02) 805.28.86
Libreria Scientifica
Dott. Lucio de Biasio 'Aeiou'
Via Coronelli, 6
20146 Milano   Tel. (02) 48.95.45.52
Telefax: (02) 48.95.45.48

JAPAN – JAPON
OECD Publications and Information Centre
Landic Akasaka Building
2-3-4 Akasaka, Minato-ku
Tokyo 107   Tel. (81.3) 3586.2016
Telefax: (81.3) 3584.7929

KOREA – CORÉE
Kyobo Book Centre Co. Ltd.
P.O. Box 1658, Kwang Hwa Moon
Seoul   Tel. 730.78.91
Telefax: 735.00.30

MALAYSIA – MALAISIE
Co-operative Bookshop Ltd.
University of Malaya
P.O. Box 1127, Jalan Pantai Baru
59700 Kuala Lumpur
Malaysia   Tel. 756.5000/756.5425
Telefax: 757.3661

MEXICO – MEXIQUE
Revistas y Periodicos Internacionales S.A. de C.V.
Florencia 57 - 1004
Mexico, D.F. 06600   Tel. 207.81.00
Telefax : 208.39.79

NETHERLANDS – PAYS-BAS
SDU Uitgeverij Plantijnstraat
Externe Fondsen
Postbus 20014
2500 EA's-Gravenhage   Tel. (070) 37.89.880
Voor bestellingen: Telefax: (070) 34.75.778

NEW ZEALAND
NOUVELLE-ZÉLANDE
Legislation Services
P.O. Box 12418
Thorndon, Wellington   Tel. (04) 496.5652
                              Telefax: (04) 496.5698

NORWAY – NORVÈGE
Narvesen Info Center – NIC
Bertrand Narvesens vei 2
P.O. Box 6125 Etterstad
0602 Oslo 6   Tel. (022) 57.33.00
                              Telefax: (022) 68.19.01

PAKISTAN
Mirza Book Agency
65 Shahrah Quaid-E-Azam
Lahore 54000   Tel. (42) 353.601
                              Telefax: (42) 231.730

PHILIPPINE – PHILIPPINES
International Book Center
5th Floor, Filipinas Life Bldg.
Ayala Avenue
Metro Manila   Tel. 81.96.76
                              Telex 23312 RHP PH

PORTUGAL
Livraria Portugal
Rua do Carmo 70-74
Apart. 2681
1200 Lisboa   Tel.: (01) 347.49.82/5
                              Telefax: (01) 347.02.64

SINGAPORE – SINGAPOUR
Gower Asia Pacific Pte Ltd.
Golden Wheel Building
41, Kallang Pudding Road, No. 04-03
Singapore 1334   Tel. 741.5166
                              Telefax: 742.9356

SPAIN – ESPAGNE
Mundi-Prensa Libros S.A.
Castelló 37, Apartado 1223
Madrid 28001   Tel. (91) 431.33.99
                              Telefax: (91) 575.39.98

Libreria Internacional AEDOS
Consejo de Ciento 391
08009 – Barcelona   Tel. (93) 488.30.09
                              Telefax: (93) 487.76.59

Llibreria de la Generalitat
Palau Moja
Rambla dels Estudis, 118
08002 – Barcelona
            (Subscripcions) Tel. (93) 318.80.12
            (Publicacions) Tel. (93) 302.67.23
                            Telefax: (93) 412.18.54

SRI LANKA
Centre for Policy Research
c/o Colombo Agencies Ltd.
No. 300-304, Galle Road
Colombo 3   Tel. (1) 574240, 573551-2
                              Telefax: (1) 575394, 510711

SWEDEN – SUÈDE
Fritzes Information Center
Box 16356
Regeringsgatan 12
106 47 Stockholm   Tel. (08) 690.90.90
                              Telefax: (08) 20.50.21

Subscription Agency/Agence d'abonnements :
Wennergren-Williams Info AB
P.O. Box 1305
171 25 Solna   Tel. (08) 705.97.50
                              Téléfax : (08) 27.00.71

SWITZERLAND – SUISSE
Maditec S.A. (Books and Periodicals - Livres
et périodiques)
Chemin des Palettes 4
Case postale 266
1020 Renens   Tel. (021) 635.08.65
                              Telefax: (021) 635.07.80

Librairie Payot S.A.
4, place Pépinet
CP 3212
1002 Lausanne   Tel. (021) 341.33.48
                              Telefax: (021) 341.33.45

Librairie Unilivres
6, rue de Candolle
1205 Genève   Tel. (022) 320.26.23
                              Telefax: (022) 329.73.18

Subscription Agency/Agence d'abonnements :
Dynapresse Marketing S.A.
38 avenue Vibert
1227 Carouge   Tel.: (022) 308.07.89
                              Telefax : (022) 308.07.99

See also – Voir aussi :
OECD Publications and Information Centre
August-Bebel-Allee 6
D-53175 Bonn 2 (Germany)   Tel. (0228) 959.120
                           Telefax: (0228) 959.12.17

TAIWAN – FORMOSE
Good Faith Worldwide Int'l. Co. Ltd.
9th Floor, No. 118, Sec. 2
Chung Hsiao E. Road
Taipei   Tel. (02) 391.7396/391.7397
                   Telefax: (02) 394.9176

THAILAND – THAÏLANDE
Suksit Siam Co. Ltd.
113, 115 Fuang Nakhon Rd.
Opp. Wat Rajbopith
Bangkok 10200   Tel. (662) 225.9531/2
                              Telefax: (662) 222.5188

TURKEY – TURQUIE
Kültür Yayinlari Is-Türk Ltd. Sti.
Atatürk Bulvari No. 191/Kat 13
Kavaklidere/Ankara   Tel. 428.11.40 Ext. 2458
Dolmabahce Cad. No. 29
Besiktas/Istanbul   Tel. 260.71.88
                              Telex: 43482B

UNITED KINGDOM – ROYAUME-UNI
HMSO
Gen. enquiries   Tel. (071) 873 0011
Postal orders only:
P.O. Box 276, London SW8 5DT
Personal Callers HMSO Bookshop
49 High Holborn, London WC1V 6HB
                        Telefax: (071) 873 8200
Branches at: Belfast, Birmingham, Bristol, Edin-
burgh, Manchester

UNITED STATES – ÉTATS-UNIS
OECD Publications and Information Centre
2001 L Street N.W., Suite 700
Washington, D.C. 20036-4910 Tel. (202) 785.6323
                            Telefax: (202) 785.0350

VENEZUELA
Libreria del Este
Avda F. Miranda 52, Aptdo. 60337
Edificio Galipán
Caracas 106   Tel. 951.1705/951.2307/951.1297
                  Telegram: Libreste Caracas

Subscription to OECD periodicals may also be placed through main subscription agencies.

Les abonnements aux publications périodiques de l'OCDE peuvent être souscrits auprès des principales agences d'abonnement.

Orders and inquiries from countries where Distributors have not yet been appointed should be sent to: OECD Publications Service, 2 rue André-Pascal, 75775 Paris Cedex 16, France.

Les commandes provenant de pays où l'OCDE n'a pas encore désigné de distributeur devraient être adressées à : OCDE, Service des Publications, 2, rue André-Pascal, 75775 Paris Cedex 16, France.

3-1994

OECD PUBLICATIONS, 2 rue André-Pascal, 75775 PARIS CEDEX 16
PRINTED IN FRANCE
(97 94 02 1) ISBN 92-64-14107-3 - No. 46999 1994